Edward Poste

Aristotle on fallacies

or The sophistici elenchi

Edward Poste

Aristotle on fallacies
or The sophistici elenchi

ISBN/EAN: 9783742818010

Manufactured in Europe, USA, Canada, Australia, Japa

Cover: Foto ©Andreas Hilbeck / pixelio.de

Manufactured and distributed by brebook publishing software (www.brebook.com)

Edward Poste

Aristotle on fallacies

ARISTOTLE ON FALLACIES

OR THE

SOPHISTICI ELENCHI

WITH A

TRANSLATION AND NOTES

BY

EDWARD POSTE, M.A.
FELLOW OF ORIEL COLLEGE, OXFORD

London
MACMILLAN AND CO.
1866

PREFACE.

ARISTOTLE's explanation of the nature of Fallacies, if not satisfactory, seems to be as complete and intelligible as any that has since been offered. As his doctrines, indeed, are the source and substance of those of his successors, it appeared to the translator that the student of this theory would prefer to resort for instruction to the fountain-head, if it were made more easy of access.

"Is not, however, the whole subject of Fallacies somewhat trumpery, and one that may be suffered, without much regret, to sink into oblivion?"

Possibly: but besides the doctrine of Fallacies, Aristotle offers either in this treatise, or in other passages quoted in the commentary, various glances over the world of science and opinion, various suggestions on problems which are still agitated, and a vivid picture of the ancient system of dialectic, which it is hoped may be found both interesting and instructive.

The text adopted is that of Bekker, except where emendation was absolutely necessary to the sense. Attention is called in the Notes to all changes except mere changes of punctuation.

TABLE OF CONTENTS.

CHAP.	PAGE
1. Conception and existence of sophistry	2
2. Classification of reasoning	4
3. Five branches of sophistry	6
4. First branch of sophistry. Fallacies dependent on diction	6
5. Fallacies not dependent on diction	10
6. All the fallacies may be deduced from the definition of confutation	16
7. All the fallacies arise from confusion, and must be solved by distinction	22
8. Difference of paralogism and sophistic proof . . .	24
9. Difference of pseudographema and sophistic proof . .	28
10. Examination of a division of proofs into proofs addressed to the word and proofs addressed to the thought. Distinction of dialectic and didactic	30
11. Sophistic proof is simulated pirastic, or simulated scientific, proof. Distinction of sophistic and eristic, sophistic and pseudographic, scientific and pirastic, proof	34
12. Second and third branches of sophistry. Reduction to falsehood and paradox	40
13. Fourth branch of sophistry. Reduction to tautology or pleonasm	42
14. Fifth branch of sophistry. Reduction to solecism	44

TABLE OF CONTENTS.

CHAP.	PAGE
15. Arrangement and tactics of the questioner	46
16. Utility of the study of sophistry	50
17. Rules of answering. The answerer must distinguish in all cases of ambiguity	52
18. Three kinds of solution. The solution of inconclusive reasoning is distinction: the solution of conclusive reasoning is objection or counterproof	58
19. Solution of the fallacies of homonymia and amphibolia	60
20. Solution of the fallacies of composition and division	62
21. Solution of the fallacies of prosody	64
22. Solution of the fallacies of figura dictionis	64
23. The solution of all fallacies dependent on diction contains an antithesis	70
24. Solution of the fallacies of accidens. Examination and rejection of other solutions which refer the same examples to ignoratio elenchi or homonymia	72
25. Solution of the fallacies a dicto secundum quid ad dictum simpliciter	76
26. Solution of the fallacies of ignoratio elenchi	80
27. Solution of the fallacies of petitio principii	80
28. Solution of the fallacies of consequens	80
29. Solution of the fallacies of non causa pro causa	82
30. Solution of the fallacies of plures interrogationes	82
31. Solution of reduction to tautology	84
32. Solution of reduction to solecism	84
33. Degrees of ingenuity and difficulty of solution of fallacies	86
34. Recapitulation	90
NOTES	97

TABLE OF CONTENTS.

	PAGE
APPENDIX A.	
Petitio principii	176
APPENDIX B.	
Non causa pro causa	186
APPENDIX C.	
Enstasis when a premiss is false	192
APPENDIX D.	
Λοιποὶ Ἀρχαί, or method-founding principles	203

§ 1. The dialectic maxims or loci are premisses of universal application 203

§ 2. How far do the maxims of dialectic coincide with the axioms of science? The axioms are indispensable to all reasoning, necessary, and self-evident truths: the maxims have not these characters . 207

§ 3. Peculiar principles of science and dialectic. Examination of Mill's theory of definition . . . 209

§ 4. The maxims are instrumental or auxiliary truths. When dialectic is purely logical, the loci or topical conceptions are the materials as well as the instruments of proof 210

§ 5. Examination of Whately's distinction of logical and extra-logical fallacies 211

§ 6. The maxims are metaphysical or ontological propositions 212

§ 7. The loci or maxims may all be grouped under the category of relation, or deduced from the definitions of the predicables or from the definition of definition 214

§ 8. Dialectic is based on two definitions: the definition of proof supplies the loci of solution; the definition of definition supplies the loci of invention . . 217

§ 9. An earlier system attempted to obtain the loci of invention as well as the loci of solution from the definition of proof 219

TABLE OF CONTENTS.

§ 10. Dialectic like science is based on definitions, but on definitions of a different order from those which are the basis of science. Dialectic like art is based on definitions of the final cause, and its maxims are rather imperative than declaratory . . . 221

§ 11. The definitions on which science is based are causal propositions; therefore the branch of dialectic employed to investigate the first principles of science should be founded on the definition of causation . 223

§ 12. Comparison of dialectic with the modern method of scientific induction 227

§ 13. Are definitions or the first principles of science susceptible of demonstration? 232

§ 14. Specimens of dialectic maxims formulated by the schoolmen 236

APPENDIX E.
Limited competence of pirastic 239

APPENDIX F.
Quadrature of the circle by Hippocrates, Antipho, and Bryso 245

ΠΕΡΙ ΣΟΦΙΣΤΙΚΩΝ

I. Περὶ δὲ τῶν σοφιστικῶν ἐλέγχων καὶ τῶν φαινομένων μὲν ἐλέγχων ὄντων δὲ παραλογισμῶν ἀλλ' οὐκ ἐλέγχων λέγωμεν, ἀρξάμενοι κατὰ φύσιν ἀπὸ τῶν πρώτων. Ὅτι μὲν οὖν οἱ μὲν εἰσὶ συλλογισμοί, οἱ δ' οὐκ ὄντες δοκοῦσι, φανερόν· ὥσπερ γὰρ καὶ ἐπὶ τῶν ἄλλων τοῦτο γίνεται διά τινος ὁμοιότητος, καὶ ἐπὶ τῶν λόγων ὡσαύτως ἔχει. Καὶ γὰρ τὴν ἕξιν οἱ μὲν ἔχουσιν εὖ οἱ δὲ φαίνονται, φυλετικῶς φυσήσαντες καὶ ἐπισκευάσαντες αὑτούς, καὶ καλοὶ οἱ μὲν διὰ κάλλος οἱ δὲ φαίνονται, κομμώσαντες αὑτούς. Ἐπί τε τῶν ἀψύχων ὡσαύτως· καὶ γὰρ τούτων τὰ μὲν ἄργυρος τὰ δὲ χρυσός ἐστιν ἀληθῶς, τὰ δ' ἔστι μὲν οὔ, φαίνεται δὲ κατὰ τὴν αἴσθησιν, οἷον τὰ μὲν λιθαργύρινα καὶ τὰ καττιτέρινα ἀργυρᾶ, τὰ δὲ χολοβάφινα χρυσᾶ. Τὸν αὐτὸν δὲ τρόπον καὶ συλλογισμὸς καὶ ἔλεγχος ὁ μὲν ἔστιν, ὁ δ' οὐκ ἔστι μέν, φαίνεται δὲ διὰ τὴν ἀπειρίαν· οἱ γὰρ ἄπειροι ὥσπερ ἂν ἀπέχοντες πόρρωθεν θεωροῦσιν. Ὁ μὲν γὰρ συλλογισμὸς ἐκ τινῶν ἐστι τεθέντων ὥστε λέγειν ἕτερόν τι ἐξ ἀνάγκης τῶν κειμένων διὰ τῶν κειμένων· ἔλεγχος δὲ συλλογισμὸς μετ' ἀντιφάσεως τοῦ συμπεράσματος. Οἱ δὲ τοῦτο ποιοῦσι μὲν οὔ, δοκοῦσι δὲ διὰ πολλὰς αἰτίας· ὧν εἷς τόπος εὐφυέστατός ἐστι καὶ δημοσιώτατος ὁ διὰ τῶν ὀνομάτων. Ἐπεὶ γὰρ οὐκ ἔστιν αὐτὰ τὰ πράγματα διαλέγεσθαι φέροντας, ἀλλὰ τοῖς ὀνόμασιν ἀντὶ τῶν πραγμάτων χρώμεθα συμβόλοις, τὸ συμβαῖνον ἐπὶ τῶν ὀνομάτων καὶ ἐπὶ τῶν πραγμάτων ἡγούμεθα συμβαίνειν, καθάπερ ἐπὶ τῶν ψήφων τοῖς λογιζομένοις. Τὸ δ' οὐκ ἔστιν ὅμοιον. Τὰ μὲν γὰρ ὀνόματα πεπέρανται καὶ

ΕΛΕΓΧΩΝ.

1. We propose to treat of Sophistical Confutations and those seeming confutations which are not really confutations but paralogisms[1]; and we thus begin, following the natural order of inquiry.

The existence, over and above real proofs, of seeming but unreal proofs is evident. As in other departments resemblance generates semblance, so in reasoning. Bodily vigour is sometimes genuine, sometimes, as in the tribal choruses, simulated by the aid of dress: beauty is sometimes natural, sometimes counterfeited by cosmetics. So in lifeless objects: some bodies are genuine silver or gold, others are not silver or gold but seem such to the sense; as litharge[5] and tin seem to be silver, and yellow metal seems to be gold. So Proof and Confutation are either real or only seem to be such to the inexperienced. For the inexperienced resemble persons who view from a distance. Proof is a tissue of propositions so related that we of necessity assert some further proposition as their consequence[6]. Confutation is a proof whose conclusion is the contradictory of a given thesis. Some proofs and confutations have not really these characters, but seem to have them from various causes; and one multitudinous and widespread division are those that owe their semblance to names. For, not being able to point to the things themselves that we reason about, we use names instead of the realities as their symbols, and then the consequences in the names appear to be consequences in the realities, as the consequences in the counters appear to the calculator to be consequences in the objects represented by the counters. But it is not so. For names, whether simple or

τὸ τῶν λόγων· πλῆθος, τὰ δὲ πράγματα τὸν ἀριθμὸν ἄπειρά ἐστιν. Ἀναγκαῖον οὖν πλείω τὸν αὐτὸν λόγον καὶ τοὔνομα τὸ ἓν σημαίνειν. Ὥσπερ οὖν κἀκεῖ οἱ μὴ δεινοὶ τὰς ψήφους φέρειν ὑπὸ τῶν ἐπιστημόνων παρακρούονται, τὸν αὐτὸν τρόπον καὶ ἐπὶ τῶν λόγων οἱ τῶν ὀνομάτων τῆς δυνάμεως ἄπειροι παραλογίζονται καὶ αὐτοὶ διαλεγόμενοι καὶ ἄλλων ἀκούοντες [10]. Διὰ μὲν οὖν ταύτην τὴν αἰτίαν καὶ τὰς λεχθησομένας ἔστι καὶ συλλογισμὸς καὶ ἔλεγχος φαινόμενος μὲν οὐκ ὢν δέ.

Ἐπεὶ δ' ἐστί τισι μᾶλλον πρὸ ἔργου τὸ δοκεῖν εἶναι σοφοῖς ἢ τὸ εἶναι καὶ μὴ δοκεῖν (ἔστι γὰρ ἡ σοφιστικὴ φαινομένη σοφία οὖσα δ' οὔ, καὶ ὁ σοφιστὴς χρηματιστὴς ἀπὸ φαινομένης σοφίας ἀλλ' οὐκ οὔσης), δῆλον ὅτι ἀναγκαῖον τούτοις καὶ τὸ τοῦ σοφοῦ ἔργον δοκεῖν ποιεῖν μᾶλλον ἢ ποιεῖν καὶ μὴ δοκεῖν. Ἔστι δ' ὡς ἓν πρὸς ἓν εἰπεῖν ἔργον περὶ ἕκαστον τοῦ εἰδότος ἀψευδεῖν μὲν αὐτὸν περὶ ὧν οἶδε, τὸν δὲ ψευδόμενον ἐμφανίζειν δύνασθαι. Ταῦτα δ' ἐστὶ τὸ μὲν ἐν τῷ δύνασθαι δοῦναι λόγον, τὸ δ' ἐν τῷ λαβεῖν[11]. Ἀνάγκη οὖν τοὺς βουλομένους σοφιστεύειν τὸ τῶν εἰρημένων λόγων γένος ζητεῖν πρὸ ἔργου γάρ ἐστιν· ἡ γὰρ τοιαύτη δύναμις [12] ποιήσει φαίνεσθαι σοφόν, οὗ τυγχάνουσι τὴν προαίρεσιν ἔχοντες.

Ὅτι μὲν οὖν ἔστι τι τοιοῦτον λόγων γένος, καὶ ὅτι τοιαύτης ἐφίενται δυνάμεως οὓς καλοῦμεν σοφιστάς, δῆλον· πόσα δ' ἐστὶν εἴδη τῶν λόγων τῶν σοφιστικῶν, καὶ ἐκ πόσων τὸν ἀριθμὸν ἡ δύναμις αὕτη συνέστηκε, καὶ πόσα μέρη τυγχάνει τῆς πραγματείας ὄντα, καὶ περὶ τῶν ἄλλων τῶν συντελούντων εἰς τὴν τέχνην ταύτην ἤδη λέγωμεν.

II. Ἔστι δὴ τῶν ἐν τῷ διαλέγεσθαι λόγων τέτταρα γένη, διδασκαλικοὶ καὶ διαλεκτικοὶ καὶ πειραστικοὶ καὶ ἐριστικοί.

Διδασκαλικοὶ μὲν οἱ ἐκ τῶν οἰκείων ἀρχῶν ἑκάστου μαθήματος καὶ οὐκ ἐκ τῶν τοῦ ἀποκρινομένου δοξῶν συλλογιζόμενοι (δεῖ γὰρ πιστεύειν τὸν μανθάνοντα),

Διαλεκτικοὶ δ' οἱ ἐκ τῶν ἐνδόξων συλλογιστικοὶ ἀντιφάσεως,

complex, are finite, realities infinite; so that a multiplicity of things is signified by the same simple or complex name. As, then, in calculation, those who are unskilled in manipulating the counters are deceived by those who are skilled, so in reasoning, those who are unacquainted with the power of names are deceived by paralogisms both when they are parties to the controversy and when they form the audience. From this cause, and others to be enumerated, there exist proofs and confutations that are apparent but unreal.

Now it answers the purpose of some persons rather to seem to be philosophers and not to be than to be and not to seem; for Sophistry is seeming but unreal philosophy, and the Sophist a person who makes money by the semblance of philosophy without the reality; and for his success it is requisite to seem to perform the function of the philosopher without performing it rather than to perform it without seeming to do so. Now, if we define by a single characteristic, the function of a man who knows is to declare the truth and expose error respecting what he knows. The former of these powers is ability to stand examination in a subject, the latter is ability to examine another who professes to know it. Those, then, who wish to practise as Sophists will aim at the kind of reasonings we have described, for it suits their purpose, as the faculty of thus reasoning produces a semblance of philosophy, which is the end they propose.

The existence, then, of such a mode of reasoning, and the fact that such a faculty is the aim of the persons we call Sophists[13], is manifest. The various kinds of sophistical reasoning, the branches of the sophistical faculty, the various elements of the sophistical profession, and the other components of the art, remain to be examined[14].

II. REASONINGS in the form of dialogue may be divided into four orders, Didactic, Dialectic, Pirastic, and Eristic[1].

Didactic reasonings conclude from the scientific principles appropriate to a subject, and not from the answerer's opinions, for the learner is required to believe[2]:

Dialectic employ as premisses probable propositions and conclude in contradiction to a thesis:

ΠΕΡΙ ΣΟΦΙΣΤΙΚΩΝ

Πειραστικοὶ δ' οἱ ἐκ τῶν δοκούντων τῷ ἀποκρινομένῳ καὶ ἀναγκαίων εἰδέναι τῷ προσποιουμένῳ ἔχειν τὴν ἐπιστήμην (ὃν τρόπον δέ, διώρισται ἐν ἑτέροις).

Ἐριστικοὶ δ' οἱ ἐκ τῶν φαινομένων ἐνδόξων μὴ ὄντων δὲ συλλογιστικοὶ ἢ φαινόμενοι συλλογιστικοί.

Περὶ μὲν οὖν τῶν ἀποδεικτικῶν ἐν τοῖς Ἀναλυτικοῖς εἴρηται, περὶ δὲ τῶν διαλεκτικῶν καὶ πειραστικῶν ἐν τοῖς ἄλλοις· περὶ δὲ τῶν ἀγωνιστικῶν καὶ ἐριστικῶν νῦν λέγωμεν.

III. Πρῶτον δὴ ληπτέον πόσων στοχάζονται οἱ ἐν τοῖς λόγοις ἀγωνιζόμενοι καὶ διαφιλονεικοῦντες. Ἔστι δὲ πέντε ταῦτα τὸν ἀριθμόν, ἔλεγχος καὶ ψεῦδος καὶ παράδοξον καὶ σολοικισμὸς καὶ πέμπτον τὸ ποιῆσαι ἀδολεσχῆσαι τὸν προσδιαλεγόμενον (τοῦτο δ' ἐστὶ τὸ πολλάκις ἀναγκάζεσθαι ταὐτὸ λέγειν)· ἢ τὸ μὴ ὄν, ἀλλὰ τὸ φαινόμενον ἕκαστον εἶναι τούτων. Μάλιστα μὲν γὰρ προαιροῦνται φαίνεσθαι ἐλέγχοντες, δεύτερον δὲ ψευδόμενόν τι δεικνύναι, τρίτον εἰς παράδοξον ἄγειν, τέταρτον δὲ σολοικίζειν ποιεῖν (τοῦτο δ' ἐστὶ τὸ ποιῆσαι τῇ λέξει βαρβαρίζειν ἐκ τοῦ λόγου τὸν ἀποκρινόμενον), τελευταῖον δὲ τὸ πλεονάκις ταὐτὸ λέγειν.

IV. Τρόποι δ' εἰσὶ τοῦ μὲν ἐλέγχειν δύο· οἱ μὲν γάρ εἰσι παρὰ τὴν λέξιν, οἱ δ' ἔξω τῆς λέξεως. Ἔστι δὲ τὰ μὲν παρὰ τὴν λέξιν ἐμποιοῦντα τὴν φαντασίαν ἓξ τὸν ἀριθμόν· ταῦτα δ' ἐστὶν ὁμωνυμία, ἀμφιβολία, σύνθεσις, διαίρεσις, προσῳδία, σχῆμα λέξεως. Τούτου δὲ πίστις ἥ τε διὰ τῆς ἐπαγωγῆς καὶ συλλογισμός, ἄν τε ληφθῇ τις ἄλλος, καὶ ὅτι τοσαυταχῶς ἂν τοῖς αὐτοῖς ὀνόμασι καὶ λόγοις μὴ ταὐτὸ δηλώσαιμεν.

Εἰσὶ δὲ παρὰ μὲν τὴν ὁμωνυμίαν οἱ τοιοίδε τῶν λόγων, οἷον ὅτι μανθάνουσιν οἱ ἐπιστάμενοι· τὰ γὰρ ἀποστοματιζόμενα[1] μανθάνουσιν οἱ γραμματικοί. Τὸ γὰρ μανθάνειν ὁμώνυμον, τό τε ξυνιέναι χρώμενον τῇ ἐπιστήμῃ καὶ τὸ λαμβάνειν ἐπιστήμην.

Καὶ πάλιν ὅτι τὰ κακὰ ἀγαθά· τὰ γὰρ δέοντα ἀγαθά, τὰ δὲ κακὰ δέοντα[2]. Διττὸν γὰρ τὸ δέον, τὸ τ' ἀναγκαῖον, ὃ συμ-

Pirastic employ as premises the opinions of the answerer on points that ought to be known by the pretender to science, with the limitations elsewhere mentioned³:

Eristic conclude from premises which seem but are not probable, or only seem to conclude from probable premises.

Demonstrative reasonings having been discussed in the Analytica⁴, Dialectic and Pirastic elsewhere, contentious and Eristic reasonings remain to be investigated.

III. We must first enumerate the objects aimed at when disputants are contentious and fight for victory. They are five: to confute the opponent, to drive him into false proposition, to drive him into paradox, to reduce him to solecism, and to reduce him to pleonasm, that is, to superfluous repetition: or the semblance of any one of these achievements without the reality. The end most desired is to confute the answerer, the next to shew that he holds a false opinion, the third to lead him into paradox, the fourth to land him in solecism, that is, to shew that his expression involves a violation of the laws of grammar, the fifth to force him to unmeaning repetition.

IV. Seeming confutations fall under two divisions; those where the semblance depends on language, and those where it is independent of language. Language produces a false semblance of ratiocination from six causes; the ambiguity of a term, the ambiguity of a proposition, the possibility of wrong disjunction, the possibility of wrong conjunction, the possibility of wrong accentuation, and similarity of termination. This classification may either be established by inspection of instances, or may be deduced (not to exclude other modes of deduction) from the fact that there are just so many ways by which a single term or proposition may have a plurality of meanings.

Ambiguous terms may be found in the following instances:— Those that learn are those that already know, for it is those that know the use of the alphabet who learn (can write or spell) what is dictated. "Learn" is ambiguous, signifying either to appreciate, that is, to employ knowledge, or to acquire knowledge.

Again:—Evil is good, for what is necessary is good, and evil is necessary. "Necessary" is ambiguous, meaning either the result

βαίνει πολλάκις καὶ ἐπὶ τῶν κακῶν (ἔστι γὰρ κακόν τι ἀναγκαῖον), καὶ τἀγαθὰ δὲ δέοντά φαμεν εἶναι.

Ἔτι τὸν αὐτὸν καθῆσθαι καὶ ἑστάναι, καὶ κάμνειν καὶ ὑγιαίνειν. Ὅσπερ γὰρ ἀνίστατο, ἕστηκεν, καὶ ὥσπερ ὑγιάζετο, ὑγιαίνει· ἀνίστατο δ' ὁ καθήμενος καὶ ὑγιάζετο ὁ κάμνων⁵. Τὸ γὰρ τὸν κάμνοντα ὁτιοῦν ποιεῖν ἢ πάσχειν οὐχ ἓν σημαίνει, ἀλλ' ὁτὲ μὲν ὅτι ὁ νῦν κάμνων ἢ καθήμενος, ὁτὲ δ' ὃς ἔκαμνε πρότερον. Πλὴν ὑγιάζετο⁶ μὲν καὶ κάμνων καὶ ὁ κάμνων ὑγιαίνει δ' οὐ κάμνων ἀλλ' ὁ κάμνων οὐ νῦν ἀλλὰ πρότερον.

Παρὰ δὲ τὴν ἀμφιβολίαν οἱ τοιοίδε, τὸ βούλεσθαι λαβεῖν με τοὺς πολεμίους.

Καὶ ἆρ' ὅ τις γινώσκει, τοῦτο γινώσκει; καὶ γὰρ τὸν γινώσκοντα καὶ τὸ γινωσκόμενον ἐνδέχεται ὡς γινώσκοντα σημῆναι τούτῳ τῷ λόγῳ⁵.

Καὶ ἆρα ὃ ὁρᾷ τις, τοῦτο ὁρᾷ; ὁρᾷ δὲ τὸν κίονα, ὥστε ὁρᾷ ὁ κίων⁶.

Καὶ ἆρα ὃ σὺ φῂς εἶναι, τοῦτο σὺ φῂς εἶναι; φῂς δὲ λίθον εἶναι, σὺ ἄρα φῂς λίθος εἶναι⁷.

Καὶ ἆρ' ἔστι σιγῶντα λέγειν; διττὸν γὰρ καὶ τὸ σιγῶντα λέγειν, τό τε τὸν λέγοντα σιγᾶν καὶ τὸ τὰ λεγόμενα⁸.

Εἰσὶ δὲ τρεῖς τρόποι τῶν παρὰ τὴν ὁμωνυμίαν καὶ τὴν ἀμφιβολίαν, εἷς μὲν ὅταν ἢ ὁ λόγος ἢ τοὔνομα κυρίως σημαίνῃ πλείω, οἷον ἀετὸς καὶ κύων· εἷς δὲ ὅταν εἰωθότες ὦμεν οὕτω λέγειν· τρίτος δὲ ὅταν τὸ συντεθὲν πλείω σημαίνῃ, κεχωρισμένον δὲ ἁπλῶς, οἷον τὸ ἐπίσταται γράμματα. Ἑκάτερον μὲν γάρ, εἰ ἔτυχεν, ἕν τι σημαίνει, τὸ ἐπίσταται καὶ τὰ γράμματα· ἄμφω δὲ πλείω, ἢ τὸ τὰ γράμματα αὐτὰ ἐπιστήμην ἔχειν ἢ τῶν γραμμάτων ἄλλον.

Ἡ μὲν οὖν ἀμφιβολία καὶ ὁμωνυμία παρὰ τούτους τοὺς τρόπους ἐστίν, παρὰ δὲ τὴν σύνθεσιν τὰ τοιάδε, οἷον τὸ δύνασθαι καθήμενον βαδίζειν καὶ μὴ γράφοντα γράφειν. Οὐ γὰρ ταὐτὸ σημαίνει, ἂν διελών τις εἴπῃ καὶ συνθείς, ὡς δυνατὸν τὸν καθήμενον βαδίζειν καὶ μὴ γράφοντα γράφειν· καὶ τοῦθ' ὡσαύτως ἄν τις συνθῇ, τὸν μὴ γράφοντα γράφειν· σημαίνει γὰρ

of antecedent conditions, and this may be evil, or the condition of a desirable result, which is a good.

Again :—The same person is standing and sitting, and is an invalid and restored to health. For he who rose up is standing, and he who was getting well is restored to health. But it was the sitter who rose up, and the invalid who was getting well. Invalid and sitter mean respectively more than one person, both him who is now an invalid or sitting, and him who was formerly an invalid or sitting. He who is getting well may be now an invalid, but he who is restored to health can only have been formerly an invalid.

Of ambiguous propositions the following are instances. I hope that you the enemy may slay.

Whom one knows, he knows. Either the person knowing or the person known is here affirmed to know.

What one sees, that one sees: one sees a pillar: ergo, that one pillar sees.

What you *are* holding, that you are: you are holding a stone: ergo, a stone you are.

Is a speaking of the silent possible? "The silent" denotes either the speaker or the subject of speech.

There are three kinds of ambiguity of term or proposition. The first is when there is an equal linguistic propriety in several interpretations; the second when one is improper but customary; the third when the ambiguity arises in the combination of elements that are themselves unambiguous, as in "knowing letters." "Knowing" and "letters" are perhaps separately unambiguous, but in combination may imply either that the letters are known or that they themselves have knowledge. Such are the modes in which propositions and terms may be ambiguous.

Wrong conjunction is the source of fallacy in the following instances. A man can walk when sitting or write when not writing. The meaning is different according as "sitting" is joined with

ὡς ἔχει δύναμιν τοῦ μὴ γράφοντα γράφειν⁹. Ἐὰν δὲ μὴ συνθῇ, ὅτι ἔχει δύναμιν, ὅτε οὐ γράφει, τοῦ γράφειν. Καὶ μανθάνει νῦν γράμματα, εἴπερ ἐμάνθανεν ἃ ἐπίσταται¹⁰. Ἔτι τὸ ἓν μόνον δυνάμενον φέρειν πολλὰ δύνασθαι φέρειν. Παρὰ δὲ τὴν διαίρεσιν, ὅτι τὰ πίντ' ἐστὶ δύο καὶ τρία, καὶ περιττὰ καὶ ἄρτια. Καὶ τὸ μεῖζον ἴσον· τοσοῦτον γὰρ καὶ ἔτι πρός. Ὁ γὰρ αὐτὸς λόγος διῃρημένος καὶ συγκείμενος οὐκ ἀεὶ ταὐτὸ σημαίνειν ἂν δόξειεν, οἷον " ἐγώ σ' ἔθηκα δοῦλον ὄντ' ἐλεύθερον¹²," καὶ τὸ " πεντήκοντ' ἀνδρῶν ἑκατὸν λίπε δῖος Ἀχιλλεύς."

Παρὰ δὲ τὴν προσῳδίαν ἐν μὲν τοῖς ἄνευ γραφῆς διαλεκτικοῖς οὐ ῥᾴδιον ποιῆσαι λόγον, ἐν δὲ τοῖς γεγραμμένοις καὶ ποιήμασι μᾶλλον, οἷον καὶ τὸν Ὅμηρον ἔνιοι διορθοῦνται πρὸς τοὺς ἐλέγχοντας ὡς ἀτόπως εἰρηκότα " τὸ μὲν οὗ καταπύθεται ὄμβρῳ." Λύουσι γὰρ αὐτὸ τῇ προσῳδίᾳ, λέγοντες τὸ οὔ ὀξύτερον. Καὶ τὸ περὶ τὸ ἐνύπνιον τοῦ Ἀγαμέμνονος, ὅτι οὐκ αὐτὸς ὁ Ζεὺς εἶπεν " δίδομεν δέ οἱ εὖχος ἀρέσθαι," ἀλλὰ τῷ ἐνυπνίῳ ἐνετέλλετο διδόναι. Τὰ μὲν οὖν τοιαῦτα παρὰ τὴν προσῳδίαν ἐστίν.

Οἱ δὲ παρὰ τὸ σχῆμα τῆς λέξεως συμβαίνουσιν, ὅταν τὸ μὴ ταὐτὸ ὡσαύτως ἑρμηνεύηται, οἷον τὸ ἄρρεν θῆλυ ἢ τὸ θῆλυ ἄρρεν, ἢ τὸ μεταξὺ θάτερον τούτων, ἢ πάλιν τὸ ποιὸν ποσὸν ἢ τὸ ποσὸν ποιόν, ἢ τὸ ποιοῦν πάσχον ἢ τὸ διακείμενον ποιεῖν, καὶ τἆλλα δ', ὡς διήρηται πρότερον. Ἔστι γὰρ τὸ μὴ τῶν ποιεῖν ὂν ὡς τῶν ποιεῖν τι τῇ λέξει σημαίνειν. Οἷον τὸ ὑγιαίνειν ὁμοίως τῷ σχήματι τῆς λέξεως λέγεται τῷ τέμνειν ἢ οἰκοδομεῖν· καίτοι τὸ μὲν ποιόν τι καὶ διακείμενόν πως δηλοῖ, τὸ δὲ ποιεῖν τι. Τὸν αὐτὸν δὲ τρόπον καὶ ἐπὶ τῶν ἄλλων.

V. Οἱ μὲν οὖν παρὰ τὴν λέξιν ἔλεγχοι ἐκ τούτων τῶν τόπων εἰσίν· τῶν δ' ἔξω τῆς λέξεως παραλογισμῶν εἴδη ἐστὶν ἑπτά, ἓν μὲν παρὰ τὸ συμβεβηκός, δεύτερον δὲ τὸ ἁπλῶς ἢ μὴ ἁπλῶς ἀλλὰ πῇ ἢ ποῦ ἢ ποτὲ ἢ πρός τι λέγεσθαι, τρίτον δὲ τὸ παρὰ τὴν τοῦ ἐλέγχου ἄγνοιαν, τέταρτον δὲ τὸ παρὰ τὸ ἑπό-

"can" or with "walk," and "not writing" with "can" or with "write."

He knows the alphabet he had to learn.

The lesser weight if you can hardly lift the greater weight you easily can lift.

Of wrong disjunction the following are instances. Five is two and three: therefore five is even and odd [11]. The greater is equal to the less, for the greater is as much as the less—and something more. For the same words have different meanings when joined and disjoined; as, I made thee a slave originally free. Fifty warriors with Achilles fought a hundred of them bit the dust.

Accentuation in unwritten discussion can hardly furnish a fallacious reasoning, but only in written controversy and criticism on the poets. Homer [13], for instance, is emended against those who condemn the expression, "part thereof is rotten by the rain." Some meet the criticism by substituting an acute accent for the circumflex, making him say, "nought thereof is rotten by the rain." Again, in Agamemnon's dream, instead of making Jove say, "I grant him triumph o'er his foes," they make Jove command the dream to promise Agamemnon triumph o'er his foes [14]. These arguments, then, turn on accentuation.

Similarity of termination produces fallacy when unlike things have names with a like inflexion, a male object a feminine name, a female object a masculine name, or a neuter a masculine or feminine; or when a quantity has a name with the termination of a quality, or a quality a name with the termination of a quantity, or an agent a name with the termination of a patient, or a state a name with the termination of an action, and so on throughout the categories before enumerated [14]. For the name of what is not an action may terminate like a name of action, as "ailing" resembles in inflexion "cutting" and "building," though it expresses a quality or state, while they express actions, and so in the other categories.

V. LANGUAGE, then, furnishes occasion for seeming confutations in the modes we have mentioned. Independent of language, there are seven classes of paralogism arising from the equation of subject and accident; from the confusion of an absolute statement with a statement limited in manner, place,

μενον, πέμπτον δὲ τὸ παρὰ τὸ ἐν ἀρχῇ λαμβάνειν, ἕκτον δὲ τὸ μὴ αἴτιον ὡς αἴτιον τιθέναι, ἕβδομον δὲ τὸ τὰ πλείω ἐρωτήματα ἓν ποιεῖν.

Οἱ μὲν οὖν παρὰ τὸ συμβεβηκὸς [1] παραλογισμοί εἰσιν, ὅταν ὁμοίως ὁτιοῦν ἀξιωθῇ τῷ πράγματι καὶ τῷ συμβεβηκότι ὑπάρχειν. Ἐπεὶ γὰρ τῷ αὐτῷ πολλὰ συμβέβηκεν, οὐκ ἀνάγκη πᾶσι τοῖς κατηγορουμένοις, καὶ καθ' οὗ κατηγορεῖται, ταὐτὰ πάντα ὑπάρχειν. Οἷον εἰ ὁ Κορίσκος ἕτερον ἀνθρώπου, αὐτὸς αὑτοῦ ἕτερος· ἔστι γὰρ ἄνθρωπος. Ἢ εἰ Σωκράτους ἕτερος, ὁ δὲ Σωκράτης ἄνθρωπος, ἕτερον ἀνθρώπου φασὶν ὡμολογηκέναι διὰ τὸ συμβεβηκέναι, οὗ ἔφησεν ἕτερον εἶναι, τοῦτον εἶναι ἄνθρωπον.

Οἱ δὲ παρὰ τὸ ἁπλῶς τόδε ἢ πῇ λέγεσθαι καὶ μὴ κυρίως, ὅταν τὸ ἐν μέρει λεγόμενον ὡς ἁπλῶς εἰρημένον ληφθῇ, οἷον εἰ τὸ μὴ ὄν ἐστι δοξαστόν, ὅτι τὸ μὴ ὄν ἐστιν· οὐ γὰρ ταὐτὸν εἶναί τί τι καὶ εἶναι ἁπλῶς. Ἢ πάλιν ὅτι τὸ ὂν οὐκ ἔστιν ὄν, εἰ τῶν ὄντων τι μή ἐστιν, οἷον εἰ μὴ ἄνθρωπος. Οὐ γὰρ ταὐτὸ μὴ εἶναί τι καὶ ἁπλῶς μὴ εἶναι· φαίνεται δὲ διὰ τὸ πάρεγγυς τῆς λέξεως, καὶ μικρὸν διαφέρειν τὸ εἶναί τι τοῦ εἶναι καὶ τὸ μὴ εἶναί τι τοῦ μὴ εἶναι. Ὁμοίως δὲ καὶ τὸ παρὰ τὸ πῇ καὶ τὸ ἁπλῶς. Οἷον εἰ ὁ Ἰνδὸς ὅλος μέλας ὤν λευκός ἐστι τοὺς ὀδόντας· λευκὸς ἄρα καὶ οὐ λευκός ἐστιν. Ἢ εἰ ἄμφω πῇ, ὅτι ἅμα τὰ ἐναντία ὑπάρχει. Τὸ δὲ τοιοῦτον ἐπ' ἐνίων μὲν παντὶ θεωρῆσαι ῥᾴδιον, οἷον εἰ λαβὼν τὸν Αἰθίοπα εἶναι μέλανα, τοὺς ὀδόντας ἔροιτ' εἰ λευκός· εἰ οὖν ταύτῃ λευκός, ὅτι μέλας καὶ οὐ μέλας οἴοιτο διειλέχθαι, συλλογιστικῶς τελειώσας τὴν ἐρώτησιν. Ἐπ' ἐνίων δὲ λανθάνει πολλάκις, ἐφ' ὅσων, ὅταν πῇ λέγηται, κἂν τὸ ἁπλῶς δόξειεν ἀκολουθεῖν, καὶ ἐν ὅσοις μὴ ῥᾴδιον θεωρῆσαι πότερον αὐτῶν κυρίως ἀποδοτέον. Γίνεται δὲ τὸ τοιοῦτον ἐν οἷς ὁμοίως ὑπάρχει τὰ ἀντικείμενα· δοκεῖ γὰρ ἢ ἄμφω ἢ μηδέτερον δοτέον ἁπλῶς εἶναι κατηγορεῖν, οἷον εἰ τὸ μὲν ἥμισυ λευκὸν τὸ δ' ἥμισυ μέλαν, πότερον λευκὸν ἢ μέλαν;

time, or relation; from an inadequate notion of confutation; from a conversion of consequent and antecedent; from begging the question; from taking what is not a cause for a cause; and, lastly, from putting many questions as one.

The equation of subject and accident occasions fallacy when it is assumed that subject and accident have all their attributes in common. For a subject has many accidents, and it is not necessary that the accidents and the subject should have all their attributes in common. For example, if a man is not Coriscus it does not follow that Coriscus is not Coriscus because Coriscus is a man⁵: nor, because Coriscus is not Socrates and Socrates is a man, does it follow that Coriscus is not a man, because Socrates, who is denied of Coriscus, is an accident of man³.

Confusion of absolute, and qualified or limited, statements gives rise to fallacy when the mere copula is taken as affirming absolute existence; when, for instance, from the premiss, that what is not, is believable, we infer that what is not, is; for the copula affirms merely a relation, not absolute existence: or, again, if we infer that what is, is not, because it is not a man or some particular thing; for not to be a particular thing is not the same as absolutely not to be. The semblance of identity is produced by the similarity of the expressions and the slightness of the difference between the enunciation of existence and attribution, or of non-existence and non-attribution, or between restricted and unrestricted predication. If, for instance, the Indian is black generally, but white in respect of his teeth, it may be argued that he is white and not white; or, if he has both attributes in different respects, that contraries coexist. The difference in some cases is easily perceived; as, for instance, if from the premisses that the Ethiopian is black, and that his teeth are white, one should fancy he had proved that he is black and not black, putting the propositions into syllogistic form. But it is often difficult to detect, when a qualified premiss is conceded but the unqualified proposition seems to follow⁴, and when it is difficult to say which alternative is properly affirmed; as happens when opposite qualities equally exist; for it seems as if either both or neither may be absolutely affirmed. If, for instance, half is white and half is black, which is the whole to be called, white or black⁵?

ΠΕΡΙ ΣΟΦΙΣΤΙΚΩΝ

Οἱ δὲ παρὰ τὸ μὴ διωρίσθαι τί ἐστι συλλογισμὸς ἢ τί ἔλεγχος, ἀλλὰ παρὰ τὴν ἔλλειψιν γίνονται τοῦ λόγου. Ἔλεγχος μὲν γὰρ ἀντίφασις τοῦ αὐτοῦ καὶ ἑνός, μὴ ὀνόματος ἀλλὰ πράγματος, καὶ ὀνόματος μὴ συνωνύμου ἀλλὰ τοῦ αὐτοῦ, ἐκ τῶν δοθέντων, ἐξ ἀνάγκης, μὴ συναριθμουμένου τοῦ ἐν ἀρχῇ, κατὰ ταὐτὸ καὶ πρὸς ταὐτὸ καὶ ὡσαύτως καὶ ἐν τῷ αὐτῷ χρόνῳ. Τὸν αὐτὸν δὲ τρόπον καὶ τὸ ψεύσασθαι περί τινος. Ἔνιοι δὲ ἀπολιπόντες τι τῶν λεχθέντων φαίνονται ἐλέγχειν, οἷον ὅτι ταὐτὸ διπλάσιον καὶ οὐ διπλάσιον· τὰ γὰρ δύο τοῦ μὲν ἑνὸς διπλάσια, τῶν δὲ τριῶν οὐ διπλάσια. Ἢ εἰ τὸ αὐτὸ τοῦ αὐτοῦ διπλάσιον καὶ οὐ διπλάσιον, ἀλλ' οὐ κατὰ ταὐτό· κατὰ μὲν γὰρ τὸ μῆκος διπλάσιον, κατὰ δὲ τὸ πλάτος οὐ διπλάσιον. Ἢ εἰ τοῦ αὐτοῦ καὶ κατὰ ταὐτὸ καὶ ὡσαύτως, ἀλλ' οὐχ ἅμα· διόπερ ἐστὶ φαινόμενος ἔλεγχος. Ἕλκοι δ' ἄν τις τοῦτον καὶ εἰς τοὺς παρὰ τὴν λέξιν.

Οἱ δὲ παρὰ τὸ ἐν ἀρχῇ λαμβάνειν γίνονται μὲν οὕτως καὶ τοσαυταχῶς ὁσαχῶς ἐνδέχεται τὸ ἐξ ἀρχῆς αἰτεῖσθαι, φαίνονται δ' ἐλέγχειν διὰ τὸ μὴ δύνασθαι συνορᾶν τὸ ταὐτὸν καὶ τὸ ἕτερον.

Ὁ δὲ παρὰ τὸ ἑπόμενον ἔλεγχος διὰ τὸ οἴεσθαι ἀντιστρέφειν τὴν ἀκολούθησιν. Ὅταν γὰρ τοῦδε ὄντος ἐξ ἀνάγκης τοδὶ ᾖ, καὶ τοῦδε ὄντος οἴονται καὶ θάτερον εἶναι ἐξ ἀνάγκης. Ὅθεν καὶ αἱ περὶ τὴν δόξαν ἐκ τῆς αἰσθήσεως ἀπάται γίνονται. Πολλάκις γὰρ τὴν χολὴν μέλι ὑπέλαβον διὰ τὸ ἕπεσθαι τὸ ξανθὸν χρῶμα τῷ μέλιτι· καὶ ἐπεὶ συμβαίνει τὴν γῆν ὕσαντος γίνεσθαι διάβροχον, κἂν ᾖ διάβροχος, ὑπολαμβάνομεν ὗσαι. Τὸ δ' οὐκ ἀναγκαῖον. Ἔν τε τοῖς ῥητορικοῖς αἱ κατὰ τὸ σημεῖον ἀποδείξεις ἐκ τῶν ἑπομένων εἰσίν. Βουλόμενοι γὰρ δεῖξαι ὅτι μοιχός, τὸ ἑπόμενον ἔλαβον, ὅτι καλλωπιστὴς ἢ ὅτι νύκτωρ ὁρᾶται πλανώμενος. Πολλοῖς δὲ ταῦτα μὲν ὑπάρχει, τὸ δὲ κατηγορούμενον οὐχ ὑπάρχει. Ὁμοίως δὲ καὶ ἐν τοῖς συλλογιστικοῖς, οἷον ὁ Μελίσσου λόγος ὅτι ἄπειρον τὸ ἅπαν, λαβὼν τὸ μὲν ἅπαν ἀγένητον (ἐκ γὰρ μὴ ὄντος οὐδὲν ἂν γενέσθαι), τὸ δὲ γενόμενον ἐξ ἀρχῆς γενέσθαι. Εἰ μὴ οὖν

Other fallacies arise from not defining proof or confutation, and neglecting some element of the definition. To confute is to contradict one and the same predicate, not only the name but also the reality, and not only a synonymous name but the identical name, as a necessary consequence of the premisses, not including the point to be proved, in the identical respect, relation, manner, and time in which the predicate is affirmed by the opponent. The same limitations are required in defining false proposition. Sometimes a man omits one of the elements, and then appears to confute, proving, for instance, that the same thing is double and not double, because two is the double of one and not the double of three; or that the same is double and not double of the same correlative but not in the same respect, double in length but not in breadth; or double of the same correlative in the same respect and manner but not at the same time, whereby the proof is vitiated. With some violence we might put this class under the head of fallacies dependent on language.

Fallacies from assuming the conclusion fall into as many classes as there are modes of assuming the conclusion. The semblance of proof arises from the difficulty of deciding what is different or identical[7].

A consequent gives rise to fallacy because the consecution of consequent and antecedent seems reciprocal. If B follows from A we imagine that A must follow from B. Hence mistaken perception in sensation, as when gall is mistaken for honey because it is yellow; and because rain wets the ground, wetness of the ground is supposed a proof of rain. In rhetorical argument proof by signs[8] is based on consequences, as a man is proved to be an adulterer by the characteristics of the adulterer, dressing elaborately or wandering at night, which facts may be true while the accusation is false. So in dialectic reasoning. Melissus in his proof of the infinite extension of the universe assumes that the universe is not generated, because from nothing nothing can be generated, and that what is generated has a beginning (is finite in space), and concludes that the universe has no beginning, and therefore is infinite in space. This does not follow. Because whatever is generated has a beginning,

γέγονεν, ἀρχὴν οὐκ ἔχει τὸ πᾶν, ὥστ' ἄπειρον. Οὐκ ἀνάγκη δὲ τοῦτο συμβαίνειν· οὐ γὰρ εἰ τὸ γενόμενον ἅπαν ἀρχὴν ἔχει, καὶ εἴ τι ἀρχὴν ἔχει, γέγονεν, ὥσπερ οὐδ' εἰ ὁ πυρέττων θερμός, καὶ τὸν θερμὸν ἀνάγκη πυρέττειν.

Ὁ δὲ παρὰ τὸ μὴ αἴτιον ὡς αἴτιον, ὅταν προσληφθῇ τὸ ἀναίτιον ὡς παρ' ἐκεῖνο γινομένου τοῦ ἐλέγχου. Συμβαίνει δὲ τὸ τοιοῦτον ἐν τοῖς εἰς τὸ ἀδύνατον συλλογισμοῖς· ἐν τούτοις γὰρ ἀναγκαῖον ἀναιρεῖν τι τῶν κειμένων. Ἐὰν οὖν ἐγκαταριθμηθῇ ἐν τοῖς ἀναγκαίοις ἐρωτήμασι πρὸς τὸ συμβαῖνον ἀδύνατον, δόξει παρὰ τοῦτο γίνεσθαι πολλάκις ὁ ἔλεγχος, οἷον ὅτι οὐκ ἔστι ψυχὴ καὶ ζωὴ ταὐτόν· εἰ γὰρ φθορᾷ γένεσις ἐναντίον, καὶ τῇ τινὶ φθορᾷ ἔσται τις γένεσις ἐναντίον· ὁ δὲ θάνατος φθορά τις καὶ ἐναντίον ζωῇ, ὥστε γένεσις ἡ ζωὴ καὶ τὸ ζῆν γίνεσθαι· τοῦτο δ' ἀδύνατον· οὐκ ἄρα ταὐτὸν ἡ ψυχὴ καὶ ἡ ζωή. Οὐ δὴ συλλελόγισται· συμβαίνει γάρ, κἂν μή τις ταὐτὸ φῇ τὴν ζωὴν τῇ ψυχῇ, τὸ ἀδύνατον, ἀλλὰ μόνον ἐναντίον ζωὴν μὲν θανάτῳ, ὄντι φθορᾷ, φθορᾷ δὲ γένεσιν. Ἀσυλλόγιστοι μὲν οὖν ἁπλῶς οὐκ εἰσὶν οἱ τοιοῦτοι λόγοι, πρὸς δὲ τὸ προκείμενον ἀσυλλόγιστοι. Καὶ λανθάνει πολλάκις οὐχ ἧττον αὐτοὺς τοὺς ἐρωτῶντας τὸ τοιοῦτον.

Οἱ μὲν οὖν παρὰ τὸ ἑπόμενον καὶ παρὰ τὸ μὴ αἴτιον λόγοι τοιοῦτοί εἰσιν· οἱ δὲ παρὰ τὸ τὰ δύο ἐρωτήματα ἐν ποιεῖν, ὅταν λανθάνῃ πλείω ὄντα, καὶ ὡς ἑνὸς ὄντος ἀποδοθῇ ἀπόκρισις μία. Ἐπ' ἐνίων μὲν οὖν ῥᾴδιον ἰδεῖν ὅτι πλείω, καὶ ὅτι οὐ δοτέον ἀπόκρισιν, οἷον πότερον ἡ γῆ θάλαττά ἐστιν ἢ ὁ οὐρανός[10]; ἐπ' ἐνίων δ' ἧττον, καί, ὡς ἑνὸς ὄντος, ἢ ὁμολογοῦσι τῷ μὴ ἀποκρίνεσθαι τὸ ἐρωτώμενον, ἢ ἐλέγχεσθαι φαίνονται, οἷον ἆρ' οὗτος καὶ οὗτός ἐστιν ἄνθρωπος; ὥστ' ἄν τις τύπτῃ τοῦτον καὶ τοῦτον, ἄνθρωπον ἀλλ' οὐκ ἀνθρώπους τυπτήσει. Ἢ πάλιν, ὧν τὰ μέν ἐστιν ἀγαθὰ τὰ δ' οὐκ ἀγαθά, πάντα ἀγαθὰ ἢ οὐκ ἀγαθά; ὁπότερον γὰρ ἂν φῇ, ἔστι μὲν ὡς ἔλεγχον ἢ ψεῦδος φαινόμενον

it need not be that whatever has a beginning is generated, i. e. that whatever is not generated has no beginning: just as, because every man in a fever is hot, it does not follow that every man who is hot is in a fever.

We mistake for a cause what is not a cause when an irrelevant proposition has been foisted into an argument as if it were one of the necessary premisses. This is practised in reductio ad impossibile, for it is here that the proposition confuted is one of the premisses. If, then, a foreign proposition be introduced among the premisses required to furnish an impossible consequence, it may be mistaken for the cause of that impossible consequence. Thus, to prove that Life and the Soul are not identical, a man assumes that the opposite of destruction is generation, and therefore the opposite of a particular destruction is a particular generation. But Death is a particular destruction and its opposite is Life. Life therefore is generation, and to live is to be generated. This is absurd: therefore Life and the Soul are not identical. There is no sequence here: for, independently of the identification of Life and the Soul, the impossible conclusion follows from the premisses that Life is the opposite of Death, that Death is destruction, and that the opposite of destruction is generation. Such an argument is not entirely inconclusive; but it does not bear on the point in dispute, and of this the confuter himself is often unconscious[a].

The conversion of consequent and antecedent and false imputation of a result to a cause gives rise to fallacies in the way we have explained: the union of several questions in one occasions a fallacy when the plurality of questions is not detected and no single answer is true. It is sometimes easy to see that there is more than one question, and that a single answer should not be given; for instance, Is the ocean surrounded by the earth, and the earth by the sky? Sometimes it is not; and the answerer, supposing that the question is single, either confesses defeat by silence, or exposes himself to seeming confutation. For instance, Is A and B a man? Yes. Then if you strike A and B you strike not men but a man. Again; if part is good and part evil, is the whole good or evil? Whichever you answer you are open to a seeming confutation or conviction of

ΠΕΡΙ ΣΟΦΙΣΤΙΚΩΝ

δόξειεν ἂν ποιεῖν· τὸ γὰρ φάναι τῶν μὴ ἀγαθῶν τι εἶναι ἀγαθὸν ἢ τῶν ἀγαθῶν μὴ ἀγαθὸν ψεῦδος. Ὁτὲ δὲ προσληφθέντων τινῶν κἂν ἔλεγχος γίνοιτο ἀληθινός, οἷον εἴ τις δοίη ὁμοίως ἓν καὶ πολλὰ λέγεσθαι λευκὰ καὶ γυμνὰ καὶ τυφλά. Εἰ γὰρ τυφλὸν τὸ μὴ ἔχον ὄψιν πεφυκὸς δ' ἔχειν, καὶ τυφλὰ ἔσται τὰ μὴ ἔχοντα ὄψιν πεφυκότα δ' ἔχειν. Ὅταν οὖν τὸ μὲν ἔχῃ τὸ δὲ μὴ ἔχῃ, τὰ ἄμφω ἔσται ἢ ὁρῶντα ἢ τυφλά· ὅπερ ἀδύνατον.

VI. Ἢ δὴ οὕτως διαιρετέον τοὺς φαινομένους συλλογισμοὺς καὶ ἐλέγχους, ἢ πάντας ἀνακτέον εἰς τὴν τοῦ ἐλέγχου ἄγνοιαν, ἀρχὴν ταύτην ποιησαμένους· ἔστι γὰρ ἅπαντας ἀναλῦσαι τοὺς λεχθέντας τρόπους εἰς τὸν τοῦ ἐλέγχου διορισμόν. Πρῶτον μὲν εἰ ἀσυλλόγιστοι· δεῖ γὰρ ἐκ τῶν κειμένων συμβαίνειν τὸ συμπέρασμα, ὥστε λέγειν ἐξ ἀνάγκης ἀλλὰ μὴ φαίνεσθαι. Ἔπειτα καὶ κατὰ τὰ μέρη τοῦ διορισμοῦ.

Τῶν μὲν γὰρ ἐν τῇ λέξει οἱ μέν εἰσι παρὰ τὸ διττόν, οἷον ἥ τε ὁμωνυμία καὶ ὁ λόγος καὶ ἡ ὁμοιοσχημοσύνη (σύνηθες γὰρ τὸ πάντα ὡς τόδε τι σημαίνειν), ἡ δὲ σύνθεσις καὶ διαίρεσις καὶ προσῳδία τῷ μὴ τὸν αὐτὸν εἶναι τὸν λόγον ἢ τοὔνομα διαφέρον. Ἔδει δὲ καὶ τοῦτο, καθάπερ καὶ τὸ πρᾶγμα ταὐτόν, εἰ μέλλει ἔλεγχος ἢ συλλογισμὸς ἔσεσθαι, οἷον εἰ λώπιον, μὴ ἱμάτιον συλλογίσασθαι ἀλλὰ λώπιον. Ἀληθὲς μὲν γὰρ κἀκεῖνο, ἀλλ' οὐ συλλελόγισται, ἀλλ' ἔτι ἐρωτήματος δεῖ, ὅτι ταὐτὸν σημαίνει, πρὸς τὸν ζητοῦντα τὸ διὰ τί.

Οἱ δὲ παρὰ τὸ συμβεβηκὸς ὁρισθέντος τοῦ συλλογισμοῦ φανεροὶ γίνονται. Τὸν αὐτὸν γὰρ ὁρισμὸν δεῖ καὶ τοῦ ἐλέγχου γίνεσθαι, πλὴν προσκεῖσθαι τὴν ἀντίφασιν· ὁ γὰρ ἔλεγχος συλλογισμὸς ἀντιφάσεως. Εἰ οὖν μή ἐστι συλλογισμὸς τοῦ συμβεβηκότος, οὐ γίνεται ἔλεγχος. Οὐ γὰρ εἰ τούτων ὄντων ἀνάγκη τόδ' εἶναι, τοῦτο δ' ἐστὶ λευκόν, ἀνάγκη λευκὸν εἶναι διὰ τὸν συλλογισμόν³. Οὐδ' εἰ τὸ τρίγωνον δυοῖν ὀρθαῖν ἴσας

false statement, for the statement that good is evil, or evil is good, is false. Sometimes indeed the addition of a premiss would give room for a genuine confutation: e.g. if you grant that the same circumstances justify us in calling a single thing and a number of things white, or naked, or blind, because if one animal is blind when deprived of sight which it naturally has, a number of animals are blind when deprived of sight which they naturally have. If, then, one is blind and another sees, both or neither will be blind or see: which is false[11].

VI. We may either divide seeming proofs and confutations into these classes, or reduce them all to a false conception of confutation, laying down the true conception as a basis. For all the fallacies we enumerated may be resolved into offences against the definition of confutation; for either the reasonings are inconclusive; whereas the premisses ought to involve the conclusion, of necessity and not merely in appearance; or they fail to satisfy the remaining elements of the definition.

Of those that depend on language some fail in the singleness of the object signified, as those occasioned by the ambiguity of term or proposition or similarity of termination; the last of which classes contains many fallacies that depend on our custom of speaking of attributes in the terms proper to substances[1]. Those from conjunction, disjunction, and accentuation want even that singleness of name or proposition which, as well as singleness of the thing signified, is required in proof and confutation. If, for instance, the thesis speaks of cloaks, the conclusion of the confutation must not speak of mantles but of cloaks. The conclusion may be true of cloaks when the other word is employed, but the reasoning is unfinished, and requires a further proposition that the words are synonymous, if the answerer demands to have it explained how he is refuted[1].

The equation of subject and accident will be seen to offend against the definition of proof, which is that of confutation minus the condition of contradiction. For confutation is disproof, or contradictory proof. If, then, in proof we cannot identify subject and accident, no more can we conclude of the subject whatever is true of the accident, or vice versa, in confutation. If the premiss states a fact of the subject A, and

ἔχει, συμβέβηκε δ' αὐτῷ σχήματι εἶναι ἢ πρώτῳ ἢ ἀρχῇ, ὅτι σχῆμα ἢ ἀρχὴ ἢ πρῶτον τοῦτο. Οὐ γὰρ ᾗ σχῆμα οὐδ' ᾗ πρῶτον, ἀλλ' ᾗ τρίγωνον, ἡ ἀπόδειξις. Ὁμοίως δὲ καὶ ἐπὶ τῶν ἄλλων. "Ωστ' εἰ ὁ ἔλεγχος συλλογισμός τις, οὐκ ἂν εἴη ὁ κατὰ συμβεβηκὸς ἔλεγχος. Ἀλλὰ παρὰ τοῦτο καὶ οἱ τεχνῖται καὶ ὅλως οἱ ἐπιστήμονες ὑπὸ τῶν ἀνεπιστημόνων ἐλέγχονται· κατὰ συμβεβηκὸς γὰρ ποιοῦνται τοὺς συλλογισμοὺς πρὸς τοὺς εἰδότας. Οἱ δ' οὐ δυνάμενοι διαιρεῖν ἢ ἐρωτώμενοι διδόασιν ἢ οὐ δόντες οἴονται δεδωκέναι.

Οἱ δὲ παρὰ τὸ πῇ καὶ ἁπλῶς, ὅτι οὐ τοῦ αὐτοῦ ἡ κατάφασις καὶ ἡ ἀπόφασις. Τοῦ γὰρ πῇ λευκοῦ τὸ πῇ οὐ λευκόν, τοῦ δ' ἁπλῶς λευκοῦ τὸ ἁπλῶς οὐ λευκὸν ἀπόφασις. Εἰ οὖν δόντος πῇ εἶναι λευκὸν ὡς ἁπλῶς εἰρημένου λαμβάνει, οὐ ποιεῖ ἔλεγχον, φαίνεται δὲ διὰ τὴν ἄγνοιαν τοῦ τί ἐστιν ἔλεγχος.

Φανερώτατοι δὲ πάντων οἱ πρότερον λεχθέντες παρὰ τὸν τοῦ ἐλέγχου διορισμόν· διὸ καὶ προσηγορεύθησαν οὕτως· παρὰ γὰρ τοῦ λόγου τὴν ἔλλειψιν ἡ φαντασία γίνεται, καὶ διαιρουμένοις οὕτως κανὸν ἐπὶ πᾶσι τούτοις θετέον τὴν τοῦ λόγου ἔλλειψιν".

Οἵ τε παρὰ τὸ λαμβάνειν τὸ ἐν ἀρχῇ καὶ τὸ ἀναίτιον ὡς αἴτιον τιθέναι δῆλοι διὰ τοῦ ὁρισμοῦ. Δεῖ γὰρ τὸ συμπέρασμα τῷ ταῦτ' εἶναι συμβαίνειν', ὅπερ οὐκ ἦν ἐν τοῖς ἀναιτίοις· καὶ πάλιν μὴ ἀριθμουμένου τοῦ ἐξ ἀρχῆς, ὅπερ οὐκ ἔχουσιν οἱ παρὰ τὴν αἴτησιν τοῦ ἐν ἀρχῇ.

Οἱ δὲ παρὰ τὸ ἑπόμενον μέρος εἰσὶ τοῦ συμβεβηκότος· τὸ γὰρ ἑπόμενον συμβέβηκε, διαφέρει δὲ τοῦ συμβεβηκότος, ὅτι τὸ μὲν συμβεβηκός ἐστιν ἐφ' ἑνὸς μόνου λαβεῖν, οἷον ταὐτὸ εἶναι τὸ ξανθὸν καὶ μέλι καὶ τὸ λευκὸν καὶ κύκνον, τὸ δὲ παρεπόμενον ἀεὶ ἐν πλείοσιν· τὰ γὰρ ἑνὶ ταὐτῷ ταὐτὰ καὶ ἀλλήλοις

white is an accident of A, it does not follow that the fact is true of all that is white. If a triangle contains angles equal to two right angles, and figure, element, or principle is an accident of triangle, it does not follow that every figure, element, or principle contains angles equal to two right angles. For it is not figure, element, or principle, but triangle, that is essentially connected with this property by the demonstration[4]. And so in other cases. Wherefore, if confutation is a species of proof, a reasoning that assumes the equivalence of subject and accident cannot be a confutation. It is by this assumption that artists and men of science are confuted by the unscientific. The latter assume the subject and accident to be interchangeable, and the men of science, knowing the essential subject of a law and unready at distinction, either acknowledge the equivalence or imagine it has been acknowledged[5].

Fallacies from not distinguishing absolute and limited statements fail to deny the identical predicate that is affirmed in the thesis. The true negation of partially white is, not partially white; of totally white, not totally white. If, therefore, the admission that an object is partially white is used as an admission that it is totally white, the confutation of the thesis that it is not totally white is only apparent, and depends on a false notion of confutation.

Most readily referrible to misconception of confutation are the class which we mentioned as such before, and which hence received their special denomination, for their semblance arises from the want of a definition, though in making such a class we must admit that its differentia is a character common to all the classes.

Assuming the point in issue, and treating as a cause what is not a cause, are at once excluded by the definition of proof; for the conclusion must be a consequence of the premisses, which it is not when we mistake the cause; and must not be assumed among the premisses, as it is in begging the question.

Fallacies from the consequent are a species of those from the accident, and differ from other fallacies from accident because the latter identify the accident with a single subject, as, for instance, yellow with honey, and white with swan; while fallacies from a consequent connect the consequent with two

ἀξιοῦμεν εἶναι ταὐτά· διὸ γίνεται παρὰ τὸ ἑπόμενον ἔλεγχος. Ἔστι δ' οὐ πάντως ἀληθές, οἷον ἂν ᾖ λευκὸν κατὰ συμβεβηκὸς καὶ γὰρ ἡ χιὼν καὶ ὁ κύκνος τῷ λευκῷ ταὐτόν. Ἢ πάλιν, ὡς ἐν τῷ Μελίσσου λόγῳ, τὸ αὐτὸ εἶναι λαμβάνει τὸ γεγονέναι καὶ ἀρχὴν ἔχειν, ἢ τὸ ἴσοις γίνεσθαι καὶ ταὐτὸ μέγεθος λαμβάνειν. Ὅτι γὰρ τὸ γεγονὸς ἔχει ἀρχήν, καὶ τὸ ἔχον ἀρχὴν γεγονέναι ἀξιοῖ, ὡς ἄμφω ταὐτὰ ὄντα τῷ ἀρχὴν ἔχειν, τό τε γεγονὸς καὶ τὸ πεπερασμένον. Ὁμοίως δὲ καὶ ἐπὶ τῶν ἴσων γινομένων· εἰ τὰ τὸ αὐτὸ μέγεθος καὶ ἓν λαμβάνοντα ἴσα γίνεται, καὶ τὰ ἴσα γινόμενα ἓν μέγεθος λαμβάνει. Ὥστε τὸ ἑπόμενον λαμβάνει. Ἐπεὶ οὖν ὁ παρὰ τὸ συμβεβηκὸς ἔλεγχος ἐν τῇ ἀγνοίᾳ τοῦ ἐλέγχου, φανερὸν ὅτι καὶ ὁ παρὰ τὸ ἑπόμενον. Ἐπισκεπτέον δὲ τοῦτο καὶ ἄλλως.

Οἱ δὲ παρὰ τὸ τὰ πλείω ἐρωτήματα ἓν ποιεῖν ἐν τῷ μὴ διαρθροῦν ἡμᾶς ἢ μὴ διαιρεῖν τὸν τῆς προτάσεως λόγον. Ἡ γὰρ πρότασίς ἐστιν ἓν καθ' ἑνός. Ὁ γὰρ αὐτὸς ὅρος ἑνὸς μόνου καὶ ἁπλῶς τοῦ πράγματος, οἷον ἀνθρώπου καὶ ἑνὸς μόνου ἀνθρώπου ὁμοίως δὲ καὶ ἐπὶ τῶν ἄλλων. Εἰ οὖν μία πρότασις ἡ ἓν καθ' ἑνὸς ἀξιοῦσα, καὶ ἁπλῶς ἔσται πρότασις ἡ τοιαύτη ἐρώτησις. Ἐπεὶ δ' ὁ συλλογισμὸς ἐκ πρωτάσεων, ὁ δ' ἔλεγχος συλλογισμός, καὶ ὁ ἔλεγχος ἔσται ἐκ προτάσεων. Εἰ οὖν ἡ πρότασις ἓν καθ' ἑνός, φανερὸν ὅτι καὶ οὗτος ἐν τῇ τοῦ ἐλέγχου ἀγνοίᾳ· φαίνεται γὰρ εἶναι πρότασις ἡ οὐκ οὖσα πρότασις. Εἰ μὲν οὖν δέδωκεν ἀπόκρισιν ὡς πρὸς μίαν ἐρώτησιν, ἔσται ἔλεγχος, εἰ δὲ μὴ δέδωκεν ἀλλὰ φαίνεται, φαινόμενος ἔλεγχος. Ὥστε πάντες οἱ τόποι πίπτουσιν εἰς τὴν τοῦ ἐλέγχου ἄγνοιαν, οἱ μὲν οὖν παρὰ τὴν λέξιν, ὅτι φαινομένη ἀντίφασις, ὅπερ ἦν ἴδιον τοῦ ἐλέγχου, οἱ δ' ἄλλοι παρὰ τὸν τοῦ συλλογισμοῦ ὅρον.

VII. Ἡ δ' ἀπάτη γίνεται τῶν μὲν παρὰ τὴν ὁμωνυμίαν καὶ τὸν λόγον τῷ μὴ δύνασθαι διαιρεῖν τὸ πολλαχῶς λεγόμενον

antecedents. When two terms are identified with a third, the axiom identifies them with one another; and it is this identification which gives rise to the fallacy from consequent. The axiom is not true if the identity in the premisses is only of subject and accident, else snow and swan, which have each an accidental identity with white, would be identical. Again:—the argument of Melissus identifies what is generated with what has a beginning, and equality with having received the same magnitude. Because all that is generated has a beginning he assumes that all that has a beginning is generated, and, having identified what has a beginning; with the finite in space, infers that all the finite in space is generated. So with equality. Because things which receive the same magnitude are equal, he assumes that things which are equal have received the same magnitude. That is to say, he converts two antecedents with the same consequent and thereby identifies the two antecedents. If, then, the fallacy from accident depends on a false idea of confutation, so does that from consequent. This topic must be handled again.

Fallacies from the union of several questions in one may be shewn to be illegitimate by developing the definition of proposition. Propositions conjoin a single subject and single predicate; for the definition of a class is the same as the definition of a single thing, that of man, for instance, as that of a single man, and so on. If, then, a single proposition conjoins a single subject and predicate, so does the class of proposition[a]. Now, as proof is composed of propositions, and confutation is proof, confutation must be composed of propositions. If, then, propositions ought to conjoin single subjects and predicates, the fallacies that fail in this shew a false conception of confutation, for they are composed of seeming but not genuine propositions. If an answer was given to a single question, there is a real confutation; if it only seemed to be given, a seeming confutation. All fallacies, then, are resolvable into a false conception of confutation; because some contain no genuine contradiction, which is peculiar to confutation, and others fail to satisfy the definition of proof.

VII. In fallacies by ambiguous terms and propositions the deception arises from our inability to discriminate the different

ΠΕΡΙ ΣΟΦΙΣΤΙΚΩΝ

(ἔνια γὰρ οὐκ εὔπορον διελεῖν, οἶον τὸ ἓν καὶ τὸ ὂν καὶ τὸ ταὐτόν), τῶν δὲ παρὰ σύνθεσιν καὶ διαίρεσιν τῷ μηδὲν οἴεσθαι διαφέρειν συντιθέμενον ἢ διαιρούμενον τὸν λόγον, καθάπερ ἐπὶ τῶν πλείστων. Ὁμοίως δὲ καὶ τῶν παρὰ τὴν προσῳδίαν· οὐ γὰρ ἄλλο δοκεῖ σημαίνειν ἀνιέμενος καὶ ἐπιτεινόμενος ὁ λόγος, ἐπ' οὐδενὸς ἢ οὐκ ἐπὶ πολλῶν. Τῶν δὲ παρὰ τὸ σχῆμα διὰ τὴν ὁμοιότητα τῆς λέξεως. Χαλεπὸν γὰρ διελεῖν ποῖα ὡσαύτως καὶ ποῖα ὡς ἑτέρως λέγεται· σχεδὸν γὰρ ὁ τοῦτο δυνάμενος ποιεῖν ἐγγύς ἐστι τοῦ θεωρεῖν τἀληθές. Μάλιστα δ' ἐπίσταται[2] συνεπινεύειν, ὅτι πᾶν τὸ κατηγορούμενόν τινος ὑπολαμβάνομεν τόδε τι καὶ ὡς ἓν ὑπακούομεν· τῷ γὰρ ἑνὶ καὶ τῇ οὐσίᾳ μάλιστα δοκεῖ παρέπεσθαι τὸ τόδε τι καὶ τὸ ὄν. Διὸ καὶ τῶν παρὰ τὴν λέξιν οὗτος ὁ τρόπος θετέος, πρῶτον μὲν ὅτι μᾶλλον ἡ ἀπάτη γίνεται μετ' ἄλλων σκοπουμένοις ἢ καθ' αὑτούς (ἡ μὲν γὰρ μετ' ἄλλου σκέψις διὰ λόγων, ἡ δὲ καθ' αὑτὸν οὐχ ἧττον δι' αὐτοῦ τοῦ πράγματος), εἶτα καὶ καθ' αὑτὸν ἀπατᾶσθαι συμβαίνει, ὅταν ἐπὶ τοῦ λόγου ποιῆται τὴν σκέψιν· ἔτι ἡ μὲν ἀπάτη ἐκ τῆς ὁμοιότητος, ἡ δ' ὁμοιότης ἐκ τῆς λέξεως. Τῶν δὲ παρὰ τὸ συμβεβηκὸς διὰ τὸ μὴ δύνασθαι διακρίνειν τὸ ταὐτὸν καὶ τὸ ἕτερον καὶ ἓν καὶ πολλά, μηδὲ τοῖς ποίοις τῶν κατηγορημάτων πάντα ταὐτὰ καὶ τῷ πράγματι συμβέβηκεν. Ὁμοίως δὲ καὶ τῶν παρὰ τὸ ἑπόμενον· μέρος γάρ τι τοῦ συμβεβηκότος τὸ ἑπόμενον. Ἔτι καὶ ἐπὶ πολλῶν φαίνεται καὶ ἀξιοῦται οὕτως, εἰ τόδε ἀπὸ τοῦδε μὴ χωρίζεται, μηδ' ἀπὸ θατέρου χωρίζεσθαι θάτερον. Τῶν δὲ παρὰ τὴν ἔλλειψιν τοῦ λόγου καὶ τῶν παρὰ τὸ πῇ καὶ ἁπλῶς ἐν τῷ παρὰ μικρὸν ἡ ἀπάτη· ὡς γὰρ οὐδὲν προσσημαῖνον τὸ τὶ ἢ πῇ ἢ πῶς ἢ τὸ νῦν καθόλου συγχωροῦμεν. Ὁμοίως δὲ καὶ ἐπὶ τῶν τὸ ἐν ἀρχῇ λαμβανόντων καὶ τῶν ἀναιτίων, καὶ ὅσοι τὰ πλείω ἐρωτήματα ὡς ἓν ποιοῦσιν· ἐν ἅπασι γὰρ ἡ ἀπάτη διὰ τὸ παρὰ μικρόν· οὐ γὰρ διακριβοῦμεν οὔτε τῆς προτάσεως οὔτε τοῦ συλλογισμοῦ τὸν ὅρον διὰ τὴν εἰρημένην αἰτίαν.

VIII. Ἐπεὶ δ' ἔχομεν παρ' ὅσα γίνονται οἱ φαινόμενοι συλλογισμοί, ἔχομεν καὶ παρ' ὁπόσα οἱ σοφιστικοὶ γένοιντ' ἂν

significations of an equivocal word, for it is sometimes no easy
task to classify the meanings of an equivocal word; for instance,
of Unity, Being, Identity. In fallacies of conjunction and
disjunction it arises from overlooking the difference produced
by the conjunction or disjunction, because in other cases it is
unimportant. So in fallacies of accentuation, because the tone
or pitch of the voice is generally indifferent to the sense¹. In
fallacies from similarity of termination the deception is due to
the similarity, for it is hard to define when similar forms of
expression indicate similar or dissimilar realities, and he who
can do it must be far advanced in the pursuit of truth. We are
seduced into error by our aptness to suppose that every predicate is determinate and single and that something single and
substantive is implied by determination and existence. This
class, then, must be reckoned among the fallacies from language:
firstly, because the deception is more common in reasoning with
others than in reasoning by ourselves; for in reasoning with
others we think the words, in reasoning by ourselves we think
the realities²: secondly, because in our solitary reasonings we are
more likely to be deceived when we think by words: thirdly,
because the deception arises from resemblance, and this lies in
the words. In fallacies from accident the deception arises from
inability to discriminate what is identical and different, one and
plural, and what predicates and subjects have or have not all
attributes in common. So in fallacies from consequent; for a
consequent is a species of accident, and in many cases it seems
to be true and is treated as an axiom that, if A never exists
without B, B never exists without A. In fallacies from not
defining confutation and from identifying absolute and limited
propositions the deception is due to the minuteness of the
difference⁴. We suppose the qualification of manner, mode,
relation, time, to be unimportant, and grant the unqualified
proposition. And so in begging the question, and misassigning
the cause, and uniting many propositions in one. In all these
the minuteness of the difference creates the deception, for it
makes us fail to entirely satisfy the definition of proposition and
proof⁵.

VIII. Possessing the sources of seeming proof we possess the
sources of sophistic proof and confutation¹. By sophistic con-

συλλογισμοὶ καὶ ἔλεγχοι. Λέγω δὲ σοφιστικὸν ἔλεγχον καὶ συλλογισμὸν οὐ μόνον τὸν φαινόμενον συλλογισμὸν ἢ ἔλεγχον, μὴ ὄντα δέ, ἀλλὰ καὶ τὸν ὄντα μέν, φαινόμενον δὲ οἰκεῖον τοῦ πράγματος². Εἰσὶ δ' οὗτοι οἱ μὴ κατὰ τὸ πρᾶγμα ἐλέγχοντες καὶ δεικνύντες ἀγνοοῦντας, ὅπερ ἦν τῆς πειραστικῆς. Ἔστι δ' ἡ πειραστικὴ μέρος τῆς διαλεκτικῆς· αὕτη δὲ δύναται συλλογίζεσθαι ψεῦδος δι' ἄγνοιαν τοῦ διδόντος τὸν λόγον. Οἱ δὲ σοφιστικοὶ ἔλεγχοι, ἂν καὶ συλλογίζωνται τὴν ἀντίφασιν, οὐ ποιοῦσι δῆλον εἰ ἀγνοεῖ· καὶ γὰρ τὸν εἰδότα ἐμποδίζουσι τούτοις τοῖς λόγοις.

Ὅτι δ' ἔχομεν αὐτοὺς τῇ αὐτῇ μεθόδῳ, δῆλον· παρ' ὅσα γὰρ φαίνεται τοῖς ἀκούουσιν ὡς ἠρωτημένα συλλελογίσθαι, παρὰ ταῦτα κἂν τῷ ἀποκρινομένῳ δόξειεν, ὥστ' ἔσονται συλλογισμοὶ ψευδεῖς διὰ τούτων ἢ πάντων ἢ ἐνίων· ὃ γὰρ μὴ ἐρωτηθεὶς οἴεται δεδωκέναι, κἂν ἐρωτηθεὶς θείη. Πλὴν ἐπί γέ τινων ἅμα συμβαίνει προσερωτᾶν τὸ ἐνδεὲς καὶ τὸ ψεῦδος ἐμφανίζειν, οἷον ἐν τοῖς παρὰ τὴν λέξιν καὶ τὸν σολοικισμόν. Εἰ οὖν οἱ παραλογισμοὶ τῆς ἀντιφάσεως παρὰ τὸν φαινόμενον ἔλεγχόν εἰσι, δῆλον ὅτι παρὰ τοσαῦτα ἂν καὶ τῶν ψευδῶν εἴησαν συλλογισμοὶ παρ' ὅσα καὶ ὁ φαινόμενος ἔλεγχος. Ὁ δὲ φαινόμενος παρὰ τὰ μόρια τοῦ ἀληθινοῦ· ἑκάστου γὰρ ἐκλείποντος φανείη ἂν ἔλεγχος, οἷον ὁ παρὰ τὸ μὴ συμβαῖνον διὰ τὸν λόγον, ὁ εἰς τὸ ἀδύνατον, καὶ ὁ τὰς δύο ἐρωτήσεις μίαν ποιῶν παρὰ τὴν πρότασιν, καὶ ἀντὶ τοῦ καθ' αὑτὸ ὁ παρὰ τὸ συμβεβηκός, καὶ τὸ τούτου μόριον, ὃ παρὰ τὸ ἑπόμενον· ἔτι τὸ μὴ ἐπὶ τοῦ πράγματος ἀλλ' ἐπὶ τοῦ λόγου συμβαίνειν· εἶτ' ἀντὶ τοῦ καθόλου τὴν ἀντίφασιν καὶ κατὰ ταὐτὸ καὶ πρὸς ταὐτὸ καὶ ὡσαύτως παρά τε τὸ ἐπί τι ἢ παρ' ἕκαστον τούτων· ἔτι παρὰ τὸ μὴ ἐναριθμουμένου τοῦ ἐν ἀρχῇ λαμβάνειν⁴. Ὥστ' ἔχοιμεν ἂν παρ' ὅσα γίνονται οἱ παραλογισμοί⁵· παρὰ πλείω μὲν γὰρ οὐκ ἂν εἶεν, παρὰ δὲ τὰ εἰρημένα ἔσονται πάντες.

futation, I mean not only proof or confutation which is seeming but unreal, but that which though real is seemingly but not really appropriate to the subject-matter. Such are those which fail to confute and prove ignorance within the peculiar sphere of the subject, which is the function of Pirastic. Pirastic is a branch of Dialectic, and arrives at a false conclusion owing to the ignorance of the person examined. Sophistic confutations, even when they prove the contradictory of a thesis, do not prove the ignorance of the respondent, for they may be brought to bear against the scientific.

We know the sources of inappropriate proofs by the same method as those of unreal proofs. For the same causes that induce an audience to imagine the premisses admitted and the conclusion proved, will induce the respondent to imagine so, and will furnish the premisses of a false proof; because, what a man has not been asked but thinks he has granted, he would grant if he were asked. Only sometimes we no sooner ask for the wanting premiss than we unmask its falsehood, as often occurs in verbal fallacies and in reductions to solecism. If, then, the paralogisms of contradiction are equal in number to the conditions of confutation that may be unfulfilled, the modes of sophistic confutation will be equally numerous[3]. Paralogism arises from not fulfilling any of the elements into which true confutation may be decomposed. Any one that may be wanting will leave only a semblance of confutation. For instance, when the cause is misassigned in reduction to impossibility, there is no sequence: when two questions are put as one, there is no genuine proposition: when we replace a subject by its accident, we substitute for a term something else than its whole essence: when we convert a consequent we do the same, for this fallacy is a subdivision of the last: when the diction is fallacious, the sequence is not in the reality but in the words: when the conclusion is irrelevant, or limitations are neglected, the contradiction instead of being absolute and total is partial and restricted, or the terms are not taken in the same respect, relation, manner: and when we beg the question the premisses are not independent of the conclusion. We know, then, how many causes of sophistic proof there are, for there cannot be more than we have enumerated.

ΠΕΡΙ ΣΟΦΙΣΤΙΚΩΝ

Ἔστι δ' ὁ σοφιστικὸς ἔλεγχος οὐχ ἁπλῶς ἔλεγχος, ἀλλὰ πρός τινα· καὶ ὁ συλλογισμὸς ὡσαύτως. Ἂν μὲν γὰρ μὴ λάβῃ ὅ τε παρὰ τὸ ὁμώνυμον ἓν σημαίνειν, καὶ ὁ παρὰ τὴν ὁμοιοσχημοσύνην τὸ μόνον τόδε*, καὶ οἱ ἄλλοι ὡσαύτως, οὔτ' ἔλεγχοι οὔτε συλλογισμοὶ ἔσονται, οὔθ' ἁπλῶς οὔτε πρὸς τὸν ἐρωτώμενον· ἐὰν δὲ λάβωσι, πρὸς μὲν τὸν ἐρωτώμενον ἔσονται, ἁπλῶς δ' οὐκ ἔσονται· οὐ γὰρ ἓν σημαῖνον εἰλήφασιν, ἀλλὰ φαινόμενον, καὶ παρὰ τοῦδε.

IX. Παρὰ πόσα δ' ἐλέγχονται οἱ ἐλεγχόμενοι, οὐ δεῖ πειρᾶσθαι λαμβάνειν ἄνευ τῆς τῶν ὄντων ἐπιστήμης ἁπάντων. Τοῦτο δ' οὐδεμιᾶς ἐστὶ τέχνης· ἄπειροι γὰρ ἴσως αἱ ἐπιστῆμαι, ὥστε δῆλον ὅτι καὶ αἱ ἀποδείξεις. Ἔλεγχοι δ' εἰσὶ καὶ ἀληθεῖς· ὅσα γὰρ ἔστιν ἀποδεῖξαι, ἔστι καὶ ἐλέγξαι τὸν θέμενον τὴν ἀντίφασιν τοῦ ἀληθοῦς, οἷον εἰ σύμμετρον τὴν διάμετρον ἔθηκεν, ἐλέγξειεν ἄν τις τῇ ἀποδείξει ὅτι ἀσύμμετρος. Ὥστε πάντων δεήσει ἐπιστήμονας εἶναι· οἱ μὲν γὰρ ἔσονται παρὰ τὰς ἐν γεωμετρίᾳ ἀρχὰς καὶ τὰ τούτων συμπεράσματα, οἱ δὲ παρὰ τὰς ἐν ἰατρικῇ, οἱ δὲ παρὰ τὰς τῶν ἄλλων ἐπιστημῶν. Ἀλλὰ μὴν καὶ οἱ ψευδεῖς ἔλεγχοι ὁμοίως ἐν ἀπείροις· καθ' ἑκάστην γὰρ τέχνην ἐστὶ ψευδὴς συλλογισμός, οἷον κατὰ γεωμετρίαν ὁ γεωμετρικὸς καὶ κατὰ ἰατρικὴν ὁ ἰατρικός. Λέγω δὲ τὸ κατὰ τὴν τέχνην τὸ κατὰ τὰς ἐκείνης ἀρχάς. Δῆλον οὖν ὅτι οὐ πάντων τῶν ἐλέγχων ἀλλὰ τῶν παρὰ τὴν διαλεκτικὴν ληπτέον τοὺς τόπους· οὗτοι γὰρ κοινοὶ πρὸς ἅπασαν τέχνην καὶ δύναμιν. Καὶ τὸν μὲν καθ' ἑκάστην ἐπιστήμην ἔλεγχον τοῦ ἐπιστήμονός ἐστι θεωρεῖν, εἴτε μὴ ὢν φαίνεται εἴ τ' ἔστι, διὰ τί ἔστι· τὸν δ' ἐκ τῶν κοινῶν καὶ ὑπὸ μηδεμίαν τέχνην τῶν διαλεκτικῶν. Εἰ γὰρ ἔχομεν ἐξ ὧν οἱ ἔνδοξοι συλλογισμοὶ περὶ ὁτιοῦν, ἔχομεν ἐξ ὧν οἱ ἔλεγχοι· ὁ γὰρ ἔλεγχός ἐστιν ἀντιφάσεως συλλογισμός, ὥστ' ἢ εἷς ἢ δύο συλλογισμοὶ ἀντιφάσεως ἔλεγχός ἐστιν. Ἔχομεν ἄρα παρ' ὁπόσα πάντες εἰσὶν οἱ τοιοῦτοι, εἰ δὲ ταῦτ' ἔχομεν, καὶ τὰς λύσεις ἔχομεν· αἱ γὰρ τούτων ἐνστάσεις λύσεις εἰσίν, ἔχομεν δὲ παρ' ὁπόσα γίνονται*. Καὶ τοὺς φαινομένους*, φαινομένους δὲ οὐχ ὁτῳοῦν ἀλλὰ τοῖς τοιοῖσδε· ἀόριστα γάρ ἐστιν,

A sophistic confutation is not an absolute confutation or a confutation of the thesis, but only relative to the answerer; and so of sophistic proof. Unless it is granted that the ambiguous term has a single meaning, and that the similar termination expresses a similar reality, and so on, there is no confutation or proof either absolute or relative to the answerer. If it is granted, there is relative proof, but not absolute, for the meaning is not single, but only seemingly so, and none but this respondent would admit it to be so [7].

IX. ALL the sources of confutation could not be enumerated without universal knowledge, which belongs to no single art. Sciences and demonstrations are possibly infinite, and confutations may be valid, for every demonstration confutes the contradictory thesis. The thesis, for instance, that the diagonal and side of the square are commensurate is confuted by the demonstration that they are incommensurate. To enumerate, then, all true confutations would require omniscience: for some confutations will be composed of principles and theorems of geometry, others of medicine, others of other sciences. Moreover false confutations are infinite; for every art has false proofs peculiar to it [1], geometry, geometrical proofs; physiology, physiological proofs. By peculiar I mean, moving exclusively in the sphere of its characteristic principles. Our present task, then, is to trace the sources not of all confutations but of all dialectical confutations; for these are limited in number, though common to every art and faculty. Scientific confutations whether seeming or real, and if real, the reasons why they are real, must be investigated by the man of science [2]. The dialectician must investigate the common confutations, that belong exclusively to no particular sphere. If we know the sources of probable proofs that are common to every sphere, we know the sources of the common confutations. For confutation is contradictory proof, and one or two proofs with a contradictory conclusion are confutation. We have enumerated the sources of all these [3], and, if so, we have enumerated the solutions; for the objections to these principles are the solutions, and we have explained the forms of objection. The dialectician must also enumerate the sources of apparent proofs, apparent, that is, not

ἐάν τις σκοπῇ παρ' ὁπόσα φαίνωνται τοῖς τυχοῦσιν. Ὥστε φανερὸν ὅτι τοῦ διαλεκτικοῦ ἐστὶ τὸ δύνασθαι λαβεῖν παρ' ὅσα γίνεται διὰ τῶν κοινῶν ἢ ἂν ἔλεγχος ἢ φαινόμενος ἔλεγχος, καὶ ἡ διαλεκτικὸς ἢ φαινόμενος διαλεκτικὸς ἢ πειραστικός.

X. Οὐκ ἔστι δὲ διαφορὰ τῶν λόγων ἣν λέγουσί τινες, τὸ εἶναι τοὺς μὲν πρὸς τοὔνομα λόγους, ἑτέρους δὲ πρὸς τὴν διάνοιαν· ἄτοπον γὰρ τὸ ὑπολαμβάνειν ἄλλους μὲν εἶναι πρὸς τοὔνομα λόγους, ἑτέρους δὲ πρὸς τὴν διάνοιαν, ἀλλ' οὐ τοὺς αὐτούς. Τί γάρ ἐστι τὸ μὴ πρὸς τὴν διάνοιαν ἀλλ' ἢ ὅταν μὴ χρῆται τῷ ὀνόματι, ἐφ' ᾧ οἰόμενος ἐρωτᾶσθαι² ὁ ἐρωτώμενος ἔδωκεν; τὸ δ' αὐτὸ τοῦτό ἐστι καὶ πρὸς τοὔνομα. Τὸ δὲ πρὸς τὴν διάνοιαν, ὅταν ἐφ' ᾧ ἔδωκεν διανοηθείς. Εἰ δή τις πλείω σημαίνοντος τοῦ ὀνόματος οἴοιτο ἓν σημαίνειν καὶ ὁ ἐρωτῶν καὶ ὁ ἐρωτώμενος, οἷον ἴσως τὸ ὂν ἢ τὸ ἓν πολλὰ σημαίνει, ἀλλὰ καὶ ὁ ἀποκρινόμενος καὶ ὁ ἐρωτῶν Ζήνων ἓν οἰόμενος εἶναι ἠρώτησε, καὶ ἔστιν ὁ λόγος ὅτι ἓν πάντα, οὗτος πρὸς τοὔνομα ἔσται ἢ πρὸς τὴν διάνοιαν τοῦ ἐρωτωμένου διειλεγμένος; Εἰ δέ γέ τις πολλὰ οἴεται σημαίνειν³, δῆλον ὅτι οὐ πρὸς τὴν διάνοιαν. Πρῶτον μὲν γὰρ περὶ τοὺς τοιούτους ἐστὶ λόγους τὸ πρὸς τοὔνομα καὶ πρὸς τὴν διάνοιαν ὅσοι πλείω σημαίνουσιν, εἶτα περὶ ὁντινοῦν ἐστίν· οὐ γὰρ ἐν τῷ λόγῳ ἐστὶ τὸ πρὸς τὴν διάνοιαν εἶναι, ἀλλ' ἐν τῷ τὸν ἀποκρινόμενον ἔχειν πως πρὸς τὰ δεδομένα.

Εἶτα πρὸς τοὔνομα πάντας ἐνδέχεται αὐτοὺς εἶναι. Τὸ γὰρ πρὸς τοὔνομα τὸ μὴ πρὸς τὴν διάνοιαν εἶναί ἐστιν ἐνταῦθα. Εἰ γὰρ μὴ πάντες, ἔσονταί τινες ἕτεροι οὔτε πρὸς τοὔνομα οὔτε πρὸς τὴν διάνοιαν· οἱ δέ φασι πάντας, καὶ διαιροῦνται ἢ πρὸς τοὔνομα ἢ πρὸς τὴν διάνοιαν εἶναι πάντας, ἄλλους δ' οὔ. Ἀλλὰ μὴν ὅσοι συλλογισμοί εἰσι παρὰ τὸ πλεοναχῶς, τούτων εἰσί τινες οἱ παρὰ τοὔνομα. Ἀτόπως μὲν γὰρ καὶ εἴρηται τὸ παρὰ τοὔνομα φάναι πάντας τοὺς παρὰ τὴν λέξιν· ἀλλ' οὖν εἰσί τινες παραλογισμοὶ οὐ τῷ τὸν ἀποκρινόμενον πρὸς τούτους

to any idiot, but to people of average intelligence: for it would be an endless work to inquire into the sources of every idiotic belief. The dialectician, then, has to discover what in the principles common to all spheres of thought are the sources of confutation whether real or apparent, that is, whether dialectic or seemingly dialectic, and whether pirastic or seemingly pirastic.

X. REASONINGS cannot be divided, as some propose, into reasonings addressed to the word and reasonings addressed to the thought[1]. It is a strange error to suppose that reasonings addressed to the word and reasonings addressed to the thought form distinct classes and are not the same reasonings under different circumstances. For not to address the thought is not to apply a name to the object which the respondent thought he was asked about when he made a concession, and is equivalent to addressing the word. To address the thought is to apply the name to the object which the respondent thought about when he granted the premiss. If, then, a name is ambiguous, but supposed to be unambiguous by the questioner as well as the answerer: as, for instance, Being and Unity are ambiguous, but were supposed to be unambiguous both by the answerer and by Zeno the questioner in the argument to prove the unity of all Being: was this argument addressed to the word, or was it not rather addressed to the thought? If, on the contrary, the respondent thinks a term ambiguous when it is unambiguous the reasoning is clearly not addressed to his thought. For the possibility of being addressed to the word, or addressed to the thought, though it belongs primarily to fallacies of ambiguous term, belongs secondarily to all reasonings; because it does not depend on the nature of the reasoning but on the state of the respondent's mind.

It follows that all reasonings, valid and invalid, may belong to the class addressed to the word; for in this doctrine all those reasonings are addressed to the word which are not addressed to the thought. Else there would be a third class, neither addressed to the word nor addressed to the thought; but we are told that there is not, and that the division is exhaustive. But in truth reasonings addressed to the word are properly confined to fallacies of ambiguous term; and it is an abuse of language to extend the name even to all fallacies in diction. We hold,

ἔχειν πως, ἀλλὰ τῷ τοιονδὶ ἐρώτημα τὸν λόγον αὐτὸν ἔχειν, ὃ πλείω σημαίνει.

Ὅλως τε ἄτοπον τὸ περὶ ἐλέγχου διαλέγεσθαι, ἀλλὰ μὴ πρότερον περὶ συλλογισμοῦ, ὁ γὰρ ἔλεγχος συλλογισμός ἐστιν. Ὥστε χρὴ καὶ περὶ συλλογισμοῦ πρότερον ἢ περὶ ψευδοῦς ἐλέγχου· ἔστι γὰρ ὁ τοιοῦτος ἔλεγχος φαινόμενος συλλογισμὸς ἀντιφάσεως. Διὸ ἢ ἐν τῷ συλλογισμῷ ἔσται τὸ αἴτιον ἢ ἐν τῇ ἀντιφάσει (προσκεῖσθαι γὰρ δεῖ τὴν ἀντίφασιν), ὁτὲ δ' ἐν ἀμφοῖν, ἂν ᾖ φαινόμενος ἔλεγχος. Ἔστι δὲ ὁ μὲν τοῦ σιγῶντα λέγειν ἐν τῇ ἀντιφάσει, οὐκ ἐν τῷ συλλογισμῷ, ὁ δέ, ἃ μὴ ἔχοι τις, δοῦναι, ἐν ἀμφοῖν, ὁ δὲ ὅτι ἡ Ὁμήρου ποίησις σχῆμα διὰ τοῦ κύκλου ἐν τῷ συλλογισμῷ. Ὁ δ' ἐν μηδετέρῳ ἀληθὴς συλλογισμός.

Ἀλλὰ δή, ὅθεν ὁ λόγος ἦλθε, πότερον οἱ ἐν τοῖς μαθήμασι λόγοι πρὸς τὴν διάνοιάν εἰσιν, ἢ οὔ; καὶ εἴ τινι δοκεῖ πολλὰ σημαίνειν τὸ τρίγωνον, καὶ ἔδωκε μὴ ὡς τοῦτο τὸ σχῆμα ἐφ' οὗ συνεπεράνατο ὅτι δύο ὀρθαί, πότερον πρὸς τὴν διάνοιαν οὗτος διείλεκται τὴν ἐκείνου, ἢ οὔ;

Ἔτι εἰ πολλὰ μὲν σημαίνει τοὔνομα, ὁ δὲ μὴ νοεῖ μηδ' οἴεται, πῶς οὗτος οὐ πρὸς τὴν διάνοιαν διείλεκται; Ἢ πῶς δεῖ ἐρωτᾶν πλὴν διδόναι διαίρεσιν; Εἶτ' ἐρωτήσειέ τις· εἰ ἔστι σιγῶντα λέγειν ἢ οὔ, ἢ ἔστι μὲν ὡς οὔ, ἔστι δ' ὡς ναί, εἰ δή τις δοίη μηδαμῶς ὁ δὲ διαλεχθείη, ἆρ' οὐ πρὸς τὴν διάνοιαν διείλεκται; καίτοι ὁ λόγος δοκεῖ τῶν παρὰ τοὔνομα εἶναι.

Οὐκ ἄρα ἐστὶ γένος τι λόγων τὸ πρὸς τὴν διάνοιαν. Ἀλλ' οἱ μὲν πρὸς τοὔνομά εἰσι καὶ τοιοῦτοι οὐ πάντες, οὐχ ὅτι οἱ ἔλεγχοι, ἀλλ' οὐδ' οἱ φαινόμενοι ἔλεγχοι. Εἰσὶ γὰρ καὶ μὴ παρὰ τὴν λέξιν φαινόμενοι ἔλεγχοι, οἷον οἱ παρὰ τὸ συμβεβηκὸς καὶ ἕτεροι.

then, that there are certain paralogisms of equivocation which do not depend on the state of the respondent's mind, but on the reasoning itself containing a term that is ambiguous.

Again: we ought not to examine confutation before we have examined proof; for confutation is a species of proof. We ought a fortiori to examine proof before we examine false confutation, which is the seeming proof of a contradictory. Its fault must be either in the proof, or in the contradiction, or in both, if the confutation is not genuine. In the argument that the outspoken may be silent, it lies in the contradiction, not in the proof. In the argument that a man can give away what he has not got, it lies in both. In the argument that the Homeric poems are a figure because they are a circle, it lies in the proof. Where there is no fault in either, the confutation is genuine[1].

But to resume[5]; is it true that mathematical reasonings are always addressed to the thought? If the respondent thought triangle ambiguous, and granted the premiss in a different acceptation from that in which it was afterwards proved to contain angles equal to two right angles; surely it cannot be said that the reasoning was addressed to his thought?

If, on the other hand[6], a name is ambiguous, and the respondent thinks it unambiguous, is not the reasoning addressed to his thought? If not, how ought the question to be framed in order that the reasoning may be addressed to the thought, if it is not enough to suggest to the answerer that he may draw a distinction? If the opponent puts the question: Is it possible or impossible for the silent to be outspoken, or possible in one sense, impossible in another? and the respondent answers, It is not possible in any sense, whereupon the opponent proves it is: surely his reasoning is addressed to the thought of the respondent? This argument, however, they class among those addressed to the word.

We conclude that there is no distinct class of reasonings addressed to the thought as opposed to reasonings addressed to the word. There is a class of reasonings addressed to the word, but it does not include all confutations, nor even all fallacious confutations[8]; for some are independent of language, those, for instance, among others, that depend on the identification of subject and accident[9].

34 ΠΕΡΙ ΣΟΦΙΣΤΙΚΩΝ

Εἰ δέ τις ἀξιοῖ διαιρεῖν, ὅτι λέγω δὲ σιγῶντα λέγειν τὰ μὲν ὡδὶ τὰ δ' ὡδί· ἀλλὰ τοῦτό γ' ἐστὶ πρῶτον μὲν ἄτοπον τὸ ἀξιοῦν (ἐνίοτε γὰρ οὐ δοκεῖ τὸ ἐρωτώμενον πολλαχῶς ἔχειν, ἀδύνατον δὲ διαιρεῖν ὃ μὴ οἴεται)· ἔπειτα τὸ διδάσκειν τί ἄλλο ἔσται; Φανερὸν γὰρ ποιήσει ὡς ἔχει τῷ μήτ' ἐσκεμμένῳ μήτ' εἰδότι μήθ' ὑπολαμβάνοντι ὅτι ἄλλως λέγεται. Ἐπεὶ καὶ ἐν τοῖς μὴ διπλοῖς τί κωλύει τοῦτο ποιεῖν[10]; Ἆρα ἴσαι αἱ μονάδες ταῖς δυάσιν ἐν τοῖς τέτταρσιν; Εἰσὶ δὲ δυάδες αἱ μὲν ὡδὶ ἐνοῦσαι αἱ δὲ ὡδί. Καὶ ἆρα τῶν ἐναντίων μία ἐπιστήμη ἢ οὔ; Ἔστι δ' ἐναντία τὰ μὲν γνωστὰ τὰ δ' ἄγνωστα. Ὥστ' ἔοικεν ἀγνοεῖν ὁ τοῦτο ἀξιῶν ὅτι ἕτερον τὸ διδάσκειν τοῦ διαλέγεσθαι, καὶ ὅτι δεῖ τὸν μὲν διδάσκοντα μὴ ἐρωτᾶν ἀλλ' αὐτὸν δῆλα ποιεῖν, τὸν δ' ἐρωτᾶν.

XI. Ἔτι τὸ φάναι ἢ ἀποφάναι ἀξιοῦν οὐ δεικνύντος ἐστίν, ἀλλὰ πεῖραν λαμβάνοντος. Ἡ γὰρ πειραστικὴ ἐστι διαλεκτική τις καὶ θεωρεῖ οὐ τὸν εἰδότα ἀλλὰ τὸν ἀγνοοῦντα καὶ προσποιούμενον. Ὁ μὲν οὖν κατὰ τὸ πρᾶγμα θεωρῶν τὰ κοινὰ διαλεκτικός, ὁ δὲ τοῦτο φαινομένως ποιῶν σοφιστικός.

Καὶ συλλογισμὸς ἐριστικὸς καὶ σοφιστικός ἐστιν εἷς μὲν ὁ φαινόμενος συλλογισμός περὶ ὧν[1] ἡ διαλεκτικὴ πειραστική ἐστι, κἂν ἀληθὲς τὸ συμπέρασμα ᾖ· τοῦ γὰρ διὰ τί ἀπατητικός ἐστι· καὶ ὅσοι μὴ ὄντες κατὰ τὴν ἑκάστου μέθοδον παραλογισμοὶ[2] δοκοῦσιν εἶναι κατὰ τὴν τέχνην. Τὰ γὰρ ψευδογραφήματα οὐκ ἐριστικά (κατὰ γὰρ τὰ ὑπὸ τὴν τέχνην οἱ παραλογισμοί), οὐδέ γ' εἴ τί ἐστι ψευδογράφημα περὶ ἀληθές[3], οἷον τὸ Ἱπποκράτους ἢ ὁ τετραγωνισμὸς ὁ διὰ τῶν μηνίσκων. Ἀλλ' ὡς Βρύσων ἐτετραγώνιζε τὸν κύκλον, εἰ καὶ τετραγωνίζεται ὁ κύκλος, ἀλλ' ὅτι οὐ κατὰ τὸ πρᾶγμα[4], διὰ τοῦτο σοφιστικός.

If, in order that the reasoning may be addressed to the thought, the questioner is required to draw the distinction himself, and say, for instance, that the silence of the outspoken may either mean this, or it may mean that; the requirement cannot be enforced, for the questioner does not always suspect the ambiguity himself, and he cannot distinguish what he thinks unambiguous. Secondly, would not this be didactic reasoning? For it discloses the truth to an answerer who has neither previously considered nor discovered nor formed any belief about the ambiguity. And why not equally in the reasonings where no ambiguity is involved give him similar information? As thus: "Are the units in four equal to the twos? Bear in mind that the twos may be taken either distributively or collectively."—"Is there one science of contraries? Bear in mind that some contraries are knowable, others unknowable." This requirement, then, implies an ignorance of the difference between didactic and dialectic reasoning, and of the principle that, while the teacher does not ask but informs, the dialectician asks [11].

XI. Again:—to challenge the respondent to affirm or deny is not the part of Didactic or the teacher, but the part of Pirastic or the examiner. For Pirastic is a species of Dialectic, and probes, not knowledge but, ignorance and false pretensions to knowledge. To do this by applying universal principles within a special sphere is dialectic: to do it in semblance only is sophistic.

Accordingly, one kind of eristic or sophistic proof is proof which seems appropriate, though really inappropriate, to the problem which Dialectic undertakes under the form of Pirastic, whether or not it has a true conclusion; for even then it is illusive as to the reason. A second are those proofs which are not confined to the special method of a science, though they pretend to be scientific. For the Pseudographema, or the misapplication of peculiar scientific principles, is not eristic, because confined to a special sphere, whether of art or science; e.g. the reasoning of Hippocrates, or the squaring of the circle by lunules. But Bryso's method of squaring the circle, even if successful, is not mathematical, and is therefore not a pseudographema but a sophism. Proof, then, that falsely pretends to

ΠΕΡΙ ΣΟΦΙΣΤΙΚΩΝ

Ὥστε ὅ τε περὶ τῶνδε φαινόμενος συλλογισμὸς ἐριστικὸς λόγος, καὶ ὁ κατὰ τὸ πρᾶγμα φαινόμενος συλλογισμός, κἂν ᾖ συλλογισμός, ἐριστικὸς λόγος· φαινόμενος γάρ ἐστι κατὰ τὸ πρᾶγμα, ὥστ' ἀπατητικὸς καὶ ἄδικος.

Ὥσπερ γὰρ ἡ ἐν ἀγῶνι ἀδικία εἶδός τι ἔχει καὶ ἔστιν ἀδικομαχία τις, οὕτως ἐν ἀντιλογίᾳ ἀδικομαχία ἡ ἐριστική ἐστιν· ἐκεῖ τε γὰρ οἱ πάντως νικᾶν προαιρούμενοι πάντων ἅπτονται καὶ ἐνταῦθα οἱ ἐριστικοί. Οἱ μὲν οὖν τῆς νίκης αὐτῆς χάριν τοιοῦτοι ἐριστικοὶ ἄνθρωποι καὶ φιλέριδες δοκοῦσιν εἶναι, οἱ δὲ δόξης χάριν τῆς εἰς χρηματισμὸν σοφιστικοί· ἡ γὰρ σοφιστική ἐστιν, ὥσπερ εἴπομεν, χρηματιστική τις ἀπὸ σοφίας φαινομένης, διὸ φαινομένης ἀποδείξεως ἐφίενται. Καὶ τῶν λόγων τῶν αὐτῶν μέν εἰσιν οἱ φιλέριδες καὶ σοφισταί, ἀλλ' οὐ τῶν αὐτῶν ἕνεκεν. Καὶ λόγος ὁ αὐτὸς μὲν ἔσται σοφιστικὸς καὶ ἐριστικός, ἀλλ' οὐ κατὰ ταὐτόν, ἀλλ' ᾗ μὲν νίκης φαινομένης, ἐριστικός, ᾗ δὲ σοφίας, σοφιστικός· καὶ γὰρ ἡ σοφιστική ἐστι φαινομένη σοφία τις ἀλλ' οὐκ οὖσα.

Ὁ δ' ἐριστικός ἐστί πως οὕτως ἔχων πρὸς τὸν διαλεκτικὸν ὡς ὁ ψευδογράφος πρὸς τὸν γεωμετρικόν· ἐκ γὰρ τῶν αὐτῶν τῇ διαλεκτικῇ παραλογίζεται καὶ ὁ ψευδογράφος τῷ γεωμέτρῃ[5]. Ἀλλ' ὁ μὲν οὐκ ἐριστικός, ὅτι ἐκ τῶν ἀρχῶν καὶ συμπερασμάτων τῶν ὑπὸ τὴν τέχνην ψευδογραφεῖ· ὁ δ' ὑπὸ τὴν διαλεκτικὴν περὶ μὲν τἆλλα ὅτι ἐριστικός ἐστι δῆλον[6]. Οἷον ὁ τετραγωνισμὸς ὁ μὲν διὰ τῶν μηνίσκων οὐκ ἐριστικός, ὁ δὲ Βρύσωνος ἐριστικός· καὶ τὸν μὲν οὐκ ἔστι μετενεγκεῖν ἀλλ' ἢ πρὸς γεωμετρίαν μόνον διὰ τὸ ἐκ τῶν ἰδίων εἶναι ἀρχῶν, τὸν δὲ πρὸς πολλούς, ὅσοι μὴ ἴσασι τὸ δυνατὸν ἐκ ἑκάστῳ καὶ τὸ ἀδύνατον· ἁρμόσει γάρ[7]. Ἢ ὡς Ἀντιφῶν ἐτετραγώνιζεν. Ἢ εἴ τις μὴ φαίη βέλτιον εἶναι ἀπὸ δείπνου περιπατεῖν διὰ τὸν Ζήνωνος λόγον, οὐκ ἰατρικός· κοινὸς γάρ.

Εἰ μὲν οὖν πάντῃ ὁμοίως εἶχεν ὁ ἐριστικὸς πρὸς τὸν δια-

ΕΛΕΓΧΩΝ.

be piraslic, or relevant to the problem, is eristic, and so is proof that falsely pretends to be scientific, even though it be conclusive; for, pretending to proceed from scientific knowledge, it is deceptive and illegitimate.

Trials of force or skill are sometimes the occasions of unfair play and illegitimate fighting: and Eristic is illegitimate fighting in disputation. The competitor who is bent on victory at all hazards sticks at no artifice; no more does the eristic reasoner. If victory is his final motive, he is called contentious and eristic; if professional reputation and lucre, sophistic. For Sophistic is, as I said before, a money-making art, that trades on the semblance of philosophy, and therefore aims at producing the semblance of demonstration. The contentious disputant and the sophist use the same kind of arguments, but not from the same motive; and the same kind of argument is sophistic and eristic in different aspects. If semblance of victory is the motive, it is eristic; if the semblance of wisdom, sophistic; for sophistry is the semblance of philosophy without the reality.

The eristic reasoner to a certain extent bears the same relation to the dialectician as the false geometer bears to the true geometer: for he draws his principles from the same source as the dialectician, and the false geometer from the same source as the true geometer. The false geometer is not eristic, because his premisses are exclusively drawn from the principles and theorems of a science, while Eristic constructs syllogisms from the principles of Dialectic. They may, however, handle the same problem. The mode of squaring the circle by lunules, for instance, is not eristic, but Bryso's is eristic. The one cannot be applied beyond the sphere of geometry, because it is based on geometrical principles; the other can be employed against all disputants who do not know what is possible or impossible in their respective spheres, for it applies to subjects different in kind. The same may be said of Antipho's method of squaring the circle. If, again, a person controverted the expediency of walking after dinner by Zeno's proof of the impossibility of motion, such an argument would not be medical, because it has a catholic application.

If the relation of Eristic and Dialectic was exactly similar

λεκτικὸν τῷ ψευδογράφῳ πρὸς τὸν γεωμέτρην, οὐκ ἂν ἦν περὶ ἐκείνων ἐριστικός. Νῦν δ' οὐκ ἔστιν ὁ διαλεκτικὸς περὶ γένος τι ὡρισμένον, οὐδὲ δεικτικὸς οὐδενός, οὐδὲ τοιοῦτος οἷος ὁ καθόλου[9]. Οὔτε γάρ ἐστιν ἅπαντα ἐν ἑνί τινι γένει, οὔτε εἰ εἴη, οἷόν τε ὑπὸ τὰς αὐτὰς ἀρχὰς εἶναι τὰ ὄντα. "Ωστ' οὐδεμία τέχνη τῶν δεικνυουσῶν τινα φύσιν ἐρωτητική[10] ἐστιν· οὐ γὰρ ἔξεστιν ὁποτερονοῦν τῶν μορίων δοῦναι· συλλογισμὸς γὰρ οὐ γίνεται ἐξ ἀμφοῖν. Ἡ δὲ διαλεκτικὴ ἐρωτητική ἐστιν. Εἰ δ' ἐδείκνυεν, εἰ καὶ μὴ πάντα, ἀλλὰ τά γε πρῶτα καὶ τὰς οἰκείας ἀρχὰς οὐκ ἂν ἠρώτα. Μὴ διδόντος γὰρ οὐκ ἂν ἔτι εἶχεν ἐξ ὧν ἔτι διαλέξεται πρὸς τὴν ἔνστασιν.

Ἡ δ' αὐτὴ καὶ πειραστική. Οὐδὲ γὰρ ἡ πειραστικὴ τοιαύτη ἐστὶν οἷα ἡ γεωμετρία, ἀλλ' ἣν ἂν ἔχοι καὶ μὴ εἰδώς τις. Ἔξεστι γὰρ πεῖραν λαβεῖν καὶ τὸν μὴ εἰδότα τὸ πρᾶγμα τοῦ μὴ εἰδότος, εἴπερ καὶ δίδωσιν οὐκ ἐξ ὧν οἶδεν οὐδ' ἐκ τῶν ἰδίων, ἀλλ' ἐκ τῶν ἑπομένων, ὅσα τοιαῦτά ἐστιν ἃ εἰδότα μὲν οὐδὲν κωλύει μὴ εἰδέναι τὴν τέχνην, μὴ εἰδότα δ' ἀνάγκη ἀγνοεῖν. Ὥστε φανερὸν ὅτι οὐδενὸς ὡρισμένου ἡ πειραστικὴ ἐπιστήμη ἐστίν. Διὸ καὶ περὶ πάντων ἐστί· πᾶσαι γὰρ αἱ τέχναι χρῶνται καὶ κοινοῖς τισίν. Διὸ πάντες καὶ οἱ ἰδιῶται τρόπον τινὰ χρῶνται τῇ διαλεκτικῇ καὶ πειραστικῇ· πάντες γὰρ μέχρι τινὸς ἐγχειροῦσιν ἀνακρίνειν τοὺς ἐπαγγελλομένους. Ταῦτα δ' ἐστὶ τὰ κοινά· ταῦτα γὰρ οὐδὲν ἧττον ἴσασιν αὐτοί, κἂν δοκῶσι λίαν ἔξω λέγειν. Ἐλέγχουσιν οὖν ἅπαντες ἀτέχνως γὰρ μετέχουσι τούτου οὗ ἐντέχνως ἡ διαλεκτική ἐστι, καὶ ὁ τέχνῃ συλλογιστικῇ πειραστικὸς διαλεκτικός. Ἐπεὶ δ' ἐστὶ πολλὰ μὲν ταῦτα καὶ κατὰ πάντων, οὐ τοιαῦτα δ' ὥστε φύσιν[12] τινὰ εἶναι καὶ γένος, ἀλλ' οἷον αἱ ἀποφάσεις, τὰ δ' οὐ τοιαῦτα ἀλλὰ ἴδια, ἔστιν ἐκ τούτων περὶ ἁπάντων πεῖραν λαμβάνειν,

ΕΛΕΓΧΩΝ.   39

to that of the false and the true geometer, there could not be
eristic arguments on geometrical problems. But the fact is
that Dialectic has no definite sphere, and demonstrates nothing
categorically, and investigates no essential theorems. For there
is no genus that embraces all Being, and, if there were, there
could be no common principles of all Being⁹. No science that
demonstrates categorically any positive theorem can interrogate
or offer to accept either alternative, for either alternative would
not furnish a proof. Dialectic interrogates. If it had to demonstrate any theorems, it could not trust, at least for the
elements and special principles of the proof, to interrogation:
for if they were denied by the respondent, it could have no
weapons to oppose to his objection.

Pirastic is a Dialectic: for it is not a speciality like geometry,
but a faculty that may be possessed by the unscientific. He
who does not know may examine the pretensions of another who
does not know: for the theses and premisses granted by the respondent are not scientific truths nor theorems from which the
primary laws may be obtained by analysis ¹¹, but consequences
or derivative facts, which are such that, while to know them does
not prove knowledge of the primary laws, not to know them
proves ignorance. Pirastic, then, is not knowledge of any definite
sphere, and therefore is conversant with every sphere: for all
sciences have certain common elements or catholic principles.
Accordingly, even the unscientific employ Dialectic and Pirastic,
for all persons to a certain extent assume to test pretensions
to knowledge. Pirastic and Dialectic are the application of
those catholic principles, and these the unscientific possess as
well as the scientific, though their expression of them may be
very defective in precision. Accordingly, all practise confutation. Unmethodically they perform the work which Dialectic
performs methodically, and the examination of false pretensions
by methodical reasoning is Dialectic. Such principles are numerous, and applicable to every province, but have no positive
nature, and form no determinate genus, resembling, in this
respect, negations: others, on the contrary, are limited to
special spheres. The former enable us to examine pretensions
in any province, and compose what is a kind of art, though

καὶ εἶναι τέχνην τινά, καὶ μὴ τοιαύτην εἶναι οἷαι αἱ δεικνύουσαι. Διόπερ ὁ ἐριστικὸς οὐκ ἔστιν οὕτως ἔχων πάντῃ ὡς ὁ ψευδογράφος· οὐ γὰρ ἔσται παραλογιστικὸς ἐξ ὡρισμένου τινὸς γένους ἀρχῶν, ἀλλὰ περὶ πᾶν γένος ἔσται ὁ ἐριστικός. Τρόποι μὲν οὖν εἰσὶν οὗτοι τῶν σοφιστικῶν ἐλέγχων· ὅτι δ' ἐστὶ τοῦ διαλεκτικοῦ τὸ θεωρῆσαι περὶ τούτων καὶ δύνασθαι ταῦτα ποιεῖν, οὐ χαλεπὸν ἰδεῖν· ἡ γὰρ περὶ τὰς προτάσεις μέθοδος ἅπασαν ἔχει ταύτην τὴν θεωρίαν.

XII. Καὶ περὶ μὲν τῶν ἐλέγχων εἴρηται τῶν φαινομένων· περὶ δὲ τοῦ ψευδόμενόν τι δεῖξαι καὶ τὸν λόγον εἰς ἄδοξον ἀγαγεῖν (τοῦτο γὰρ ἦν δεύτερον τῆς σοφιστικῆς προαιρέσεως) πρῶτον μὲν οὖν ἐκ τοῦ πυνθάνεσθαί πως καὶ διὰ τῆς ἐρωτήσεως συμβαίνει μάλιστα. Τὸ γὰρ πρὸς μηδὲν ὁρίσαντα κείμενον ἐρωτᾶν θηρευτικόν ἐστι τούτων· εἰκῇ γὰρ λέγοντες ἁμαρτάνουσι μᾶλλον· εἰκῇ δὲ λέγουσιν, ὅταν μηδὲν ἔχωσι προκείμενον. Τό τε ἐρωτᾶν πολλά, κἂν ὡρισμένον ᾖ πρὸς ὃ διαλέγεται, καὶ τὸ τὰ δοκοῦντα λέγειν ἀξιοῦν ποιεῖ τιν' εὐπορίαν τοῦ εἰς ἄδοξον ἀγαγεῖν ἢ ψεῦδος· ἐάν τε ἐρωτώμενος φῇ ἢ ἀποφῇ τούτων τι, ἄγειν πρὸς ἃ ἐπιχειρήματος εὐπορεῖ. Δυνατὸν δὲ νῦν ἧττον κακουργεῖν διὰ τούτων ἢ πρότερον· ἀπαιτοῦνται γὰρ τί τοῦτο πρὸς τὸ ἐν ἀρχῇ. Στοιχεῖον δὲ τοῦ τυχεῖν ἢ ψεύδους τινὸς ἢ ἀδόξου τὸ μηδεμίαν εὐθὺς ἐρωτᾶν θέσιν, ἀλλὰ φάσκειν ἐρωτᾶν μαθεῖν βουλόμενον· χώραν γὰρ ἐπιχειρήματος ἡ σκέψις ποιεῖ. Πρὸς δὲ τὸ ψευδόμενον δεῖξαι ἴδιος τόπος ὁ σοφιστικός, τὸ ἄγειν πρὸς τοιαῦτα πρὸς ἃ εὐπορεῖ λόγων. Ἔσται δὲ καὶ καλῶς καὶ μὴ καλῶς τοῦτο ποιεῖν, καθάπερ ἐλέχθη πρότερον.

Πάλιν πρὸς τὸ παράδοξα λέγειν σκοπεῖν ἐκ τίνος γένους ὁ διαλεγόμενος, εἶτ' ἐπερωτᾶν ὃ τοῖς πολλοῖς οὗτοι λέγουσι παράδοξον· ἔστι γὰρ ἑκάστοις τι τοιοῦτον. Στοιχεῖον δὲ τούτων τὸ τὰς ἑκάστων εἰληφέναι θέσεις ἐν ταῖς προτάσεσιν[e]. Λύσις δὲ καὶ τούτων ἡ προσήκουσα φέρεται τὸ ἐμφανίζειν ὅτι οὐ διὰ τὸν λόγον συμβαίνει τὸ ἄδοξον· ἀεὶ δὲ τοῦτο καὶ βούλεται ὁ ἀγωνιζόμενος.

Ἔτι δ' ἐκ τῶν βουλήσεων καὶ τῶν φανερῶν δοξῶν. Οὐ

very unlike the sciences that demonstrate. Eristic reasoning, then, is not exactly similar to false geometry; for it does not consist of paralogisms drawn from a limited sphere of principles, but of proofs drawn from catholic principles applicable to every sphere [13].

Such are the modes of sophistic confutation. The investigation of them and power to apply them belong to Dialectic: for all these matters belong to the method of Proposition.

XII. Unreal confutation has been examined. False or paradoxical statement, the second aim of the Sophist, is obtained by the mode of questioning and interrogating; by questioning, for instance, without previous definition of the problem. For random answers are more likely to be wrong, and answers are made at random when there is no point in issue. If there is a definite point in issue, it is useful to multiply questions and request the respondent to give his genuine opinion, and if he states candidly his beliefs and disbeliefs, to lead him on to controversial ground[1]. This fraud is less practicable now, for the answerer will demand, What has this to do with the question? Another rule for obtaining a false or paradoxical statement is not to put a proposition with confidence, but to pretend to ask from a desire to learn: for consultation gives an opening to attack. Another artifice for proving error is to lead the discussion on to debatable ground. This may be done fairly in some cases, as we have already mentioned.

Again:—paradox may be elicited by considering to what school the respondent belongs, and proposing some tenet of the school that the world pronounces to be a paradox; for there are such tenets in every school. For this purpose it is useful to have made a collection of paradoxes. The proper solution is to shew that the paradox has no connexion with the thesis, as the disputant pretends.

Another source of paradox is the opposition of secret wishes

γὰρ ταὐτὰ βούλονταί τε καὶ φασίν, ἀλλὰ λέγουσι μὲν τοὺς εὐσχημονεστάτους τῶν λόγων, βούλονται δὲ τὰ φαινόμενα λυσιτελεῖν, οἷον τεθνάναι καλῶς μᾶλλον ἢ ζῆν ἡδέως φασὶ δεῖν καὶ πένεσθαι δικαίως μᾶλλον ἢ πλουτεῖν αἰσχρῶς, βούλονται δὲ τἀναντία. Τὸν μὲν οὖν λέγοντα κατὰ τὰς βουλήσεις εἰς τὰς φανερὰς δόξας ἀκτέον, τὸν δὲ κατὰ ταύτας εἰς τὰς ἀποκεκρυμμένας· ἀμφοτέρως γὰρ ἀναγκαῖον παράδοξα λέγειν· ἢ γὰρ πρὸς τὰς φανερὰς ἢ πρὸς τὰς ἀφανεῖς δόξας ἐροῦσιν ἐναντία.

Πλεῖστος δὲ τόπος ἐστὶ τοῦ ποιεῖν παράδοξα λέγειν, ὥσπερ καὶ ὁ Καλλικλῆς ἐν τῷ Γοργίᾳ γέγραπται λέγων, καὶ οἱ ἀρχαῖοι δὲ πάντες ᾤοντο συμβαίνειν, παρὰ τὸ κατὰ φύσιν καὶ κατὰ τὸν νόμον· ἐναντία γὰρ εἶναι φύσιν καὶ νόμον, καὶ τὴν δικαιοσύνην κατὰ νόμον μὲν εἶναι καλὸν κατὰ φύσιν δ' οὐ καλόν. Δεῖν οὖν πρὸς μὲν τὸν εἰπόντα κατὰ φύσιν κατὰ νόμον ἀπαντᾶν, πρὸς δὲ τὸν κατὰ νόμον ἐπὶ τὴν φύσιν ἄγειν· ἀμφοτέρως γὰρ εἶναι λέγειν παράδοξα. *Ἦν δὲ τὸ μὲν κατὰ φύσιν αὐτοῖς τὸ ἀληθές, τὸ δὲ κατὰ νόμον τὸ τοῖς πολλοῖς δοκοῦν. Ὥστε δῆλον ὅτι κἀκεῖνοι, καθάπερ καὶ οἱ νῦν, ἢ ἐλέγξαι ἢ παράδοξα λέγειν τὸν ἀποκρινόμενον ἐπεχείρουν ποιεῖν.

Ἔνια δὲ τῶν ἐρωτημάτων ἔχει ἀμφοτέρως ἄδοξον εἶναι τὴν ἀπόκρισιν, οἷον πότερον τοῖς σοφοῖς ἢ τῷ πατρὶ δεῖ πείθεσθαι, καὶ τὰ συμφέροντα πράττειν ἢ τὰ δίκαια, καὶ ἀδικεῖσθαι αἱρετώτερον ἢ βλάπτειν. Δεῖ δ' ἄγειν εἰς τὰ τοῖς πολλοῖς καὶ τοῖς σοφοῖς ἐναντία, ἐὰν μὲν λέγῃ τις ὡς οἱ περὶ τοὺς λόγους, εἰς τὰ τοῖς πολλοῖς, ἐὰν δ' ὡς οἱ πολλοί, ἐπὶ τὰ τοῖς ἐν λόγῳ. Φασὶ γὰρ οἱ μὲν ἐξ ἀνάγκης τὸν εὐδαίμονα δίκαιον εἶναι· τοῖς δὲ πολλοῖς ἄδοξον τὸ βασιλέα μὴ εὐδαιμονεῖν. Ἔστι δὲ τὸ εἰς τὰ οὕτως ἄδοξα συνάγειν τὸ αὐτὸ τῷ εἰς τὴν κατὰ φύσιν καὶ κατὰ νόμον ὑπεναντίωσιν ἄγειν· ὁ μὲν γὰρ νόμος δόξα τῶν πολλῶν, οἱ δὲ σοφοὶ κατὰ φύσιν καὶ κατ' ἀλήθειαν λέγουσιν.

XIII. Καὶ τὰ μὲν παράδοξα ἐκ τούτων δεῖ ζητεῖν τῶν τόπων· περὶ δὲ τοῦ ποιῆσαι ἀδολεσχεῖν, ὃ μὲν λέγομεν τὸ ἀδολεσχεῖν, εἰρήκαμεν ἤδη. Πάντες δὲ οἱ τοιοίδε λόγοι τοῦτο βούλονται

and open professions. Men profess all that is noble while their wishes are set on their material interests. They profess that a glorious death is better than a pleasurable life, and honourable poverty than sordid opulence; but their wishes are not in harmony with their words. If the thesis is in accordance with their real desires, the respondent should be confronted with their public professions; if it is in accordance with these, he should be confronted with their real desires. In either case he must fall into paradox and contradict their public or private opinions.

An abundant source of paradox is what Callicles in the Gorgias is represented as pointing out, and which was familiar to all the ancient disputants, the discrepancy of nature and law. They considered the two to be opposite, and justice, for instance, to be beautiful by law, but not by nature: so that if the thesis conforms to nature, it must be confronted with law; if conformable to law, with nature. In either case the respondent must fall into paradox. The ancients meant by nature, truth; by law, public opinion. Thus, like modern disputants, they aimed either to confute the respondent or to land him in paradox.

Some questions involve a paradox whichever way they are answered. Ought a man to obey the wise or his father? Ought he to do what is expedient or what is just? Is it better to be wronged or to wrong? We must lead the respondent on into the questions where the world and philosophy are at variance, and if he agrees with the philosophers, confront him with the opinions of the many; if he agrees with the many, with the judgment of the speculators. The one think that there is no happiness without virtue; the others think that happiness is the lot of every king. This method is the same as that which employs the discrepancies of nature and law: for law is current opinion; nature and truth the creed of the wise.

XIII. PARADOXES, then, are to be obtained from the sources enumerated. Pleonasm, as we have already stated, means superfluous iteration. Reduction to pleonasm is as follows.

ΠΕΡΙ ΣΟΦΙΣΤΙΚΩΝ

ποιεῖν· εἰ μηδὲν διαφέρει τὸ ὄνομα ἢ τὸν λόγον εἰπεῖν, διπλάσιον δὲ καὶ διπλάσιον ἡμίσεος ταὐτό, εἰ ἄρα ἐστὶν ἡμίσεος διπλάσιον, ἔσται ἡμίσεος ἡμίσεος διπλάσιον. Καὶ πάλιν ἂν ἀντὶ τοῦ διπλάσιον διπλάσιον ἡμίσεος τεθῇ, τρὶς ἔσται εἰρημένον, ἡμίσεος ἡμίσεος ἡμίσεος διπλάσιον. Καὶ ἀρά ἐστιν ἡ ἐπιθυμία ἡδέος; τοῦτο δ' ἐστὶν ὄρεξις ἡδέος· ἔστιν ἄρα ἡ ἐπιθυμία ὄρεξις ἡδέος ἡδέος.

Εἰσὶ δὲ πάντες οἱ τοιοῦτοι τῶν λόγων ἔν τε τοῖς πρός τι, ὅσα μὴ μόνον τὰ γένη ἀλλὰ καὶ αὐτὰ πρός τι λέγεται, καὶ πρὸς τὸ αὐτὸ καὶ ἓν ἀποδίδοται. Οἷον ἥ τε ὄρεξις τινὸς ὄρεξις καὶ ἡ ἐπιθυμία τινὸς ἐπιθυμία, καὶ τὸ διπλάσιον τινὸς διπλάσιον καὶ διπλάσιον ἡμίσεος. Καὶ ὅσων ἡ οὐσία¹ οὐκ ὄντων πρός τι ὅλως, ὧν εἰσὶν ἕξεις ἢ πάθη ἤ τι τοιοῦτον, ἐν τῷ λόγῳ αὐτῶν προσδηλοῦται, κατηγορουμένων ἐπὶ τούτοις. Οἷον τὸ περιττὸν ἀριθμὸς μέσον ἔχων ἔστι δ' ἀριθμὸς περιττός· ἔστιν ἄρα ἀριθμὸς μέσον ἔχων ἀριθμός. Καὶ εἰ τὸ σιμὸν κοιλότης ῥινός ἐστιν, ἔστι δὲ ῥὶς σιμή, ἔστιν ἄρα ῥὶς ῥὶς κοίλη. Φαίνονται δὲ ποιεῖν οὐ ποιοῦντες ἐνίοτε διὰ τὸ μὴ προσπυνθάνεσθαι εἰ σημαίνει τι καθ' αὑτὸ λεχθὲν τὸ διπλάσιον ἢ οὐδέν, καὶ εἴ τι σημαίνει, πότερον τὸ αὐτὸ ἢ ἕτερον, ἀλλὰ τὸ συμπέρασμα λέγειν εὐθύς. Ἀλλὰ φαίνεται διὰ τὸ τὸ ὄνομα ταὐτὸ εἶναι ταὐτὸ καὶ σημαίνειν.

XIV. Σολοικισμὸς δ' οἷον μέν ἐστιν εἴρηται πρότερον. Ἔστι δὲ τοῦτο καὶ ποιεῖν καὶ μὴ ποιοῦντα φαίνεσθαι καὶ ποιοῦντα μὴ δοκεῖν, καθάπερ ὁ Πρωταγόρας ἔλεγεν, εἰ ὁ μῆνις καὶ ὁ πήληξ ἄρρεν ἐστίν· ὁ μὲν γὰρ λέγων οὐλομένην σολοικίζει μὲν κατ' ἐκεῖνον, οὐ φαίνεται δὲ τοῖς ἄλλοις, ὁ δὲ οὐλόμενον φαίνεται μὲν ἀλλ' οὐ σολοικίζει. Δῆλον οὖν ὅτι κἂν τέχνῃ τις τοῦτο δύναιτο ποιεῖν· διὸ πολλοὶ τῶν λόγων οὐ συλλογιζόμενοι σολοικισμὸν φαίνονται συλλογίζεσθαι, καθάπερ ἐν τοῖς ἐλέγχοις.

Εἰσὶ δὲ πάντες σχεδὸν οἱ φαινόμενοι σολοικισμοὶ παρὰ τὸ τόδε, καὶ ὅταν ἡ πτῶσις¹ μήτε ἄρρεν μήτε θῆλυ δηλοῖ ἀλλὰ τὸ μεταξύ. Τὸ μὲν οὗτος ἄρρεν σημαίνει, τὸ δ' αὕτη θῆλυ· τὸ δὲ τοῦτο θέλει μὲν τὸ μεταξὺ σημαίνειν, πολλάκις δὲ σημαίνει

Let us assume that an equivalent expression may always be
substituted for a term. If, then, the double is double of its
half, and double is equivalent to double of its half, it follows
by substitution, that the double is double of its half of its half,
and, by further substitution, double of its half of its half of
its half. Again, if appetite is appetite of pleasure and appetite
is equivalent to desire of pleasure, appetite is desire of pleasure
of pleasure.

All these reasonings turn on relatives where both the genus
and the species[1] is a relative and has the same correlative: as
desire and appetite are both relatives and have the same
correlative, pleasure; and double and double of half are both
relatives and have the same correlative, half. Or they turn
on terms which are not properly relatives but whose definition
expresses the subject of which they are states, affections, or
other attributes. E. g. if odd is equivalent to number that
has a middle unit, odd number is number number that has a
middle unit; and if aquiline is equivalent to hooked nose, an
aquiline nose is a hooked nose nose. The reduction to pleonasm
is not genuine when the premiss has not been granted that the
relative has a meaning by itself and means the same when
joined with the correlative[3]. The conclusion is drawn without
this premiss: because the term being the same, it is assumed
to have the same meaning in both cases.

XIV. Solecism we explained before to be barbarism in
language. It may be either real and apparent, or real and
unapparent, or apparent and unreal, as Protagoras said. If
wrath and helmet are masculine nouns, he who gives them
a feminine concord commits a real but unapparent solecism;
he who gives them a masculine concord commits an apparent
but unreal solecism. This appearance can be methodically produced; and there are methods which apparently but not really
convict of solecism, as there are methods of apparent but not
real confutation.

Almost all seeming solecisms depend on the neuter pronoun
That, and the masculine or feminine names of objects that are
not really male or female but neuter. He denotes a male, She
a female, That properly denotes a neuter, but often really

κἀκείνων ἑκάτερον, οἷον τί τοῦτο; Καλλιόπη, ξύλον, Κορίσκος. Τοῦ μὲν οὖν ἄρρενος καὶ τοῦ θήλεος διαφέρουσιν αἱ πτώσεις ἅπασαι, τοῦ δὲ μεταξὺ αἱ μὲν αἱ δ' οὔ. Δοθέντος δὴ πολλάκις τούτο, συλλογίζονται ὡς εἰρημένου τούτον ὁμοίως δὴ καὶ ἄλλην πτῶσιν ἀντ' ἄλλης. Ὁ δὲ παραλογισμὸς γίνεται διὰ τὸ κοινὸν εἶναι τὸ τοῦτο πλειόνων πτώσεων· τὸ γὰρ τοῦτο σημαίνει ὁτὲ μὲν οὗτος ὁτὲ δὲ τοῦτον. Δεῖ δ' ἐναλλὰξ σημαίνειν, μετὰ μὲν τοῦ ἔστι τὸ οὗτος, μετὰ δὲ τοῦ εἶναι τὸ τοῦτον, οἷον ἔστι Κορίσκος, εἶναι Κορίσκον. Καὶ ἐπὶ τῶν θηλείων ὀνομάτων ὡσαύτως, καὶ ἐπὶ τῶν λεγομένων μὲν σκευῶν, ἐχόντων δὲ θηλείας ἢ ἄρρενος κλῆσιν. Ὅσα γὰρ εἰς τὸ ο καὶ τὸ ν τελευτᾷ, ταῦτα μόνα σκεύους ἔχει κλῆσιν, οἷον ξύλον, σχοινίον, τὰ δὲ μὴ οὕτως ἄρρενος ἢ θήλεος, ὧν ἔνια φέρομεν ἐπὶ τὰ σκεύη, οἷον ἀσκὸς μὲν ἄρρεν τοὔνομα, κλίνη δὲ θῆλυ. Διόπερ καὶ ἐπὶ τῶν τοιούτων ὡσαύτως τὸ ἔστι καὶ τὸ εἶναι διοίσει. Καὶ τρόπον τινὰ ὅμοιός ἐστιν ὁ σολοικισμὸς τοῖς παρὰ τὸ τὰ μὴ ὅμοια ὁμοίως λεγομένοις² ἐλέγχοις. Ὥσπερ γὰρ ἐκείνοις ἐπὶ τῶν πραγμάτων, τούτοις ἐπὶ τῶν ὀνομάτων συμπίπτει σολοικίζειν· ἄνθρωπος γὰρ καὶ λευκὸν καὶ πρᾶγμα καὶ ὄνομά ἐστιν. Φανερὸν οὖν ὅτι τὸν σολοικισμὸν πειρατέον ἐκ τῶν εἰρημένων πτώσεων συλλογίζεσθαι.

Εἴδη μὲν οὖν ταῦτα τῶν ἀγωνιστικῶν λόγων καὶ μέρη τῶν εἰδῶν καὶ τρόποι οἱ εἰρημένοι. Διαφέρει δ' οὐ μικρόν, ἐὰν ταχθῇ πως τὰ περὶ τὴν ἐρώτησιν πρὸς τὸ λανθάνειν, ὥσπερ ἐν τοῖς διαλεκτικοῖς. Ἐφεξῆς οὖν τοῖς εἰρημένοις ταῦτα πρῶτον λεκτέον.

XV. Ἔστι δὴ πρὸς τὸ ἐλέγχειν¹ ἓν μὲν μῆκος· χαλεπὸν γὰρ ἅμα πολλὰ συνορᾶν· εἰς δὲ τὸ μῆκος τοῖς προειρημένοις στοιχείοις χρηστέον. Ἒν δὲ τάχος· ὑστερίζοντες γὰρ ἧττον προορῶσιν. Ἔτι δ' ὀργὴ καὶ φιλονικία· ταραττόμενοι γὰρ ἧττον δύνανται φυλάττεσθαι πάντες· στοιχεῖα δὲ τῆς ὀργῆς τό τε φανερὸν ἑαυτὸν ποιεῖν βουλόμενον ἀδικεῖν καὶ τὸ παράπαν ἀναισχυντεῖν. Ἔτι τὸ ἐναλλὰξ τὰ ἐρωτήματα τιθέναι, ἐάν τε πρὸς ταὐτὸ πλείους τις ἔχῃ λόγους, ἐάν τε καὶ ὅτι οὕτως καὶ

denotes a male or female. What is that? That is Calliope:
That is wood: That is Coriscus. The cases of masculine and
feminine nouns are always distinguishable; not so those of
neuters. When That in the premiss represents He, we may
argue as if it represented Him, and vice versa: and a fallacy
will arise from this variety of representation. It alternately
represents He or Him, according as it accompanies the infinitive or indicative mood. So it either represents She or Her,
and either the nominative or the accusative of neuter objects
which have masculine or feminine names. For neuter objects
ought to have names ending in On, and the other terminations
ought to denote the male or female sex, but are sometimes applied
to neuters, as askos (wine-skin) has a masculine termination,
kline (bed) a feminine. The names of these objects, just like
proper masculines and feminines, change their inflexion according as they accompany the indicative or infinitive, that is, distinguish the nominative and accusative cases. Reduction to
solecism resembles the fallacies that arise from similarity of
termination or Figura dictionis. There we are cheated in the
category of the things, here in the cases of their names[3], for
man and white are both names and things. Solecism, then, is
proved under the circumstances we have indicated.

We have now enumerated the branches of sophistic disputation and their subdivisions and methods. For concealment of
his purpose, Arrangement is important to the sophist as to the
dialectician. We therefore proceed to treat of Arrangement[4].

XV. LENGTH is favourable to concealment; for it is hard to
see the mutual relations of a long series of propositions. Length
is to be produced by the methods already mentioned[2]. Quickness facilitates concealment, for the answerer has not time to
foresee consequences. So, too, anger and the heat of dispute;
for any mental discomposure puts us off our guard. Anger may
be produced by effrontery and open attempts to cheat. So, too,
alternately proposing the premisses either of different arguments
for the same conclusion, or of arguments to prove opposite conclusions, for the answerer has to guard against different and

ὅτι οὐχ οὕτως· ἅμα γὰρ συμβαίνει ἢ πρὸς πλείω ἢ πρὸς τἀναντία ποιεῖσθαι τὴν φυλακήν. Ὅλως δὲ πάντα τὰ πρὸς τὴν κρύψιν λεχθέντα πρότερον χρήσιμα καὶ πρὸς τοὺς ἀγωνιστικοὺς λόγους· ἡ γὰρ κρύψις ἐστὶ τοῦ λαθεῖν χάριν, τὸ δὲ λαθεῖν τῆς ἀπάτης.

Πρὸς δὲ τοὺς ἀνανεύοντας ἅττ' ἂν οἰηθῶσιν εἶναι πρὸς τὸν λόγον, ἐξ ἀποφάσεως ἐρωτητέον, ὡς τοὐναντίον βουλόμενον, ἢ καὶ ἐξ ἴσου ποιοῦντα τὴν ἐρώτησιν· ἀδήλου γὰρ ὄντος τοῦ τί βούλεται λαβεῖν ἧττον δυσκολαίνουσιν. Ὅταν τ' ἐπὶ τῶν μερῶν διδῷ τις τὸ καθ' ἕκαστον, ἐπάγοντα τὸ καθόλου πολλάκις οὐκ ἐρωτητέον, ἀλλ' ὡς δεδομένῳ χρηστέον· ἐνίοτε γὰρ οἴονται καὶ αὐτοὶ δεδωκέναι καὶ τοῖς ἀκούουσι φαίνονται διὰ τὴν τῆς ἐπαγωγῆς μνείαν, ὡς οὐκ ἂν ἠρωτημένα μάτην. Ἐν οἷς τε μὴ ὀνόματι σημαίνεται τὸ καθόλου, ἀλλὰ τῇ ὁμοιότητι χρηστέον πρὸς τὸ συμφέρον· λανθάνει γὰρ ἡ ὁμοιότης πολλάκις. Πρός τε τὸ λαβεῖν τὴν πρότασιν τοὐναντίον παραβάλλοντα χρὴ πυνθάνεσθαι· οἷον, εἰ δέοι λαβεῖν ὅτι δεῖ πάντα τῷ πατρὶ πείθεσθαι, πότερον ἅπαντα δεῖ πείθεσθαι τοῖς γονεῦσιν ἢ πάντ' ἀπειθεῖν; καὶ τὰ ὀλιγάκις ὀλίγα· πότερον πολλὰ συγχωρητέον ἢ ὀλίγα; Μᾶλλον γάρ, εἴπερ ἀνάγκη, δόξειεν ἂν εἶναι πολλά· παρατιθεμένων γὰρ ἐγγὺς τῶν ἐναντίων, καὶ μείζω καὶ μεγάλα φαίνεται καὶ χείρω καὶ βελτίω τοῖς ἀνθρώποις.

Σφόδρα δὲ καὶ πολλάκις ποιεῖ δοκεῖν ἐληλέγχθαι τὸ μάλιστα σοφιστικὸν συκοφάντημα τῶν ἐρωτώντων, τὸ μηδὲν συλλογισαμένους μὴ ἐρώτημα ποιεῖν τὸ τελευταῖον, ἀλλὰ συμπεραντικῶς εἰπεῖν, ὡς συλλελογισμένους, οὐκ ἄρα τὸ καὶ τό.

Σοφιστικὸν δὲ καὶ τὸ, κειμένου παραδόξου, τὸ φαινόμενον ἀξιοῦν ἀποκρίνεσθαι, προκειμένου τοῦ δοκοῦντος ἐξ ἀρχῆς, καὶ τὴν ἐρώτησιν τῶν τοιούτων οὕτω ποιεῖσθαι, πότερόν σοι δοκεῖ; Ἀνάγκη γάρ, ἂν ᾖ τὸ ἐρώτημα ἐξ ὧν ὁ συλλογισμός, ἢ ἔλεγχον ἢ παράδοξον γίνεσθαι, δόντος μὲν ἔλεγχον, μὴ δόντος δὲ μηδὲ δοκεῖν φάσκοντος ἄδοξον, μὴ δόντος δὲ δοκεῖν δ' ὁμολογοῦντος ἐλεγχοειδές.

Ἔτι καθάπερ καὶ ἐν τοῖς ῥητορικοῖς, καὶ ἐν τοῖς ἐλεγκτικοῖς

opposite dangers. Generally all the dialectic methods of concealment¹ are available in contentious reasoning, for concealment is a means of fraud.

When the answerer denies whatever he fancies helps the argument, you must ask the negative, as if you wanted the opposite of what you really do, or affect indifference. When doubtful what you want to obtain he has less scope for mere obstruction. Often when the particulars of an induction are granted, the universal should not be asked but employed as if granted: for the answerer will fancy he has granted it and so will the audience, as they will recollect the induction and assume the particulars were not asked without a purpose. The absence of a single name for the subject of the generalization is advantageous to the questioner, for the similarity will often be undetected⁴. To obtain a proposition you should contrast it with the opposite. If, for instance, you want to obtain the premiss, that a man should obey his father in all things, you should ask, Should a man obey or disobey his parents in all things; and if you want the premiss that a small number multiplied by a small number is a large number, you should ask whether it is a small number or a large number; for if compelled to elect, one would rather pronounce it a large number. For the juxtaposition of contraries increases their apparent quantity and value.

An appearance of confutation is often produced by a sophistic fraud, when the questioner, without having proved any thing, instead of asking the final proposition, asserts it in the form of a conclusion, as if he had disproved the thesis⁶.

It is sophistic, too, when the thesis is a paradox⁷, to ask in proposing the premisses for the respondent's genuine opinion, as if the thesis was his genuine opinion, and to put all the questions in this shape: Is it your real opinion, et cetera. If the question is a premiss of the proof, the answerer must either be confuted or led into paradox: if he grants the premiss, he must be confuted: if he says it is not his real opinion, he utters a paradox: if he refuses to grant the premiss, though he allows it to be his opinion, it looks as if he were confuted.

Again, as in Rhetoric so in Dialectic, discrepancies should

ΠΕΡΙ ΣΟΦΙΣΤΙΚΩΝ

ὁμοίως τὰ ἐναντιώματα θεωρητέον ἢ πρὸς τὰ ὑφ' ἑαυτοῦ λεγόμενα, ἢ πρὸς οὓς ὁμολογεῖ καλῶς λέγειν ἢ πράττειν, ἔτι πρὸς τοὺς δοκοῦντας τοιούτους, ἢ πρὸς τοὺς ὁμοίους, ἢ πρὸς τοὺς πλείστους, ἢ πρὸς πάντας. Ὥσπερ τε καὶ ἀποκρινόμενοι πολλάκις, ὅταν ἐλέγχωνται, ποιοῦσι διττόν, ἂν μέλλῃ συμβαίνειν ἐλεγχθήσεσθαι, καὶ ἐρωτῶντας χρηστέον ποτὲ τούτῳ πρὸς τοὺς ἐνισταμένους, ἂν ὡδὶ μὲν συμβαίνῃ ὡδὶ δὲ μή, ὅτι οὕτως εἴληφεν, οἷον ὁ Κλεοφῶν ποιεῖ ἐν τῷ Μανδροβούλῳ. Δεῖ δὲ καὶ ἀφισταμένους τοῦ λόγου τὰ λοιπὰ τῶν ἐπιχειρημάτων ἐπιτέμνειν[9], καὶ τὸν ἀποκρινόμενον, ἂν προαισθάνηται, προενίστασθαι καὶ προαγορεύειν. Ἐπιχειρητέον δ' ἐνίοτε καὶ πρὸς ἄλλα τοῦ εἰρημένου, ἐκεῖνο ἐκλαβόντας, ἐὰν μὴ πρὸς τὸ κείμενον ἔχῃ τις ἐπιχειρεῖν· ὅπερ ὁ Λυκόφρων ἐποίησε προβληθέντος λύραν ἐγκωμιάζειν. Πρὸς δὲ τοὺς ἀπαιτοῦντας πρός τι ἐπιχειρεῖ[10], ἐπειδὴ δοκεῖ δεῖν ἀποδιδόναι τὴν αἰτίαν, λεχθέντων δ' ἐνίων εὐφυλακτότερον τὸ καθόλου συμβαῖνον ἐν τοῖς ἐλέγχοις, λέγειν τὴν ἀντίφασιν, ὅ τι ἔφησεν ἀποφῆσαι, ἢ ὃ ἀπέφησε φῆσαι, ἀλλὰ μὴ ὅτι τῶν ἐναντίων ἡ αὐτὴ ἐπιστήμη ἢ οὐχ ἡ αὐτή. Οὐ δεῖ δὲ τὸ συμπέρασμα προτατικῶς ἐρωτᾶν· ἔνια δ' οὐδ' ἐρωτητέον, ἀλλ' ὡς ὁμολογουμένῳ χρηστέον.

XVI. Ἐξ ὧν μὲν οὖν αἱ ἐρωτήσεις, καὶ πῶς ἐρωτητέον ἐν ταῖς ἀγωνιστικαῖς διατριβαῖς, εἴρηται· περὶ δὲ ἀποκρίσεως, καὶ πῶς χρὴ λύειν, καὶ τί καὶ πρὸς τίνα χρῆσιν οἱ τοιοῦτοι τῶν λόγων ὠφέλιμοι, μετὰ ταῦτα λεκτέον.

Χρήσιμοι μὲν οὖν εἰσὶ πρὸς μὲν φιλοσοφίαν διὰ δύο. Πρῶτον μὲν γὰρ ὡς ἐπὶ τὸ πολὺ γινόμενοι παρὰ τὴν λέξιν ἄμεινον ἔχειν ποιοῦσι πρὸς τὸ ποσαχῶς ἕκαστον λέγεται, καὶ ποῖα ὁμοίως καὶ ποῖα ἑτέρως ἐπί τε τῶν πραγμάτων συμβαίνει καὶ ἐπὶ τῶν ὀνομάτων. Δεύτερον δὲ πρὸς τὰς καθ' αὑτὸν ζητήσεις· ὁ γὰρ ὑφ' ἑτέρου ῥᾳδίως παραλογιζόμενος καὶ τοῦτο μὴ αἰσθανόμενος κἂν αὐτὸς ὑφ' αὑτοῦ τοῦτο πάθοι πολλάκις. Τρίτον δὲ καὶ τὸ λοιπὸν ἔτι πρὸς δόξαν, τὸ περὶ πάντα γεγυμνάσθαι δοκεῖν καὶ μηδενὸς ἀπείρως ἔχειν· τὸ γὰρ κοινωνοῦντα λόγων ψέγειν λόγους, μηδὲν ἔχοντα διορίζειν περὶ τῆς φαυλότητος

be developed between the thesis and the tenets either of the
answerer or of those whom he acknowledges to be high authorities, or of those who are generally so acknowledged, or of
those of his own school, or of those of the majority of people, or
of those of all mankind". And as the answerer avoids imminent
confutation by drawing distinctions, so the questioner who fore-
sees an objection that applies in one sense and not in another,
should explain that he means the proposition in the unobjection-
able sense, like Cleophon in the Mandrobulus. And digressing
from the argument in hand he should by anticipation restrict
the bearing of his other arguments, and the answerer similarly
should meet his other arguments by anticipatory protestation
and objection. Sometimes the questioner must attack a proposition different from the thesis, by means of misinterpretation,
if he cannot attack the thesis, as Lycophron did when required
to deliver an encomium on the lyre. If the answerer demands
what is the drift of a question, as the law is that the object of
a question must be assigned on demand, and a definite answer
might put him on his guard against the intended confutation,
he should be told that the object is to prove the contradictory of
his thesis, the affirmative of his negative, or the negative of his
affirmative; not that the object is to prove, say, that contraries
fall under the same science, or that they fall under different
sciences. The conclusion should not be asked as a proposition. Some premisses should not be asked but assumed as
granted.

XVI. We have expounded the sources of questions and the
modes of questioning in contentious disputation. We have
now to discuss answers and solution and the use of this
theory.

It is useful to the lover of truth for two reasons. As it
chiefly turns on language, it teaches us the various signification
of words and the different sequences in the world of words and
the world of realities. Again, it corrects our solitary reasonings; for he who is easily led by an opponent into undetected
paralogisms, will often fall of himself into similar errors.
Thirdly, it is useful to save us from the imputation of want of
culture. For if we censure a mode of disputation without being

αὐτῶν, ὑποψίαν δίδωσι τοῦ δοκεῖν δυσχεραίνειν οὐ διὰ τἀληθὲς ἀλλὰ δι' ἀπειρίαν.

Ἀποκρινομένοις δὲ πῶς ἀπαντητέον πρὸς τοὺς τοιούτους λόγους, φανερόν, εἴπερ ὀρθῶς εἰρήκαμεν πρότερον ἐξ ὧν εἰσὶν οἱ παραλογισμοί, καὶ τὰς ἐν τῷ πυνθάνεσθαι πλεονεξίας ἱκανῶς διείλομεν. Οὐ ταὐτὸν δ' ἐστὶ λαβόντα τε τὸν λόγον ἰδεῖν καὶ λῦσαι τὴν μοχθηρίαν, καὶ ἐρωτώμενον ἀπαντᾶν δύνασθαι ταχέως. Ὃ γὰρ ἴσμεν, πολλάκις μετατιθέμενον ἀγνοοῦμεν. Ἔτι δ', ὥσπερ ἐν τοῖς ἄλλοις τὸ θᾶττον καὶ τὸ βραδύτερον ἐκ τοῦ γεγυμνάσθαι γίνεται μᾶλλον, οὕτω καὶ ἐπὶ τῶν λόγων ἔχει, ὥστε, ἂν δῆλον μὲν ἡμῖν ᾖ, ἀμελέτητοι δ' ὦμεν, ὑστεροῦμεν τῶν καιρῶν πολλάκις. Συμβαίνει δέ ποτε καθάπερ ἐν τοῖς διαγράμμασιν· καὶ γὰρ ἐκεῖ ἀναλύσαντες ἐνίοτε συνθεῖναι πάλιν ἀδυνατοῦμεν· οὕτω καὶ ἐν τοῖς ἐλέγχοις εἰδότες παρ' ὃ ὁ λόγος συμβαίνει συνεῖραι, διαλῦσαι¹ τὸν λόγον ἀποροῦμεν.

XVII. Πρῶτον μὲν οὖν, ὥσπερ συλλογίζεσθαί φαμεν ἐνδόξως ποτὲ μᾶλλον ἢ ἀληθῶς προαιρεῖσθαι δεῖν, οὕτω καὶ λυτέον ποτὲ μᾶλλον ἐνδόξως ἢ κατὰ τἀληθές. Ὅλως γὰρ πρὸς τοὺς ἐριστικοὺς μαχετέον οὐχ ὡς ἐλέγχοντας ἀλλ' ὡς φαινομένους· οὐ γάρ φαμεν συλλογίζεσθαί γε αὐτούς, ὥστε πρὸς τὸ μὴ δοκεῖν διορθωτέον. Εἰ γάρ ἐστιν ὁ ἔλεγχος ἀντίφασις μὴ ὁμώνυμος ἔκ τινων, οὐδὲν ἂν δέοι διαιρεῖσθαι πρὸς τἀμφίβολα καὶ τὴν ὁμωνυμίαν· οὐ γὰρ ποιεῖ συλλογισμόν. Ἀλλ' οὐδενὸς ἄλλου χάριν προσδιαιρετέον ἀλλ' ἢ ὅτι τὸ συμπέρασμα φαίνεται ἐλεγχοειδές. Οὔκουν τὸ ἐλεγχθῆναι ἀλλὰ τὸ δοκεῖν εὐλαβητέον, ἐπεὶ τό γ' ἐρωτᾶν ἀμφίβολα καὶ τὰ παρὰ τὴν ὁμωνυμίαν, ὅσαι τ' ἄλλαι τοιαῦται παρακρούσεις, καὶ τὸν ἀληθινὸν ἔλεγχον ἀφανίζει καὶ τὸν ἐλεγχόμενον καὶ μὴ ἐλεγχόμενον ἄδηλον ποιεῖ. Ἐπεὶ γὰρ ἔξεστιν ἐπὶ τέλει συμπερανομένου μὴ ὅπερ ἔφησεν ἀποφῆσαι λέγειν, ἀλλ' ὁμωνύμως, εἰ καὶ ὅτι μάλιστ' ἔτυχεν ἐπὶ ταὐτὸν φέρων, ἄδηλον εἰ ἐλήλεγκται· ἄδηλον γὰρ εἰ ἀληθῆ λέγει νῦν. Εἰ δὲ διελὼν ἤρετο τὸ ὁμώνυμον ἢ τὸ ἀμφίβολον, οὐκ ἂν ἄδηλος ἦν ὁ ἔλεγχος. Ὅ τ' ἐπιζητοῦσι νῦν μὲν ἧττον πρότερον δὲ μᾶλλον οἱ ἐριστικοί, τὸ ἢ

able to specify its vices, our censure may be suspected of proceeding not from insight but from prejudice.

The manner in which the answerer should encounter this kind of argumentation is plain, if we have rightly enumerated the sources of paralogism and the frauds of the questioner. But it is not the same thing to be able on examination to see through an argument and correct its error, and to be able under interrogation to oppose it with promptitude. What we know has often only to change its position to become unknown to us. Here, too, as elsewhere, quickness and slowness depend on practice: and if we understand a sophism but want practice, we shall often be too late to apply our knowledge. And the same occurs as in geometrical reasoning: here we sometimes accomplish an analysis but cannot succeed in the synthesis: so in disputation we may know the principle of a sophism, and yet be unable to arrest it in the process of formation.

XVII. To begin :—as the show instead of the reality of proof may sometimes, in my opinion, be properly intended, so may the show instead of the reality of solution. For eristic confutation is not genuine but only apparent. There is no genuine proof but only the appearance of proof to be dissipated. If confutation is the evolution of an unequivocal contradiction from certain premisses, to avoid confutation there is no need of distinction when a term is equivocal, because it leads to no genuine contradiction, and the sole motive for distinguishing when we answer is to avoid the appearance. It is the shadow not the substance of disproof that has to be repelled. Indeed equivocal propositions and terms and the other fraudulent artifices may mask genuine confutation and make it uncertain whether a man is confuted when he really is. For as the answerer may say when the questioner has constructed his proof, that the thesis is only contradicted by means of an equivocation, even though he really used a word in the same signification as the questioner, it is not certain whether he is confuted, for it is not certain that his averment is false. Whereas if the questioner had drawn a distinction when he put the equivocal question, there would have been no uncertainty about the confutation, and the requirement, less insisted on now than formerly in eristic, that the answer

ναί ἢ οὒ ἀποκρίνεσθαι τὸν ἐρωτώμενον, ἐγίνετ' ἄν. Νῦν δὲ διὰ τὸ μὴ καλῶς ἐρωτᾶν τοὺς πυνθανομένους ἀνάγκη προσαποκρίνεσθαί τι τὸν ἐρωτώμενον, διορθοῦντα τὴν μοχθηρίαν τῆς προτάσεως, ἐπεὶ διελομένου γε ἱκανῶς ἢ ναί ἢ οὒ ἀνάγκη λέγειν τὸν ἀποκρινόμενον.

Εἰ δέ τις ὑπολήψεται τὸν κατὰ ὁμωνυμίαν ἔλεγχον εἶναι, τρόπον τινὰ οὐκ ἔσται διαφυγεῖν τὸ ἐλέγχεσθαι τὸν ἀποκρινόμενον· ἐπὶ γὰρ τῶν ὁρατῶν¹ ἀναγκαῖον ὃ ἔφησεν ἀποφῆσαι ὄνομα, καὶ ὃ ἀπέφησε φῆσαι. Ὡς γὰρ διορθοῦνταί τινες, οὐδὲν ὄφελος. Οὐ γὰρ Κορίσκον φασὶν εἶναι μουσικὸν καὶ ἄμουσον, ἀλλὰ τοῦτον τὸν Κορίσκον μουσικὸν καὶ τοῦτον τὸν Κορίσκον ἄμουσον. Ὁ γὰρ αὐτὸς ἔσται λόγος τὸ τοῦτον τὸν Κορίσκον¹ τῷ τοῦτον τὸν Κορίσκον ἄμουσον εἶναι ἢ μουσικόν· ὅπερ ἅμα φησί τε καὶ ἀπόφησιν. Ἀλλ' ἴσως οὐ ταὐτὸ σημαίνει· οὐδὲ γὰρ ἐκεῖ τοὔνομα. Ὥστε τί διαφέρει; Εἰ δὲ τῷ μὲν τὸ ἁπλῶς λέγειν Κορίσκον ἀποδώσει, τῷ δὲ προσθήσει τὸ τινὰ ἢ τόνδε, ἄτοπον· οὐδὲν γὰρ μᾶλλον θατέρῳ· ὁποτέρῳ γὰρ ἄν, οὐδὲν διαφέρει.

Οὐ μὴν ἀλλ' ἐπειδὴ ἄδηλος μέν ἐστιν ὁ μὴ διορισάμενος τὴν ἀμφιβολίαν πότερον ἐλήλεγκται ἢ οὐκ ἐλήλεγκται, δέδοται δ' ἐν τοῖς λόγοις τὸ διελεῖν, φανερὸν ὅτι τὸ μὴ διορίσαντα δοῦναι τὴν ἐρώτησιν ἀλλ' ἁπλῶς ἁμάρτημά ἐστιν, ὥστε κἂν εἰ μὴ αὐτός, ἀλλ' ὅ γε λόγος ἐληλεγμένῳ ὅμοιός ἐστιν. Συμβαίνει μέντοι πολλάκις ὁρῶντας τὴν ἀμφιβολίαν ἀκνεῖν διαιρεῖσθαι διὰ τὴν πυκνότητα τῶν τὰ τοιαῦτα προτεινόντων, ὅπως μὴ πρὸς ἅπαν δοκῶσι δυσκολαίνειν· εἶτ' οὐκ ἂν οἰηθέντων παρὰ τοῦτο γενέσθαι τὸν λόγον, πολλάκις ἀπήντησε παράδοξον. Ὥστ' ἐπειδὴ δέδοται διαιρεῖν, οὐκ ὀκνητέον, καθάπερ ἐλέχθη πρότερον.

Εἰ δὲ τὰ δύο ἐρωτήματα μὴ ἓν ποιεῖ τις⁴ ἐρώτημα, οὐδ' ἂν ὁ παρὰ τὴν ὁμωνυμίαν καὶ τὴν ἀμφιβολίαν ἐγίνετο παραλογισμός, ἀλλ' ἢ ἔλεγχος ἢ οὔ. Τί γὰρ διαφέρει ἐρωτῆσαι εἰ Καλλίας καὶ Θεμιστοκλῆς μουσικοί εἰσιν ἢ εἰ ἀμφοτέροις ἓν ὄνομα ἦν ἑτέροις οὖσιν; εἰ γὰρ πλείω δηλοῖ ἑνός, πλείω

must be simply Yes or No, would then be practicable. As it is, the unfairness of the questions compels us to add something to them in our answer to correct their views: though, if the distinction was properly made by the questioner, the answer should be simply Yes or No.

If it is held that equivocal terms lead to genuine confutation, it is impossible for the answerer to avoid confutation. Where the same proper name denotes several individuals, he must perforce nominally deny what he affirmed, and affirm what he denied. The correction that some have proposed is ineffectual. Not Coriscus, they say, is musical and unmusical, but this Coriscus is musical and this Coriscus is unmusical. Here " this Coriscus" and " this Coriscus" are the same terms, and have contradictory predicates. " But they do not mean the same person." No more did the simple name: so that nothing is gained. To call one of them simply Coriscus, and the other, this or that Coriscus, is unjustifiable; for why should one rather than the other have the distinctive addition, when their right to it is equal?

As it is uncertain when we have not drawn the distinction whether we are confuted or no, and we have the right to draw distinctions, to grant a premiss absolutely and without distinction is an error, and makes the answerer, or at least his answer, appear to be confuted. It often happens that we see an ambiguity but hesitate to distinguish, because the occasions are so numerous, for fear of seeming to be perversely obstructive. Then, never having suspected that a given point would be the hinge of the argument, we are surprised into paradox. As, then, we have the right of distinguishing, we must use it unhesitatingly, as I said before[3].

In equivocation if two questions were not put as one, there would be no paralogism, but either a genuine confutation or not even a seeming one. What is the difference between asking whether Callias and Themistocles are musical, and asking the same question about two different persons of the same name?

ἠρώτησεν. Εἰ οὖν μὴ ὀρθὸν πρὸς δύο ἐρωτήσεις μίαν ἀπόκρισιν ἀξιοῦν λαμβάνειν ἁπλῶς, φανερὸν ὅτι οὐδενὶ προσήκει τῶν ὁμωνύμων ἀποκρίνεσθαι ἁπλῶς, οὐδ' εἰ κατὰ πάντων ἀληθές, ὥσπερ ἀξιοῦσί τινες. Οὐδὲν γὰρ τοῦτο διαφέρει ἢ εἰ ἤρετο, Κορίσκος καὶ Καλλίας πότερον οἴκοι εἰσὶν ἢ οὐκ οἴκοι, εἴτε παρόντων ἀμφοῖν εἴτε μὴ παρόντων· ἀμφοτέρως γὰρ πλείους αἱ προτάσεις· οὐ γὰρ εἰ ἀληθὲς εἰπεῖν, διὰ τοῦτο μία ἡ ἐρώτησις. Ἐγχωρεῖ γὰρ καὶ μυρία ἕτερα ἐρωτηθέντα ἐρωτήματα ἅπαντα ἢ ναὶ ἢ οὒ ἀληθὲς εἶναι λέγειν· ἀλλ' ὅμως οὐκ ἀποκριτέον μιᾷ ἀποκρίσει· ἀναιρεῖται γὰρ τὸ διαλέγεσθαι. Τοῦτο δ' ὅμοιον ὡς εἰ καὶ τὸ αὐτὸ ὄνομα τεθείη τοῖς ἑτέροις. Εἰ οὖν μὴ δεῖ πρὸς δύο ἐρωτήσεις μίαν ἀπόκρισιν διδόναι, φανερὸν ὅτι οὐδ' ἐπὶ τῶν ὁμωνύμων τὸ ναί ἢ οὒ λεκτέον. Οὐδὲ γὰρ ὁ εἰπὼν ἀποκέκριται ἀλλ' εἴρηκεν. Ἀλλ' ἀξιοῦνταί πως ἐν τοῖς διαλεγομένοις διὰ τὸ λανθάνειν τὸ συμβαῖνον.

Ὥσπερ οὖν εἴπομεν, ἐπειδήπερ οὐδ' ἔλεγχοί τινες ὄντες δοκοῦσιν εἶναι, κατὰ τὸν αὐτὸν τρόπον καὶ λύσεις δόξουσιν εἶναί τινες οὐκ οὖσαι λύσεις ἃς δή φαμεν ἐνίοτε μᾶλλον δεῖν φέρειν ἢ τὰς ἀληθεῖς ἐν τοῖς ἀγωνιστικοῖς λόγοις καὶ τῇ πρὸς τὸ διττὸν ἀπαντήσει. Ἀποκριτέον δ' ἐπὶ μὲν τῶν δοκούντων τὸ ἔστω λέγοντα· καὶ γὰρ οὕτως ἥκιστα γίνοιτ' ἂν παρεξέλεγχος· ἂν δέ τι παράδοξον ἀναγκάζηται λέγειν, ἐνταῦθα μάλιστα προσθετέον τὸ δοκεῖν· οὕτω γὰρ ἂν οὔτ' ἔλεγχος οὔτε παράδοξον γίνεσθαι δόξειεν.

Ἐπεὶ δὲ πῶς αἰτεῖται τὸ ἐν ἀρχῇ δῆλον, οἴονται δὲ πάντες, ἂν ᾖ σύνεγγυς, ἀναιρετέον καὶ μὴ συγχωρητέον εἶναί ἕνια ὡς τὸ ἐν ἀρχῇ αἰτοῦντος, ὅταν τι τοιοῦτον ἀξιοῖ τις ὃ ἀναγκαῖον μὲν συμβαίνειν ἐκ τῆς θέσεως, ᾖ δὲ ψεῦδος ἢ ἄδοξον, ταὐτὸ λεκτέον· τὰ γὰρ ἐξ ἀνάγκης συμβαίνοντα τῆς αὐτῆς εἶναι δοκεῖ θέσεως. Ἔτι ὅταν τὸ καθόλου μὴ ὀνόματι ληφθῇ ἀλλὰ παραβολῇ, λεκτέον ὅτι οὐχ ὡς ἐδόθη οὐδ' ὡς προύτεινε λαμβάνει· καὶ γὰρ παρὰ τοῦτο γίνεται πολλάκις ἔλεγχος. Ἐξειργόμενον δὲ τούτων ἐπὶ τὸ μὴ καλῶς δεδεῖχθαι πορευτέον, ἀπαντῶντα κατὰ τὸν εἰρημένον διορισμόν.

If the persons are two, the question is two. If, then, it is
wrong to give a single answer to two questions, it is wrong to
give a simple answer to an equivocal question, even when it is
true in every signification, as some say you ought. It is just
the same as asking, are Coriscus and Callias at home? In either
case, whether both are at home or neither, there are two questions. The truth of a single predicate to several subjects does
not make the questions one. Ten thousand questions might all
be answerable by one single Yes or No, and yet it would not be
a single answer: else there could be no dialectic. And the same
is true if many subjects have one name. If, then, a plurality of
questions must not receive a single answer, no more must an
ambiguous proposition be answered Yes or No. This is not
really an answer but a speech. It is made sometimes from not
foreseeing the consequences.

As there are unreal but seeming confutations, so, as we said
before, there are unreal but seeming solutions, which must sometimes be employed in preference to the true[5] in contentious
disputation and replying to arguments based on equivocation.
When we admit premisses which we believe, we should use the
formula, Granted, for this will preclude accessory confutation.
When to save our thesis from confutation we must maintain a
paradox, we should profess it to be our genuine opinion; thus
we avoid confutation and efface the character of paradox.

We have explained what begging the question means, and it
is allowed that when assumptions are closely connected with the
issue we may deny them and refuse to concede them as premisses on the plea that they beg the question: similarly, if a
necessary consequence of the thesis is false and improbable, we
should use the same plea, for a necessary consequence seems to
be part of the thesis. Again, if the subject of a premiss obtained
by generalization is nameless, and only indicated by comparison,
we must say that what was propounded and granted was not
the principle now employed, for this is often the case[7]. Excluded from these courses we must attempt to shew that the
proof fails in some of the elements which we enumerated.

ΠΕΡΙ ΣΟΦΙΣΤΙΚΩΝ

Ἐν μὲν οὖν τοῖς κυρίως λεγομένοις ὀνόμασιν ἀνάγκη ἀποκρίνεσθαι ἢ ἁπλῶς ἢ διαιρούμενον. Ἃ δὲ συνυπονοοῦντες τίθεμεν, οἷον ὅσα μὴ σαφῶς ἀλλὰ κολοβῶς ἐρωτᾶται, παρὰ τοῦτο συμβαίνει ὁ ἔλεγχος, οἷον ἆρ᾽ ὃ ἂν ᾖ Ἀθηναίων, κτῆμά ἐστιν Ἀθηναίων; Ναί. Ὁμοίως δὲ καὶ ἐπὶ τῶν ἄλλων. Ἀλλὰ μὴν ὁ ἄνθρωπός ἐστι τῶν ζῴων; Ναί. Κτῆμα ἄρα ὁ ἄνθρωπος τῶν ζῴων. Τὸν γὰρ ἄνθρωπον τῶν ζῴων λέγομεν, ὅτι ζῷόν ἐστι, καὶ Λύσανδρον τῶν Λακώνων, ὅτι Λάκων. Δῆλον οὖν ὡς ἐν οἷς ἀσαφὲς τὸ προτεινόμενον οὐ συγχωρητέον ἁπλῶς.

Ὅταν δὲ δυοῖν ὄντοιν θατέρου μὲν ὄντος ἐξ ἀνάγκης θάτερον εἶναι δοκῇ, θατέρου δὲ τοῦτο μὴ ἐξ ἀνάγκης, ἐρωτώμενον πρότερον δεῖ τὸ ἔλαττον διδόναι· χαλεπώτερον γὰρ συλλογίσασθαι ἐκ πλειόνων. Ἐὰν δ᾽ ἐπιχειρῇ ὅτι τῷ μέν ἐστιν ἐναντίον τῷ δ᾽ οὐκ ἔστιν, ἂν ὁ λόγος ἀληθὴς ᾖ, ἐναντίον φάναι, ὄνομα δὲ μὴ κεῖσθαι τοῦ ἑτέρου.

Ἐπεὶ δ᾽ ἔνια μὲν ὧν λέγουσιν οἱ πολλοὶ τὸν μὴ συγχωροῦντα ψεύδεσθαι ἂν φαῖεν ἔνια δ᾽ οὔ, οἷον ὅσα ἀμφιδοξοῦσιν (πότερον γὰρ φθαρτὴ ἢ ἀθάνατος ἡ ψυχὴ τῶν ζῴων, οὐ διώρισται τοῖς πολλοῖς)· ἐν οἷς οὖν ἄδηλον ποτέρως εἴωθε λέγεσθαι τὸ προτεινόμενον, πότερον ὡς αἱ γνῶμαι (καλοῦσι γὰρ γνώμας καὶ τὰς ἀληθεῖς δόξας καὶ τὰς ὅλας ἀποφάνσεις"), ἢ ὡς ἡ διάμετρος ἀσύμμετρος, ἔτι οὐ τἀληθὲς ἀμφιδοξεῖται, μάλιστα μεταφέρων ἄν τις λανθάνοι τὰ ὀνόματα περὶ τούτων (διὰ μὲν γὰρ τὸ ἄδηλον εἶναι ποτέρως ἔχει τἀληθές", οὐ δόξει σοφίζεσθαι, διὰ δὲ τὸ ἀμφιδοξεῖν οὐ δόξει ψεύδεσθαι), ἡ δὲ μεταφορὰ ποιήσει τὸν λόγον ἀνεξέλεγκτον.

Ἔτι ὅσα ἂν τις προαισθάνηται τῶν ἐρωτημάτων, προενστατέον καὶ προαγορευτέον· οὕτω γὰρ ἂν μάλιστα τὸν πυνθανόμενον κωλύσειεν.

XVIII. Ἐπεὶ δ᾽ ἐστὶν ἡ μὲν ὀρθὴ λύσις ἐμφάνισις ψευδοῦς συλλογισμοῦ, παρ᾽ ὁποίαν ἐρώτησιν συμβαίνει τὸ ψεῦδος, ὁ δὲ ψευδὴς συλλογισμὸς λέγεται διχῶς (ἢ γὰρ εἰ συλλελόγισται ψεῦδος, ἢ εἰ μὴ ὢν συλλογισμὸς δοκεῖ εἶναι συλλογισμός), εἴη ἂν ἥ τε εἰρημένη νῦν λύσις καὶ ἡ τοῦ φαινομένου συλλογισμοῦ

Properly expressed questions may be answered simply or with a distinction: the understood but unexpressed portions of obscure or elliptical questions are the harbours of fallacy. Do you grant that what is of the Athenians is the property of the Athenians? Yes. And so in other cases? Yes. Is not man of the animals? Yes. Man therefore is the property of the animals. But man is said to be of the animals because he is an animal, as Lysander is said to be of the Spartans because he is a Spartan. Obscure questions, then, are not to be granted without distinction.

When of two propositions the truth of the first involves the truth of the second but not reciprocally, if we have the option we should grant the truth of the second. For the questioner will have to argue with greater trouble and at greater length. If he tries to prove that one term has an opposite, another not; if he is right, we should say, they both have, but in one case it is nameless.

The world has some opinions which it considers it false to contradict, in others it is undecided and permits contradiction, as, for instance, on the question whether the soul is mortal or immortal. Sometimes, again, the natural interpretation of a thesis is doubtful: whether, that is to say, it is to be taken in a metaphorical sense, like a proverb, which is a practical aphorism in a figurative dress, or in a literal sense, like the mathematical theorem that the diagonal of a square is incommensurate to the side. In such a case, when moreover the doctrine is problematic and the world is undecided, we may safely adopt a metaphorical interpretation: the doubtfulness of the meaning saves our interpretation from seeming sophistic, the indecision of the world saves our assertion from seeming false, and the presence of metaphor is a bar to confutation.

Foreseen questions should be anticipated by protestations and distinctions; for this disconcerts the questioner.

XVIII. ONE true solution of a false proof is the indication of the false premiss that causes the false conclusion. False proof, however, not only means a conclusive proof with a false conclusion, but also an inconclusive though apparent proof[1]. Another solution, then, will be the indication of the premiss

παρὰ τί φαίνεται τῶν ἐρωτημάτων διόρθωσις. Ὥστε συμβαίνει τῶν λόγων τοὺς μὲν συλλελογισμένους ἀνελόντα, τοὺς δὲ φαινομένους διελόντα λύειν. Πάλιν δ' ἐπεὶ τῶν συλλελογισμένων λόγων οἱ μὲν ἀληθὲς οἱ δὲ ψεῦδος ἔχουσι τὸ συμπέρασμα, τοὺς μὲν κατὰ τὸ συμπέρασμα ψευδεῖς διχῶς ἐνδέχεται λύειν· καὶ γὰρ τῷ ἀνελεῖν τι τῶν ἠρωτημένων, καὶ τῷ δεῖξαι τὸ συμπέρασμα ἔχον οὐχ οὕτως· τοὺς δὲ κατὰ τὰς προτάσεις τῷ ἀνελεῖν τι μόνον· τὸ γὰρ συμπέρασμα ἀληθές. Ὥστε τοῖς βουλομένοις λύειν λόγον πρῶτον μὲν σκεπτέον εἰ συλλελόγισται ἢ ἀσυλλόγιστος, εἶτα πότερον ἀληθὲς τὸ συμπέρασμα ἢ ψεῦδος, ὅπως ἢ διαιροῦντες ἢ ἀναιροῦντες λύωμεν, καὶ ἀναιροῦντες ἢ ὡδὶ ἢ ὡδε, καθάπερ ἐλέχθη πρότερον. Διαφέρει δὲ πλεῖστον ἐρωτώμενόν τε καὶ μὴ λύειν λόγον· τὸ μὲν γὰρ προϊδεῖν χαλεπόν, τὸ δὲ κατὰ σχολὴν ἰδεῖν ῥᾷον.

XIX. Τῶν μὲν οὖν παρὰ τὴν ὁμωνυμίαν καὶ τὴν ἀμφιβολίαν ἐλέγχων οἱ μὲν ἔχουσι τῶν ἐρωτημάτων τι πλείω σημαῖνον, οἱ δὲ τὸ συμπέρασμα πολλαχῶς λεγόμενον, οἷον ἐν μὲν τῷ σιγῶντα λέγειν τὸ συμπέρασμα διττόν, ἐν δὲ τῷ μὴ συνεπίστασθαι² τὸν ἐπιστάμενον ἓν τῶν ἐρωτημάτων ἀμφίβολον. Καὶ τὸ διττὸν ὁτὲ μὲν ἔστιν ὁτὲ δ' οὐκ ἔστιν, ἀλλὰ σημαίνει τὸ διττὸν τὸ μὲν ὂν τὸ δ' οὐκ ὄν.

Ὅσοις μὲν οὖν ἐν τῷ τέλει τὸ πολλαχῶς, ἂν μὴ προσλάβῃ τὴν ἀντίφασιν, οὐ γίνεται ἔλεγχος, οἷον ἐν τῷ τὸν τυφλὸν ὁρᾶν· ἄνευ γὰρ ἀντιφάσεως οὐκ ἦν ἔλεγχος. Ὅσοις δ' ἐν τοῖς ἐρωτήμασιν, οὐκ ἀνάγκη προαποφῆσαι τὸ διττόν· οὐ γὰρ πρὸς τοῦτο¹ ἀλλὰ διὰ τοῦτο ὁ λόγος. Ἐν ἀρχῇ μὲν οὖν τὸ διπλοῦν καὶ ὄνομα καὶ λόγον οὕτως ἀποκριτέον, ὅτι ἔστιν ὡς, ἔστι δ' ὡς οὔ, ὥσπερ τὸ σιγῶντα λέγειν, ὅτι ἔστιν ὡς, ἔστι δ' ὡς οὔ. Καὶ τὰ δέοντα⁴ πρακτέον ἔστιν ἅ, ἔστι δ' ἃ οὔ· τὰ γὰρ δέοντα λέγεται πολλαχῶς. Ἐὰν δὲ λάθῃ, ἐπὶ τέλει προστιθέντα τῇ ἐρωτήσει διορθωτέον⁵. Ἆρ' ἔστι⁷ σιγῶντα λέγειν; Οὔ, ἀλλὰ τόνδε σιγῶντα. Καὶ ἐν τοῖς ἔχουσι δὲ τὸ πλεοναχῶς ἐν ταῖς προτάσεσιν ὁμοίως. Οὐκ ἄρα συνεπίστανται ὅτι ἐπίστανται; Ναί, ἀλλ' οὐχ οἱ οὕτως ἐπιστάμενοι· οὐ γὰρ ταὐτόν ἐστιν ὅτι

that causes the false appearance. Conclusive proofs are solved
by contradiction of a premiss, inconclusive proofs by distinction.
Again:—conclusive proofs either have a true or a false conclusion. Those whose conclusion is false may be solved in two
ways, either by contradicting a premiss or by a counterproof
directed against the conclusion²: those whose falsity is confined
to the premisses, by contradiction alone, as the conclusion is
true. Accordingly when we wish to solve a proof we must first
look to see whether it is conclusive or inconclusive, and, if
conclusive, whether the conclusion is true or false; and then
solve it either by distinction or contradiction, and in the latter
case either by enstasis or by counterproof, as I said before³. It
is very different to solve a proof under interrogation and afterwards. To anticipate is difficult; to detect a fallacy at leisure
is easy.

XIX. When there is an ambiguity in a term or a proposition
of a confutation, the ambiguity sometimes lies in the premisses,
sometimes in the conclusion. In the argument about speech of
the speechless the conclusion is ambiguous¹: in the argument
about the unconsciousness of knowledge a premiss is ambiguous.
The ambiguous proposition is true in the answerer's sense, false
in the opponent's.

When the ambiguity lies in the conclusion, unless the conclusion is previously denied by the respondent, there is no
confutation, as we may see in the argument about sight of
the blind², for confutation requires contradiction. When the
ambiguity lies in a premiss the semblance of confutation does
not require a previous contradiction of the ambiguous proposition; for then the ambiguous element is not the subject or
predicate of the thesis confuted, but the middle term of the
proof. The thesis should at starting be stated with a distinction, if it contains any ambiguity. We should maintain, for
instance, that speech of the speechless is possible in one sense
and not in another, and that what is necessary ought sometimes
to be done, sometimes not, as the word is ambiguous. If the
ambiguity is not at first detected, we should afterwards restrict
and correct the thesis. Is speech of the speechless impossible?
No, but speech by the speechless is. So when the ambiguity is
in the premisses. Is not knowledge conscious? Some is, that

οὐκ ἔστι συνεπίστασθαι καὶ ὅτι τοὺς ὡδὶ ἐπισταμένους οὐκ ἔστιν. Ὅλως τε μαχετέον, ἂν καὶ ἁπλῶς συλλογίζηται, ὅτι οὐκ ὃ ἔφησεν ἀπέφησε πρᾶγμα, ἀλλ' ὄνομα· ὥστ' οὐκ ἔλεγχος.

XX. Φανερὸν δὲ καὶ τοὺς παρὰ τὴν διαίρεσιν καὶ σύνθεσιν πῶς λυτέον· ἂν γὰρ διαιρούμενος καὶ συντιθέμενος ὁ λόγος ἕτερον σημαίνῃ, συμπεραινομένου τοὐναντίον λεκτέον. Εἰσὶ δὲ πάντες οἱ τοιοῦτοι λόγοι παρὰ τὴν σύνθεσιν ἢ διαίρεσιν. Ἆρ' ᾧ εἶδες σὺ τοῦτον τυπτόμενον, τούτῳ ἐτύπτετο οὗτος; καὶ ᾧ ἐτύπτετο, τούτῳ σὺ εἶδες; ἔχει μὲν οὖν τι κὰκ τῶν ἀμφιβόλων ἐρωτημάτων, ἀλλ' ἔστι παρὰ σύνθεσιν. Οὐ γάρ ἐστι διττὸν τὸ παρὰ τὴν διαίρεσιν· οὐ γὰρ ὁ αὐτὸς λόγος γίνεται διαιρούμενος, εἴπερ μὴ καὶ τὸ ὄρος καὶ ὅρος τῇ προσῳδίᾳ λεχθὲν σημαίνει ἕτερον². Ἀλλ' ἐν μὲν τοῖς γεγραμμένοις ταὐτὸν ὄνομα, ὅταν ἐκ τῶν αὐτῶν στοιχείων γεγραμμένον ᾖ καὶ ὡσαύτως, κἀκεῖ δ' ἤδη παράσημα ποιοῦνται, τὰ δὲ φθεγγόμενα οὐ ταὐτά. Ὥστ' οὐ διττὸν τὸ παρὰ διαίρεσιν. Φανερὸν δὲ καὶ ὅτι οὐ πάντες οἱ ἔλεγχοι παρὰ τὸ διττόν, καθάπερ τινές φασιν.

Διαιρετέον οὖν τῷ ἀποκρινομένῳ· οὐ γὰρ ταὐτὸν ἰδεῖν τοῖς ὀφθαλμοῖς τυπτόμενον καὶ τὸ φάναι ἰδεῖν τοῖς ὀφθαλμοῖς τυπτόμενον. Καὶ ὁ Εὐθυδήμου δὲ λόγος, ἆρ' οἶδας σὺ νῦν οὔσας ἐν Πειραιεῖ τριήρεις ἐν Σικελίᾳ ὤν; Καὶ πάλιν, ἆρ' ἔστιν ἀγαθὸν ὄντα σκυτέα μοχθηρὸν εἶναι; εἴη δ' ἄν τις ἀγαθὸς ὢν σκυτεὺς μοχθηρός· ὥστ' ἔσται ἀγαθὸς σκυτεὺς μοχθηρός. Ἆρ' ὧν αἱ ἐπιστῆμαι σπουδαῖαι, σπουδαῖα τὰ μαθήματα; τοῦ δὲ κακοῦ σπουδαῖον τὸ μάθημα⁶· σπουδαῖον ἄρα μάθημα τὸ κακόν. Ἀλλὰ μὴν καὶ κακὸν καὶ μάθημα τὸ κακόν, ὥστε κακὸν μάθημα τὸ κακόν. Ἀλλ' ἐστὶ κακῶν σπουδαία ἐπιστήμη. Ἆρ' ἀληθὲς εἰπεῖν νῦν ὅτι σὺ γέγονας; γέγονας ἄρα νῦν. Ἢ ἄλλο σημαίνει διαιρεθέν· ἀληθὲς γὰρ εἰπεῖν νῦν ὅτι σὺ γέγονας, ἀλλ' οὐ νῦν γέγονας. Ἆρ' ὡς δύνασαι καὶ ἃ

is to say, such and such a kind of knowledge; for there is a difference between the restricted and unrestricted premiss. If the questioner argues without regard to the distinction, we must contend that he has contradicted the name and not the reality, and therefore has not confuted.

XX. It is evident how fallacies of composition and division are to be solved. If the composition or division produces a difference of signification, when the opponent draws his conclusion from the premisses in one signification, we must say they bore the other. The following arguments depend on composition and division. Was the man beaten with that with which you saw him beaten, and did you see him beaten with that with which he was beaten¹? The reasoning has something of the fallacy of ambiguous proposition, but belongs to a distinct class, the fallacy of composition. We have not here a single proposition with a double meaning, for the division produces two propositions, just as the characters, oros and horos, are the sign of two different sounds, distinguished by the breathing though not by the accent. The written word may be the same when it has the same letters in the same order, though even written words are now distinguished by accents and aspirates, but the spoken words are undeniably different. The fallacy of division, then, does not consist in ambiguity, nor is ambiguity the principle of all sophism, as some have asserted².

The answerer must distinguish and point out the difference between seeing with the eyes a man beaten and seeing him beaten with the eyes. So in the argument of Euthydemus. Do you in Sicily know at this moment there are triremes in the Piræus⁴? Again: a good shoemaker can be a bad shoemaker, for a good man may be a bad shoemaker, therefore he is both a good shoemaker and a bad shoemaker⁵. Again: if the knowledge of a thing is good, it is a good thing to learn: the knowledge of evil is good, therefore evil is a good thing to learn. But evil is evil and a thing to learn, therefore it is an evil thing to learn. As it is true that the knowledge of evil is good (the fallacy must lie in the rest of the reasoning). It is true to say in the present moment you are born: then you are born in the present moment. No: the division makes a difference: it is true in the present moment that you are born but not that you are

δύνασαι, οὕτως καὶ ταῦτα ποιήσαις ἄν; οὐ κιθαρίζων δ' ἔχεις δύναμιν τοῦ κιθαρίζειν· κιθαρίσαις ἂν ἄρα οὐ κιθαρίζων. Ἡ οὐ τούτου ἔχει τὴν δύναμιν τοῦ οὐ κιθαρίζων κιθαρίζειν, ἀλλ' ὅτε οὐ ποιεῖ, τοῦ ποιεῖν. Λύουσι δέ τινες τοῦτον καὶ ἄλλως. Εἰ γὰρ ἔδωκεν ὡς δύναται ποιεῖν, οὔ φασι συμβαίνειν μὴ κιθαρίζοντα κιθαρίζειν· οὐ γὰρ πάντως ὡς δύναται ποιεῖν δεδόσθαι ποιήσειν· οὐ ταὐτὸν δ' εἶναι ὡς δύναται καὶ πάντως ὡς δύναται ποιεῖν. Ἀλλὰ φανερὸν ὅτι οὐ καλῶς λύουσιν· τῶν γὰρ παρὰ ταὐτὸν λόγων ἡ αὐτὴ λύσις, αὕτη δ' οὐχ ἁρμόσει ἐπὶ πάντας οὐδὲ πάντως ἐρωτωμένους, ἀλλ' ἔστι πρὸς τὸν ἐρωτῶντα, οὐ πρὸς τὸν λόγον.

XXI. Παρὰ δὲ τὴν προσῳδίαν λόγοι μὲν οὐκ εἰσίν, οὔτε τῶν γεγραμμένων οὔτε τῶν λεγομένων, πλὴν εἴ τινες ὀλίγοι γένοιντ' ἄν, οἷον οὗτος ὁ λόγος. Ἆρά γ' ἐστὶ τὸ οὗ καταλύεις οἰκία; Ναί. Οὐκοῦν τὸ οὐ καταλύεις τοῦ καταλύεις ἀπόφασις; Ναί. Ἔφησας δ' εἶναι τὸ οὐ καταλύεις οἰκίαν· ἡ οἰκία ἄρα ἀπόφασις. Ὡς δὴ λυτέον, δῆλον· οὐ γὰρ ταὐτὸ σημαίνει ὀξύτερον τὸ δὲ βαρύτερον ῥηθέν.

XXII. Δῆλον δὲ καὶ τοῖς παρὰ τὸ ὡσαύτως λέγεσθαι τὰ μὴ ταὐτὰ πῶς ἀπαντητέον, ἐπείπερ ἔχομεν τὰ γένη τῶν κατηγοριῶν. Ὁ μὲν γὰρ ἔδωκεν ἐρωτηθεὶς μὴ ὑπάρχειν τι τούτων ὅσα τί ἐστι σημαίνει· ὁ δ' ἔδειξεν ὑπάρχον τι τῶν πρός τι ἢ ποσῶν, δοκούντων δὲ τί ἐστι σημαίνειν διὰ τὴν λέξιν, οἷον ἐν τῷδε τῷ λόγῳ. Ἆρ' ἐνδέχεται τὸ αὐτὸ ἅμα ποιεῖν τε καὶ πεποιηκέναι; Οὔ. Ἀλλὰ μὴν ὁρᾶν γέ τι ἅμα καὶ ἑωρακέναι τὸ αὐτὸ καὶ κατὰ ταὐτὸ ἐνδέχεται. Ἆρ' ἐστί τι τῶν πάσχειν ποιεῖν τι; Οὔ. Οὐκοῦν τὸ τέμνεται καίεται αἰσθάνεται ὁμοίως λέγεται, καὶ πάντα πάσχειν τι σημαίνει· πάλιν δὲ τὸ λέγειν τρέχειν ὁρᾶν ὁμοίως ἀλλήλοις λέγεται· ἀλλὰ μὴν τό γ' ὁρᾶν αἰσθάνεσθαί τί ἐστιν, ὥστε καὶ πάσχειν τι ἅμα καὶ ποιεῖν. Εἰ δέ τις ἐκεῖ δοὺς μὴ ἐνδέχεσθαι ἅμα ταὐτὸ ποιεῖν καὶ πεποιηκέναι, τὸ ὁρᾶν καὶ ἑωρακέναι φαίη ἐγχωρεῖν, οὔπω ἐλήλεγκται, εἰ μὴ λέγοι τὸ ὁρᾶν ποιεῖν τι ἀλλὰ πάσχειν· προσδεῖ γὰρ

ΕΛΕΓΧΩΝ.

born in the present moment.—Do you do what you can and as you can? Yes. Not harping, you can harp. You harp, then, not harping. No: you have not the power to harp not harping, but when not harping you have the power to harp.

The solution some propose is different. If it is granted that a man does a thing as he can, they say it does not follow that he harps not harping, because it was not granted that he does the thing in all the ways in which he can. The solution is clearly bad, for fallacies identical in principle should admit of the same solution; but this solution will not apply to other fallacies similar in principle, nor to every mode of interrogation. It is a solution relative to the individual arguer, not to the argument.

XXI. ACCENTUATION scarcely gives rise to any fallacy either in writing or speaking, but a few might be invented like the following:—A house is where you lodge (οὖ with circumflex and aspirate), you do not lodge (οὐ with unwritten grave accent and soft breathing) is a negation, therefore a house is a negation. The solution is plain, for the word is not the same when the accent is grave and when it is circumflex.

XXII. It is plain that we must solve fallacies from similarity of expression by pointing out the difference of category denoted by similar words. The thesis denies the existence of a substance, and the questioner proves the existence of a relation or quantity that seems to be a substance from the form of expression. For instance: can we be making and have made one and the same thing? No[1]. Why, we can be seeing and have seen one and the same thing. Can an action be a passion? No. Why, to be cut, to be burnt, to be affected by a sensible object, are similar expressions, and all denote passions. Again, to say, to run, to see, are similar expressions. Now to see is to be affected by a sensible object, therefore it is both an action and a passion. In the former example, if I asserted in my thesis that one could not be making and have made the same thing, and granted that one could be seeing what one has seen, I am not confuted unless I grant that seeing is making. This additional premiss is required, but the hearer thinks that when I

F

τούτου τοῦ ἐρωτήματος· ἀλλ' ὑπὸ τοῦ ἀκούοντος ὑπολαμβάνεται δεδωκέναι, ὅτε τὸ τέμνειν ποιεῖν τι καὶ τὸ τετμηκέναι πεποιηκέναι ἔδωκε, καὶ ὅσα ἄλλα ὁμοίως λέγεται. Τὸ γὰρ λοιπὸν αὐτὸς προστίθησιν ὁ ἀκούων ὡς ὁμοίως λεγόμενον· τὸ δὲ λέγεται μὲν οὐχ ὁμοίως, φαίνεται δὲ διὰ τὴν λέξιν. Τὸ αὐτὸ δὲ συμβαίνει ὅπερ ἐν ταῖς ὁμωνυμίαις· οἴεται γὰρ ἐν τοῖς ὁμωνύμοις ὁ ἀγνὼς τῶν λόγων ὃ ἔφησεν ἀποφῆσαι πρᾶγμα, οὐκ ὄνομα· τὸ δὲ ἔτι προσδεῖ ἐρωτήματος, εἰ ἐφ' ἓν βλέπων λέγει τὸ ὁμώνυμον· οὕτως γὰρ δόντος ἔσται ἔλεγχος.

Ὅμοιοι δὲ καὶ οἵδε οἱ λόγοι τούτοις, εἰ ὅ τις ἔχων ὕστερον μὴ ἔχει ἀπέβαλεν· ὁ γὰρ ἕνα μόνον ἀποβαλὼν ἀστράγαλον οὐχ ἕξει δέκα ἀστραγάλους. Ἢ ὃ μὲν μὴ ἔχει πρότερον ἔχων, ἀποβέβληκεν, ὅσον δὲ μὴ ἔχει ἢ ὅσα, οὐκ ἀνάγκη τοσαῦτα ἀποβαλεῖν. Ἐρωτήσας οὖν ὃ ἔχει, συνάγει ἐπὶ τοῦ ὅσα· τὰ γὰρ δέκα ποσά. Εἰ οὖν ἤρετο ἐξ ἀρχῆς εἰ ὅσα τις μὴ ἔχει πρότερον ἔχων, ἆρά γε ἀποβέβληκε τοσαῦτα, οὐδεὶς ἂν ἔδωκεν, ἀλλ' ἢ τοσαῦτα ἢ τούτων τι. Καὶ ὅτι δοίη ἄν τις ὃ μὴ ἔχει· οὐ γὰρ ἔχει ἕνα μόνον ἀστράγαλον. Ἢ οὐ δέδωκεν ὃ οὐκ εἶχεν, ἀλλ' ὡς οὐκ εἶχε, τὸν ἕνα. Τὸ γὰρ μόνον οὐ τόδε σημαίνει οὐδὲ τοιόνδε οὐδὲ τοσόνδε, ἀλλ' ὡς ἔχει πρός τι, οἷον ὅτι οὐ μετ' ἄλλου. Ὥσπερ οὖν εἰ ἤρετο ἆρ' ὃ μή τις ἔχει δοίη ἄν, μὴ φάντος δὲ ἔροιτο εἰ δοίη ἄν τίς τι ταχέως μὴ ἔχων ταχέως, φήσαντος δὲ συλλογίζοιτο ὅτι δοίη ἂν τις ὃ μὴ ἔχει. Καὶ φανερὸν ὅτι οὐ συλλελόγισται· τὸ γὰρ ταχέως οὐ τόδε διδόναι ἀλλ' ὧδε διδόναι ἐστίν· ὡς δὲ μὴ ἔχει τις, δοίη ἄν, οἷον ἡδέως ἔχων δοίη ἂν λυπηρῶς.

Ὅμοιοι δὲ καὶ οἱ τοιοίδε πάντες. Ἆρ' ᾧ μὴ ἔχει χειρὶ τύπτοι ἄν; ἢ ᾧ μὴ ἔχει ὀφθαλμῷ ἴδοι ἄν; οὐ γὰρ ἔχει ἕνα μόνον. Λύουσι μὲν οὖν τινὲς λέγοντες καὶ ὡς ἔχει ἕνα μόνον καὶ ὀφθαλμὸν καὶ ἀλλ' ὁτιοῦν ὁ πλείω ἔχων. Οἱ δὲ καὶ ὡς ὃ ἔχει ἔλαβεν· ἐδίδου γὰρ μίαν μόνον οὗτος ψῆφον καὶ οὗτός

granted that to be cutting is to be making, and to have cut to have made, I also granted that the remaining forms denote corresponding categories. The hearer himself grants that the remainder have a similar signification, whereas the signification is different, though the forms are similar. What happens in the fallacies of ambiguous term happens here. In the fallacies of ambiguous term the uninitiated fancy that the reality is contradicted as well as the name, whereas confutation requires a further admission, that one reality is denoted by the ambiguous name. If the answerer grants this, he is confuted.

Similar to these reasonings are the following. What one had at first and has no longer he need not have lost, for if he had ten dice and loses one he has no longer ten. No. What he had at first and has no longer he must have lost; though he need not have lost as much or as many as he had at first. The thesis spoke of the substance that he has no longer, the conclusion speaks of the quantity. If it had been asked, when a man has a certain number of things at first and not subsequently, must he have lost them all? it would have been answered, No, he need not have lost them all, but he must have lost some of them. Again:—A man may give away what he has not got, for he may have many and give away only one. No. He does not give away a thing which he has not got, but a thing which is not related in the giving as it was in the having, if he had many and gives only one, for *only* denotes neither substance, nor quality, nor quantity, but relation, namely dissociation from others. When the thesis is that a man cannot give what he has not got, if it is granted that a man may give quickly what he has not got quickly, and I infer that a man may give what he has not got, my argument is inconclusive: for quickly does not denote substance but manner, and the manner of giving may be different from the manner of having; for a man may have with pleasure what he gives with pain.

Similar, too, are the following:—Suppose the thesis to be, a man cannot see with an eye he has not nor strike with a hand he has not. But a two-eyed or two-handed man has not only one eye or hand but may see or strike with only one. Some meet the argument by contradicting the premiss which denies that a man has only one eye or anything else when he has more

γ' ἔχει, φασί, μίαν μόνην παρὰ τούτου ψῆφον. Οἱ δ' εὐθὺς τὴν ἐρώτησιν³ ἀναιροῦντες, ὅτι ἐνδέχεται ὃ μὴ ἔλαβεν ἔχειν, οἷον οἶνον λαβόντα ἡδύν, διαφθαρέντος ἐν τῇ λήψει, ἔχειν ὀξύν. Ἀλλ' ὅπερ ἐλέχθη καὶ πρότερον, οὗτοι πάντες οὐ πρὸς τὸν λόγον ἀλλὰ πρὸς τὸν ἄνθρωπον λύουσιν. Εἰ γὰρ ἦν αὕτη λύσις, δόντα τὸ ἀντικείμενον οὐχ οἷόν τε λύειν, καθάπερ ἐπὶ τῶν ἄλλων· οἷον, εἰ ἔστι μὲν ὃ ἔστι δ' ὃ οὔ ἡ λύσις, ἄν ἁπλῶς δῷ λέγεσθαι, συμπεραίνεται· ἐὰν δὲ μὴ συμπεραίνηται, οὐκ ἄν εἴη λύσις· ἐν δὲ τοῖς προειρημένοις πάντων διδομένων οὐδέ φαμεν γίνεσθαι συλλογισμόν.

Ἔτι δὲ καὶ οἵδ' εἰσὶ τούτων τῶν λόγων. Ἆρ' ὃ γέγραπται, ἔγραφέτο⁶; Γέγραπται δὲ νῦν ὅτι σὺ κάθησαι, ψευδὴς λόγος· ἦν δ' ἀληθής, ὅτ' ἐγράφετο· ἅμα ἄρα ἐγράφετο ψευδὴς καὶ ἀληθής. Τὸ γὰρ ψευδῆ ἢ ἀληθῆ λόγον ἢ δόξαν εἶναι οὐ τόδε ἀλλὰ τοιόνδε σημαίνει· ὁ γὰρ αὐτὸς λόγος καὶ ἐπὶ τῆς δόξης. Καὶ ἆρ' ὃ μανθάνει ὁ μανθάνων, τοῦτ' ἐστὶν ὃ μανθάνει; μανθάνει δέ τις τὸ βραδὺ ταχύ. Οὐ τοίνυν ὃ μανθάνει ἀλλ' ὡς μανθάνει εἴρηκεν. Καὶ ἆρ' ὃ βαδίζει τις πατεῖ; βαδίζει δὲ τὴν ἡμέραν ὅλην. Ἢ οὐχ ὃ βαδίζει ἀλλ' ὅτε βαδίζει εἴρηκεν. Οὐδ' ὅταν τὴν κύλικα πίνειν, ὃ πίνει ἀλλ' ἐξ οὗ. Καὶ ἆρ' ὅ τις οἶδεν, ἢ μαθὼν ἢ εὑρὼν οἶδεν; ὧν δὲ τὸ μὲν εὗρε τὸ δ' ἔμαθε, τὰ ἄμφω οὐδέτερον. Ἢ ὃ μὲν ἅπαν, ἃ δὲ οὐχ ἅπαντα¹. Καὶ

ΕΛΕΓΧΩΝ.

than one. Or suppose the thesis to be, What a man has received and not parted with he possesses; and the premisses, He received only one ballot, but, having several before, does not possess only one: conclusion, Therefore he does not possess what he received. Some solve this by contradicting a premiss, and maintaining that he possesses only one from this donor: others by contradicting the thesis, and asserting that it is possible not to possess what one received; to receive sound wine, for instance, and if it was injured in the storage, to possess sour. All these solutions, like some mentioned before, are addressed, not to the argument but to the arguer. In every true solution, an admission contradicting the allegation of the solution would make the confutation valid, as in the other examples. For instance, if the solution is a distinction, an admission that the premiss is true without distinction would make the conclusion valid. Where a valid conclusion does not follow from the contradictory of the solution, that solution cannot be true. In the above examples, even if all is supplied which the proposed solutions allege to be wanting, there still is no conclusion[4].

The following arguments belong to the same class. Suppose the thesis to be, that the same statement cannot be both true and false. Then because what is written was written a certain time ago, and what is written, namely, that you are seated, is false now, though true when it was written; the arguer concludes that what was written was both true and false. But the falsity or truth of a statement is not its substance (what is written) but its quality: and so of opinion. Again:—what a man learns is what he learns: a man learns a slow march quick (quickly), therefore quick is slow. Here the subject which a man learns is confused with the rate of his learning. Again:—what one walks he tramples on: a man walks a day; therefore he tramples on the day. Here we change from space to time. Again:—when a man is said to drink a cup, the expression confuses the vessel and the wine. Again:—suppose the thesis to be, that the same thing cannot be both known and unknown; then because all that a man knows he knows either by teaching or discovery; and if part of his knowledge was taught him, and part discovered, the whole was neither taught nor discovered, I conclude that the whole was both known and unknown. The

ὅτι ἔστι τις τρίτος ἄνθρωπος· παρ' αὐτὸν καὶ τοὺς καθ' ἕκαστον. Τὸ γὰρ ἄνθρωπος καὶ ἅπαν τὸ κοινὸν οὐ τόδε τι, ἀλλὰ τοιόνδε τι ἢ πρός τι ἢ πῶς ἢ τῶν τοιούτων τι σημαίνει. Ὁμοίως δὲ καὶ ἐπὶ τοῦ Κορίσκος καὶ Κορίσκος μουσικός, πότερον ταὐτὸν ἢ ἕτερον; τὸ μὲν γὰρ τόδε τι τὸ δὲ τοιόνδε σημαίνει, ὥστ' οὐκ ἔστιν αὐτὸ ἐκθέσθαι*. Οὐ τὸ ἐκτίθεσθαι δὲ ποιεῖ τὸν τρίτον ἄνθρωπον, ἀλλὰ τὸ ὅπερ τόδε τι εἶναι συγχωρεῖν. Οὐ γὰρ ἔσται τόδε τι εἶναι ὅπερ Καλλίας καὶ ὅπερ ἄνθρωπός ἐστιν. Οὐδ' εἴ τις τὸ ἐκτιθέμενον μὴ ὅπερ τόδε τι εἶναι λέγοι ἀλλ' ὅπερ ποιόν, οὐδὲν διοίσει· ἔσται γὰρ τὸ παρὰ τοὺς πολλοὺς ἕν τι, οἷον ὁ ἄνθρωπος. Φανερὸν οὖν ὅτι οὐ δοτέον τόδε τι εἶναι τὸ κοινῇ κατηγορούμενον ἐπὶ πᾶσιν, ἀλλ' ἤτοι ποιὸν ἢ πρός τι ἢ ποσὸν ἢ τῶν τοιούτων τι σημαίνειν.

XXIII. Ὅλως δ' ἐν τοῖς παρὰ τὴν λέξιν λόγοις δεῖ κατὰ τὸ ἀντικείμενον ἔσται ἡ λύσις ἢ παρ' ὅ ἐστιν ὁ λόγος. Οἷον εἰ παρὰ σύνθεσιν ὁ λόγος, ἡ λύσις διελόντι, εἰ δὲ παρὰ διαίρεσιν, συνθέντι. Πάλιν εἰ παρὰ προσῳδίαν ὀξεῖαν, ἡ βαρεῖα προσῳδία λύσις, εἰ δὲ παρὰ βαρεῖαν, ἡ ὀξεῖα. Εἰ δὲ παρ' ὁμωνυμίαν, ἔστι τὸ ἀντικείμενον ὄνομα εἰπόντα λύειν, οἷον εἰ ἔμψυχον¹ συμβαίνει λέγειν, ἀποφήσαντα μὴ εἶναι, δηλοῦν ὡς ἔστιν ἔμψυχον εἰ δ' ἄψυχον ἔφησεν, ὁ δ' ἔμψυχον συνελογίσατο, λέγειν ὡς ἔστιν ἄψυχον. Ὁμοίως δὲ καὶ ἐπὶ τῆς ἀμφιβολίας. Εἰ δὲ παρ' ὁμοιότητα λέξεως, τὸ ἀντικείμενον ἔσται λύσις. Ἆρ' ὃ μὴ ἔχει, δοίη ἄν τις; Ἢ οὐχ ὃ μὴ ἔχει, ἀλλ' ὡς οὐκ ἔχει, οἷον ἕνα μόνον ἀστράγαλον. Ἆρ' ὃ ἐπίσταται, ἢ μαθὼν ἢ εὑρὼν ἐπίσταται; Ἀλλ' οὐχ ἃ ἐπίσταται. Καὶ εἰ ὃ βαδίζει πατεῖ, ἀλλ' οὐχ ὅτε. Ὁμοίως δὲ καὶ ἐπὶ τῶν ἄλλων.

solution is, that the premiss asserted, that all he knew distributively, not all collectively, was from one of these sources. Again, the proof of a third order of man, besides the individual man and the ideal man, depends on the confusion of category. For man and other generic terms are not names of substances, but of quality, or relation, or mode, or some other accident. So in the problem whether Coriscus and the musician Coriscus are different or the same, one term expresses a substance, the other a quality which cannot be really isolated. It is not, however, the isolation that produces the third order of man, but the assumption that the generic man is a substance, for without this, what is common to Callias and the generic man could not seem to be a substance. And what is isolated may be considered as not a substance, but merely a quality, without any logical inconvenience, for we shall still have a one besides the many, for instance, the generic man [9]. We must maintain, then, that genera are not names of substances, but merely names of qualities, or relations, or quantities, or other accidents [10].

XXIII. WHEN language is the source of fallacy, the opposite interpretation to that which produces the fallacy furnishes the solution. If composition produces the fallacy, division gives the solution; if division, composition. If acute accentuation creates the fallacy, grave accentuation supplies the solution; if grave, acute. If an ambiguous term is misinterpreted, give the opposite interpretation. If the thesis said a thing was animate, and the terms prove it inanimate, interpret them so as to leave it animate: if your thesis said it was inanimate, and the terms prove it animate, interpret them so as to leave it inanimate: and so with ambiguous propositions. If similarity of expression leads to confutation by one interpretation, the opposite interpretation provides the solution. If the thesis is, that a man cannot give what he does not possess, then your concession must be explained to be, that the possessor of many things who gives only one, gives, not a thing that he does not possess, but a thing that is not related to other gifts as it was to other possessions. Each element of a man's knowledge is known either by tradition or by discovery, not the sum total. A man tramples the way he goes, not the time. And so in the other cases.

ΠΕΡΙ ΣΟΦΙΣΤΙΚΩΝ

XXIV. Πρὸς δὲ τοὺς παρὰ τὸ συμβεβηκὸς μία μὲν ἡ αὐτὴ λύσις πρὸς ἅπαντας. Ἐπεὶ γὰρ ἀδιόριστόν ἐστι τὸ πότε λεκτέον ἐπὶ τοῦ πράγματος, ὅταν ἐπὶ τοῦ συμβεβηκότος ὑπάρχῃ, καὶ ἐπ' ἐνίων μὲν δοκεῖ καὶ φασίν, ἐπ' ἐνίων δ' οὔ φασιν ἀναγκαῖον εἶναι, ῥητέον οὖν συμβιβασθέντας ὁμοίως πρὸς ἅπαντας ὅτι οὐκ ἀναγκαῖον. Ἔχειν δὲ δεῖ προφέρειν τὸ οἷον. Εἰσὶ δὲ πάντες οἱ τοιοίδε τῶν λόγων παρὰ τὸ συμβεβηκός. Ἆρ' οἶδας ὃ μέλλω σε ἐρωτᾶν; Ἆρ' οἶδας τὸν προσιόντα ἢ τὸν ἐγκεκαλυμμένον; Ἆρ' ὁ ἀνδριὰς σόν ἐστιν ἔργον, ἢ σὸς ὁ κύων πατήρ; Ἆρα τὰ ὀλιγάκις ὀλίγα ὀλίγα; Φανερὸν γὰρ ἐν ἅπασι τούτοις ὅτι οὐκ ἀνάγκη τὸ κατὰ τοῦ συμβεβηκότος καὶ κατὰ τοῦ πράγματος ἀληθεύεσθαι· μόνοις γὰρ τοῖς κατὰ τὴν οὐσίαν ἀδιαφόροις καὶ ἓν οὖσιν ἅπαντα δοκεῖ ταὐτὰ ὑπάρχειν. Τῷ δ' ἀγαθῷ οὐ ταὐτόν ἐστιν ἀγαθῷ τ' εἶναι καὶ μέλλοντι ἐρωτᾶσθαι, οὐδὲ τῷ προσιόντι ἢ ἐγκεκαλυμμένῳ προσιόντι τε εἶναι καὶ Κορίσκῳ. Ὥστ' οὐκ εἰ οἶδα τὸν Κορίσκον, ἀγνοῶ δὲ τὸν προσιόντα, τὸν αὐτὸν οἶδα καὶ ἀγνοῶ· οὐδ' εἰ ταῦτ' ἐστὶν ἐμόν, ἔστι δ' ἔργον, ἐμόν ἐστιν ἔργον, ἀλλ' ἢ κτῆμα ἢ πρᾶγμα ἢ ἄλλο τι. Τὸν αὐτὸν δὲ τρόπον καὶ ἐπὶ τῶν ἄλλων.

Λύουσι δέ τινες ἀναιροῦντες· τὴν ἐρώτησιν φασὶ γὰρ ἐνδέχεσθαι ταὐτὸ πρᾶγμα εἰδέναι καὶ ἀγνοεῖν, ἀλλὰ μὴ κατὰ ταὐτό· τὸν οὖν προσιόντα οὐκ εἰδότες, τὸν δὲ Κορίσκον εἰδότες, ταὐτὸ μὲν εἰδέναι καὶ ἀγνοεῖν φασίν, ἀλλ' οὐ κατὰ ταὐτό. Καίτοι πρῶτον μέν, καθάπερ ἤδη εἴπομεν, δεῖ τῶν παρὰ ταὐτὸ λόγων τὴν αὐτὴν εἶναι διόρθωσιν· αὕτη δ' οὐκ ἔσται, ἄν τις μὴ ἐπὶ τοῦ εἰδέναι ἀλλ' ἐπὶ τοῦ εἶναι ἢ πῶς ἔχειν τὸ αὐτὸ ἀξίωμα λαμβάνῃ, οἷον εἰ ὅδε ἐστὶ πατήρ, ἔστι δὲ σός· εἰ

XXIV. All fallacies from the equation of subject and accident admit of the same solution. It is undetermined when the subject has the attributes of its accident, and sometimes it is believed and maintained to have them, sometimes not. We must therefore reply to every conclusion based on this principle, that it does not follow; and we must be prepared with an example [1]. The following arguments depend on the equation of subject and accident. You do not know what I am going to ask you about; I am going to ask you about the nature of the Summum Bonum; therefore you do not know the nature of the Summum Bonum [2]. You do not know the person approaching with a muffled face; he is Coriscus: therefore you do not know Coriscus [3]. The statue is a workmanship; the statue is yours: therefore the statue is your workmanship. The dog is yours; the dog is a father: therefore the dog is your father [4]. A small number multiplied by a small number is a large number. Then a four multiplied by a four is a large number; but a four multiplied by a four is a four; therefore a four is a large number [5]. What is true of the accident is not of necessity true of the subject (and vice versa): for only those things whose entire essence is one and indistinguishable have all their attributes in common. But being the Summum Bonum is not exactly the same as being about to be asked: nor is approaching with a muffled face exactly the same as being Coriscus. So if I know Coriscus and not the person approaching, it does not follow that I know and do not know the same person: and if this is mine, and a workmanship, it is not my workmanship, but my chattel or property; and so in the other cases.

Some solve the difficulty by distinguishing the thesis and making the fallacy consist of Ignoratio elenchi. They say we may know and not know the same thing but not in the same respect: that, if you know Coriscus and do not know who approaches, you know and do not know the same person, but not in respect of the same predicate. But, in the first place, as I said before [7], all fallacies on the same principle ought to receive the same solution. Now this solution would not apply if we argued, not about knowledge, but about existence or relation: if, for instance, because this slave is a father and this slave is yours, I argued that he is your

γὰρ ἐπ' ἐνίων ταῦτ' ἐστὶν ἀληθὲς καὶ ἐνδέχεται ταὐτὸ εἰδέναι καὶ ἀγνοεῖν, ἀλλ' ἐνταῦθα οὐδὲν κοινωνεῖ τὸ λεχθέν. Οὐδὲν δὲ κωλύει τὸν αὐτὸν λόγον πλείους μοχθηρίας ἔχειν· ἀλλ' οὐχ ἡ πάσης ἁμαρτίας ἐμφάνισις λύσις ἐστίν· ἐγχωρεῖ γὰρ ὅτι μὲν ψεῦδος συλλελόγισται δεῖξαί τινα, παρ' ὃ δὲ μὴ δεῖξαι, οἷον τὸν Ζήνωνος λόγον, ὅτι οὐκ ἔστι κινηθῆναι. Ὥστε καὶ εἴ τις ἐπιχειροίη συνάγειν ὡς ἀδύνατον, ἁμαρτάνει, κἂν εἰ μυριάκις ᾖ συλλελογισμένος· οὐ γάρ ἐστιν αὕτη λύσις. Ἦν γὰρ ἡ λύσις ἐμφάνισις ψευδοῦς συλλογισμοῦ, παρ' ὃ ψευδής· εἰ οὖν μὴ συλλελόγισται ἢ καὶ ἀληθὲς ἢ ψεῦδος ἐπιχειρεῖ συνάγειν, ἡ ἐκείνου δήλωσις λύσις ἐστίν. Ἴσως δὲ καὶ τοῦτ' ἐπ' ἐνίων οὐδὲν κωλύει συμβαίνειν· πλὴν ἐπί γε τούτων οὐδὲ τοῦτο δόξειεν ἄν· καὶ γὰρ τὸν Κορίσκον ὅτι Κορίσκος οἶδε, καὶ τὸ προσιὸν ὅτι προσιόν. Ἐνδέχεσθαι δὲ δοκεῖ τὸ αὐτὸ εἰδέναι καὶ μή, οἷον ὅτι μὲν λευκὸν εἰδέναι, ὅτι δὲ μουσικὸν μὴ γνωρίζειν, οὕτω γὰρ τὸ αὐτὸ οἶδε καὶ οὐκ οἶδεν· ἀλλ' οὐ κατὰ ταὐτόν. Τὸ δὲ προσιὸν καὶ Κορίσκον, καὶ ὅτι προσιὸν καὶ ὅτι Κορίσκος, οἶδεν.

Ὁμοίως δ' ἁμαρτάνουσι καὶ οἱ λύοντες, ὅτι ἅπας ἀριθμὸς ὀλίγος, ὥσπερ οὓς εἴπομεν· εἰ γὰρ μὴ συμπεραινομένου, τοῦτο παραλιπόντες, ἀληθὲς συμπεπεράνθαι φασί, πάντα γὰρ εἶναι καὶ πολὺν καὶ ὀλίγον, ἁμαρτάνουσιν.

Ἔνιοι δὲ καὶ τῷ διττῷ λύουσι τοὺς συλλογισμούς, οἷον ὅτι σός ἐστι πατὴρ ἢ υἱὸς ἢ δοῦλος. Καίτοι φανερὸν ὡς εἰ παρὰ τὸ πολλαχῶς λέγεσθαι φαίνεται ὁ ἔλεγχος, δεῖ τοὔνομα ἢ τὸν λόγον κυρίως εἶναι πλειόνων· τὸ δὲ τῶδ' εἶναι τοῦδε τέκνον οὐδεὶς λέγει κυρίως, εἰ δεσπότης ἐστὶ τέκνου· ἀλλὰ παρὰ τὸ συμβεβηκὸς ἡ σύνθεσίς[10] ἐστιν. Ἆρ' ἐστὶ τοῦτο σόν; Ναί. Ἔστι δὲ τοῦτο τέκνον· σὸν ἄρα τοῦτο τέκνον ὅτι συμβέβηκεν εἶναι καὶ σὸν καὶ τέκνον· ἀλλ' οὐ σὸν τέκνον.

Καὶ τὸ εἶναι τῶν κακῶν τι ἀγαθόν· ἡ γὰρ φρόνησίς ἐστιν ἐπιστήμη τῶν κακῶν. Τὸ δὲ τοῦτο τούτων εἶναι οὐ λέγεται πολλαχῶς, ἀλλὰ κτῆμα. Εἰ δ' ἄρα πολλαχῶς (καὶ γὰρ τὸν ἄνθρωπον τῶν ζῴων φαμὲν εἶναι, ἀλλ' οὔ τι κτῆμα) καὶ ἐάν τι

ΕΛΕΓΧΩΝ. 75

father. Though the solution is applicable with some predicates, and the same thing, for instance, may be known and unknown in different respects, with other predicates it is inapplicable. In the second place, the same argument may have several faults, but it is not the exposure of any fault that is solution; for the falsity of the conclusion may be demonstrated without explaining why the reasoning is fallacious. To solve Zeno's proof of the impossibility of motion, we ought not to try to prove the opposite; for though we gave ten thousand valid proofs, this would be no solution; for it would not disclose where the vice of his argument lay. If an argument is inconclusive, or concludes what is true or false from false premisses, the exposure of this vice is solution. In the third place, though this distinction of the thesis may be admissible in other cases, it is not admissible here: for here you know that Coriscus is Coriscus, and that he who approaches approaches. But the same subject can only be known and not known in respect of different predicates; known, for instance, to be white, and not known to be musical. Here the same person is known to be Coriscus and not known to be Coriscus, or known to approach and not known to approach.

So it is wrong to solve the fallacy about number by retracting the thesis that a number cannot be both great and small. When an argument is inconclusive, to overlook the want of cogency, and maintain the truth of the conclusion, is bad logic.

Some class these fallacies under the head of Equivocation, maintaining, for instance, that yours means either your father, your son, or your slave. But a term or proposition is only ambiguous when it has a plurality of proper significations; and this man's child cannot properly signify a child that is this man's slave. It is the equation of subject and accident that produces the fallacious combination. Is it yours? Yes. Is it a child? Yes. Then it is your child. No. It is yours, and a child, but not your child.

So too the proof that some of evil is good, (for wisdom is knowledge of evil,) is referred to the class of ambiguity. But the expression *of* a thing (the genitive case) is not ambiguous, as it only properly denotes property (has a possessive force). Granting, however, that the genitive is ambiguous, (for when

πρὸς τὰ κακὰ λέγηται ὥς τινός, διὰ τοῦτο τῶν κακῶν ἐστίν, ἀλλ' οὐ τοῦτο τῶν κακῶν[11]; Παρὰ τὸ πῇ οὖν καὶ ἁπλῶς φαίνεται. Καίτοι ἐνδέχεται ἴσως ἀγαθὸν εἶναί τι τῶν κακῶν διττῶς, ἀλλ' οὐκ ἐπὶ τοῦ λόγου τούτου, ἀλλ' εἴ τι δοῦλον εἴη ἀγαθὸν μοχθηροῦ, μᾶλλον. Ἴσως δ' οὐδ' οὕτως· οὐ γὰρ εἰ ἀγαθὸν καὶ τούτου, ἀγαθὸν τούτου ἅμα. Οὐδὲ τὸ τὸν ἄνθρωπον φάναι τῶν ζῴων εἶναι οὐ λέγεται πολλαχῶς· οὐ γὰρ εἴ ποτέ τι σημαίνομεν ἀφελόντες, τοῦτο λέγεται πολλαχῶς· καὶ γὰρ τὸ ἥμισυ εἰπόντες τοῦ ἔπους δός μοι Ἰλιάδα σημαίνομεν, οἷον τὸ μῆνιν ἄειδε θεά.

XXV. Τοὺς δὲ παρὰ τὸ κυρίως τόδε ἢ πῇ ἢ ποῦ ἢ πῶς ἢ πρός τι λέγεσθαι καὶ μὴ ἁπλῶς, λυτέον σκοποῦντι τὸ συμπέρασμα πρὸς τὴν ἀντίφασιν, εἰ ἐνδέχεται τούτων τι πεπονθέναι. Τὰ γὰρ ἐναντία καὶ τὰ ἀντικείμενα καὶ φάσιν καὶ ἀπόφασιν ἁπλῶς μὲν ἀδύνατον ὑπάρχειν τῷ αὐτῷ, πῇ μέντοι ἑκάτερον ἢ πρός τι ἢ πῶς, ἢ τὸ μὲν πῇ τὸ δ' ἁπλῶς, οὐδὲν κωλύει. Ὥστ' εἰ τόδε μὲν ἁπλῶς τόδε δὲ πῇ, οὔπω ἔλεγχος. Τοῦτο δ' ἐν τῷ συμπεράσματι θεωρητέον πρὸς τὴν ἀντίφασιν.

Εἰσὶ δὲ πάντες οἱ τοιοῦτοι λόγοι τοῦτ' ἔχοντες. Ἆρ' ἐνδέχεται τὸ μὴ ὂν εἶναι; Ἀλλὰ μὴν ἔστι γέ τι μὴ ὄν. Ὁμοίως δὲ καὶ τὸ ὂν οὐκ ἔσται· οὐ γὰρ ἔσται τι τῶν ὄντων. Ἆρ' ἐνδέχεται τὸν αὐτὸν ἅμα εὐορκεῖν καὶ ἐπιορκεῖν; Ἆρ' ἐγχωρεῖ τὸν αὐτὸν ἅμα τῷ αὐτῷ πείθεσθαι καὶ ἀπειθεῖν; Ἢ οὔτε τὸ εἶναί τι καὶ εἶναι ταὐτόν; τὸ δὲ μὴ ὂν οὐκ, εἰ ἔστι τι, καὶ ἔστιν ἁπλῶς· οὔτ' εἰ εὐορκεῖ τόδε ἢ τῇδε, ἀνάγκη καὶ εὐορκεῖν· ὁ δ' ὀμόσας ἐπιορκήσειν εὐορκεῖ ἐπιορκῶν τοῦτο μόνον, εὐορκεῖ δὲ οὔ· οὐδ' ὁ ἀπειθῶν πείθεται, ἀλλά τι πείθεται. Ὅμοιος δ' ὁ λόγος καὶ περὶ τοῦ ψεύδεσθαι τὸν αὐτὸν ἅμα καὶ ἀληθεύειν· ἀλλὰ διὰ τὸ μὴ εἶναι εὐθεώρητον, ποτέρως ἄν τις ἀποδοίη τὸ ἁπλῶς ἀληθεύειν ἢ ψεύδεσθαι, δύσκολον φαίνεται. Κωλύει δ' αὐτὸν οὐδὲν ἁπλῶς μὲν εἶναι ψευδῆ, πῇ δ' ἀληθῆ ἢ τινός, καὶ εἶναι

ΕΛΕΓΧΩΝ.

we say man is of the animals we mean he is a species, not the property, of the animals; that is to say, the genitive may have either a possessive or a partitive force,) still when we express the relation of wisdom to evils by putting evils into the genitive, we do not mean that wisdom is absolutely of evils, but that wisdom is a correlative, namely, the knowledge of evils. The fallacy then lies not in ambiguity but in the confusion of absolute and restricted propositions. If, however, the expression that there is a good of evils, is not ambiguous when we affirm that wisdom is of evils, do we not obtain an ambiguous conclusion when we assume a good slave belonging to bad masters? Perhaps not even then, for a thing that is good and of the bad is not therefore a good of the bad [12]. The expression that man is of the animals is not ambiguous [13], for ellipsis is not ambiguity, for we may call unambiguously for the Iliad by saying, "Achilles wrath [11]."

XXV. FALLACIES from the confusion of absolute or unrestricted propositions with propositions restricted in mode, place, degree, or relation, are to be solved by comparing the conclusion with the thesis, to see whether there is any restriction on either side to prevent their being contradictory [1]. For contrary, opposite, negative and affirmative predicates cannot both belong to the same subject absolutely, but may both belong restrictedly, or one restrictedly and the other absolutely. If one belongs absolutely and the other restrictedly, there is no confutation. We must therefore compare the conclusion with the thesis.

All the following arguments have this defect.—Thesis: what is not, cannot be. But what is not, is what is not.—Thesis: what is, cannot not-be. But what is, is not, for it is not some special thing.—Thesis: the same man cannot be perjured and keep his oath.—Thesis: the same man cannot at the same time obey and disobey the same command. In the first two examples to be restrictedly something and absolutely to be, are not the same. What is not, is restrictedly something, but absolutely is not. Again, a man may be unforsworn in a definite particular but not absolutely. If he swore to perjure himself and keeps his oath, he is unperjured in this particular but not absolutely. Again, he who disobeys, though not obedient absolutely, may be obedient to a particular command. So it may

ἀληθῆ τινά, ἀληθῆ δὲ μή. Ὁμοίως δὲ καὶ ἐπὶ τῶν πρός τι καὶ ποῦ καὶ πότε· πάντες γὰρ οἱ τοιοῦτοι λόγοι παρὰ τοῦτο συμβαίνουσιν. Ἆρ' ἡ ὑγίεια ἢ ὁ πλοῦτος ἀγαθόν; Ἀλλὰ τῷ ἄφρονι καὶ μὴ ὀρθῶς χρωμένῳ οὐκ ἀγαθόν· ἀγαθὸν ἆρα καὶ οὐκ ἀγαθόν. Ἆρα τὸ ὑγιαίνειν ² ἢ δύνασθαι ἐν πόλει ἀγαθόν; Ἀλλ' ἔστιν ὅτε οὐ βέλτιον· ταὐτὸν ἆρα τῷ αὐτῷ ἀγαθὸν καὶ οὐκ ἀγαθόν. Ἠ οὐδὲν κωλύει ἁπλῶς ὃν ἀγαθὸν τῷδε μὴ εἶναι ἀγαθόν, ἢ τῷδε μὲν ἀγαθόν, ἀλλ' οὐ νῦν ἢ οὐκ ἐνταῦθ' ἀγαθόν. Ἆρ' ὃ μὴ βούλοιτ' ἂν ὁ φρόνιμος, κακόν; Ἀποβαλεῖν δ' οὐ βούλεται τἀγαθόν· κακὸν ἆρα τἀγαθόν. Οὐ γὰρ ταὐτὸν εἰπεῖν τἀγαθὸν εἶναι κακὸν καὶ τὸ ἀποβαλεῖν τἀγαθόν. Ὁμοίως δὲ καὶ ὁ τοῦ κλέπτου λόγος. Οὐ γὰρ εἰ κακόν ἐστιν ὁ κλέπτης, καὶ τὸ λαβεῖν ἐστὶ κακόν· οὔκουν τὸ κακὸν βούλεται, ἀλλὰ τἀγαθόν· τὸ γὰρ λαβεῖν ἀγαθόν ². Καὶ ἡ νόσος κακόν ἐστιν, ἀλλ' οὐ τὸ ἀποβαλεῖν νόσον. Ἆρα τὸ δίκαιον τοῦ ἀδίκου καὶ τὸ δικαίως τοῦ ἀδίκως αἱρετώτερον; Ἀλλ' ἀποθανεῖν ἀδίκως αἱρετώτερον. Ἆρα δίκαιόν ἐστι τὰ αὑτοῦ ἔχειν ἕκαστον; Ἃ δ' ἄν τις κρίνῃ κατὰ δόξαν τὴν αὐτοῦ, κἂν ᾖ ψευδῆ, κύριά ἐστιν ἐκ τοῦ νόμου· τὸ αὐτὸ ἆρα δίκαιον καὶ οὐ δίκαιον. Καὶ πότερα δεῖ νικᾶν ¹ τὸν τὰ δίκαια λέγοντα ἢ τὸν τὰ ἄδικα; Ἀλλὰ μὴν καὶ τὸν ἀδικούμενον δίκαιόν ἐστιν ἱκανῶς λέγειν ἃ ἔπαθεν· ταῦτα δ' ἦν ἄδικα. Οὐ γὰρ εἰ παθεῖν τι ἀδίκως αἱρετόν, τὸ ἀδίκως αἱρετώτερον τοῦ δικαίως· ἀλλ' ἁπλῶς μὲν τὸ δικαίως, τοδὶ μέντοι οὐδὲν κωλύει ἀδίκως ἢ δικαίως. Καὶ τὸ ἔχειν τὰ αὑτοῦ δίκαιον, τὸ δὲ τἀλλότρια οὐ δίκαιον· κρίσιν μέντοι ταύτην δικαίαν εἶναι οὐδὲν κωλύει, οἷον ἂν ᾖ κατὰ δόξαν τοῦ κρίναντος· οὐ γὰρ εἰ δίκαιον τοδὶ ἢ ὡδί, καὶ ἁπλῶς δίκαιον. Ὁμοίως δὲ καὶ ἄδικα ὄντα οὐδὲν κωλύει λέγειν γε αὐτὰ δίκαιον εἶναι· οὐ γὰρ εἰ λέγειν δίκαιον, ἀνάγκη δίκαια εἶναι, ὥσπερ οὐδ' εἰ ὠφέλιμον λέγειν, ὠφέλιμα. Ὁμοίως δὲ καὶ ἐπὶ τῶν δικαίων. Ὥστ' οὐκ εἰ τὰ λεγόμενα ἄδικα, ὁ λέγων ἄδικα νικᾷ· λέγει γὰρ ἃ λέγειν ἐστὶ δίκαια, ἁπλῶς δὲ καὶ παθεῖν ἄδικα.

be proved that the same person at the same moment may utter truth and falsehood. The doubt whether a proposition ought to be called absolutely true or absolutely false causes the only difficulty. A statement may be absolutely false and partially true, that is, partially but not absolutely true. There may be similar restrictions in relation to time, and place, as in the following arguments: Health and wealth are good, but to the fool and person who misuses them they are evil. Therefore they are both good and evil.—Office and political power are good, but to the same person there is a time when they are evil. The same thing therefore is both good and evil. But a thing may be good absolutely, yet not to this individual; or good to this individual, yet not at this time and place. Again, What the wise avoids is evil; he avoids lost good; therefore good is evil. No. Good is not evil but an evil thing to lose. The argument about the thief is like this. The thief is an evil but a good person to catch; so that we desire what is good, not what is evil, when we desire his capture. So sickness is an evil and a good thing to get rid of. Again, right is better than wrong, and to act rightly than to act wrongly: but it is better to be put to death wrongly.—It is just that a man should have his own: but a conscientious judgment, though it adjudicates a man's property to his neighbour, is just. The same thing therefore is just and unjust.—Judgment should be given for the party asserting rights, not for the party asserting wrongs. But the victim of injustice ought to obtain judgment when he relates his grievances, that is, his wrongs. With reference to the last three examples, we may observe that to suffer wrongly may be preferable, though what is done wrongly is not absolutely preferable to what is done rightly. What is done rightly is absolutely preferable; what is done wrongly only in certain special particulars. Again, it is absolutely just that a man should have his own, and not just that he should have what is his neighbour's; though such an adjudication is just in a qualified sense, if honest. But what is just in this sense is not absolutely just. Again, wrongs may be right to allege, and the rightness of the allegation does not make them rights any more than the expediency of the allegation makes them expedient, and vice versa. Although, then, the things alleged are wrongs,

ΠΕΡΙ ΣΟΦΙΣΤΙΚΩΝ

XXVI. Τοῖς δὲ παρὰ τὸν ὁρισμὸν γινομένοις τοῦ ἐλέγχου, καθάπερ ὑπεγράφη πρότερον, ἀπαντητέον σκοποῦσι τὸ συμπέρασμα πρὸς τὴν ἀντίφασιν, ὅπως ἔσται τὸ αὐτὸ καὶ κατὰ τὸ αὐτὸ καὶ πρὸς τὸ αὐτὸ καὶ ὡσαύτως καὶ ἐν τῷ αὐτῷ χρόνῳ. Ἐὰν δ᾽ ἐν ἀρχῇ προσέρηται, οὐχ ὁμολογητέον ὡς ἀδύνατον τὸ αὐτὸ εἶναι διπλάσιον καὶ μὴ διπλάσιον, ἀλλὰ φατέον, μὴ μέντοι ὡδί, ὥς ποτ᾽ ἦν τὸ ἐλέγχεσθαι διωμολογημένον. Εἰσὶ δὲ πάντες οἵδ᾽ οἱ λόγοι παρὰ τὸ τοιοῦτο. Ἆρ᾽ ὁ εἰδὼς ἕκαστον ὅτι ἕκαστον, οἶδε τὸ πρᾶγμα, καὶ ὁ ἀγνοῶν ὡσαύτως; Εἰδὼς δέ τις τὸν Κορίσκον ὅτι Κορίσκος, ἀγνοοίη ἂν ὅτι μουσικός, ὥστε ταὐτὸ ἐπίσταται καὶ ἀγνοεῖ. Ἆρα τὸ τετράπηχυ τοῦ τριπήχεος μεῖζον; Γένοιτο δ᾽ ἂν ἐκ τριπήχους τετράπηχυ κατὰ τὸ μῆκος· τὸ δὲ μεῖζον ἐλάττονος μεῖζον· αὐτὸ ἄρα αὑτοῦ μεῖζον καὶ ἔλαττον.

XXVII. Τοὺς δὲ παρὰ τὸ αἰτεῖσθαι καὶ λαμβάνειν τὸ ἐν ἀρχῇ πυνθανομένῳ μέν, ἂν ᾖ δῆλον, οὐ δοτέον, οὐδ᾽ ἂν ἔνδοξον ᾖ, λέγοντα τἀληθές. Ἂν δὲ λάθῃ, τὴν ἄγνοιαν διὰ τὴν μοχθηρίαν τῶν τοιούτων λόγων εἰς τὸν ἐρωτῶντα μεταστρεπτέον ὡς οὐ διειλεγμένον· ὁ γὰρ ἔλεγχος ἄνευ τοῦ ἐξ ἀρχῆς. Εἶθ᾽ ὅτι ἐδόθη οὐχ ὡς τούτῳ χρησομένου, ἀλλ᾽ ὡς πρὸς τοῦτο συλλογισομένου τοὐναντίον, ἢ ἐπὶ τῶν παρεξελέγχων.

XXVIII. Καὶ τοὺς διὰ τοῦ παρεπομένου συμβιβάζοντας ἐπ᾽ αὐτοῦ τοῦ λόγου δεικτέον. Ἔστι δὲ διττὴ ἡ τῶν ἑπομένων ἀκολούθησις. Ἡ γὰρ ὡς τῷ ἐν μέρει τὸ καθόλου, οἷον ἀνθρώπῳ ζῷον· ἀξιοῦται γάρ, εἰ τόδε μετὰ τοῦδε, καὶ τόδ᾽ εἶναι μετὰ τοῦδε. Ἡ κατὰ τὰς ἀντιθέσεις· εἰ γὰρ τόδε τῷδε ἀκολουθεῖ, τῷ ἀντικειμένῳ τὸ ἀντικείμενον. Παρ᾽ ὃ καὶ ὁ τοῦ Μελίσσου λόγος· εἰ γὰρ τὸ γεγονὸς ἔχει ἀρχήν, τὸ ἀγένητον

it is not wrong allegations that carry the judgment, for the things are right to allege though absolutely wrongs and wrong to undergo.

XXVI. Fallacies that omit some element in the definition of confutation, as was suggested above, must be solved by examining whether the conclusion is contradictory of the thesis, and regards the same terms, in the same portion, in the same relation, in the same manner, in the same time. The thesis when first advanced should admit that the same thing may be double and not double in any way that falls short of the conditions of contradiction. The following arguments depend on this. He who knows a subject to have a predicate knows the subject, and so he who is ignorant. If, then, I know that Coriscus is Coriscus, and am ignorant that he is musical, I know and am ignorant of the same subject.—A thing four cubits high is higher than a thing three cubits high: but what is three cubits high may grow to be four cubits high. What is greater is greater than what is less. The same thing, therefore, may be greater and less than itself, and in respect of the same dimension, namely height.

XXVII. In fallacies from begging and assuming the point in issue, if we are aware in time we should deny the proposition, even though it is probable, and say, as we fairly may, that it cannot be granted but must be proved. If it escaped us, the badness of the reasoning enables us to turn round and impute the blunder to the opponent, who ought to have known that it is no confutation to assume a contradictory proposition: and we may say that we admitted the proposition, not as a premiss but as a thesis to be confuted, or as a premiss, not of the main reasoning, but of a by-confutation[1].

XXVIII. Fallacies from the relation of antecedent and consequent can only be exposed when the false conclusion is drawn. There are two modes of falsely inferred sequence. Either when animal, the universal, follows from man, the particular, it is inferred that man, the particular, reciprocally follows from animal, the universal: or, the relation of the contradictories of the antecedent and consequent is supposed to correspond directly to the relation of the antecedent and consequent. If A, that is, follows B, it is assumed that not-A follows not-B, as in Melissus' argu-

ἀξιοῖ μὴ ἔχειν, ὥστ' εἰ ἀγένητος ὁ οὐρανός, καὶ ἄπειρος. Τὸ δ' οὐκ ἔστιν· ἀνάπαλιν γὰρ ἡ ἀκολούθησις.

XXIX. Ὅσοι τε παρὰ τὸ προστιθέναι τι συλλογίζονται, σκοπεῖν εἰ ἀφαιρουμένου συμβαίνει μηδὲν ἧττον τὸ ἀδύνατον, κἄπειτα τοῦτο ἐμφανιστέον, καὶ λεκτέον ὡς ἔδωκεν οὐχ ὡς δοκοῦν ἀλλ' ὡς πρὸς τὸν λόγον, ὁ δὲ κέχρηται οὐδὲν πρὸς τὸν λόγον.

XXX. Πρὸς δὲ τοὺς τὰ πλείω ἐρωτήματα ἓν ποιοῦντας εὐθὺς ἐν ἀρχῇ διοριστέον. Ἐρώτησις γὰρ μία πρὸς ἣν μία ἀπόκρισίς ἐστιν, ὥστ' οὔτε πλείω καθ' ἑνὸς οὔτε ἓν κατὰ πολλῶν, ἀλλ' ἓν καθ' ἑνὸς φατέον ἢ ἀποφατέον. Ὥσπερ δὲ ἐπὶ τῶν ὁμωνύμων ὁτὲ μὲν ἀμφοῖν ὁτὲ δ' οὐδετέρῳ ὑπάρχει, ὥστε μὴ ἁπλοῦ ὄντος τοῦ ἐρωτήματος ἁπλῶς ἀποκρινομένοις οὐδὲν συμβαίνει πάσχειν, ὁμοίως καὶ ἐπὶ τούτων. Ὅταν μὲν οὖν τὰ πλείω τῷ ἑνὶ ἢ τὸ ἐν τοῖς πολλοῖς ὑπάρχῃ, τῷ ἁπλῶς δόντι καὶ ἁμαρτόντι ταύτην τὴν ἁμαρτίαν οὐδὲν ὑπεναντίωμα συμβαίνει· ὅταν δὲ τῷ μὲν τῷ δὲ μή, ἢ πλείω κατὰ πλειόνων, καὶ ἔστιν ὡς ὑπάρχει ἀμφότερα ἀμφοτέροις, ἔστι δ' ὡς οὐχ ὑπάρχει πάλιν, ὥστε τοῦτ' εὐλαβητέον. Οἷον ἐν τοῖσδε τοῖς λόγοις. Εἰ τὸ μέν ἐστιν ἀγαθὸν τὸ δὲ κακόν, ὅτι ταῦτά[1] ἀληθὲς εἰπεῖν ἀγαθὸν καὶ κακὸν καὶ πάλιν μήτ' ἀγαθὸν μήτε κακόν· οὐκ ἔστι γὰρ ἑκάτερον ἑκάτερον, ὥστε ταὐτὸ ἀγαθὸν καὶ κακὸν καὶ οὔτ' ἀγαθὸν οὔτε κακόν. Καὶ εἰ ἕκαστον αὐτὸ αὑτῷ ταὐτόν καὶ ἄλλου ἕτερον· ἐπεὶ δ'[2] οὐκ ἄλλοις ταὐτά, ἀλλ' αὑτοῖς, καὶ ἕτερα αὐτῶν, ταὐτὰ ἑαυτοῖς ἕτερα καὶ ταὐτά. Ἔτι εἰ τὸ μὲν ἀγαθὸν κακὸν γίνεται, τὸ δὲ κακὸν ἀγαθόν ἐστιν, δύο γένοιτ' ἄν[3].

ment. If the generated is limited he assumes that the ungenerated is unlimited: that is to say, because, if the heavens are infinite in space, they are eternal in time, he assumes that, if they are eternal in time, they are infinite in space. But this is not so; for the sequence of the contradictories of an antecedent and consequent is the inverse of the original sequence.

XXIX. In fallacies where a superfluous proposition is foisted in as the cause of an absurd conclusion, we must examine whether the suppression of the premiss would interrupt the conclusion; and after shewing that it does not, we may add that the premisses which really cause it were not granted because they were believed, but because the questioner seemed to wish to use them against the thesis, which he has failed to do.

XXX. Several questions put as one should be met at once by decomposition of the complex question into its elements. Only a single question admits of a single answer: so that neither several predicates of one subject, nor one predicate of several subjects, but only one predicate of one subject ought to be affirmed or denied in a single answer. When we have an ambiguous subject, sometimes a predicate is true of both or neither of the things signified; and though the question is equivocal, a simple answer exposes us to no confutation. The same thing happens when many questions are asked. When several predicates are true of one subject, or one predicate of several subjects, a single answer, though a dialectical error, involves us in no confutation. But if a predicate is true of one subject and not of others, or several predicates are propounded of several subjects, and each is true of each but not all of all, a single answer involves confutation and must be refused. For instance, if A is good and B evil, if we say that A and B are good and evil, we may be interpreted to say that the same things are good and evil and neither good nor evil, for A is not evil and B is not good. Again, if A differs from B, and we say that A and B are the same as themselves or different from themselves, we may be interpreted to mean that A is different from A or that A is the same as B. Again, if A becomes good and B becomes evil, and we say that A and B become good and evil, we may be interpreted to mean that each becomes both good and evil. Again, if A and B are unequal, and we say

Δυοῖν τε καὶ ἀνίσων ἑκάτερον αὐτὸ αὑτῷ ἴσον, ὥστε ἴσα καὶ ἄνισα αὐτὰ αὑτοῖς.

Ἐμπίπτουσι μὲν οὖν οὗτοι καὶ εἰς ἄλλας λύσεις· καὶ γὰρ τὸ ἄμφω καὶ τὸ ἅπαντα πλείω σημαίνει· οὔκουν ταὐτόν, πλὴν ὄνομα, συμβαίνει φῆσαι καὶ ἀποφῆσαι· τοῦτο δ' οὐκ ἦν ἔλεγχος. Ἀλλὰ φανερὸν ὅτι μὴ μιᾶς ἐρωτήσεως τῶν πλειόνων γινομένων, ἀλλ' ἓν καθ' ἑνὸς φάντος ἢ ἀποφάντος, οὐκ ἔσται τὸ ἀδύνατον.

XXXI. Περὶ δὲ τῶν ἀπαγόντων εἰς ταὐτὸ πολλάκις εἰπεῖν, φανερὸν ὡς οὐ δοτέον τῶν πρός τι λεγομένων σημαίνειν τι χωριζομένας καθ' αὑτὰς τὰς κατηγορίας, οἷον διπλάσιον ἄνευ τοῦ διπλάσιον ἡμίσεος[1], ὅτι ἐμφαίνεται. Καὶ γὰρ τὰ δέκα ἐν τοῖς ἑνὸς δέουσι δέκα καὶ τὸ ποιῆσαι ἐν τῷ μὴ ποιῆσαι, καὶ ὅλως ἐν τῇ ἀποφάσει ἡ φάσις· ἀλλ' ὅμως οὐκ εἴ τις λέγοι τοδὶ μὴ εἶναι λευκόν, λέγει αὐτὸ λευκὸν εἶναι. Τὸ δὲ διπλάσιον οὐδὲ σημαίνει οὐδὲν ἴσως, ὥσπερ οὐδὲ τὸ ἐν τῇ ἀποφάσει[2]· εἰ δ' ἄρα καὶ σημαίνει, ἀλλ' οὐ ταὐτὸ καὶ συνῃρημένον. Οὐδ' ἡ ἐπιστήμη ἐν τῷ εἴδει, οἷον εἰ ἔστιν ἡ ἰατρικὴ ἐπιστήμη, ὅπερ τὸ κοινόν· ἐκεῖνο δ' ἦν ἐπιστήμη ἐπιστητοῦ.

Ἐν δὲ τοῖς δι' ὧν δηλοῦται κατηγορουμένοις ταὐτὸ[3] λεκτέον, ὡς οὐ τὸ αὐτὸ χωρὶς καὶ ἐν τῷ λόγῳ τὸ δηλούμενον. Τὸ γὰρ κοῖλον κοινῇ μὲν τὸ αὐτὸ δηλοῖ ἐπὶ τοῦ σιμοῦ καὶ τοῦ ῥοικοῦ, προστιθέμενον δὲ οὐδὲν κωλύει, ἀλλὰ τὸ μὲν τῇ ῥινὶ τὸ δὲ τῷ σκέλει σημαίνει[4]· ἔνθα μὲν γὰρ τὸ σιμόν, ἔνθα δὲ τὸ ῥαιβὸν σημαίνει· καὶ οὐδὲν διαφέρει εἰπεῖν ῥὶς σιμὴ ἢ ῥὶς κοίλη. Ἔτι οὐ δοτέον τὴν λέξιν κατ' εὐθύ· ψεῦδος γάρ ἐστιν. Οὐ γάρ ἐστι τὸ σιμὸν ῥὶς κοίλη ἀλλὰ ῥινὸς τοδί, οἷον πάθος, ὥστ' οὐδὲν ἄτοπον, εἰ ἡ ῥὶς ἡ σιμὴ ῥίς ἐστιν ἔχουσα κοιλότητα ῥινός.

XXXII. Περὶ δὲ τῶν σολοικισμῶν, παρ' ὅ τι μὲν φαίνονται συμβαίνειν, εἴπομεν πρότερον, ὡς δὲ λυτέον, ἐπ' αὐτῶν τῶν λόγων ἔσται φανερόν. Ἅπαντες γὰρ οἱ τοιοίδε τοῦτο βούλονται κατασκευάζειν. Ἆρ' ὃ λέγεις ἀληθῶς, καὶ ἔστι τοῦτο ἀληθῶς; Φῂς δ' εἶναί τι λίθον· ἔστιν ἄρα τι λίθον. Ἢ τὸ

they are equal to themselves, we may be interpreted to say that they are equal to one another.

These fallacies admit of other solutions, for *themselves* and *all* are ambiguous, meaning either each respectively or all promiscuously. So that only the same name, not the same thing, is affirmed and denied of the same subject; which, we agreed, is no confutation. If however a single answer is not given, but a single predicate affirmed or denied of a single subject, no semblance of confutation can be fabricated⁴.

XXXI. REDUCTIONS to pleonasm must be opposed by denying that a relative name has any meaning when separated from the correlative, as double separated from half in the phrase double of half, though it appears as a factor in the expression. For ten is a factor in the expression ten minus one, and doing in the expression not-doing, and the affirmative in all negative expressions: yet to deny a thing to be white is not to affirm it to be white. Double then, extracted and isolated, has no meaning any more than the affirmative in the negative expression: or, if it has a meaning, not the same as the factors combined. So when we name a specific science, say, medical science, the factor science is not the same as the genus science, for the latter is correlative to the general object of science.

When the subject of an attribute enters the definition of the attribute, we must say that the attribute does not mean the same when conjoined with the subject and when separate. For though curved, the generic element, is only part of the meaning of aquiline and bandy when they are isolated, yet when these terms are joined to nose and leg they may lose the other part of their meaning; for aquiline nose and bandy leg mean no more than hooked nose and crooked leg. Further, we must deny the accuracy of the definition of aquiline and bandy; for aquiline is not a hooked nose, but a nasal quality or shape; and it is not strange that an aquiline nose should be a nose having a nasal curvature⁵.

XXXII. APPARENT solecisms depend on the cause that has been explained. The mode of solving them will be manifest in an example. The following arguments attempt to prove solecism. S (nominative) is (M) that (nominative) which (accusative) you truly affirm S (accusative) to be. You affirm S (accu-

ΠΕΡΙ ΣΟΦΙΣΤΙΚΩΝ

λέγειν λίθον οὐκ ἔστι λέγειν ὃ ἀλλ' ὅν, οὐδὲ τοῦτο ἀλλὰ τοῦτον. Εἰ οὖν ἔροιτό τις, ἆρ' ὃν ἀληθῶς λέγεις, ἔστι τοῦτον, οὐκ ἂν δοκοίη ἑλληνίζειν, ὥσπερ οὐδ' εἰ ἔροιτο, ἆρ' ἣν λέγεις εἶναι, ἔστιν οὗτος; Ξύλον δ' εἰπεῖν² οὗτος, ἢ ὅσα μήτε θῆλυ μήτ' ἄρρεν σημαίνει, οὐδὲν διαφέρει. Διὸ καὶ οὐ γίνεται σολοικισμός, εἰ ὃ λέγεις εἶναι, ἔστι τοῦτο; ξύλον δὲ λέγεις εἶναι· ἔστιν ἄρα ξύλον. Ὁ δὲ λίθος καὶ τὸ οὗτος ἄρρενος ἔχει κλῆσιν. Εἰ δή τις ἔροιτο, ἆρ' οὗτός ἐστιν αὕτη; εἶτα πάλιν, τί δ'; οὐχ οὗτός ἐστι Κορίσκος; εἶτ' εἴπειεν, ἔστιν ἄρα οὗτος αὕτη, οὐ συλλελόγισται τὸν σολοικισμόν, οὐδ' εἰ τὸ Κορίσκος σημαίνει ὅπερ αὕτη, μὴ δίδωσι δὲ ὁ ἀποκρινόμενος, ἀλλὰ δεῖ τοῦτο προσερωτηθῆναι. Εἰ δὲ μήτ' ἔστιν μήτε δίδωσιν, οὐ συλλελόγισται οὔτε τῷ ὄντι οὔτε πρὸς τὸν ἠρωτημένον. Ὁμοίως οὖν δεῖ κἀκεῖ τὸν λίθον σημαίνειν οὗτος³. Εἰ δὲ μήτε ἔστι μήτε δίδοται, οὐ λεκτέον τὸ συμπέρασμα· φαίνεται δὲ παρὰ τὸ τὴν ἀνόμοιαν πτῶσιν τοῦ ὀνόματος ὁμοίαν φαίνεσθαι. Ἆρ' ἀληθές ἐστιν εἰπεῖν ὅτι ἔστιν αὕτη, ὅπερ εἶναι φὴς αὐτήν; Εἶναι δὲ φῂς ἀσπίδα· ἔστιν ἄρα αὕτη ἀσπίδα. Ἢ οὐκ ἀνάγκη, εἰ μὴ τὸ αὕτη ἀσπίδα σημαίνει ἀλλ' ἀσπίς, τὸ δ' ἀσπίδα ταύτην. Οὐδ' εἰ ὃ φῂς εἶναι τοῦτον, ἐστὶν οὗτος, φῂς δ' εἶναι Κλέωνα, ἔστιν ἄρα οὗτος Κλέωνα· οὐ γὰρ ἔστιν οὗτος Κλέωνα· εἴρηται γὰρ ὅτι ὃ φημι εἶναι τοῦτον, ἔστιν οὗτος, οὐ τοῦτον· οὐδὲ γὰρ ἂν ἑλληνίζοι οὕτως τὸ ἐρώτημα λεχθέν. Ἆρ' ἐπίστασαι τοῦτο; τοῦτο δ' ἐστὶ λίθος· ἐπίστασαι ἄρα λίθος. Ἢ οὐ ταὐτὸ σημαίνει τὸ τοῦτο ἐν τῷ ἆρ' ἐπίστασαι τοῦτο καὶ ἐν τῷ τοῦτο δὲ λίθος, ἀλλ' ἐν μὲν τῷ πρώτῳ τοῦτον, ἐν δὲ τῷ ὑστέρῳ οὗτος. Ἆρ' οὗ ἐπιστήμην ἔχεις, ἐπίστασαι τοῦτο; ἐπιστήμην δ' ἔχεις λίθου· ἐπίστασαι ἄρα λίθου. Ἢ τὸ μὲν τούτου λίθου λέγεις, τὸ δὲ τοῦτον λίθον ἐδόθη δ', οὐ ἐπιστήμην ἔχεις, ἐπίστασθαι, οὐ τούτου, ἀλλὰ τοῦτο, ὥστ' οὐ λίθου ἀλλὰ λίθον. Ὅτι μὲν οὖν οἱ τοιοῦτοι τῶν λόγων οὐ συλλογίζονται σολοικισμὸν ἀλλὰ φαίνονται, καὶ διὰ τί τε φαίνονται καὶ πῶς ἀπαντητέον πρὸς αὐτούς, φανερὸν ἐκ τῶν εἰρημένων.

sative) to be *P* (accusative). Therefore *S* (nominative) is *P* (accusative). No. When *P* the predicate is masculine, the neuter pronouns *that* and *which* may be replaced by masculine pronouns which distinguish the nominative and accusative cases[1]. If I asserted with masculine pronouns, *S* (nominative) is that (accusative) which you truly maintain it to be, I should speak ungrammatically, just as much as if I said a woman is he whom you affirm her to be. Neuter predicates do not distinguish the nominative and accusative, and give rise to no apparent solecism. It is the masculine and feminine forms, whether the object denoted is really masculine and feminine or not, that occasion solecism. If I am impugning the thesis No man is a woman, and obtain the premiss, Coriscus is a man, if I say at once therefore a man is a woman, I have not proved the solecism, assuming Coriscus to be a woman, unless this premiss is granted by express concession. If Coriscus is not a woman, and not admitted to be a woman, I have not proved my conclusion either absolutely or relatively to this opponent. So in the first example it must be expressly granted as a major premiss, that *M* nominative is *P* the accusative: if it is not really so, and is not granted to be so, the conclusion does not follow. It seems to follow because in the neuter pronouns the nominative and accusative are not distinguished. The nominative of *S* is (*M*) the nominative of the noun whose accusative you affirm the accusative of *S* to be. You affirm the accusative of *S* to be the accusative of *P*. Therefore the nominative of *S* is the accusative of *P*. This is a *non sequitur;* for the nominative of *S* was affirmed in the minor premiss to be the nominative of a certain name. Again, from the premisses: This man (nominative) is he (nominative) whom (accusative) you affirm him (accusative) to be: you affirm him (accusative) to be Cleona (accusative); it does not follow that this man (nominative) is Cleona (accusative), for the major premiss does not affirm that he (nominative) whom you affirm him to be is Cleona (accusative), and the minor premiss affirmed that *S* (nominative) was he (nominative) not him (accusative), and any other expression would have been ungrammatical. You know *M* (accusative): *M* (nominative) is *P* (nominative); therefore you know *P* (nominative). No. *M* is ambiguous: in one premiss it is

ΠΕΡΙ ΣΟΦΙΣΤΙΚΩΝ

XXXIII. Δεῖ δὲ καὶ κατανοεῖν ὅτι πάντων τῶν λόγων οἱ μέν εἰσι ῥᾴους κατιδεῖν οἱ δὲ χαλεπώτεροι, παρὰ τί καὶ ἐν τίνι παραλογίζονται τὸν ἀκούοντα, πολλάκις οἱ αὐτοὶ ἐκείνοις ὄντες. Τὸν αὐτὸν γὰρ λόγον δεῖ καλεῖν τὸν παρὰ ταὐτὸ γινόμενον· ὁ αὐτὸς δὲ λόγος τοῖς μὲν παρὰ τὴν λέξιν τοῖς δὲ παρὰ τὸ συμβεβηκὸς τοῖς δὲ παρ' ἕτερον δόξειεν ἂν εἶναι διὰ τὸ μεταφερόμενον· ἕκαστον μὴ ὁμοίως εἶναι δῆλον. Ὥσπερ οὖν ἐν τοῖς παρὰ τὴν ὁμωνυμίαν, ὅσπερ δοκεῖ τρόπος εὐηθέστατος εἶναι τῶν παραλογισμῶν, τὰ μὲν καὶ τοῖς τυχοῦσίν ἐστι δῆλα (καὶ γὰρ οἱ λόγοι σχεδὸν οἱ γελοῖοι πάντες εἰσὶ παρὰ τὴν λέξιν, οἷον ἀνὴρ ἐφέρετο κατὰ κλίμακος δίφρον, καὶ ὅπου στέλλεσθε; πρὸς τὴν κεραίαν. Καὶ ποτέρα τῶν βοῶν ἔμπροσθεν τέξεται; οὐδετέρα, ἀλλ' ὄπισθεν ἄμφω. Καὶ καθαρὸς ὁ βορέας; οὐ δῆτα· ἀπεκτόνηκε γὰρ τὸν πτωχὸν καὶ τὸν ὠνούμενον'. Ἆρ' Εὔαρχος; οὐ δῆτα, ἀλλ' Ἀπολλωνίδης. Τὸν αὐτὸν δὲ τρόπον καὶ τῶν ἄλλων σχεδὸν οἱ πλεῖστοι.) Τὰ δὲ καὶ τοὺς ἐμπειροτάτους φαίνεται λανθάνειν· σημεῖον δὲ τούτων ὅτι μάχονται πολλάκις περὶ τῶν ὀνομάτων, οἷον πότερον ταὐτὸν σημαίνει κατὰ πάντων τὸ ὂν καὶ τὸ ἓν ἢ ἕτερον. Τοῖς μὲν γὰρ δοκεῖ ταὐτὸν σημαίνειν τὸ ὂν καὶ τὸ ἕν· οἱ δὲ τὸν Ζήνωνος λόγον καὶ Παρμενίδου λύουσι διὰ τὸ πολλαχῶς φάναι τὸ ἓν λέγεσθαι καὶ τὸ ὄν. Ὁμοίως δὲ καὶ περὶ τοῦ συμβεβηκότος καὶ περὶ τῶν ἄλλων ἕκαστον· οἱ μὲν ἔσονται ῥᾴους ἰδεῖν οἱ δὲ χαλεπώτεροι τῶν λόγων καὶ λαβεῖν ἐν τίνι γένει, καὶ πότερον ἔλεγχος ἢ οὐκ ἔλεγχος, οὐ ῥᾴδιον ὁμοίως περὶ πάντων.

Ἔστι δὲ δριμὺς λόγος ὅστις ἀπορεῖν ποιεῖ μάλιστα· δάκνει γὰρ αὐτὸς μάλιστα. Ἀπορία δ' ἐστὶ διττή, ἡ μὲν ἐν τοῖς συλλελογισμένοις, ὅ τι ἀνέλῃ τις τῶν ἐρωτημάτων, ἡ δ' ἐν τοῖς

ΕΛΕΓΧΩΝ. 69

nominative in the other accusative. What (genitive) you have perception of, that (accusative) you perceive. You have perception of a stone (genitive); therefore you perceive of a stone (genitive). No. Of that (genitive) is of a stone, and the premiss was, what you have perception of, not of that but, that (accusative) you perceive. Therefore you perceive—not of a stone but—a stone. These arguments then do not really prove solecism: why they seem to do so, and how they are to be solved, is plain from what has been said[4].

XXXIII. It must be observed that in some arguments it is easy, in others difficult, to detect what and wherein is the fallacy, even when the arguments are identical. Arguments may be called identical when they depend on the same principle or belong to the same class. An identical argument may by one be referred to the head of equivocation; by another to the equation of subject and accident, by another to another principle, because in its successive application to different spheres the principle is not equally patent or disguised. For instance, fallacies of ambiguity are supposed to be the easiest of detection[2], and some are obvious to the dullest, for almost all repartees and ridiculous turns depend on this principle[3]. Thus: Down stairs a man tumbled (carried)—a chair.—Whither are you bound? (Where do you fasten the sails when you take them in?) To the yard arm.—Which cow will calve before (the other)? Neither; both behind.—Is it a set (pure) Boreas? No: he has killed a beggar.—Who was the purchaser? Evarchus? No: Apollonides (extravagant): and so on. Others even the acutest fail to detect. A proof of this is the number of controversies that depend on words; for instance, on the ambiguity of Unity and Being. Some suppose these terms to be univocal; others solve the arguments of Zeno and Parmenides by shewing them to be equivocal. In the same way fallacies that depend on the equation of subject and accident and the other principles are sometimes easy sometimes hard of detection. The classification, too, of a fallacy, and the decision whether an argument is fallacious or not, vary in difficulty.

The cleverest argument is that which causes most doubt and embarrassment. Doubt is of two kinds: in dialectic reasoning we doubt which proposition is false; in eristic reasoning we

ἐριστικοῖς, πῶς εἴπῃ· τις τὸ προταθέν. Διόπερ ἐν τοῖς συλλογιστικοῖς οἱ δριμύτεροι λόγοι ζητεῖν μᾶλλον ποιοῦσιν. Ἔστι δὲ συλλογιστικὸς μὲν λόγος δριμύτατος, ἂν ἐξ ὅτι μάλιστα δοκούντων ὅτι μάλιστα ἔνδοξον ἀναιρῇ. Εἷς γὰρ ὢν ὁ λόγος μετατιθεμένης¹ τῆς ἀντιφάσεως ἅπαντας ὁμοίως ἕξει τοὺς συλλογισμούς· δεῖ γὰρ ἐξ ἐνδόξων ὁμοίως ἔνδοξον ἀναιρήσει ἢ κατασκευάσει, διόπερ ἀπορεῖν ἀναγκαῖον. Μάλιστα μὲν οὖν ὁ τοιοῦτος δριμύς, ὁ ἐξ ἴσου τὸ συμπέρασμα ποιῶν τοῖς ἐρωτήμασι, δεύτερος δ᾽ ὁ ἐξ ἁπάντων ὁμοίων· οὗτος γὰρ ὁμοίως ποιήσει ἀπορεῖν ὁποῖον τῶν ἐρωτημάτων ἀναιρετέον. Τοῦτο δὲ χαλεπόν· ἀναιρετέον μὲν γάρ, ὃ τι δ᾽ ἀναιρετέον, ἄδηλον.

Τῶν δ᾽ ἐριστικῶν δριμύτατος μὲν ὁ πρῶτον εὐθὺς ἄδηλος πότερον συλλελόγισται ἢ οὔ, καὶ πότερον παρὰ ψεῦδος ἢ διαίρεσίν ἐστιν ἡ λύσις, δεύτερος δὲ τῶν ἄλλων ὁ δῆλος μὲν ὅτι παρὰ διαίρεσιν ἢ ἀναίρεσίν ἐστι, μὴ φανερὸς δ᾽ ὢν διὰ τίνος τῶν ἠρωτημένων ἀναίρεσιν ἢ διαίρεσιν λυτέος ἐστίν, ἀλλὰ πότερον αὕτη παρὰ τὸ συμπέρασμα ἢ παρά τι τῶν ἐρωτημάτων ἐστίν.

Ἐνίοτε μὲν οὖν ὁ μὴ συλλογισθεὶς λόγος εὐήθης ἐστίν, ἐὰν ᾖ λίαν ἄδοξα ἢ ψευδῆ τὰ λήμματα· ἐνίοτε δ᾽ οὐκ ἄξιος καταφρονεῖσθαι. Ὅταν μὲν γὰρ ἐλλείπῃ τι τῶν τοιούτων ἐρωτημάτων, περὶ οὗ ὁ λόγος καὶ δι᾽ ὅ, καὶ μὴ προσλαβὼν τοῦτο καὶ μὴ συλλογισάμενος εὐήθης ὁ συλλογισμός· ὅταν δὲ τῶν ἔξωθεν, οὐκ εὐκαταφρόνητος οὐδαμῶς, ἀλλ᾽ ὁ μὲν λόγος ἐπιεικής, ὁ δ᾽ ἐρωτῶν ἠρώτηκεν οὐ καλῶς.

Ἔστι τε, ὥσπερ λύειν ὁτὲ μὲν πρὸς τὸν λόγον ὁτὲ δὲ πρὸς τὸν ἐρωτῶντα καὶ τὴν ἐρώτησιν ὁτὲ δὲ πρὸς οὐδέτερον τούτων, ὁμοίως καὶ ἐρωτᾶν ἔστι καὶ συλλογίζεσθαι καὶ πρὸς τὴν θέσιν καὶ πρὸς τὸν ἀποκρινόμενον καὶ πρὸς τὸν χρόνον, ὅταν ᾖ πλείονος χρόνου δεομένη ἡ λύσις ἢ τοῦ παρόντος καιροῦ τὸ διαλεχθῆναι πρὸς τὴν λύσιν.

XXXIV. Ἐκ πόσων μὲν οὖν καὶ ποίων γίνονται τοῖς διαλεγομένοις οἱ παραλογισμοί, καὶ πῶς δείξομέν τε ψευδόμενον καὶ παράδοξα λέγειν ποιήσομεν, ἔτι δ᾽ ἐκ τίνων συμβαίνει ὁ σολοικισμός¹, καὶ πῶς ἐρωτητέον καὶ τίς ἡ τάξις τῶν ἐρωτη-

doubt how a proposition ought to be worded. Accordingly dialectic paradoxes are the more stimulative of inquiry. The cleverest dialectic argument is that both of whose premisses are extremely probable, while the thesis confuted is also extremely probable. Then a single syllogism by successive substitution of the contradictory of the conclusion for one of the premisses makes three syllogisms of equal probability and improbability, in each of which highly probable premisses lead to an equally improbable conclusion, which must occasion embarrassment. The cleverest, then, is one where the improbability of the conclusion equals the probability of the premisses: the next is where the premisses are equally probable; for then we shall doubt which of them ought to be denied. One must be false, but we have no indication which[8]. The cleverest eristic reasoning is where the preliminary decision is difficult, whether the reasoning is conclusive or inconclusive: that is, whether the solution is by negation or distinction. The next is where the doubt is, not whether the solution is by negation or distinction but, which proposition is to be denied or distinguished, and whether it is one of the premisses or the conclusion that requires distinction[9].

An imperfect proof is contemptible when the premisses are very improbable or false, but it may be respectable. If some of the propositions about the subject or predicate or middle term are wanting, and are neither assumed nor proved, the argumentation is quite a failure; but when they are assumed without proof and only some preliminary premisses are wanting, the argument is respectable though badly developed[10].

As solution is either addressed to the proof, or to the prover and his questions, or to neither; so questions and proof may be addressed either to the thesis, the answerer, or the time, when the solution requires more time than is allowed, or the questioner has time for a rejoinder[11].

XXXIV. The number and nature of the sources of paralogism, the means of eliciting false or paradoxical propositions, the mode of producing solecism, the mode of questioning, and the arrangement of questions, the utility of this kind of argu-

μάτων, ἔτι πρὸς τί χρήσιμοι πάντες εἰσὶν οἱ τοιοῦτοι λόγοι, καὶ περὶ ἀποκρίσεως ἁπλῶς τε πάσης καὶ πῶς λυτέον τοὺς λόγους καὶ τοὺς σολοικισμούς, εἰρήσθω περὶ ἁπάντων ἡμῖν ταῦτα. Λοιπὸν δὲ περὶ τῆς ἐξ ἀρχῆς προθέσεως ἀναμνήσασιν εἰπεῖν τι βραχὺ περὶ αὐτῆς καὶ τέλος ἐπιθεῖναι τοῖς εἰρημένοις.

Προειλόμεθα μὲν οὖν εὑρεῖν δύναμίν τινα συλλογιστικὴν περὶ τοῦ προβληθέντος ἐκ τῶν ὑπαρχόντων ὡς ἐνδοξοτάτων· τοῦτο γὰρ ἔργον ἐστὶ τῆς διαλεκτικῆς καθ' αὐτὴν καὶ τῆς πειραστικῆς. Ἐπεὶ δὲ προσκατασκευάζεται πρὸς αὐτὴν διὰ τὴν τῆς σοφιστικῆς γειτνίασιν, ὡς οὐ μόνον πεῖραν δύναται λαβεῖν διαλεκτικῶς ἀλλὰ καὶ ὡς εἰδώς, διὰ τοῦτο οὐ μόνον τὸ λεχθὲν ἔργον ὑπεθέμεθα τῆς πραγματείας, τὸ λόγον δύνασθαι λαβεῖν, ἀλλὰ καὶ ὅπως λόγον ὑπέχοντες φυλάξομεν τὴν θέσιν ὡς δι' ἐνδοξοτάτων ὁμοτρόπως. Τὴν δ' αἰτίαν εἰρήκαμεν τούτου, ἐπεὶ καὶ διὰ τοῦτο Σωκράτης ἠρώτα, ἀλλ' οὐκ ἀπεκρίνετο· ὡμολόγει γὰρ οὐκ εἰδέναι. Δεδήλωται δ' ἐν τοῖς πρότερον καὶ πρὸς πόσα καὶ ἐκ πόσων τοῦτο ἔσται, καὶ ὅθεν εὐπορήσομεν τούτων, ἔτι δὲ πῶς ἐρωτητέον ἢ τακτέον τὴν ἐρώτησιν πᾶσαν, καὶ περί τε ἀποκρίσεων καὶ λύσεων τῶν πρὸς τοὺς συλλογισμούς. Δεδήλωται δὲ καὶ περὶ τῶν ἄλλων, ὅσα τῆς αὐτῆς μεθόδου τῶν λόγων ἐστίν. Πρὸς δὲ τούτοις περὶ τῶν παραλογισμῶν διεληλύθαμεν, ὥσπερ εἰρήκαμεν ἤδη πρότερον. Ὅτι μὲν οὖν ἔχει τέλος ἱκανῶς ἃ προειλόμεθα, φανερόν.

Δεῖ δ' ἡμᾶς μὴ λεληθέναι τὸ συμβεβηκὸς περὶ ταύτην τὴν πραγματείαν. Τῶν γὰρ εὑρισκομένων ἁπάντων τὰ μὲν παρ' ἑτέρων ληφθέντα πρότερον πεπονημένα κατὰ μέρος ἐπιδέδωκεν ὑπὸ τῶν παραλαβόντων ὕστερον· τὰ δ' ἐξ ὑπαρχῆς εὑρισκόμενα μικρὰν τὸ πρῶτον ἐπίδοσιν λαμβάνειν εἴωθε, χρησιμωτέραν μέντοι πολλῷ τῆς ὕστερον ἐκ τούτων αὐξήσεως. Μέγιστον γὰρ ἴσως ἀρχὴ παντός, ὥσπερ λέγεται· διὸ καὶ χαλεπώτατον· ὅσῳ γὰρ κράτιστον τῇ δυνάμει, τοσούτῳ μικρότατον ὂν τῷ μεγέθει χαλεπώτατόν ἐστιν ὀφθῆναι. Ταύτης δ' εὑρημένης ῥᾷον τὸ προστιθέναι καὶ συναύξειν τὸ λοιπόν ἐστιν· ὅπερ καὶ περὶ τοὺς ῥητορικοὺς λόγους συμβέβηκε, σχεδὸν δὲ

mentation, the mode of answering and solving confutations and solecisms, have been successively examined. We may now recal to mind our original design and, with a few brief observations, bring our treatise to a close.

Our aim was the invention of a method of reasoning on any problem from the most probable premisses that can be found[2]. This is the proper function of Dialectic and Pirastic. But it arrogates a further province from its vicinity to Sophistic, professing not only to test knowledge with the resources of Dialectic, but also to maintain any thesis with the infallibility of science. Besides, therefore, the above-named function, the examination of pretensions to knowledge, we included in the faculty we were investigating the power of defending any thesis by probable premisses without self-contradiction[3]. The reason is what we mentioned before[4], as may be seen from the fact that Socrates only questioned and never answered, because he confessed ignorance. We indicated the number of problems[5] and the sources or repertories of proof[6], the right mode of questioning and arrangement[7], the right mode of answering and solution, and the other matters pertaining to the system; and we afterwards treated, as was just remarked, of paralogism. The task, then, which we undertook is completed.

A fact, however, in the history of this art is worthy of notice. Inventions are either the final shaping of what has been partly elaborated by others, or they are original discoveries and but roughly shaped. The latter are the more important. The first step, according to the proverb, is the grand thing and the most difficult; for first beginnings are as small and inconspicuous as

καὶ περὶ τὰς ἄλλας πάσας τέχνας. Οἱ μὲν γὰρ τὰς ἀρχὰς εὑρόντες παντελῶς ἐπὶ μικρόν τι προήγαγον· οἱ δὲ νῦν εὐδοκιμοῦντες παραλαβόντες παρὰ πολλῶν οἷον ἐκ διαδοχῆς κατὰ μέρος προαγαγόντων οὕτως ηὐξήκασι, Τισίας μὲν μετὰ τοὺς πρώτους, Θρασύμαχος δὲ μετὰ Τισίαν, Θεόδωρος δὲ μετὰ τοῦτον, καὶ πολλοὶ πολλὰ συνενηνόχασι μέρη· διόπερ οὐδὲν θαυμαστὸν ἔχειν τι πλῆθος τὴν τέχνην. Ταύτης δὲ τῆς πραγματείας οὐ τὸ μὲν ἦν τὸ δ' οὐκ ἦν προεξειργασμένον, ἀλλ' οὐδὲν παντελῶς ὑπῆρχεν. Καὶ γὰρ τῶν περὶ τοὺς ἐριστικοὺς λόγους μισθαρνούντων ὁμοία τις ἦν ἡ παίδευσις τῇ Γοργίου πραγματείᾳ. Λόγους γὰρ οἱ μὲν ῥητορικοὺς οἱ δὲ ἐρωτητικοὺς ἐδίδοσαν ἐκμανθάνειν, εἰς οὓς πλειστάκις ἐμπίπτειν ᾠήθησαν ἑκάτεροι τοὺς ἀλλήλων λόγους. Διόπερ ταχεῖα μὲν ἄτεχνος δ' ἦν ἡ διδασκαλία τοῖς μανθάνουσι παρ' αὐτῶν· οὐ γὰρ τέχνην ἀλλὰ τὰ ἀπὸ τῆς τέχνης διδόντες παιδεύειν ὑπελάμβανον, ὥσπερ ἂν εἴ τις ἐπιστήμην φάσκων παραδώσειν ἐπὶ τὸ μηδὲν πονεῖν τοὺς πόδας, εἶτα σκυτοτομικὴν μὲν μὴ διδάσκοι, μηδ' ὅθεν δυνήσεται πορίζεσθαι τὰ τοιαῦτα, δοίη δὲ πολλὰ γένη παντοδαπῶν ὑποδημάτων· οὗτος γὰρ βεβοήθηκε μὲν πρὸς τὴν χρείαν, τέχνην δ' οὐ παρέδωκεν. Καὶ περὶ μὲν τῶν ῥητορικῶν ὑπῆρχε πολλὰ καὶ παλαιὰ τὰ λεγόμενα, περὶ δὲ τοῦ συλλογίζεσθαι παντελῶς οὐδὲν εἴχομεν πρότερον ἄλλο λέγειν, ἀλλ' ἢ τριβῇ[11] ζητοῦντες πολὺν χρόνον ἐπονοῦμεν. Εἰ δὲ φαίνεται θεασαμένοις ὑμῖν ὡς ἐκ τοιούτων ἐξ ἀρχῆς ὑπαρχόντων ἔχειν ἡ μέθοδος ἱκανῶς παρὰ τὰς ἄλλας πραγματείας τὰς ἐκ παραδόσεως ηὐξημένας, λοιπὸν ἂν εἴη πάντων ὑμῶν ἢ τῶν ἠκροαμένων ἔργον τοῖς μὲν παραλελειμμένοις τῆς μεθόδου συγγνώμην τοῖς δ' εὑρημένοις πολλὴν ἔχειν χάριν.

they are potent. When they are once accomplished the remainder is easily added or developed. This was the history of rhetorical composition and of most other arts. The original inventors made but small progress. The great modern professors inherited from their predecessors many successive improvements and added others. Tisias after the first inventors, Thrasymachus after Tisias, Theodorus after Thrasymachus, and many others, contributed various portions. Accordingly, it is no wonder that the art has now a certain amplitude[4]. But the system I have expounded had not been partially, though imperfectly, elaborated by others: its very foundations had to be laid[9]. The education given to their pupils by the paid teachers of Eristic was like that given by Gorgias to his pupils in Rhetoric. Ready-made speeches[10], oratorical or interrogatory, which were considered to cover the topics of the rival professors, were given to the pupil to be learnt by heart. The training accordingly was rapid but unscientific. Instead of art, the products of art were communicated, and this was called education. One might as well have promised to communicate an art for protecting the feet, and, instead of teaching the art of shoemaking, have presented the learner with an assortment of shoes. This would be supplying his wants but not teaching him an art. But the teachers of rhetoric inherited many principles that had been long ascertained; dialectic had absolutely no traditional doctrines. Our researches were tentative, long, and troublesome. If, then, starting from nothing, the system bears a comparison with others that have been developed by division of labour in successive generations, candid criticism will be readier to commend it for the degree of completeness to which it has attained than to find fault with it for falling short of perfection.

NOTES.

CHAPTER I.

1] For the difference between a sophistic proof and a paralogism see ch. viii.

2] For the meaning of ἕξις, compare Topica, 8. 2: Προσφέρουσι γὰρ ὅτι τῇ ὑγιείᾳ, ἐλάττονι ὄντι ἀγαθῷ τῆς εὐεξίας, μεῖζον κακὸν ἀντίκειται, τὴν γὰρ νόσον μεῖζον κακὸν εἶναι τῆς καχεξίας. '(Against the assumption that the greater evil is opposed to the greater good), they adduce the enstasis that health, a lesser good than bodily vigour, has a greater evil for its opposite; for sickness is a greater evil than want of bodily vigour.' And Topica, 5. 7: Ὁμοίως ἔχει ἰατρός τε πρὸς τὸ ποιητικὸς ὑγιείας εἶναι καὶ γυμναστὴς πρὸς τὸ ποιητικὸν εὐεξίας. 'The function of the gymnastic trainer is the production of bodily vigour, as the function of the physician is the production of health.'

3] Φυλέτικῶς. This seems an allusion to the choral exhibitions at Athens. Each tribe (φυλή), through its choragus, furnished a chorus, and was emulous for its reputation, which depended on its εὐανδρία, i. e. σωμάτων μέγεθος καὶ ῥώμη, the size and strength of the choristers, as well as their vocal powers, εὐφωνία. Xenophon, Mem. 3. 3. Οἱ φυλέται, therefore, implied in φυλετικῶς, are οἱ χορευταί.

4] Κομμώσαντες. In the Gorgias sophistic is said to be the counterpart or analogon of κομμωτική, a fraudulent art, which by means of shape and colour and sleekness and dress counterfeits the beauty and good condition which are properly produced by gymnastic. Κομμωτική is to γυμναστική, and ὀψοποιητική is to ἰατρική, as σοφιστική is to νομοθετική, or ῥητορική is to δικαστική.

H

5] Λιθάργυρος, 'a compound of silver and lead; or, vitrified lead collected in separating lead and silver.' *Liddell and Scott.*

6] We have a similar definition in Topics, I. I, where speech (λόγος) is made the genus: "Ἔστι δὴ συλλογισμὸς λόγος ἐν ᾧ τεθέντων τινῶν ἕτερόν τι τῶν κειμένων ἐξ ἀνάγκης συμβαίνει διὰ τῶν κειμένων.

7] Understand after ὦν, not αἰτιῶν, but ἐλέγχων. Τόποι is here used for γένος, for, speaking properly, the τόπος or αἰτία is τὰ ὀνόματα, the ἔλεγχοι are διὰ τῶν ὀνομάτων.

8] Τὰ πράγματα φέροντας, 'moving, manipulating, the objects,' appears to be a metaphor derived from the phrase τὰς ψήφους φέρειν, which shortly follows.

9] Λόγος may mean an argument, or a proposition, or a definition, or a circumlocution. It usually means an argument, but when in close antithesis to ὄνομα it means a circumlocution or a complex, as opposed to a simple, term.

10] Οἱ ἀκούοντες are the audience present at a controversy. See ch. viii, Παρ' ὅσα γὰρ φαίνεται τοῖς ἀκούουσιν ὡς ἠρωτημένα συλλελογίσθαι, παρὰ ταῦτα ἐὰν τῷ ἀποκρινομένῳ δόξειεν. Also ch. xv, 'Ενίοτε γὰρ οἴονται καὶ αὐτοὶ δεδωκέναι καὶ τοῖς ἀκούουσι φαίνονται. On this point an unknown paraphrast, edited by Spengel, says the only thing that he says worth quoting: Οἱ γὰρ ἀκροαταὶ ἐν ταῖς διαλέξεσι κριταὶ τῆς νίκης τοῖς ἀγωνιζομένοις ἐτέθησαν. 'The audience present at a controversy are the judges who decide which disputant is victorious.' This writer transforms some of Aristotle's cramped statements into very sonorous periods, but is of no value as a commentator.

11] In ordinary Greek δοῦναι λόγον is to render an account, λαβεῖν λόγον to audit an account. In logical language δοῦναι λόγον is the function of the answerer, λαβεῖν λόγον of the questioner. In ch. xxxiv. the former of these functions is said to be the more sophistical branch of dialectic, because the answerer pretends to science, which the questioner disclaims. In ch. xi. it is explained how the piratic questioner, himself making no pretensions to knowledge, may be competent to examine the knowledge and expose the ignorance of the answerer. Throughout the present treatise however, in accordance with the title, it is usually the questioner that is supposed to be the sophist, and the respondent who is the honest reasoner.

CHAP. I.   NOTES.   99

12] Δύναμις, capacity, is in the intellect; προαίρεσις, purpose, in the will. The antithesis between these terms may throw light on what Aristotle conceived to be the relation between sophistic and dialectic: 'Ὁρᾶν δὲ καὶ εἴ τι τῶν ψεκτῶν ἢ φευκτῶν εἰς δύναμιν ἢ τὸ δυνατὸν ἔθηκεν, οἶον τὸν σοφιστὴν ἢ διάβολον ἢ κλέπτην τὸν δυνάμενον λάθρα τὰ ἀλλότρια κλέπτειν. Οὐδεὶς γὰρ τῶν εἰρημένων τῷ δυνατὸν εἶναί τι τούτων τοιοῦτος λέγεται· δύναται μὲν γὰρ καὶ ὁ θεὸς καὶ ὁ σπουδαῖος τὰ φαῦλα δρᾶν, ἀλλ' οὔκ εἰσὶ τοιοῦτοι· πάντες γὰρ οἱ φαῦλοι κατὰ προαίρεσιν λέγονται. Ἔτι πᾶσα δύναμις τῶν αἱρετῶν· καὶ γὰρ αἱ τῶν φαύλων δυνάμεις αἱρεταί, διὸ καὶ τὸν θεὸν καὶ τὸν σπουδαῖον ἔχειν φαμὲν αὐτάς, δυνατοὺς γὰρ εἶναι τὰ φαῦλα πράττειν. ...'Ἢ εἴ τι τῶν ἐν δύο γένεσιν ἢ πλείοσιν εἰς θάτερον ἔθηκεν. Ἔνια γὰρ οὐκ ἔστιν εἰς ἓν γένος θεῖναι, οἶον τὸν φένακα καὶ τὸν διάβολον· οὔτε γὰρ ὁ προαιρούμενος ἀδυνατῶν δέ, οὔθ' ὁ δυνάμενος μὴ προαιρούμενος δέ, διάβολοι ἢ φέναξ, ἀλλ' ὁ ἄμφω ταῦτα ἔχων· ὥστ' οὐ θετέον εἰς ἓν γένος ἀλλ' εἰς ἀμφότερα τὰ εἰρημένα. Topics, 4. 5. ' We should look to see whether a thing to be blamed or shunned has been referred to the genus Ability or Able. Whether, for instance, the sophist, calumniator, or thief has been defined to be a man able to appropriate secretly his neighbour's property, et cetera. It is not ability to perform these things to which these names are given, for God and the virtuous have ability to do evil though not the inclination; it is on account of his volition that we call a person bad. Again, every power is a thing to be desired, even the power to do evil, and this accordingly we ascribe to God and the virtuous, for we suppose they have the power without the will.... Again, we must observe whether a species that falls under two or several genera has been referred solely to one, for some things cannot be placed in a single genus, as, for instance, the impostor and calumniator: for neither the will without the power nor the power without the will makes the impostor or calumniator, but both united. They ought therefore to have a double genus.' Πρὸς δὲ τούτοις ὅτι τῆς αὐτῆς [ἐστι τέχνης] τό τε πιθανὸν καὶ τὸ φαινόμενον ἰδεῖν πιθανόν, ὥσπερ καὶ ἐπὶ τῆς διαλεκτικῆς συλλογισμόν τε καὶ φαινόμενον συλλογισμόν· ὁ γὰρ σοφιστικὸς οὔκ ἐν τῇ δυνάμει ἀλλ' ἐν τῇ προαιρέσει. Πλὴν ἐνταῦθα μὲν ἔσται ὁ μὲν κατὰ τὴν ἐπιστήμην ὁ δὲ κατὰ τὴν προαίρεσιν ῥήτωρ, ἐκεῖ δὲ σοφιστὴν μὲν κατὰ τὴν προαίρεσιν, διαλεκτικὸς δὲ οὐ κατὰ τὴν προαίρεσιν ἀλλὰ

H 2

κατὰ τὴν δύναμιν. Rhetoric, I. 1. 'Again, it is the function of a single art to investigate the means of both true and false persuasion, as dialectic examines both genuine and apparent proof. For a man is not a sophist who has the power to deceive without the will. In the sphere of oratory, however, [there is a want of distinctive names, for] both the science of wrong persuasion and the science combined with the purpose of wrong persuasion are called rhetoric; whereas in the sphere of disputation [the power plus] the will to deceive is called sophistic, the power without the will, dialectic.' Ἔτι δὲ τἀναντία δεῖ δύνασθαι πείθειν, καθάπερ καὶ ἐν τοῖς συλλογισμοῖς, οὐχ ὅπως ἀμφότερα πράττωμεν, οὐ γὰρ δεῖ τὰ φαῦλα πείθειν, ἀλλ' ἵνα μήτε λανθάνῃ πῶς ἔχει, καὶ ὅπως ἄλλου χρωμένου τοῖς λόγοις μὴ δικαίως αὐτοὶ λύειν ἔχωμεν. Τῶν μὲν οὖν ἄλλων τεχνῶν οὐδεμία τἀναντία συλλογίζεται, ἡ δὲ διαλεκτικὴ καὶ ἡ ῥητορικὴ μόναι τοῦτο ποιοῦσιν, ὁμοίως γάρ εἰσιν ἀμφότεραι τῶν ἐναντίων. Τὰ μέντοι ὑποκείμενα πράγματα οὐχ ὁμοίως ἔχει, ἀλλ' ἀεὶ τἀληθῆ καὶ τὰ βελτίω τῇ φύσει εὐσυλλογιστότερα καὶ πιθανώτερα, ὡς ἁπλῶς εἰπεῖν. Rhet. I. 1. 'The power of maintaining opposite conclusions is desirable in rhetoric as well as in dialectic, not that we may practise both its branches, for we must not persuade to evil, but that we may understand the process, and, if another makes a sinister use of reason, may counteract his sophistries. No science proves contrary conclusions except dialectic and rhetoric, which are equally related to the right and the wrong conclusion. Facts, however, are not equally favourable to both; for the true theorems and just conclusions are supplied by nature with more evidence and means of persuasion than the contrary, as a general rule.' From these passages and ch. xxxiv. it appears that the present treatise may be considered as the last book of the Topics, or general treatise on dialectic; from ch. ii, however, it appears to be an independent substantive treatise.

13] Did the sophist ever exist? Was there ever a class of people who professed to be philosophers and to educate, but, instead of method or a system of reasoned truth, only knew and only taught, under the name of philosophy, the game of eristic? When we read Whately's Logic we see that to him the sophist he so often mentions is merely an ideal, the personification of a bad argument. Grote says, the only reality corresponding to

the name are the disjecti membra sophistæ in all of us, the errors incidental to human frailty in the search after truth. But, if we accept the testimony of Aristotle, there were certain definite individuals who, by the common consent of the thinking Hellenic world, had coined more fallacies than is permitted to human infirmity, and were consequently recognized by the educated as utterers of counterfeit wisdom, clever charlatans, intellectual Cagliostros, pseudo-philosophers, because indifferent to the truth. We must not suppose that the name was applied to thinkers merely because their opinions were heterodox or unpalatable to their contemporaries; for it was never applied, as far as I am aware, to Leucippus or Democritus. The question, however, is more interesting to the historian than to the logician. To the logician, sophistry, like dialectic and science and philosophy, is merely an ideal.

14] The kinds of sophistical reasoning are enumerated in ch. iv. and v, the branches of the faculty in ch. iii, the elements of the profession, if different from the last, may be the functions of questioning and answering, the other components of the art are arrangement and the remaining topics treated in ch. xv. and xvii.

CHAPTER II.

1] A fourfold division of reasonings has been given in the Topics, but instead of pirastic the pseudographema (for which see ch. xi) is mentioned. Ἀπόδειξις μὲν οὖν ἐστὶν ὅταν ἐξ ἀληθῶν καὶ πρώτων ὁ συλλογισμὸς ᾖ, ἢ ἐκ τοιούτων ἃ διά τινων πρώτων καὶ ἀληθῶν τῆς περὶ αὐτὰ γνώσεως τὴν ἀρχὴν εἴληφε. Διαλεκτικὸς δὲ συλλογισμὸς ὁ ἐξ ἐνδόξων συλλογιζόμενος.... Ἐριστικὸς δ' ἐστὶ συλλογισμὸς ὁ ἐκ φαινομένων ἐνδόξων μὴ ὄντων δέ, καὶ ὁ ἐξ ἐνδόξων ἢ φαινομένων ἐνδόξων φαινόμενος.... ὁ μὲν οὖν πρότερος τῶν ῥηθέντων ἐριστικῶν συλλογισμῶν καὶ συλλογισμὸς λεγέσθω, ὁ δὲ λοιπὸς ἐριστικὸς μὲν συλλογισμός, συλλογισμὸς δ' οὔ, ἐπειδὴ φαίνεται μὲν συλλογίζεσθαι συλλογίζεται δ' οὔ. Ἔτι δὲ παρὰ τοὺς εἰρημένους ἅπαντας συλλογισμοὺς οἱ ἐκ τῶν περί τινας ἐπιστήμας οἰκείων γινόμενοι παραλογισμοί.... οὔτε γὰρ ἐξ ἀληθῶν καὶ πρώτων συλλογίζεται ὁ ψευδογραφῶν οὔτ' ἐξ ἐνδόξων.... ἀλλ' ἐκ τῶν οἰκείων μὲν τῇ ἐπιστήμῃ λημμάτων οὐκ ἀληθῶν δὲ τὸν συλλογισμὸν ποιεῖται. Topica, 1. 1.

'Demonstrative proof is based on true and elementary premisses, or on theorems that have been proved by true and elementary premisses. Dialectic proof is based on probable premisses.... Eristic proof is based on premisses which seem but are not probable, or is seeming but not real proof based on probable or seemingly probable premisses.... The former kind may be called absolutely proof, the latter is not proof without qualification but eristic proof, for it is only simulated proof. Different from all these are the paralogisms based on premisses peculiar to a certain sphere of subject-matter.... for the premisses of the geometrical paralogism are neither elementary truths nor probabilities.... but are propositions peculiar to a certain sphere and false.'

2] This famous dictum should be compared with other passages which require less faith on the part of the learner. Τῷ μὲν γὰρ μανθάνοντι θετέον ἀεὶ τὰ δοκοῦντα, καὶ γὰρ οὐδ' ἐπιχειρεῖ ψεῦδος οὐδεὶς διδάσκειν. Topics, 8. 5. 'A learner should admit whatever he believes, for no teacher tries to prove what is false.' Elsewhere we are told that the learner, or answerer in didactic, should be less ready to concede premisses than the answerer in dialectic. Ὅταν δ' ᾖ πρὸς τὸ ἀξίωμα καὶ τὴν πρότασιν μεῖζον ἔργον διαλεχθῆναι ἢ τὴν θέσιν, διαπορήσειεν ἄν τις πότερον θετέον τὰ τοιαῦτα ἢ οὔ. Εἰ γὰρ μὴ θήσει ἀλλ' ἀξιώσει καὶ πρὸς τοῦτο διαλέγεσθαι, μεῖζον προστάξει τοῦ ἐν ἀρχῇ κειμένου εἰ δὲ θήσει, πιστεύσει ἐξ ἧττον πιστῶν. Εἰ μὲν οὖν δεῖ μὴ χαλεπώτερον τὸ πρόβλημα ποιεῖν, θετέον, εἰ δὲ διὰ γνωριμωτέρων συλλογίζεσθαι, οὐ θετέον. Ἡ τῷ μὲν μανθάνοντι οὐ θετέον ἂν μὴ γνωριμώτερον ᾖ, τῷ δὲ γυμναζομένῳ θετέον ἂν ἀληθὲς μόνον φαίνηται. Ὥστε φανερὸν ὅτι οὐχ ὁμοίως ἐρωτῶντί τε καὶ διδάσκοντι ἀξιωτέον τιθέναι. Topics, 8. 3. 'If a premiss is harder to prove than the conclusion, ought it, or ought it not, to be granted by the answerer? If he refuses to grant it and requires it to be proved, he imposes a task more difficult than the original problem; if he grants it, the grounds of proof will be less evident than the conclusion. If the problem ought not to be made more difficult, the premiss should be granted; if the grounds of proof should be more evident than the conclusion, it should not be granted. We decide that a learner should grant no premiss that is not more evident than the conclusion; the dialectician who argues for practice should grant any which

appears true. The same rules, then, do not apply to dialectic and didactic.'

3] The only extant passage in which Aristotle defines the nature of pirastic premisses is in ch. xi. This cannot possibly be referred to by the words ἐν ἑτέροις. These words then indicate a lost work on Pirastic.

4] This treatise, then, was written after the Analytica Posteriora, which treats of Demonstration. The first chapter of the Analytica Priora refers to the Topica, which was therefore written previously, as we might have judged from comparing the degree of precision with which the process of reasoning is handled in the two treatises. But the eighth book of the Topica refers to the Analytica Priora (see chap. 11 and 13). This book therefore must have been added subsequently. The seventh book of the Topica may seem to refer to the Analytica Posteriora: ἐκ τίνων δὲ δεῖ [ὅρον] κατασκευάζειν, διώρισται μὲν ἐν ἑτέροις ἀκριβέστερον, πρὸς δὲ τὴν προκειμένην μέθοδον οἱ αὐτοὶ τόποι χρήσιμοι. Topica, 7. 3. But in the Analytica Posteriora the rules for establishing a definition are not given under the form of loci, and the words ἐν ἑτέροις may refer to some other treatise. The Sophistici Elenchi was written before the Hermeneutica, which refers to it in ch. 11, under the name of τὰ τοπικά. The seventeenth chapter of the second book of the Analytica Priora refers to the Sophistici Elenchi under the name of τὰ τοπικά. This chapter therefore, and probably others in the second book, must have been added subsequently, as the mass of the treatise was written before the Sophistici Elenchi. The Rhetoric was written after the Topica and Analytica Priora, which it refers to in the second chapter of the first book. It speaks of τὰ ἐριστικά in the twenty-fifth chapter of the second book, but, to judge from the inferior precision with which it handles the subject of fallacies, was probably written before the Sophistici Elenchi.

CHAPTER IV.

1] Verbal fallacies of course vanish in translation. In the following translations much licence has been taken, and the result is but lame.

Γραμματική is defined to be the art of reading and writing: ἐπιστήμη τοῦ γράψαι τὸ ὑπαγορευθὲν καὶ τοῦ ἀναγνῶναι. Topica, 6. 5. The teacher was said to ἀποστοματίζειν, or ὑπαγορεύειν, when he dictated a word to be written or spelt. The boy who caught and understood the word, that is, who could exactly appreciate a complex sound and decompose it into its letters or elementary sounds, was said in the language of the school to μανθάνειν. He was γραμματικός, master of alphabetic science. The example is taken from the Euthydemus of Plato (§§ 12–18): it may be thus analysed. Suppose that the thesis to be confuted is ὁ μανθάνων ἀνεπιστήμων. We have two syllogisms:—

Major,	ὁ μανθάνων τὰ ἀποστοματιζόμενα	γραμματικός·
Minor,	ὁ μανθάνων τὰ ἀποστοματιζόμενα	μανθάνει·
Conclusion, ∴	ὁ μανθάνων	γραμματικός.

Again:

Major,	ὁ γραμματικός	ἐπιστήμων·
Minor,	ὁ μανθάνων	γραμματικός·
Conclusion, ∴	ὁ μανθάνων	ἐπιστήμων.

The minor term (μανθάνων) is ambiguous.

2]
Major,	τὰ δέοντα	ἀγαθά·
Minor,	τὰ κακὰ	δέοντα·
Conclusion, ∴	τὰ κακὰ	ἀγαθά.

The middle term is ambiguous.

3]
Major,	ὅσπερ ἀνίστατο	ἕστηκε·
Minor,	ὁ καθήμενος	ἀνίστατο·
Conclusion, ∴	ὁ καθήμενος	ἕστηκε.

The minor term is ambiguous.

Major,	ὅσπερ ὑγιάζετο	ὑγιαίνει·
Minor,	ὁ κάμνων	ὑγιάζετο·
Conclusion, ∴	ὁ κάμνων	ὑγιαίνει.

The minor term is ambiguous.

Whately is inclined to rest the claims of logic to consideration on the services she performs in teaching us the seat of the ambiguities on which fallacies are built. This, he repeatedly informs us, is the middle term. The above examples may shew on how precarious a foundation he rests the claims of logic.

CHAP. IV. NOTES. 105

4] Read ὑγιάζεται. In the next line we have MS. authority for omitting the article before πρότερον.

5] Supplying a minor we obtain this fallacy:—

Major,   τοῦτο ὅ τις γινώσκει   γινώσκει·
Minor,   ἡ γραφαὶ   τοῦτο ὅ τις γινώσκει·
Conclusion, ∴ ἡ γραφαὶ   γινώσκουσι.

The major premiss is taken to mean,
    αὗται ἅς τις γινώσκει   γινώσκουσι.

It really means,
    τίς γινώσκει ταύτας ἅς γινώσκει.

There are therefore more than three terms, or we may say that the middle is ambiguous. For a justification of the employment of the feminine and masculine pronouns in the analysis of this and the following fallacies, see ch. xxxii.

6] Major,   τοῦτο ὃ ὁρᾷ τις   ὁρᾷ·
   Minor,   ὁ κίων   τοῦτο ὃ ὁρᾷ τις·
   Conclusion, ∴ ὁ κίων   ὁρᾷ.

The major premiss is ambiguous. It really means, τοῦτον, ὃν ὁρᾷ τις, ὁρᾷ: but it is taken to mean, οὗτος, ὃν ὁρᾷ τις, ὁρᾷ.

7] Major,   τὸ φῂς εἶναι οὗτος
         ὃν σὺ φῂς εἶναι ἔστι τὸ φῂς εἶναι λίθον
   Minor,   σὺ φῂς εἶναι τοῦτον ὃν σὺ φῂς εἶναι·
   Conclusion, ∴ σὺ φῂς εἶναι λίθος.

The middle is ambiguous if we employ the word τοῦτο, but if, as above, we use the masculine gender, there are two distinct terms, one containing οὗτος, the other τοῦτον.

8] Suppose the thesis to be: Speaking of the speechless or silent is impossible. We have the syllogism,

Major,   Speaking of iron tools is possible:
Minor,   Speaking of iron tools is speaking of the silent:
Conclusion, Speaking of the silent is possible.

Here the conclusion follows, but, as the minor term is ambiguous, does not contradict the thesis. A disputant in the Euthydemus denies the minor premiss, asserting that if we go by a factory at work, we shall find that iron tools are the reverse of silent: ’Ἀλλά μοι δοκεῖς, Εὐθύδημε, οὐ καθεύδων ἐπικεκοιμῆσθαι, καὶ εἰ οἶόν τε, λέγοντα μηδέν, λέγειν, καὶ σὺ τοῦτο ποιεῖν. Ἦ γὰρ οὐχ οἷόν τε, ἔφη ὁ Διονυσόδωρος, σιγῶντα λέγειν; Οὐδ’ ὁπωστιοῦν, ἦ δ’ ὃς

ὁ Κτήσιππος. "Ὅταν οὖν λίθους λέγῃς καὶ ξύλα καὶ σιδήρια, οὐ σιγῶντα λέγεις; Οὔκουν εἴ γε ἐγώ, ἔφη, παρέρχομαι ἐν τοῖς χαλκείοις, ἀλλὰ φθεγγόμενα καὶ βοῶντα μέγιστον τὰ σιδήρια λέγεται ἐάν τις ἄψηται. Euthydemus, § 67.

9] There is something wrong here. We may either omit καὶ μὴ γράφοντα γράφειν, or καὶ τοῦθ' ὡσαύτως ἂν τις συνθῇ, τὸν μὴ γράφοντα γράφειν.

10] Here again we require emendation. We obtain a moderate amount of sense if we read, καὶ μανθάνων γράμματα ἅπερ μανθάνει ἐπιστάται.

11] Major,   Two and three (distributively) are even and odd;
    Minor,   Two and three (collectively) are five;
    Conclusion, ∴ Five is even and odd.

Whately adds:—
    Major,   All the angles of a triangle are equal to two right angles;
    Minor,   *ABC* is an angle of a triangle;
    Conclusion, ∴ *ABC* is equal to two right angles.

How does the fallacy of conjunction differ from the fallacy of disjunction? Whately says, when the middle is taken collectively in the major premiss and distributively in the minor, we have the fallacy of division; when it is taken distributively in the major and collectively in the minor, the fallacy of composition. So when some other term and not the middle is ambiguous, we might say the fallacy was one of division or composition, according as the term was taken collectively in the premiss and distributively in the conclusion or vice versa.

Thus, Major,   Three and two are two numbers;
    Minor,   Three and two are five;
    Conclusion, ∴ Five is two numbers;
would be a fallacy of composition; whereas,
    Major,   Five is one number;
    Minor,   Three and two are five;
    Conclusion, ∴ Three and two are one number;
would be a fallacy of division. This is intelligible, but cannot have been Aristotle's view, for his first example of division would, according to Whately's test, be a fallacy of composition. The

point is hardly worth deciding; for the fallacies in diction may well be regarded as a single species, or at the utmost as two, homonymia and figura dictionis.

12] Buhle, comparing Terence's line in the Andria,

Scia. Feci ex servo ut esses libertus mihi,

infers that this is a line of Menander. But if our chronologies are correct and this line was quoted by Aristotle, it was older than Menander. For we are told that Aristotle died in B.C. 322, and that Menander's first play was acted when he was still an ephebus, i. e. between 18 and 20 years old, in B.C. 321.

13] To find any fault (ἁμαρτία) in Homer was thought to be a paradox, and adverse criticisms on him seem to have been considered a branch of dialectic or eristic. The critic treated the poet as pirastic treats the pretenders to other arts and sciences, that is, he attempted to prove by the poet's utterances that he was not a master of the art which he professed. Though, if such criticisms were, as they ought to have been, based on principles peculiar to æsthetic science, when false, they would have been pseudographic (see chap. xi), not sophistic. Perhaps, however, the person confuted was not the poet, but the rhapsode, who often attributed universal science to Homer. In the Poetics, chap. 25, five loci (εἴδη) of such criticisms (ἐπιτιμήσεις, προβλήματα) are given, and twelve solutions. Some of the criticisms are referred to the sophistic loci of accentuation, homonymia, amphibolia, division, ignoratio elenchi; but the text is very corrupt.

14] The defence of these two passages by a change of accentuation is attributed in the Poetics to Hippias of Thasos. The first occurs in Iliad 23. 328; the second does not occur in Agamemnon's dream, but in Iliad 21. 297, where Achilles is encouraged by Poseidon. We may infer that our present form of the text had not been established in the time of Aristotle.

15] See Topics, 1. 9.

CHAPTER V.

1] Συμβεβηκὸς here is opposed to οὐσία, and means not only what is usually called accident, but every predicate except definition or the whole essence of the subject. See ch. xxiv, where the fallacy of accidens is discussed: Μόνοις γὰρ τοῖς κατὰ τὴν

οὐσίαν ἀδιαφόροις καὶ ἓν οὖσιν ἅπαντα δοκεῖ ταὐτὰ ὑπάρχειν. 'Only those terms whose essence is one and indistinguishable have all their predicates in common.' The words ἓν οὖσιν shew that even genus is to be regarded as accident. Compare 'Ἀληθὲς γὰρ πᾶν τὸ ἀνθρώπῳ εἶναι ζῴῳ εἶναι, ὥσπερ καὶ πάντα ἄνθρωπον ζῷον, ἀλλ' οὐχ οὕτως ὥστε ἓν εἶναι. Analytica Posteriora, 2. 4. 'Humanity is animality and man is animal, but the ideas are only partially, not totally, identical.'

2] Major, ἄνθρωπος οὐ Κορίσκος·
 Minor, Κορίσκος ἄνθρωπος·
 Conclusion, ∴ Κορίσκος οὐ Κορίσκος.
We have an undistributed middle.

3] Major, Σωκράτης ἄνθρωπος·
 Minor, Κορίσκος οὐ Σωκράτης·
 Conclusion, ∴ Κορίσκος οὐκ ἄνθρωπος.
We have an illicit process of the major.

In the Euthydemus it is stated that Socrates is the son of Sophroniscus, and that Patrocles is the son of the mother of Socrates by her former husband, Chæredemus. The sophist then attempts to prove that either Sophroniscus or Chæredemus is not a father. Οὐκοῦν, ἦ δ' ὅς, ἕτερος ἦν Χαιρέδημος τοῦ πατρός; Τοὐμοῦ γ', ἔφην ἐγώ. Ἆρ' οὖν πατὴρ ἦν ἕτερος ὢν πατρός; ἢ σὺ εἶ ὁ αὐτὸς τῷ λίθῳ; Δέδοικα μὲν ἔγωγ', ἔφην, μὴ φανῶ ὑπὸ σοῦ ὁ αὐτός· οὐ μέντοι μοι δοκῶ. Οὐκοῦν ἕτερος εἶ, ἔφη, τοῦ λίθου; Ἕτερος μέντοι. Ἄλλο τι οὖν ἕτερος, ἢ δ' ὅς, ὢν λίθου οὐ λίθος εἶ; καὶ ἕτερος ὢν χρυσοῦ οὐ χρυσὸς εἶ; Ἔστι ταῦτα. Οὐκοῦν καὶ ὁ Χαιρέδημος, ἔφη, ἕτερος ὢν πατρὸς οὐκ ἂν πατὴρ εἴη. Ἔοικεν, ἦν δ' ἐγώ, οὐ πατὴρ εἶναι. Εἰ γὰρ δή που, ἔφη, πατήρ ἐστιν ὁ Χαιρέδημος, ὑπολαβὼν ὁ Εὐθύδημος, πάλιν αὖ ὁ Σωφρονίσκος ἕτερος ὢν πατρὸς οὐ πατήρ ἐστιν, ὥστε σύ, ὦ Σώκρατες, ἀπάτωρ εἶ. Euthydemus, § 62. 'Chæredemus then, said he, was other than a father?—Than mine, said I.—Then how could he be a father if he was other than a father? Are you the same as a stone?—I am afraid you will prove me so, said I, but I believe I am not.—Then you are other than a stone?—Yes.—Being other than a stone you are not a stone; and being other than gold you are not gold?—True.—Chæredemus, therefore, being other than a father is not a father.—It seems he is not a father.—At least if Chæredemus

is a father, said Euthydemus breaking in, Sophroniscus being other than a father is no father, and you, my Socrates, are fatherless.'

4] In the Topics it is given as a dialectic maxim that when a qualified assertion is true, the unqualified assertion is true; although it is allowed that the principle has numerous exceptions. Τὸν αὐτὸν δὲ τρόπον σκεπτέον καὶ ἐπὶ τοῦ κατά τι καὶ ποτὲ καὶ ποῦ· εἰ γὰρ κατά τι ἐνδέχεται, καὶ ἁπλῶς ἐνδέχεται. ... Ἔνστασις ὅτι κατά τι μὲν εἰσι φύσει σπουδαῖοι, οἷον ἐλευθέριοι ἢ σωφρονικοί, ἁπλῶς δὲ οὐκ εἰσὶ φύσει σπουδαῖοι. ... Τὸν αὐτὸν δὲ τρόπον καὶ τοῦ μὲν καλὸν τὸν πατέρα θύειν, οἷον ἐν Τριβαλλοῖς, ἁπλῶς δ' οὐ καλόν. ... Τὸ δ' ἁπλῶς ἐστιν ὃ μηδενὸς προστιθέντος ἐρεῖς ὅτι καλὸν ἔστιν ἢ τὸ ἐναντίον· οἷον τὸ τὸν πατέρα θύειν οὐκ ἐρεῖς καλὸν εἶναι, ἀλλὰ τισὶ καλὸν εἶναι, οὐκ ἄρα ἁπλῶς καλόν· ἀλλὰ τὸ τοὺς θεοὺς τιμᾶν ἐρεῖς καλὸν οὐδὲν προσθείς, ἁπλῶς γὰρ καλόν ἐστι. Topics, 2. 11. 'We should look to facts qualified in point of respect or time or place; for what is true in a certain respect is absolutely true. ... By way of enstasis it may be objected that partial virtue is inborn, as liberality or an inclination to temperance, but complete virtue is never inborn. ... Again, locally it is a duty to sacrifice one's father, as among the Triballi, but absolutely it is not a duty. ..... Absolutely means, without the addition of restrictive terms: as to sacrifice a father cannot be called a duty without the addition, among the Triballi; whereas to reverence the gods is a duty without any restriction.'

5] The opposition between absolute and relative motion or rest accounts for the conflicting statements respecting a certain doctrine of Plato in the Timæus. Well-informed writers have declared that the earth is there represented as at rest: equally well-informed writers declare that she is represented as in motion. Which of these statements is true? Both. The universe is represented as having a solid pole or axis which revolves at a certain pace in a given direction and carries round with it the rest of the universe. The earth is at the centre of the universe and would revolve with it if she were not rotating on the axis with exactly equal speed in the opposite direction, (ἰλλομένην, i.e. ἀνελιττομένην, περὶ τὸν διὰ παντὸς πόλον τεταμένον). Shall we say she is at rest or in motion? If the revolution of the axis ceased while the counter-revolution of the

earth continued, there is no doubt she would be in motion: if the counter-revolution of the earth ceased while the revolution of the axis continued, there is no doubt she would be in motion, revolving with the rest of the world. While both revolutions continue, it may be disputed whether we ought to say that she is absolutely at rest though relatively in motion, or absolutely in motion though relatively at rest. See the subject examined, with a different explanation, by Grote, in his pamphlet on the Timæus.

6] It would be a false classification (ἀλκή) to place ignoratio elenchi, and, what may be identified with it, secundum quid, among the fallacies in diction, because the similitude which produces the deception is a real similitude of facts or ideas, and not merely a similitude of words.

7] There is a chapter on petitio principii in the Analytica Priora, for which see Appendix A.

8] In the Rhetoric the fallacy of signs is enumerated as distinct from the fallacy of consequences. From which we may infer that the present treatise, containing the juster view, is the later composition.

9] The nature of the fallacy of non causa pro causa has been sufficiently explained in this chapter, but as Whately confesses that he cannot conceive what logicians mean by this term, in Appendix B we have added a chapter on the same subject from the Analytica Priora.

10] There must be something corrupt here: the translation does not follow the text.

11] What Aristotle apparently means, and what we must get from his words as best we may, is this:—An inconclusive argument with true premisses in plurium interrogationum may be converted, like any other fallacy, into a conclusive argument, that is to say, a sophistic proof (see ch. viii), by the assumption of false premisses. The premisses in this fallacy are of the following form, (ch. xxx): A and B are C and D; where what is true of A is false of B, and vice versa: whence a fallacy. If now we assume on the contrary that A and B have the same predicates, that if C or D is affirmed or denied of the one it is equally (ὁμοίως) affirmed or denied of the other, we shall have valid reasoning from a false assumption.

CHAPTER VI.

1] Substantive names (nomina substantiva) properly and primarily belong to individual substances. Language extends them, secondly, to the genera of these substances; and, thirdly, to attributes (e.g. ἰσότης, ἀνισότης). Realism ascribes substantive existence to the second of these classes, if not to the third.

2] Mill says: "Logic postulates to be allowed to assert the same meaning in any words which will express it—We require the liberty of substituting for a given assertion the same assertion in different words—We require the liberty of exchanging a proposition for any other that is equipollent with it." *Criticisms on Sir W. Hamilton*, ch. 21. This postulate he identifies with the axiom or principle of identity, which he thus expresses: "Whatever is true in one form of words is true in every other form of words which conveys the same meaning." The dialectic rule is not inconsistent with this, but only imposes on the disputant before he changes a formula the necessity of obtaining the assent of the respondent. A respondent could not refuse his assent to any reasonable proposition without exposing himself to the charge of δυσκολία, perverse obstructiveness, which was equivalent to defeat. If, however, the respondent was prepared to brave the charge of δυσκολία, the conditions imposed on the opponent must have sometimes enabled the respondent to avoid a formal confutation. Οὐ γὰρ πρὸς τὸν ἔξω λόγον ἡ ἀπόδειξις ἀλλὰ πρὸς τὸν ἐν τῇ ψυχῇ, ἐπεὶ οὐδὲ συλλογισμός. Ἀεὶ γὰρ ἔστιν ἐνστῆναι πρὸς τὸν ἔξω λόγον, ἀλλὰ πρὸς τὸν ἔσω λόγον οὐκ ἀεί. Analytica Posteriora, I. 10. 'It is not the spoken but the thought proposition that carries demonstration or even ordinary proof; for exception can always be taken to the verbal enunciation, though not always to the thought enunciated.' [I have translated as if Aristotle had written οὐ γὰρ ἐκ τοῦ ἔξω λόγου ἡ ἀπόδειξις ἀλλ' ἐκ τοῦ ἐν τῇ ψυχῇ. If πρὸς is used in its proper sense, i.e. (see ch. xix, note 4) as indicating not the premisses but the conclusion of a demonstration, we must translate: 'The conclusion of demonstration is not the spoken but the thought proposition.' But the axiom, the indemonstrable foundation of proof, of which Aristotle is speaking, could hardly be spoken

of as the conclusion of a demonstration. It seems, then, that πρός here is not used in its Aristotelian sense, but in the sense which it bears in the formulas, πρὸς τοὔνομα, πρὸς τὴν διάνοιαν, which are examined in ch. x].

3] There must be something wrong here. The translation assumes the true reading to be, Οὐ γὰρ εἰ τοῦτο ἀνάγκη τοδ' εἶναι, τοῦτο δ' ἐστὶ λευκόν, ἀνάγκη πᾶν λευκὸν τόδ' εἶναι. But if this is Aristotle's meaning it is odd that the important word πᾶν should have slipped out both of this and the following example. The fallacy in these two cases may be described as the equation of particular and universal. But this description will not apply to the examples subsequently given.

4] The same instance of an accidental conclusion is given in the Analytica Posteriora, I. 4: Καθόλου δὲ λέγω ὃ ἂν κατὰ παντός τε ὑπάρχῃ καὶ καθ' αὑτό..... τὸ καθόλου δὲ ὑπάρχει τότε ὅταν ἐπὶ τοῦ τυχόντος καὶ πρώτου δεικνύηται. Οἷον, τὸ δύο ὀρθὰς ἔχειν οὔτε τῷ σχήματί ἐστι καθόλου· καίτοι ἔστι δεῖξαι κατὰ σχήματος ὅτι δύο ὀρθὰς ἔχει, ἀλλ' οὐ τοῦ τυχόντος σχήματος, οὐδὲ χρῆται τῷ τυχόντι σχήματι ὁ δεικνύς, τὸ γὰρ τετράγωνον σχῆμα μέν, οὐκ ἔχει δὲ δύο ὀρθαῖς ἴσας· τό τ' ἰσοσκελὲς ἔχει μὲν τὸ τυχὸν δύο ὀρθαῖς ἴσας, ἀλλ' οὐ πρῶτον, ἀλλὰ τὸ τρίγωνον πρότερον. Ὁ τοίνυν τὸ τυχὸν πρῶτον δείκνυται δύο ὀρθὰς ἔχειν ἢ ὁτιοῦν ἄλλο, τούτῳ ὑπάρχει καθόλου, καὶ ἡ ἀπόδειξις καθ' αὑτὸ τούτου ἐστί, τῶν δ' ἄλλων τρόπον τινὰ οὐ καθ' αὑτό· οὐδὲ τοῦ ἰσοσκελοῦς οὐκ ἔστι καθόλου ἀλλ' ἐπὶ πλέον. 'A commensurate proposition (a proposition whose subject and predicate are distributed and coextensive) is universal and essential. .... Its subject is universal and the highest genus which can be proved to universally possess the predicate. Figure is not commensurate to the predicate, containing angles equal to two right angles, for some figures possess it but not all; nor can any figure indifferently, the tetragon, for example, be employed in the proof. Isosceles possesses it universally, but is not the highest genus which possesses it; for triangle is higher. Only the universal and highest subject is commensurate, and only such is essential: the others, including isosceles, are in a sense accidental.' The expression, ὁ δεικνύς, seems to shew that Aristotle is referring to some sophistical demonstration that had been actually propounded.

5] The frivolous examples of confutation per accidens hitherto

given seem far too flimsy meshes to embarrass the man of science, and it is here implied that, like other fallacies, they can only be valid when the premisses are false. But elsewhere we are told that it is often very difficult to discriminate between accidental or illegitimate and essential or legitimate demonstration. The geometer, to avoid confutation by accidental syllogism, is recommended to decline arguing except before a geometrical tribunal. Εἰ δὲ διαλέξεται γεωμέτρῃ ᾖ γεωμέτρης, οὗτως φανερὸν ὅτι καὶ καλῶς, ἐὰν ἐκ τούτων τι δεικνύῃ, εἰ δὲ μή, οὐ καλῶς. Δῆλον δ' ὅτι οὐδ' ἐλέγχει γεωμέτρην ἀλλ' ἢ κατὰ συμβεβηκός. Ὥστ' οὐκ ἂν εἴη ἐν ἀγεωμετρήτοις (κριταῖς) περὶ γεωμετρίας διαλεκτέον, λήσει γὰρ ὁ φαύλως διαλεγόμενος. Analytica Posteriora, I. 12. 'In controversy with a geometer only conclusions from geometrical (essential) premisses are legitimate; others, if they refute him, only refute him accidentally, and not as a geometrician. Therefore a geometrical controversy should be conducted before a tribunal of geometers; for, otherwise, ungeometrical arguments will pass without detection.' As science advances it is continually making the discovery that its earliest theorems combined terms whose connexion was merely accidental. Δεῖ δὲ μὴ λανθάνειν, ὅτι πολλάκις συμβαίνει διαμαρτάνειν, καὶ μὴ ὑπάρχειν τὸ δεικνύμενον πρῶτον καθόλου, ᾖ δοκεῖ δείκνυσθαι καθόλου πρῶτον.... Λέγω δὲ τούτου ᾖ τοῦτο ἀποδείξιν, ὅταν ᾖ πρώτου καθόλου. Εἰ οὖν τις δείξειεν ὅτι αἱ ὀρθαὶ οὐ συμπίπτουσι, δόξειεν ἂν τούτου εἶναι ἡ ἀπόδειξις κυρίως διὰ τὸ ἐπὶ πασῶν εἶναι τῶν ὀρθῶν, οὐκ ἔστι δέ· εἴπερ μὴ ὅτι ὡδὶ ἴσαι γίνεται τοῦτο, ἀλλ' ᾖ ὁπωσοῦν ἴσαι. Καὶ εἰ τρίγωνον μὴ ἦν ἄλλο ἢ ἰσοσκελές, ᾖ ἰσοσκελὲς ἂν ἐδόκει ὑπάρχειν. Καὶ τὸ ἀνάλογον ὅτι ἐναλλάξ, ᾖ ἀριθμοὶ καὶ ᾖ γραμμαὶ καὶ ᾖ στερεὰ καὶ ᾖ χρόνοι, ὥσπερ ἐδείκνυτό ποτε χωρίς, ἐνδεχόμενόν γε κατὰ πάντων μιᾷ ἀποδείξει δειχθῆναι. Ἀλλὰ διὰ τὸ μὴ εἶναι ὠνομασμένον τι πάντα ταῦτα ἕν, ἀριθμοὶ μήκη χρόνοι στερεά, καὶ εἴδει διαφέρειν ἀλλήλων, χωρὶς ἐλαμβάνετο. Νῦν δὲ καθόλου δείκνυται· οὐ γὰρ ᾖ γραμμαὶ ἢ ᾖ ἀριθμοὶ ὑπῆρχεν, ἀλλ' ᾖ τοδὶ ὃ καθόλου ὑποτίθεται ὑπάρχειν. Διὰ τοῦτο οὐδ' ἄν τις δείξῃ καθ' ἕκαστον τὸ τρίγωνον ἀποδείξει ἢ μιᾷ ἢ ἑτέρᾳ ὅτι δύο ὀρθὰς ἔχει ἕκαστον, τὸ ἰσόπλευρον χωρὶς καὶ τὸ σκαληνὸν καὶ τὸ ἰσοσκελές, οὔπω οἶδε τὸ τρίγωνον ὅτι δύο ὀρθαῖς ἴσον εἰ μὴ τὸν σοφιστικὸν τρόπον, οὐδὲ καθόλου τρίγωνον, οὐδ' εἰ μηδέν ἐστι παρὰ ταῦτα τρίγωνον ἕτερον· οὐ γὰρ ᾖ τρίγωνον οἶδεν, οὐδὲ πᾶν τρίγωνον ἀλλ' ἢ κατ' ἀριθμόν· κατ' εἶδος δ' οὐ πᾶν, καὶ εἰ μηδέν ἐστιν ὃ

οὐκ οἶδε. Anal. Post. i. 5. 'It often happens that a conclusion is not primary and commensurate, when it seems to be.... If not primary and commensurate, the demonstration is not essential. Perpendiculars to the same line are parallel; but this is not an essential proposition; for not only perpendiculars, but all lines that meet another at equal angles, are parallel. Were the isosceles the only known triangle, the property of containing angles equal to two right angles would seem essentially connected with isoscelism. The permutation of proportionals, numbers, lines, solids, times, is not essentially connected with number, time, dimension, but can be demonstrated at once of the commensurate genus. It was formerly proved in detail. They differ in species, and there was no name for their genus. When you prove in detail of each species of triangle, equilateral, scalene, isosceles, the equality of their interior angles to two right angles, you may exhaust the possible cases but your predicate is not essential and commensurate, and you have only a sophistical science. Your universal is numerical but not essential.' Conclusions from accidental premisses are not only plausible but irresistible. Καίτοι ἀπορήσειεν ἄν τις ἴσως, τίνος ἕνεκα ταῦτα (τὰ συμβεβηκότα μὴ καθ' αὑτά) δεῖ ἐρωτᾶν περὶ τούτων, εἰ μὴ ἀνάγκη τὸ συμπέρασμα εἶναι. Οὐδὲν γὰρ διαφέρει εἴ τις ἐρόμενος τὰ τυχόντα εἶτα εἴπειεν τὸ συμπέρασμα. Δεῖ δ' ἐρωτᾶν οὐχ ὡς ἀναγκαῖον εἶναι διὰ τὰ ἠρωτημένα, ἀλλ' ὅτι λέγειν ἀνάγκη τῷ ἐκεῖνα λέγοντι, καὶ ἀληθῶς λέγειν ἐὰν ἀληθὲς ᾖ ὑπάρχοντα. Analytica Posteriora, 1. 6. 'It may be asked of what use are accidental premisses in dialectic, if they do not necessitate the conclusion. Do we not first make some irrelevant remarks, and then assert the conclusion, when we argue from contingent premisses? To which we answer that they are not propounded as grounds of a categorically necessary conclusion; but because, if they are conceded, by a hypothetical necessity the conclusion is conceded; and if they are true, by a hypothetical necessity the conclusion is true.' Indeed all dialectic, as opposed to science, consists of accidental ratiocination. 'Ἀντιστρέφει δὲ μᾶλλον τὰ ἐν τοῖς μαθήμασιν, ὅτι οὐδὲν συμβεβηκὸς λαμβάνουσιν (ἀλλὰ καὶ τούτῳ διαφέρουσι τῶν ἐν τοῖς διαλόγοις) ἀλλ' ὁρισμούς. Analytica Posteriora, 1. 12. 'The convertibility of consequent and antecedent is more common in science than in

CHAP. VI. NOTES. 115

dialectic; for dialectic employs accidental premises, science only definitions.'

These conflicting views of accidental ratiocination may be reconciled by dividing it into two classes:—

1. Reasonings that are inconclusive, i. e. dialectically unsound and fallacious:
2. Reasonings that are conclusive, i. e. dialectically sound, but, as not based on appropriate principles nor satisfying the other conditions of science, unscientific.

If we refer to the instances quoted above, a proof that all figures contain angles equal to two right angles must be invalid and undialectical, and belong to the first class; but a proof that every isosceles contains them would be logically valid and dialectical but unscientific, and belong to the second class. We may observe that in the passage quoted above from An. Post. 1. 4, Aristotle only calls the latter conclusions in some sense (τρόπον τινά) accidental.

6] This is unintelligible, and the text probably corrupt.

7] Bekker reads, τῷ ταῦτ' εἶναι αἴτια τοῦ συμβαίνειν. This looks like the vestige of a paraphrase: δεῖ γὰρ ταῦτ' εἶναι αἴτια τοῦ συμβαίνειν τὸ συμπέρασμα.

8] The Hermeneutica, ch. 11, refers to this passage by the words ἐν τοῖς τοπικοῖς.

9] It is clear that the words οὖν παρὰ τὴν λέξιν should be cancelled, unless for λέξιν we read ἔλεγξιν. The slightest consideration will suffice to shew that the two classes of fallacy, in dictione and extra dictionem, do not correspond to sins against the two elements of confutation, contradiction and proof. Of the class in dictione, reasonings involving homonymia and amphibolia may, indeed, be conclusive when the ambiguity lies in the extremes, but must be inconclusive when it lies in the middle term. Of the class extra dictionem, the fallacies non causa pro causa and ignoratio elenchi fail rather in contradiction than in proof. Aristotle has elsewhere spoken correctly. In the beginning of this chapter he implies (εἰ μέλλει ἔλεγχος ἢ συλλογισμὸς ἔσεσθαι) that some of the fallacies in dictione are devoid of proof as well as of confutation (contradiction). In ch. xix. he says that homonymia and amphibolia may affect either the premises or the conclusion, i. e. either the proof or the contra-

diction. And in ch. x. he gives an instance of homonymia (epic poems are a plane figure for they are a circle) affecting the middle term, that is, the proof: and observes that figura dictionis may be treated as faulty either in the proof or in the contradiction. In ch. xxv. he seems to say that secundum quid only fails in the contradiction, but it is clear that it may fail either in the contradiction or in the sequence.

We may observe that we only give a semblance of unity to the theory of fallacies by lumping them all together under the definition of confutation, for the elements of that definition are obtained by no systematic subdivision, and form, as far as appears, a purely arbitrary and incoherent agglomeration.

CHAPTER VII.

1] A man might misplace his accents and yet be understood in Greek society, unless the misplacement produced ambiguity.

2] Ἐπίστασαι. This must be wrong. We should read ποιεῖ, or πείθει, or ἐπιστᾷ, or ἐπισπᾶται, or something equivalent. In support of the last conjecture compare, Ἆρ᾽ οὖν αὐτὸ γιγνώσκων σύμφης, ἢ σε οἷον ῥύμη τις ὑπὸ τοῦ λόγου συνειθισμένου συνεπίσπασατο πρὸς τὸ ταχὺ συμφῆσαι; Sophistes, 46. 'Have you any good reason for your assent, or has the current of the language to which you are accustomed hurried you along into an ill-considered admission?' Aristotle is thinking of realism or the theory of ideas, which he says, ch. xxii, is founded on this fallacy.

3] Reasoning to a certain extent is possible, as we see in brutes, without words. But the development of language must have been accompanied by a great increase of reasoning power. Thenceforth in all reasoning there are two parallel trains, the train of images and the train of words. When the train of words precedes it awakes the train of images, if the words are imitative, by the associative law of similarity. If the sounds are not imitative, but interjectional, that is, produced according to some physiological law by the action of the organs of sensation on the organs of expression, they afterwards suggest the sensations that produced them by the associative law of con-

tiguity in place and time. But in rapid thought the images are very imperfectly excited. The mind, emboldened by habit, ventures to trust herself to the train of words through which she can pass with great celerity without stopping to realize them by images which would encumber her and clog her motion. Rapid and powerful reasoning, then, takes place chiefly by the verbal train. Reasoning without words is more likely to occur in meditation than in conversation. See this subject discussed by Mill, *Examination of Sir W. Hamilton's Philosophy*, ch. 17.

4] This sentence shews the affinity, in Aristotle's mind, between the fallacies ignoratio elenchi and secundum quid (see note 3 to ch. viii). In this treatise (see ch. v, vi, vii) ἔλλειψις is always used to denote ignoratio elenchi. In the Rhetoric, where the fallacies are enumerated, ignoratio elenchi is not mentioned and ἔλλειψις designates the fallacy secundum quid. Ἄλλος (τόπος) παρὰ τὴν ἔλλειψιν τοῦ πότε καὶ πῶς οἷον ὅτι δικαίως Ἀλέξανδρος ἔλαβε τὴν Ἑλένην, αἵρεσις γὰρ αὐτῇ ἐδόθη παρὰ τοῦ πατρός. Οὐ γὰρ ἀεὶ ἴσως ἀλλὰ τὸ πρῶτον· καὶ γὰρ ὁ πατὴρ μέχρι τούτου κύριος. Ἢ εἴ τις φαίη τὸ τύπτειν τοὺς ἐλευθέρους ὕβριν εἶναι· οὐ γὰρ πάντως, ἀλλ' ὅταν ἄρχῃ χειρῶν ἀδίκων. Rhetoric, 2. 24. 'Another class of fallacies depends on the omission of limitations in time or manner: as the argument that Helen had a right to elope with Paris because her father granted her the option of her husband. But the option granted was not perpetual but one that determined with her first choice, for this was all her father had the power to grant. So the statement, that striking a freeman is an assault, requires limitation: for it is only an assault in him who strikes first.' The moderns have created a distinction by confining ignoratio elenchi to valid arguments with irrelevant conclusions, i. e. by confining the omitted limitations to such as affect the contradiction.

5] This chapter explains why the solution (λύσις) of an inconclusive or illogical confutation is called διαίρεσις (distinction). A conclusive or logical confutation can only be solved by shewing that one of the premisses is false (ἀναίρεσις). If this is shewn by certain simple topics, it is called enstasis; if by other topics, antisyllogism. Solution, then, is either enstasis, which includes διαίρεσις and one branch of ἀναίρεσις, or antisyllogism, which is the other branch of ἀναίρεσις. Antisyllo-

gism, being a species of solution, is the disproof of one of the opponent's premisses, not of his conclusion; for it would be an abuse of language to call the disproof of a conclusion a solution of the argument supporting that conclusion.

CHAPTER VIII.

1] Eristic proof is either inconclusive or contains a false premiss. But it is not every false premiss that makes a proof eristic. If the premiss, though unscientific, is a special proposition, referring exclusively to a particular subject-matter, the proof is dialectic. Even the general propositions that characterize dialectic, the topical maxims, must be accepted with many limitations and exceptions, for dolus latet in generalibus; and if they are applied without these limitations and exceptions they are open to enstasis, and the conclusion is false, but still, it appears, the proof is regarded as dialectic. The basis of genuine probability in these propositions saves their inaccurate application from the stigma of sophistry. The false maxims that constitute a proof eristic, that is, radically bad or vicious in principle, are thirteen false propositions corresponding to the thirteen fallacies. Οὐ γὰρ πᾶν τὸ φαινόμενον ἔνδοξον καὶ ἔστιν ἔνδοξον. Οὐδὲν γὰρ τῶν λεγομένων ἐνδόξων ἐπιπόλαιον ἔχει παντελῶς τὴν φαντασίαν, καθάπερ περὶ τὰς τῶν ἐριστικῶν λόγων ἀρχὰς συμβέβηκεν ἔχειν. Παραχρῆμα γὰρ καὶ ὡς ἐπὶ τὸ πολὺ τοῖς καὶ μικρὰ συνορᾶν δυναμένοις κατάδηλος ἐν αὐτοῖς ἡ τοῦ ψεύδους ἐστὶ φύσις. Topica, 1. 1. 'Not every semblance of truth is probability. Probability, as we use the term, has more than an absolutely superficial semblance of truth, such as may be found in the principles of eristic proof, whose falsehood a moment's consideration discloses to all but the very dullest.' Of these sophistic principles five might be identified with perversions of dialectic maxims. The principles justifying the fallacies of accidens, consequens, secundum quid, non causa pro causa, and figura dictionis may be supposed to belong to the loci of subject and accident, antecedent and consequent, whole and part, cause and effect, and conjugates or paronyms. But it must be confessed, that it appears to be juster, instead of confining the term

sophism to the application of the thirteen imaginary principles, to extend it, in pirastic at least, by the criterion, οὐ ποιεῖ δῆλον εἰ ἀγνοεῖ, to the misapplication of any dialectic maxim. For it is evident that the false conclusion in which the respondent might be landed by such a false premiss would not convict him of ignorance in any special branch of knowledge which he professed. Even if the false premiss is not a dialectic maxim, but a specific proposition, not essentially (καθ' αὑτό) connected with the subject of the problem, the pirastic confutation is sophistic. And in spite of the expressions in this chapter, it is difficult to believe that this was not Aristotle's view.

2] An argument is usually called appropriate (οἰκεῖος τοῦ πράγματος, κατὰ τὸ πρᾶγμα) when it is scientific. Οὕτω γὰρ ἔσονται καὶ αἱ ἀρχαὶ οἰκεῖαι τοῦ δεικνυμένου. Συλλογισμὸς μὲν γὰρ ἔσται καὶ ἄνευ τούτων, ἀπόδειξις δ' οὐκ ἔσται, οὐ γὰρ ποιήσει ἐπιστήμην. Analytica Posteriora, I. 2. 'Then the premisses will be appropriate to the conclusion. Otherwise the proof would not be demonstrative or scientific.' Δῆλον δ' ἐκ τούτων καὶ ὅτι εὐήθεις οἱ λαμβάνειν οἰόμενοι καλῶς τὰς ἀρχάς, ἐὰν ἔνδοξος ᾖ ἡ πρότασις καὶ ἀληθής. Οὐ γὰρ τὸ ἔνδοξον ἢ μὴ ἀρχή ἐστιν, ἀλλὰ τὸ πρῶτον τοῦ γένους περὶ ὃ δείκνυται, καὶ τἀληθὲς οὐ πᾶν οἰκεῖον. An. Post. I. 6. 'It is absurd to suppose that our assumptions are scientific principles if they are only probable and true. Principles are not probabilities but primary propositions appropriate to a given sphere, and propositions may be true but inappropriate.' Χαλεπὸν δ' ἐστὶ τὸ γνῶναι εἰ οἶδεν ἢ μή. Χαλεπὸν γὰρ τὸ γνῶναι εἰ ἐκ τῶν ἑκάστου (οἰκείων) ἀρχῶν ἴσμεν ἢ μή, ὅπερ ἐστὶ τὸ εἰδέναι. Οἰόμεθα δ', ἂν ἔχωμεν ἐξ ἀληθινῶν τινῶν συλλογισμὸν καὶ πρώτων, ἐπίστασθαι. Τὸ δ' οὐκ ἔστιν, ἀλλὰ συγγενῆ (οἰκεῖα) δεῖ εἶναι τοῖς πρώτοις. An. Post. I. 9. 'It is hard to decide when our knowledge is science, for it is hard to decide whether the premisses are appropriate, as they must be in science. We fancy when we have a proof by true and primordial premisses, that we have science: not always, for they must also be homogeneous (appropriate) to the conclusion.'

Here, however, οἰκεῖος means, not scientific, but pirastic. The premisses employed in pirastic are not in the highest sense appropriate (ἴδια) to the subject, yet have a necessary connexion with it (ἑπόμενα, see ch. xi) and so far may be called appro-

priate. They are appropriate when compared with sophistic, inappropriate when compared with scientific, proof.

3] Every inconclusive reasoning (παραλογισμός) from true premisses may be converted into conclusive reasoning (συλλογισμός) from false premisses. The fallacies become valid arguments as far as the form is concerned if we substitute for the true principles on which sound reasoning reposes false principles to cover their faults and justify their sequence. It would require great art to put such propositions into a plausible form, and seduce the respondent into the concession of them: but we can conceive it accomplished. If such principles were formulated, they would correspond to the axioms or κοιναὶ ἀρχαί of science, and the topical maxims or κοιναὶ ἀρχαί of dialectic, and would themselves constitute the κοιναὶ ἀρχαί of sophistic. As false metaphysical principles and false linguistic theorems or rules of interpretation, they would imply, in the person who conceded them, an ignorance of logic and metaphysic or linguistic, but not of any other special science. For instance, a geometer who incautiously admitted them, and was consequently confuted on a geometrical question, might be proved to be an unpractised logician, but would not be proved to be an impostor in his pretensions to geometry. Arguments, therefore, derived from such pseudo-loci are inadmissible in pirastic.

4] This recapitulation omits ignoratio elenchi, which indeed may well be omitted, for it cannot be distinguished, as Aristotle defines it, from secundum quid. Regarding it as the fallacy of irrelevant conclusions, we might suppose we found a trace of a reference to it in the word ἀντίφασιν; but this term occurs in the examination of secundum quid, ch. xxv. Some words, however, may have slipped out of the text in this recapitulation, which, as it stands, is hardly the language of articulately speaking men. It is not clear why, after his three previous enumerations of the fallacies, Aristotle recapitulates at all. Did he intend to formulate the pseudo-axioms by which the sophisms may be rehabilitated, and recite the list as a framework in which the formulas might be inserted, but afterwards find his design more troublesome of execution than he had anticipated, and leave it unexecuted?

5] For παραλογισμοὶ read σοφιστικοὶ συλλογισμοί, or rather

ψευδεῖς συλλογισμοί, for a proof may be sophistic whose premisses are true but accidental or inappropriate. If accidental proofs are to be included under the thirteen fallacious loci, the locus of accidens must embrace not only the paralogism of accidens, but also all syllogisms professing to be scientific whose terms are not coextensive; in other words, whose premisses are not commensurate (καθόλου), i. e. universal and convertible; in other words, all syllogisms that fall short of demonstration (ἀπόδειξις).

6] We should read or understand, τὸ μόνον τόδε τι σημαίνειν τὰ κατηγορούμενα, or τὸ μόνον τόδε σημαίνειν τὰ οὕτως κατηγορούμενα.

7] There are, then, three gradations:—
(1) Valid proof (συλλογισμός, or ἁπλῶς συλλογισμός).
(2) Proof by the false principles above described. This is conclusive reasoning and real reasoning, but, as deceptive, it requires some qualification, and we call it relative or sophistic proof (πρὸς τοῦτον, or σοφιστικὸς συλλογισμός).
(3) Inconclusive reasoning, that is, no proof, but the mere semblance of proof (φαινόμενος συλλογισμός, or παραλογισμός).

CHAPTER IX.

1] I. e. pseudographemas.

2] Euclid is said to have written a treatise on geometrical fallacies. To expose false argumentation, says Plato investigating didactic method in the Phædrus, we require a knowledge of the truth, and as error depends on the likeness and consequent confusion of different terms, we must be able to distinguish the terms in question by definition and division. Δεῖ ἄρα τὸν μέλλοντα ἀπατήσειν μὲν ἄλλον, αὐτὸν δὲ μὴ ἀπατήσεσθαι, τὴν ὁμοιότητα τῶν ὄντων καὶ ἀνομοιότητα ἀκριβῶς διειδέναι.—'Ανάγκη μὲν οὖν.—Ἦ οὖν οἷός τε ἔσται, ἀλήθειαν ἀγνοῶν ἑκάστου, τὴν τοῦ ἀγνοουμένου ὁμοιότητα μικράν τε καὶ μεγάλην ἐν τοῖς ἄλλοις διαγιγνώσκειν;—'Αδύνατον.—Οὐκοῦν τοῖς παρὰ τὰ ὄντα δοξάζουσι καὶ ἀπατωμένοις δῆλον ὡς τὸ πάθος τοῦτο δι' ὁμοιοτήτων τινῶν εἰσερρύη.—Γίγνεται γοῦν οὕτως.—Ἔστιν οὖν ὅπως τεχνικὸς ἔσται μεταβιβάζειν κατὰ σμικρὸν διὰ τῶν ὁμοιοτήτων, ἀπὸ τοῦ ὄντος ἑκάστοτε ἐπὶ

τοὐναντίον ἀπάγων, ἢ αὐτὸς τοῦτο διαφεύγειν, ὁ μὴ ἐγνωρικὼς ὃ ἔστιν ἕκαστον τῶν ὄντων;—Οὐ μή ποτε.—Λόγων ἄρα τέχνην, ὦ ἑταῖρε, ὁ τὴν ἀλήθειαν μὴ εἰδώς, δόξας δὲ τεθηρευκώς, γελοίαν τινά, ὡς ἔοικε, καὶ ἄτεχνον παρέξεται.—Κινδυνεύει. Phædrus, 98. 'The power of deceiving and avoiding deception requires an exact knowledge of likenesses and unlikenesses; and unless a man knows the true object, he cannot discriminate the degrees of likeness to it in other objects. As, then, false belief and error arise from likeness, the art of leading away through gradations of likeness from the true to the false, and of avoiding being thus misled, is impossible without a knowledge of realities; and an argumentative art, armed with opinions instead of knowledge, is an absurdity and not truly an art.' The knowledge that Plato requires for didactic may be divided into two portions, science and logic; corresponding to the two portions into which law is divided by the jurist, the substantive code and the code of procedure. Part will consist of specific doctrines (ἴδιαι ἀρχαί), and belongs to the man of science, Euclid or Archimedes: part of generic theorems, rather method than doctrine (κοιναὶ ἀρχαί), and belongs to the dialectician. Accordingly Aristotle bases dialectic on the definition of genuine confutation (ἀληθὴς ἔλεγχος), and makes solution proceed by division and discrimination (διαίρεσις). But, in addition to this, didactic requires similar definitions and divisions of the ἴδιαι ἀρχαί. See Appendix E on the limits of pirastic.

3] The common sources of probable proof are enumerated in the Topica.

4] Does ἔχομεν δὲ παρ' ὁπόσα γίνονται mean that the enstasis is derived from the same topics as the proof; or does it mean that in some lost chapters the varieties of enstasis had been examined? A phrase of the Rhetoric seems to establish the latter view: Αἱ δ' ἐνστάσεις φέρονται, καθάπερ ἐν τοῖς τοπικοῖς, τετραχῶς. Rhet. 2. 25.

5] Καὶ τοὺς φανερομένους [ἐλέγχους] is connected, after a long parenthesis, with τὸν δ' ἐκ τῶν κοινῶν καὶ ὑπὸ μηδεμίαν τέχνην [ἔλεγχον] τῶν διαλεκτικῶν [ἐστὶ θεωρεῖν].

CHAPTER X.

1] Of the name of the theorist now criticised, and the precise nature of his theory, we have no information; and without this information it is difficult to decide whether Aristotle's arguments are conclusive, and what is their precise drift. If we may trust a partly unintelligible fragment of Eudemus quoted by Simplicius, the theorist criticised in this chapter is no other than Plato himself: Ἔστι δὲ, ὥς ἔοικε, τὸ διορίζειν ἕκαστον ποσαχῶς λέγεται μέγα πρὸς ἀλήθειαν. Πλάτων τε γὰρ εἰσαγαγὼν τὸ δισσὸν πολλὰς ἀπορίας ἔλυσε, πράγματων ὧν νῦν οἱ σοφισταὶ καταφεύγουσιν ὥσπερ ἐπὶ τὰ εἴδη, καὶ πρὸς τούτοις τοὔνομα τῶν λόγων ἀφώρισε. Simplicius on Phys. Ausc. 1. 2. 'To distinguish the various meanings of equivocal terms is a great step in speculation. For Plato solved many difficulties by introducing the doctrine of various meanings...... and banished words from proof [distinguished reasoning addressed to the word from reasoning addressed to the thought?].' But it would be rash to place much reliance on a corrupt fragment, and it would be strange if Aristotle spoke of Plato as 'certain persons.' The theorist seems to have hit, somewhat vaguely, upon the distinction between word-thinking and object-thinking, and to have held that the source of all error is word-thinking.

The substance of Aristotle's criticism seems to be this:—

(1) The trains of word-thinking and object-thinking are parallel: the same ratiocination may belong to both trains: and it is impossible to say when it belongs to each. But if the trains constituted two classes of reasoning, they ought to be contradistinguished and mutually exclusive.

(2) Thought requires some further limitation to express object-thinking. All word-thinking is thinking. The expression, addressed to the thought, therefore, is insufficient to exclude word-thinking.

(3) The fact of being addressed to the thought is only an external relation of an argument, its relation to the respondent. But the relations of a thing may vary by the change of its correlatives, while the thing itself remains unchanged. They are its most extrinsic and accidental attributes, and cannot form the principle of its subdivision.

But, it may be answered, are there not some arguments whose essential nature is such that they cannot be represented by a train of object-thought? Yes: and these are recognized under the head of fallacies in diction. But there is another class of reasonings, independent of diction, and therefore belonging possibly to the train of object-thinking, which are yet fallacious.

2] So read for οἰόμενος ἐρωτᾶσθαι ἐφ' ᾧ.

3] After σημαίνειν insert τὸ ἓν σημαῖνον.

4] The amphibolous reasoning about speech of the speechless (ch. iv) is conclusive with an ambiguous minor term, that is, the conclusion does not contradict the thesis.

The homonymous argument about Homer has an ambiguous middle, and therefore is inconclusive.

In saying that the fallacy of the argument in figura dictionis lies both in the sequence and in the contradiction, Aristotle seems to mean, that we have the option of treating the conclusion as contradictory but not legitimate, or as legitimate but not contradictory. Thus: Thesis:—It is impossible to give what one has not got. Confutation:—It is possible to give but few, having many: to give but few, having many, is to give *as* one has not got (see ch. xxii): therefore it is possible to give *as* one has not got. This conclusion is valid, but does not contradict the thesis. The conclusion, Therefore it is possible to give *what* one has not got, contradicts the thesis but does not follow from the premisses.

The defects of accidens and consequens (illicit process and undistributed middle) and petitio principii lie in the sequence: of ignoratio elenchi and non causa pro causa in the contradiction: of secundum quid and verbal fallacies, sometimes in the contradiction, sometimes in the sequence. We may distinguish, then, between conclusive syllogism and conclusive confutation. For in the second of these classes the syllogism is conclusive, the confutation inconclusive.

5] This is a resumption of the second of his former positions: viz. that a reasoning with unambiguous terms is not addressed to the thought if the respondent thinks them ambiguous.

6] This is a resumption of the first of his former positions: viz. that a reasoning with ambiguous terms is addressed to the thought if the respondent thinks them unambiguous. What

CHAP. X.   NOTES.   125

Aristotle says amounts to this: Word-thinking is thinking; and, after one has given the respondent the option of assenting or dissenting or distinguishing, it cannot be pretended that one has not come at his real belief or thought.

7] Read εἶτα ἐρωτησάτω τις, or, εἶτα ἐρωτήσαντος.

8] This seems to imply that the theorist maintained all object-thinking to be infallible, and all confutation confined to the sphere of word-thinking, and more or less invalid.

9] Aristotle elsewhere has himself used the antithesis which he now so severely criticizes. Χρήσιμον δὲ τὸ μὲν ποσαχῶς λέγεται ἐπισκέφθαι πρὸς τὸ γίνεσθαι κατ' αὐτὸ τὸ πρᾶγμα καὶ μὴ πρὸς τὸ ὄνομα τοὺς συλλογισμούς. Ἀδήλου γὰρ ὄντος ποσαχῶς λέγεται, ἐνδέχεται μὴ ἐπὶ ταὐτὸν τόν τε ἀποκρινόμενον καὶ τὸν ἐρωτῶντα φέρειν τὴν διάνοιαν. Ἐμφανισθέντος δὲ ποσαχῶς λέγεται καὶ ἐπὶ τί φέρων τίθησι, γελοῖος ἂν φαίνοιτο ὁ ἐρωτῶν, εἰ μὴ πρὸς τοῦτο τὸν λόγον ποιοῖτο. Χρήσιμον δὲ καὶ πρὸς τὸ μὴ παραλογισθῆναι καὶ πρὸς τὸ παραλογίσασθαι ... Τοῦτο δ' οὐκ ἐπὶ πάντων δυνατόν, ἀλλ' ὅταν ᾖ τῶν πολλαχῶς λεγομένων τὰ μὲν ἀληθῆ τὰ δὲ ψευδῆ. Topica, 1. 18. 'The use to the respondent of knowing the different significations of a name is to confine the reasoning to the real object of thought and prevent it from merely bearing on the words. For if the varieties of signification are not known, the questioner and answerer may be thinking of different objects: but when the respondent has pointed out the different significations and which he intends in his premiss or thesis, it would be ridiculous in the questioner to direct his reasoning to a different object. The use to the questioner is, if the answerer is ignorant of the different significations, to construct a paralogism....This can only be done when a proposition is true in one sense and false in another.' Οὐ γὰρ πρὸς τὸν ἔξω λόγον ἡ ἀπόδειξις, ἀλλὰ πρὸς τὸν ἐν τῇ ψυχῇ, ἐπεὶ οὐδὲ συλλογισμός· ἀεὶ γὰρ ἔστιν ἐνστῆναι πρὸς τὸν ἔξω λόγον, ἀλλὰ πρὸς τὸν ἔσω λόγον οὐκ ἀεί. Analytica Posteriora, 1. 10. ' Proof and demonstration hinge, not on the expressed, but on the conceived premiss. The expressed premiss is always open to enstasis, the conceived premiss not always.' If the answerer can often oppose to the expressed premiss, ἔξω λόγος, of the questioner an enstasis which is unavailable against the intended premiss, ἔσω λόγος; surely the questioner also can often construct with the expressed concession

of the answerer or direct against his expressed thesis, ἕω λόγος, a proof which is impossible with the intended concession or unavailable against the intended thesis. "Ὅτι μὲν οὖν ἀπὸ τῆς αὐτῆς εἰσὶ διανοίας ἀμφότεροι οἱ λόγοι, δῆλον. Ἔστι δ' οὐχ ὁ αὐτὸς τρόπος πρὸς ἅπαντας τῆς ἐντεύξεως· οἱ μὲν γὰρ πειθοῦς δέονται, οἱ δὲ βίας. Ὅσοι μὲν γὰρ ἐκ τοῦ ἀπορῆσαι ὑπέλαβον οὕτως, τούτων εὐίατος ἡ ἄγνοια· οὐ γὰρ πρὸς τὸν λόγον ἀλλὰ πρὸς τὴν διάνοιαν ἡ ἀπάντησις αὐτῶν. Ὅσοι δὲ λόγου χάριν λέγουσι, τούτων δ' ἔλεγχος ἴασις τοῦ τ' ἐν τῇ φωνῇ λόγου καὶ τοῦ ἐν τοῖς ὀνόμασιν. Metaphysica, 3, 5. 'The doctrines that the same thing can be and not be, and that all opinions are true, are clearly the same in principle: but all disputants are not to be encountered by the same method, for some require persuasion, others violence. Where the opinion is the result of honest doubts it is an error which can easily be healed. For here we have to encounter not words but convictions [or, if ἀπάντησις is the act of the respondent, For here the opposition is not addressed to our words but to our meaning]. Where it is merely maintained from the love of disputation, the only remedy is confutation of the expressed and verbal thesis by the expressed and verbal concessions.' Here we have an admission from Aristotle that in certain controversies his own arguments would be addressed not to the thought of the respondent but to his words. He considers the axiom or principle of contradiction a necessary proposition and one that is necessarily believed. If, then, it is denied by a respondent and we argue in its defence, we cannot address his thought, that is, argue against his conviction, for he has no conviction to be argued against. In the passage from the Metaphysic, Aristotle speaks with confidence of confuting the contradictor of the axiom, though he admits it would be difficult: but the passage from the Analytic, which refers to the same subject, implies that the verbal triumph would remain with the respondent who denied the axiom.

The different expressions of Aristotle respecting the antithesis, addressed to the word, addressed to the thought, seem, however, to be reconcilable. He does not deny the existence of the antithesis, but denies that it constitutes a differentia of arguments (οὐκ ἔστι διαφορὰ τῶν λόγων) of so intrinsic and essential a character as to be fit to form the basis of a classification.

10] Ποιεῖν has MS. authority and seems more natural than

CHAP. XI.   NOTES.   127

παθεῖν, which is Bekker's reading. Whichever we read, the sense is the same. The following proposition is only true where both the units and twos are taken collectively. If we take either distributively, we affirm that each unit or each two is equal to four.

11] In ch. xv. the questioner is recommended to distinguish and divide and exclude from his propositions any objectionable interpretation in order to anticipate objection and obtain without trouble the necessary premisses. But of course he would only do this for his own purposes, that is, with the premisses capable of being honestly employed, not with the premisses charged with the fallacy. In ch. xvii. Aristotle goes further, and admits that a confutation, where the respondent is taken by surprise in consequence of overlooking distinctions, is not genuine: and that, at all events, if the respondent is limited to answering Yes or No, the distinctions ought to be drawn by the questioner. Νῦν δὲ διὰ τὸ μὴ καλῶς ἐρωτᾶν τοὺς πυνθανομένους ἀνάγκη προσαποκρίνεσθαί τι τὸν ἐρωτώμενον, διορθοῦντα τὴν μοχθηρίαν τῆς προτάσεως, ἐπεί, διελομένου γε ἱκανῶς, ἢ ναὶ ἢ οὒ ἀνάγκη λέγειν τὸν ἀποκρινόμενον.

Didactic reasoning differs from pirastic because the didactic reasoner is supposed to be in possession of the truth: it differs from apodictic or scientific reasoning because, apparently, there is but one genuine scientific proof of each theorem, whereas didactic reasoning must be accommodated to the capacity and character of the learner. The true problem of the Phædrus is the investigation of didactic method; which seems to prove that this dialogue was not an early Platonic composition, but written after Plato thought he had said enough on the nature of the elenchus or negative dialectic.

CHAPTER XI.

1] Φαινόμενος περὶ ὧν is the same as φαινόμενος κατὰ τὸ πρᾶγμα above, and φαινόμενος περὶ τῶνδε below. In fact, περὶ τῶνδε has probably slipped out before φαινόμενος in the present passage. A man may be confuted and yet not proved to be in the wrong on the point in dispute. He may be right in his special facts, which may alone be important, but appear to be confuted by failing to detect some slight mis-statement of a metaphysical premiss, which is ill-apprehended because it is abstract, and is

not really an element of the doctrine in question. This species of sophistic proof was discussed in ch. viii.

2] Συλλογισμοί would be a better reading, for the proofs in question are not paralogisms. Παραλογισμοί, however, may stand, for the proofs in question may be compared either with scientific proof or with the pseudographema, and the pseudographema is a paralogism (παραλογιστικὸς ἐξ ὡρισμένου τινὸς γένους ἀρχῶν below). The second species of sophistic proof simulates scientific proof as the first simulated pirastic. We have not yet had it in this treatise (except in note 5 to ch. vi), but it is alluded to in the Analytic: Ἐπίστασθαι δὲ οἰόμεθ' ἕκαστον ἀπλῶς, ἀλλὰ μὴ τὸν σοφιστικὸν τρόπον τὸν κατὰ συμβεβηκός, ὅταν τήν τ' αἰτίαν οἰώμεθα γινώσκειν δι' ἣν τὸ πρᾶγμά ἐστιν, ὅτι ἐκείνου αἰτία ἐστί, καὶ μὴ ἐνδέχεσθαι τοῦτ' ἄλλως ἔχειν. An. Post. 1. 2. 'Science absolute, as opposed to sophistic science or accidental proof, is the knowledge of the cause and necessity of a law.' Neither the cause nor the necessity can be exposed by any but essential or commensurate premisses. Accidental premisses, then, will be sophistic. Ἐπεὶ δ' ἐξ ἀνάγκης ὑπάρχει περὶ ἕκαστον γένος ὅσα θκα' αὐτὰ ὑπάρχει καὶ ᾗ ἕκαστον, φανερὸν ὅτι περὶ τῶν καθ' αὐτὰ ὑπαρχόντων αἱ ἐπιστημονικαὶ ἀποδείξεις καὶ ἐκ τῶν τοιούτων εἰσί. Τὰ μὲν γὰρ συμβεβηκότα οὐκ ἀναγκαῖα, ὥστ' οὐκ ἀνάγκη τὸ συμπέρασμα εἰδέναι διότι ὑπάρχει... τὸ δὲ διότι ἐπίστασθαι ἐστι τὸ διὰ τοῦ αἰτίου ἐπίστασθαι. Δι' αὐτὸ ἄρα δεῖ καὶ τὸ μέσον τῷ τρίτῳ καὶ τὸ πρῶτον τῷ μέσῳ ὑπάρχειν. An. Post. 1. 6. 'Essential attributes furnish the only necessary propositions and must form the premisses and conclusions of scientific demonstration. Accidents are contingent and cannot exhibit the reason or cause of a necessary law. Both the major and minor premiss, then, must be essential.' Διὰ τοῦτο οὐδ' ἂν τις δείξῃ καθ' ἕκαστον τὸ τρίγωνον ἀποδείξει ἢ μιᾷ ἢ ἑτέρᾳ ὅτι δύο ὀρθὰς ἔχει ἕκαστον, τὸ ἰσόπλευρον χωρὶς καὶ τὸ σκαληνὲς καὶ τὸ ἰσοσκελές, οὔπω οἶδε τὸ τρίγωνον ὅτι δύο ὀρθαῖς, εἰ μὴ τὸν σοφιστικὸν τρόπον, οὐδὲ καθόλου τρίγωνον, οὐδ' εἰ μηθὲν ἔστι παρὰ ταῦτα τρίγωνον ἕτερον. Οὐ γὰρ ᾗ τρίγωνον οἶδεν. An. Post. 1. 5. 'If one were to prove in detail of each species of triangle, equilateral, scalene, isosceles, the equality of their interior angles to two right angles, he might exhaust the possible cases, but his predicate would not be essential and commensurate, and he would only have a sophistical science.'

NOTES.

To complete the statement of Aristotle's view, it should be added that essential propositions are those whose predicate cannot be defined without naming the subject, or whose subject cannot be defined without naming the predicate. Καθ' αὑτὰ δὲ (λέγω) ὅσα ὑπάρχει τε ἐν τῷ τί ἐστιν, οἷον τριγώνῳ γραμμὴ καὶ γραμμῇ στιγμή. ἡ γὰρ οὐσία αὐτῶν ἐκ τούτων ἐστί, καὶ ἐν τῷ λόγῳ τῷ λέγοντι τί ἐστιν ἐνυπάρχει· καὶ ὅσοις τῶν ἐνυπαρχόντων αὐτοῖς αὐτὰ ἐν τῷ λόγῳ ἐνυπάρχουσι τῷ τί ἐστι δηλοῦντι· οἷον τὸ εὐθὺ ὑπάρχει γραμμῇ καὶ τὸ περιφερές, καὶ τὸ περιττὸν καὶ ἄρτιον ἀριθμῷ, καὶ τὸ πρῶτον καὶ σύνθετον καὶ ἰσόπλευρον καὶ ἑτερόμηκες· καὶ πᾶσι τούτοις ἐνυπάρχουσιν ἐν τῷ λόγῳ τῷ τί ἐστι λέγοντι ἔνθα μὲν γραμμὴ ἔνθα δ' ἀριθμός......Τὰ ἄρα λεγόμενα ἐπὶ τῶν ἁπλῶς ἐπιστητῶν καθ' αὑτὰ οὕτως, ὡς ἐνυπάρχειν τοῖς κατηγορουμένοις ἢ ἐνυπάρχεσθαι, δι' αὑτά τέ ἐστι καὶ ἐξ ἀνάγκης. An. Post. 1. 4. 'An attribute is essential that enters into the conception of the subject, as line enters into the conception of triangle and point of line. It helps to compose the essence of the subject, and is found in its definition. Or, it is an attribute in whose definition the subject is contained. Straight and curved are attributes of line; and even and odd, prime and compound, square and scalene, of number; and we cannot define them without mentioning the subjects they attach to, line and number......In the essential premisses, then, of absolute science, where the subject is either contained in the definition of the predicate, or contains the predicate in its own definition, the essence of the terms is the cause of their conjunction and the conjunction is necessary.' A modern logician might admit that, as a condition of science, we must have propositions of causation, and that in causal propositions the antecedent and consequent terms must bear to one another a certain definite relation; but he would insist that the test of this relation was not definition, but the inductive methods of agreement and difference. To reconcile these doctrines it would be necessary to assert that these methods are methods of definition. But even then a difference would remain. For the modern logician would be satisfied by an objective relation, discovered by experience: while Aristotle seems further to require a subjective relation, viz. such that it should be impossible to conceive one of the terms without at the same time conceiving the other.

3] I do not know what distinction is intended between ψευ-

κ

δογράφημα and ψευδογράφημα περὶ ἀληθές, unless it is that of art and science. It is evident that the quadrature of the circle by lunules was not the method of Hippocrates, as is generally supposed. His method was what Aristotle elsewhere calls the method of segments (see Appendix F). The problem of squaring the circle, i. e. of finding a square whose area shall equal that of a given circle, long occupied the scientific world, and, like the problem of perpetual motion, was a favourite arena of the unscientific long after the scientific had pronounced it insoluble. Modern mathematicians are agreed that it cannot be solved by arithmetic or geometry, the only methods of the ancients, and requires the method of infinitesimals. See an article on the quadrature of the circle, by De Morgan, in the National Encyclopedia. Aristotle seems to have suspected it was insoluble from his expression, Εἰ καὶ τετραγωνίζεται ὁ κύκλος: in the Categories he asserts that it had not been solved in his day: "Ἔτι τὸ μὲν ἐπιστητὸν ἀναιρεθὲν συναναιρεῖ τὴν ἐπιστήμην, ἡ δὲ ἐπιστήμη τὸ ἐπιστητὸν οὐ συναναιρεῖ......οἷον καὶ ὁ τοῦ κύκλου τετραγωνισμὸς εἴ γε ἔστιν, ἐπιστήμη μὲν αὐτοῦ οὐκ ἔστιν οὐδέπω, αὐτὸς δὲ ἐπιστητόν ἐστιν. Cat. 7. 'Without a knowable there can be no knowledge, but without knowledge there may be a knowable: if, for instance, the quadrature of the circle is possible, it is knowable, though at present it is not known.'

4] Κατὰ τὸ πρᾶγμα here means more than it did in the beginning of the chapter, where its force was limited by the words τὰ κοινά. There it meant, necessarily connected with a subject, though not coextensive with it. Here it is equivalent to κατὰ τὴν οἰκείαν μέθοδον, and means coextensive, or commensurate, with a given sphere.

5] So read, as the sense requires, for τὸν γεωμέτρην.

6] Here μὲν is followed by no corresponding clause, and the text is doubtless corrupt. We might add, after δῆλον, ἀλλὰ κἂν περὶ τὰ γεωμετρικὰ εἴη, or we might read, ὁ δ' ὑπὸ τὴν διαλεκτικήν. Περὶ μέντοι τἆλλα ὅτι ἐριστικός ἐστι, δῆλον, or something equivalent. In the first case τἆλλα would mean τὰ κοινά, in the second case it would mean τὰ ἴδια, or, rather, τὰ γεωμετρικά. In any case the drift is certain, viz. that the same problem, e. g. the quadrature of the circle, may be handled either in a sophism or in a pseudographeme.

7] Ἁρμόττειν, or ἐφαρμόττειν, is a technical term in describing dialectical proof. Ἔστι γὰρ οὕτω δεῖξαι ὥσπερ Βρύσων τὸν τετραγωνισμόν. Κατὰ κοινόν τι γὰρ δεικνύουσιν οἱ τοιοῦτοι λόγοι, ὃ καὶ ἑτέρῳ ὑπάρξει· διὸ καὶ ἐπ᾽ ἄλλων ἐφαρμόττουσιν οἱ λόγοι οὐ συγγενῶν. Οὐκοῦν οὐχ ᾗ ἐκεῖνο ἐπίσταται, ἀλλὰ κατὰ συμβεβηκός· οὐ γὰρ ἂν ἐφήρμοττεν ἡ ἀπόδειξις καὶ ἐπ᾽ ἄλλο γένος. An. Post. 1. 9. 'Such a proof, like Bryso's squaring of the circle, as it may conclude by a cause that is not confined to the given subject, but is found in other genera, is transferable to a heterogeneous subject-matter. But if the essence of the subject and not an accident is the cause of knowledge, the demonstration is not transferable to any other genus.' The paraphrast says, 'Ὁ δ᾽ ἀπό τινων κοινοτέρων καὶ ὑπερβαινόντων καὶ πολλοῖς ἁρμοζόντων γένεσιν ἐριστικός. For ὑπερβαινόντων [transcendent] Aristotle would have said, μεταβαινόντων. Ὥστ᾽ ἢ ἀπλῶς ἀνάγκη τὸ αὐτὸ εἶναι γένος ἢ πῇ, εἰ μέλλει ἡ ἀπόδειξις μεταβαίνειν. An. Post. 1. 7. 'Two subjects must be the same in species or genus, if a demonstration can be transferred from the one to the other.'

8] Καθόλου must be taken in the sense in which it is described in the Analytic, as equivalent to καθ᾽ αὑτό, and therefore ὁ καθόλου will mean ὁ ἐκ τῶν ἰδίων ἀρχῶν ἀποδεικτικός. Even the philosopher (ὁ φιλόσοφος) who has the most comprehensive sphere must deal with his problems commensurately and essentially (καθόλου, καθ᾽ αὑτό), and therefore is limited in his premisses and conclusions. Unlike the dialectician, he has nothing to say to geometrical problems.

9] Τὰς δ᾽ αὐτὰς ἀρχὰς ἁπάντων εἶναι τῶν συλλογισμῶν ἀδύνατον. ......Ἕτεραι γὰρ πολλῶν τῷ γένει αἱ ἀρχαὶ καὶ οὐδ᾽ ἐφαρμόττουσαι. Analytica Posteriora, 1.32. 'The principles of all deduction are not identical......They are heterogeneous and vary with the subject, and are inapplicable beyond their respective spheres.' The constitution of philosophy imagined by those who maintained the unity of first principles was probably such as we have in Hegel's system, where the laws of physic and ethic are repetitions of the laws of the development of reason laid down in the logic; or in Herbert Spencer's philosophy, where the theorems of ethical and natural science are exemplifications of the general laws of evolution and its component processes of differentiation and integration, which themselves are again affiliated

on a primary axiom of the persistence of force, a principle which very much resembles, if it is not identical with, the Aristotelian axiom.

In the Metaphysic we are told that though all being does not belong to a single genus (καθόλου, καθ' ἕν), yet as referrible to a common standard (πρὸς ἕν) it belongs to a single science, philosophy. Τὸ δὲ ὂν λέγεται μὲν πολλαχῶς, ἀλλὰ πρὸς ἓν καὶ μίαν τινὰ φύσιν, καὶ οὐχ ὁμωνύμως.... Οὐ μόνον δὲ [περὶ] τῶν καθ' ἓν λεγομένων ἐπιστήμης ἐστὶ θεωρῆσαι μιᾶς, ἀλλὰ καὶ τῶν πρὸς μίαν λεγομένων φύσιν.... Δῆλον οὖν ὅτι καὶ τὰ ὄντα μιᾶς θεωρῆσαι ᾗ ὄντα ..... καὶ εἰ μή ἐστι τὸ ὂν ἢ τὸ ἓν καθόλου καὶ ταὐτὸ ἐπὶ πάντων ἢ χωριστόν, ὥσπερ ἴσως οὐκ ἔστι. Metaphysica, 3. 2. 'The meanings of being, though heterogeneous, are referred to one standard, and the word is not equivocal. As not only homogeneous subjects, or those that are denoted by a univocal name, belong to one science, but also all that are related to a common standard, the essential attributes of being will be investigated by a single science, though being may not be a genus or a separate entity.' Dialectic resembles philosophy in the wideness of its range: Ἐπεὶ ὥσπερ ἔστι καὶ ἀριθμοῦ ᾗ ἀριθμὸς ἴδια πάθη.... ὁμοίως δὲ καὶ στερεῷ.... ἔστιν ἕτερα ἴδια, οὕτω καὶ τῷ ὄντι ᾗ ὄν ἔστι τινὰ ἴδια, καὶ ταῦτ' ἐστὶ περὶ ὧν τοῦ φιλοσόφου ἐπισκέψασθαι τἀληθές. Σημεῖον δέ· οἱ γὰρ διαλεκτικοὶ καὶ σοφισταὶ ταὐτὸν μὲν ὑποδύονται σχῆμα τῷ φιλοσόφῳ· ἡ γὰρ σοφιστικὴ φαινομένη μόνον σοφία ἐστί, καὶ οἱ διαλεκτικοὶ διαλέγονται περὶ ἁπάντων· κοινὸν δὲ πᾶσι τὸ ὄν ἐστι, διαλέγονται δὲ περὶ τούτων δῆλον ὅτι διὰ τὸ τῆς φιλοσοφίας εἶναι αὐτὰ οἰκεῖα. Περὶ μὲν γὰρ τὸ αὐτὸ γένος στρέφεται ἡ σοφιστικὴ καὶ ἡ διαλεκτικὴ τῇ φιλοσοφίᾳ, ἀλλὰ διαφέρει τῆς μὲν τῷ τρόπῳ τῆς δυνάμεως, τῆς δὲ τοῦ βίου τῇ προαιρέσει. Ἔστι δὲ ἡ διαλεκτικὴ πειραστικὴ περὶ ὧν ἡ φιλοσοφία γνωριστική, ἡ δὲ σοφιστικὴ φαινομένη, οὖσα δ' οὔ. Metaph. 3. 2. 'As number and solidity have certain essential attributes, which are examined by particular sciences, so being has certain essential attributes, which are investigated by philosophy. For dialectic and sophistic assume the garb of philosophy. Their range is universal; and being, the theme of philosophy, is universal. The other two deal with the universe of being because it is the proper sphere of philosophy. For philosophy has the same sphere as sophistic and dialectic; but differs from dialectic in the nature of her power, from sophistic

in the aim of her life: for she is scientific, while dialectic is pirastic, [or, as Grote would say, she is positive and dogmatic, while dialectic is negative and sceptical,] and sophistic a sham.' But philosophy is restricted to scientific methods, and has appropriate problems; dialectic is unrestricted in problem and process. Dialectic proof, therefore, differs not only from scientific, but also from philosophic proof: and the sophism differs from the philosophic as well as from the scientific pseudographema.

10] This seems to be the point of connexion with the preceding chapter. We saw there that some theorist had identified dialectic and didactic. But they must be distinct: for didactic, ex vi termini, proves something or other; dialectic is merely pirastic, and proves nothing. It interrogates, that is, is willing to accept a denial of any truth whatever, and therefore cannot prove any single conclusion. If, like the sciences, dialectic proved any theorems, dialectic, like the sciences, whatever other problems it left open, would refuse to allow the truth of its principles to be called in question. Didactic then, though conversational in form, is not, in the true sense of the word, ἐρωτητική. Perhaps for ὥστε we should read ἔτι or ἔπειτα; for the train of thought seems to be, that even if there were a universal science, it could not be dialectic, because dialectic interrogates.

11] In the mathematics it is possible not only by synthesis to obtain compound formulas by composition of elementary formulas, but also by analysis from formulas respecting the compound to obtain by decomposition a knowledge of the elementary factors. But though the pirastic reasoner must possess some derivative propositions respecting the subject-matter; must know, for instance, that the thesis advanced by the respondent is false, and that certain deducible consequences are impossible; yet these propositions are not such as to enable him to deduce from them by analytical reasoning the primary laws that govern the subjects and attributes in question. Otherwise pirastic would imply science; for knowledge of a conclusion as deducible from the primary laws is science. Compare, Εἰ δ' ἦν ἀδύνατον ἐκ ψευδοῦς ἀληθὲς δεῖξαι, ῥᾴδιον ἂν ἦν τὸ ἀναλύειν. Ἀντιστρέφει γὰρ ἂν ἐξ ἀνάγκης. Ἔστω γὰρ τὸ Α ὄν, τούτου δ' ὄντος ταδί ἐστιν,

ἃ οἶδα ὅτι ἔστιν, οἷον τὸ B· ἐκ τούτων ἅμα δείξω ὅτι ἔστιν ἐκεῖνο. Ἀντιστρέφει δὲ μᾶλλον τὰ ἐν τοῖς μαθήμασιν, ὅτι οὐδὲν συμβεβηκὸς λαμβάνουσιν, ἀλλὰ καὶ τούτῳ διαφέρουσι τῶν ἐν τοῖς διαλόγοις, ἀλλ' ὁρισμούς. Anal. Post. 1. 12. 'If true conclusions never resulted from false premisses, it would be easy to obtain by analytical reasoning the principles on which any theorem depends. For the principles and theorem would be related to one another as the terms of a convertible proposition. If the antecedent A involves the consequent B, when I knew the existence of B I might infer the existence of A. This reciprocal demonstration is more common in science than in dialectic, for the premisses of science are never accidents but definitions.'

12] The introduction of the word nature (φύσις) may remind us of a negative definition of logic in the pantheistic system of Hegel, where logic is defined to be reason before the creation of the world, or, reason antecedent to nature; the three successive transformations of reason being logical truth, nature, and morality. In the passage before us, however, φύσις includes moralities as well as laws of nature.

13] It appears that a pseudographema would be legitimate in pirastic: for if the respondent could not solve it, it would prove his ignorance of the science (ποιεῖ δῆλον εἰ ἀγνοεῖ, ch. viii). The pseudographema, however, does not belong to pirastic; for pirastic is not supposed to have sufficient knowledge of scientific principles to construct a pseudographema.

Pirastic proof is intermediate between sophistic proof and scientific proof. The former has no particularity (ἴδιον); the latter no universality (κοινόν); pirastic has both particularity and universality. Scientific proof cannot be extended beyond its private sphere: sophistic confutation proves no ignorance in a particular sphere: pirastic confutation tests knowledge in a particular sphere by principles applicable to every sphere. Ὁ κατὰ τὸ πρᾶγμα, i. e. ἰδίως, θεωρῶν τὰ κοινά, πειραστικός. See above. For a further examination of τὰ κοινά see Appendix D. Whately has divided fallacies into logical and extra-logical. We shall see in Appendix D that this division will not bear examination. Aristotle's division is into dialectical (σοφίσματα) and extra-dialectical or scientific (ψευδογραφήματα). If we define dialectic to be opinionative reasoning and logic the science

CHAP. XII. NOTES. 135

of proof, we may divide dialectical fallacies into logical and extra-logical, but logical will include all that Whately considers extra-logical.

CHAPTER XII.

1] Ἔτι ὁ σοφιστικὸς τρόπος, τὸ ἄγειν εἰς τοιοῦτον πρὸς ὃ εὐπορήσομεν ἐπιχειρημάτων. Τοῦτο δ' ἔσται ὁτὲ μὲν ἀναγκαῖον, ὁτὲ δὲ φαινόμενον ἀναγκαῖον, ὁτὲ δὲ οὔτε φαινόμενον οὔτε ἀναγκαῖον. Ἀναγκαῖον μὲν οὖν ὅταν, ἀρνησαμένου τοῦ ἀποκρινομένου τῶν πρὸς τὴν θέσιν τι χρησίμων, πρὸς τοῦτο τοὺς λόγους ποιῆται, τυγχάνῃ δὲ τοῦτο τοιοῦτον ὂν πρὸς ὃ εὐπορεῖν ἐστιν ἐπιχειρημάτων. Ὁμοίως δὲ καὶ ὅταν, ἀπαγωγὴν πρός τι διὰ τοῦ κειμένου ποιησάμενος, ἀναιρεῖν ἐπιχειρῇ· τούτου γὰρ ἀναιρεθέντος καὶ τὸ προκείμενον ἀναιρεῖται. Φαινόμενον δὲ ἀναγκαῖον, ὅταν φαίνηται μὲν χρήσιμον καὶ οἰκεῖον τῆς θέσεως, μὴ ᾖ δὲ, πρὸς ὃ γίγνονται οἱ λόγοι, εἴτε ἀρνησαμένου τοῦ τὸν λόγον ὑπέχοντος, εἴτε ἀπαγωγῆς ἐνδόξου διὰ τῆς θέσεως πρὸς αὐτὸ γινομένης ἀναιρεῖν ἐπιχειρεῖ αὐτά· τὸ δὲ λοιπόν, ὅταν μήτε ἀναγκαῖον ᾖ μήτε φαινόμενον πρὸς ὃ γίνονται οἱ λόγοι, ἀλλ' ὡς δὲ παρεξελέγχεσθαι συμβαίνῃ τῷ ἀποκρινομένῳ. Δεῖ δὲ εὐλαβεῖσθαι τὸν ἔσχατον τῶν ῥηθέντων τρόπων· παντελῶς γὰρ ἀπηρτημένος καὶ ἀλλότριος ἔοικεν εἶναι τῆς διαλεκτικῆς. Διὸ δεῖ καὶ τὸν ἀποκρινόμενον μὴ δυσκολαίνειν, ἀλλὰ τιθέναι τὰ μὴ χρήσιμα πρὸς τὴν θέσιν, ἐπισημαινόμενον ὅσα μὴ δοκεῖ μέν, τίθησι δέ. Μᾶλλον γὰρ ἀπορεῖν ὡς ἐπιτοπολὺ συμβαίνει τοῖς ἐρωτῶσιν, ὅταν πάντων τιθεμένων αὐτοῖς τῶν τοιούτων μὴ περαίνωσιν. Topica, 2. 5. 'There is also the sophistic method of leading the respondent on to ground where attack is easy. This is sometimes really necessary, sometimes apparently necessary, sometimes neither really nor apparently. It is really necessary when a premiss directly bearing on the thesis is denied by the respondent and happens to be easy for the questioner to argue: or when the questioner has deduced a consequence from the thesis and argues to prove its absurdity. It is apparently necessary if the proposition only appears to be an appropriate premiss or necessary consequence of the thesis. When neither really nor apparently necessary, it may give an opportunity for a collateral or by-confutation. The last method must be avoided, for it is quite alien to dialectic. When it is practised, the respondent should not be obstructive, but grant

every proposition that is unconnected with the thesis, observing that he is willing to grant it for the sake of argument, though he knows it to be false. For the questioner is the more discomfited, if notwithstanding the most liberal admissions he fails to confute the thesis.' The second case, which Aristotle implies may be practised by the dialectician, shews the affinity of dialectic and sophistic, for the locus, so far at least as it consists of reductio ad absurdum, is the fallacy of non causa pro causa.

2] i. e. ἐν τῇ τῶν προτάσεων ἐκλογῇ. See Topics, 1. 14. Though dialectic is characterized by its metaphysical principles (οὐσία), sometimes called forms of thought, yet it must always have special premisses (ἴδια), which some have called its matter, and Aristotle its materials (ὄργανα). As they are extraneous to the art of dialectic, they are dismissed in the Topics with the remark that a collection (ἐκλογή) must be made of them. They are here called pre-eminently premisses (προτάσεις), because the universal maxims, though often treated as premisses, are usually suppressed, and are often viewed not as premisses, but as regulative principles, or precepts for the conduct of argument. Στοιχεῖον or τόπος is elsewhere opposed to the εἴδη or special premisses; here the collection of εἴδη is called a στοιχεῖον. Thesis is here used not for any tenet defended by the respondent, but in the special sense of paradox. See Topica, t. 11.

CHAPTER XIII.

1] I do not see how else to translate the text. But there is no relation of genus and species in the first example: for double and double of half are not so related. We might construct a syllogism respecting duplicity, containing the relation of genus and species, thus: Double is equivalent to multiple of a half; therefore double of a half is multiple of a half of a half. But this would not involve iteration ad infinitum, like the first example.

2] Perhaps ἡ οὐσία should be cancelled. It is not a proper term to express the subject of an attribute, and the words ὧν and τούτοις shew that the nominative to προσδηλοῦται is a plural. Accordingly, Waitz proposes for ἡ οὐσία to read τὰ ὑποκείμενα.

The predicates described are one of the two classes of essential predicates investigated by science. See ch. xi, note 2.

3] Aristotle says that double, in the expression double of a half, is not exactly equivalent to double placed independently. The other fallacy consists in falsely defining odd as if it were odd number.

CHAPTER XIV.

1] For ἡ πτῶσις we require, ἡ ἄρρενος ἢ θήλεος κλῆσις, 'the masculine and feminine termination or form.' See below.

2] For λεγομένοις read λέγεσθαι, or read γινομένοις and after ὁμοίως understand λέγεσθαι or ἑρμηνεύεσθαι.

3] In figura dictionis the same form is common to different categories, e. g. the substantive name, nomen substantivum, to substances and accidents: in the fallacy of solecism the same form is common to the nominative and accusative. In figura dictionis we are cheated into an error of fact: in the fallacy of solecism we are cheated into a wrong grammatical construction. The employment of the word solecism, which properly means an impropriety of diction or a violation of grammar, to express an impropriety of action or a violation of some practical science, has become a common metaphor. Referring to ch. iv. we shall see that one of the instances of amphibolia would furnish a fallacy of solecism: Ἆρα τοῦτο, ὃ ὁρᾷ Κορίσκος, ὁρᾷ; τοῦτο δὲ εἴων· ὥστε ὁρᾷ ὁ Κορίσκος, οὐ κίονα ἀλλά, εἴων.

4] In the Rhetoric Aristotle treats of invention, expression, and arrangement. Τρία ἐστὶν ἃ δεῖ πραγματευθῆναι περὶ τὸν λόγον, ἓν μὲν ἐκ τίνων αἱ πίστεις ἔσονται, δεύτερον δὲ περὶ τὴν λέξιν, τρίτον δὲ πῶς χρὴ τάξαι τὰ μέρη τοῦ λόγου. Rhetoric, 3. 1. In the Topics he treats of invention and arrangement. Μέχρι μὲν οὖν τοῦ εὑρεῖν τὸν τόπον ὁμοίως τοῦ φιλοσόφου καὶ τοῦ διαλεκτικοῦ ἡ σκέψις. Τὸ δ' ἤδη ταῦτα τάττειν καὶ ἐρωτηματίζειν ἴδιον τοῦ διαλεκτικοῦ· πρὸς ἕτερον γὰρ πᾶν τὸ τοιοῦτον. Τῷ δὲ φιλοσόφῳ καὶ ζητοῦντι καθ' ἑαυτὸν οὐδὲν μέλει, ἐὰν ἀληθῆ μὲν ᾖ καὶ γνώριμα δι' ὧν ὁ συλλογισμός, μὴ θῇ δ' αὐτὰ ὁ ἀποκρινόμενος διὰ τὸ σύνεγγυς εἶναι τοῦ ἐξ ἀρχῆς καὶ προορᾶν τὸ συμβησόμενον· ἀλλ' ἴσως κἂν σπουδάσειεν ὅτι μάλιστα γνώριμα καὶ σύνεγγυς εἶναι τὰ ἀξιώματα· ἐκ τούτων γὰρ οἱ ἐπιστημονικοὶ συλλογισμοί. Topics, 8. 1. 'Invention of the

method of argument belongs to philosophy and dialectic alike: the arrangement and shaping of the questions to dialectic alone. The philosopher and solitary inquirer, when he has discovered true and evident premisses, has no trouble from the refusal of the respondent to grant them, because they bear immediately on the problem, and manifestly confute his thesis. He is glad to have them connected as closely and evidently as possible with the problem; for so they must be in scientific proof.' From the contents of the following chapter it appears that τάξις expresses rather tactics than simply arrangement.

CHAPTER XV.

1] For ἐλέγχειν read λανθάνειν.

2] It seems that Aristotle was capable of giving precepts for lengthiness, but they are not extant, unless he refers to what he said about unnecessary propositions in the Topica, 8. 1.

3] Various methods of concealment are given in the Topica, 8. 1. E. g. to keep back till the last moment the conclusions of the inductions and prosyllogisms that furnish the premisses of confutation (μὴ διαρθρωθέντων τῶν προτέρων συλλογισμῶν); to leave the subject of dispute and obtain concessions respecting its correlatives or paronyms (τὰ σύστοιχα); to smuggle in the important premiss with a quantity of irrelevant matter (ἐν παραβύστῳ προστιθέντες καθάπερ οἱ ψευδογραφοῦντες); &c.

4] Ἔτι διὰ τῆς ὁμοιότητος συνθάνεσθαι· καὶ γὰρ πιθανὸν καὶ λανθάνει μᾶλλον τὸ καθόλου. Οἷον ὅτι ὥσπερ ἐπιστήμη καὶ ἄγνοια τῶν ἐναντίων ἡ αὐτή, οὕτω καὶ αἴσθησις τῶν ἐναντίων ἡ αὐτή, ἢ ἀνάπαλιν, ἐπειδὴ αἴσθησις ἡ αὐτή, καὶ ἐπιστήμη. Τοῦτο δ' ἐστὶν ὅμοιον ἐπαγωγῇ, οὐ μὴν ταὐτόν γε. Ἐκεῖ μὲν γὰρ ἀπὸ τῶν καθ' ἕκαστα τὸ καθόλου λαμβάνεται, ἐπὶ δὲ τῶν ὁμοίων οὐκ ἔστι τὸ λαμβανόμενον τὸ καθόλου ὑφ' ὃ πάντα τὰ ὅμοιά ἐστι. Topica, 8. 1. 'Another method of concealment is to reason by similitude, that is, to reason directly from particulars to similar particulars. The reasoning is persuasive and the immediate premiss is not disclosed. For instance, as the intellectual appreciation or non-appreciation of contraries is identical and simultaneous, so is the sensational, and vice versa. The mode of proof resembles induction, but differs, because it does

not express the universal proposition, but passes at once to the particular conclusion.' This mode of reasoning has lately risen to distinction. Mill considers it the true or natural type of all reasoning, induction and syllogism being artificial. Grote finds here the long-sought criterion between true opinion and knowledge: true opinion, so far as it is not merely a lucky guess but founded on evidence, passing immediately from particulars to particulars without recognizing the intermediate law. See his comment on the Meno. After ἀλλὰ in the text perhaps we should add ἀνώνυμον.

5] Καὶ τὰ ὀλιγάκις ὀλίγα, so read, comparing ch. xxiv, for καὶ τὸ πολλάκις πολλά.

6] In the Rhetoric this artifice is given as the fallacy figura dictionis. Τόποι δ' εἰσὶ τῶν φαινομένων ἐνθυμημάτων εἷς μὲν ὁ παρὰ τὴν λέξιν, καὶ τούτου ἓν μὲν μέρος ὥσπερ ἐν τοῖς διαλεκτικοῖς τὸ μὴ συλλογισάμενον συμπερασματικῶς τὸ τελευταῖον εἰπεῖν, οὐκ ἄρα τὸ καὶ τό, ἀνάγκη ἄρα τὸ καὶ τό. Καὶ τὸ τοῖς ἐνθυμήμασιν [οἰκεῖον?] τὸ συνεστραμμένως καὶ ἀντικειμένως εἰπεῖν φαίνεται ἐνθύμημα. Ἡ γὰρ τοιαύτη λέξις χώρα ἐστὶν ἐνθυμήματος. Καὶ ἔοικε τὸ τοιοῦτον εἶναι παρὰ τὸ σχῆμα τῆς λέξεως. Rhet. 2. 24. 'One locus of seeming oratorical proof is diction. One division of this is, as in dialectic, without proving to conclude in the language of proof: "It follows, then, that this must be true:" "It follows, then, that that must be false." For crowded and antithetical propositions look like proof, because such diction is the vehicle of proof: and the fallacy is figura dictionis.'

7] Ἂν δ' ἑτέρου δόξαν διαφυλάττῃ ὁ ἀποκρινόμενος, δῆλον ὅτι πρὸς τὴν ἐκείνου διάνοιαν ἀποβλέποντα θετέον ἕκαστα καὶ ἀρνητέον. Διὸ καὶ οἱ κομίζοντες ἀλλοτρίας δόξας, οἷον ἀγαθὸν καὶ κακὸν εἶναι ταὐτόν, καθάπερ Ἡράκλειτός φησιν, οὐ διδόασι μὴ παρεῖναι ἅμα τῷ αὐτῷ τἀναντία, οὐχ ὡς οὐ δοκοῦν αὐτοῖς τοῦτο, ἀλλ' ὅτι καθ' Ἡράκλειτον οὕτω λεκτέον. Topics, 8. 5. 'When the respondent defends the tenet of another person, the opinions of that person are the standard of what he ought or ought not to admit. Accordingly, the advocate of a dogma which he himself does not hold,—for instance, that good and evil are identical, as Heraclitus said,—will not grant that contraries cannot coexist; not because he disbelieves it, but because it is inconsistent with the system of Heraclitus.' In the text προκείμενον seems to signify,

not, as usually, the thesis, but the conclusion of the argument, i. e. the contradictory of the thesis. So in Topica, θ. 5: 'Αδόξου γὰρ οὔσης τῆς θέσεως ἔνδοξον τὸ συμπέρασμα· ὥστε δεῖ τὰ λαμβανόμενα ἔνδοξα πάντ' εἶναι καὶ μᾶλλον ἔνδοξα τοῦ προκειμένου, εἰ μέλλει διὰ τῶν γνωριμωτέρων τὸ ἧττον γνώριμον περαίνεσθαι. 'If the thesis is improbable, the conclusion of the disproof is originally probable; therefore all the premisses ought to be probable in a still higher degree, in order to fulfil the conditions of proof.'

8] Ἄλλος (τόπος ἐνθυμήματος) ἐκ κρίσεως περὶ τοῦ αὐτοῦ ἢ ὁμοίου ἢ ἐναντίου, μάλιστα μὲν εἰ πάντες καὶ ἀεί, εἰ δὲ μή, ἀλλ' οἵ γε πλεῖστοι, ἢ σοφοὶ ἢ πάντες ἢ οἱ πλεῖστοι, ἢ ἀγαθοί, ἢ εἰ αὐτοὶ οἱ κρίνοντες, ἢ οἷς ἀποδέχονται οἱ κρίνοντες, ἢ οἷς μὴ οἷόν τε ἐναντίον κρίνειν, οἷον τοῖς κυρίοις, ἢ οἷς μὴ καλὸν τὰ ἐναντία κρίνειν, οἷον θεοῖς ἢ πατρὶ ἢ διδασκάλοις. Rhet. 2. 23. 'Another topic of argument is authority, or the decision on an identical, similar, or opposite question, either of all the world, or of the majority of the world, or of all philosophers, or of the majority of philosophers, or of the good, or of the judges, or of those whom the judges accept as authorities, or of those whose decision cannot be rescinded, as of a superior tribunal, or of those whom it is immoral to disregard, as the gods, or parents, or teachers.'

9] Τὰ ἐπιχειρήματα ἐπιτέμνειν is to cut down the propositions (ἐπιχειρήματα) so as to disarm the respondent of his enstasis. Πρὸς δὲ τοὺς ἐπισταμένους τῷ καθόλου, μὴ ἐν αὐτῷ δὲ τὴν ἔνστασιν φέροντας ἀλλ' ἐν τῷ ὁμωνύμῳ, διελόμενον ἐρωτητέον. . . . Ἐὰν δὲ μὴ ἐν τῷ ὁμωνύμῳ ἀλλ' ἐν αὐτῷ ἐπιστάμενος κωλύῃ τὴν ἐρώτησιν, ἀφαιροῦντα δεῖ ἐν ᾧ ἡ ἔνστασις προτείνειν τὸ λοιπὸν καθόλου ποιοῦντα. . . Οὐ μόνον δ' ἐπισταμένου τοῦτο ποιητέον, ἀλλὰ κἂν ἄνευ ἐνστάσεως ἀρνῆται διὰ τὸ προορᾶν τι τῶν τοιούτων· ἀφαιρεθέντος γὰρ ἐν ᾧ ἡ ἔνστασις, ἀναγκασθήσεται τιθέναι διὰ τὸ μὴ προορᾶν ἐν τῷ λοιπῷ ἐπὶ τίνος οὐχ οὕτως. Ἐὰν δὲ μὴ τιθῇ, ἀπαιτούμενος ἔνστασιν οὐ μὴ ἔχῃ ἀποδοῦναι. Topica, θ. 2. 'If the respondent opposes a premiss by an enstasis, availing himself of an equivocation, the questioner must distinguish. If the enstasis is not founded on equivocation, he must cut off from the proposition the portion open to enstasis, and propose what remains as a universal. He must do this even when the answerer adduces no enstasis, but simply denies the proposition, because he perceives the possibility of an enstasis. When the exceptionable portion has been excluded,

the proposition must be granted, for the answerer can no longer adduce an enstasis.'

10] So read for πρός τι ἐπιχειρεῖν. Compare ἀπαιτοῦνται γάρ, εἰ τοῦτο πρὸς τὸ ἐν ἀρχῇ; ch. viii.

CHAPTER XVI.

1] For διαλῦσαι read κωλῦσαι. The former would be a very ill chosen term to express a process opposite to analysis and analogous to synthesis.

CHAPTER XVII.

1] At first sight ὁρατῶν seems to be a false reading for ὁμωνύμων. But ὁρατῶν may stand. Aristotle is not speaking of all equivocation (he would hardly say that all involved inevitable confutation) but of a particular species, i.e. when one proper name belongs to several individuals. These individuals, according to Aristotle, cannot be distinguished by any artifice of nomenclature.

2] Τὸ τοῦτον τὸν Κορίσκον. So read for τὸ τὸν τὸν Κορίσκον.

3] The formulas of dialectic, now obsolete, were not long ago household terms, as the following quotation may shew:—

' Mais le quadrille aussi, Monsieur de la Garonne,
   Est un jeu du hasard.'—
                        ' Madame, *distinguo:*
   Pour l'honnête personne,
   Oh ! vraiment, *concedo ;*
   Mais pour la gent friponne,
                        Nego.'
                        Le Sage, *L'Espérance* (acted 1730).

4] For ποιεῖ τις read ἐποίει τις, or ἐποιεῖτο. It seems that some logician had maintained that a single answer should be given to an equivocal question if it is true in both interpretations, though he also held that a single answer should never be returned to several questions. Against this logician Aristotle says that every fallacy of homonymia or amphibolia may be regarded as a fallacy plurium interrogationum.

5] Aristotle asserted this before in the beginning of the

chapter, but he has not justified it, unless we take what was said about τῶν ὁρατῶν to be a justification. But this, if it proved anything, proved that sometimes there is no true solution, not that a false solution is to be preferred to the true. It is not easy to see how he could justify it, except on the ground that a fallacious solution is often cleverer than the true one, and therefore to be preferred in a trial of skill. See however ch. xxxiv, note 3.

6] Read ὅταν δὴ.

7] Ἔστι δὲ ἐπ' ἐνίων μὲν ἐπάγοντα δυνατὸν ἐρωτῆσαι τὸ καθόλου. Ἐπ' ἐνίων δὲ οὐ ῥᾴδιον διὰ τὸ μὴ κεῖσθαι ταῖς ὁμοιότησιν ὄνομα πάσαις κοινόν, ἀλλ' ὅταν δέῃ τὸ καθόλου λαβεῖν, Οὕτως ἐπὶ πάντων τῶν τοιούτων, φασί· τοῦτο δὲ διορίσαι τῶν χαλεπωτάτων, ὁποῖα τῶν προφερομένων τοιαῦτα καὶ ὁποῖα οὔ. Καὶ παρὰ τοῦτο πολλάκις ἀλλήλους παρακρούονται κατὰ τοὺς λόγους οἱ μὲν φάσκοντες ὅμοια εἶναι τὰ μὴ ὄντα ὅμοια, οἱ δὲ ἀμφισβητοῦντες τὰ ὅμοια μὴ εἶναι ὅμοια. Διὸ πειρατέον ἐπὶ πάντων τῶν τοιούτων ὀνοματοποιεῖν αὐτόν, ὅπως μήτε τῷ ἀποκρινομένῳ ἐξῇ ἀμφισβητεῖν ὡς οὐχ ὁμοίως τὸ ἐπιφερόμενον λέγεται, μήτε τῷ ἐρωτῶντι συκοφαντεῖν ὡς ὁμοίως λεγομένου ἐπειδὴ πολλὰ τῶν οὐχ ὁμοίως λεγομένων ὁμοίως φαίνεται λέγεσθαι. Topica, 8. 1. 'In induction it is sometimes difficult to word the generalization, because the point of similarity in the particulars has not been denoted in popular language by a common name. In generalizing we say, And so in all like cases, or, And so in all the members of the class. But it is excessively difficult to define the class or determine what particulars are like: and hence many fallacies arise, one party maintaining the likeness of what is unlike, the other the unlikeness of what is like. We ought therefore ourselves to invent a name for the class, that the answerer may be unable to pretend the unlikeness of what is like, or the questioner the likeness of what is unlike, for what is really unlike often appears to be like.' It is curious to see the fundamental problem of induction treated so incidentally and perfunctorily. The definition of the antecedent term of a generalization is spoken of as if it were merely the process of inventing a name. It is really the problem, which Aristotle would allow to be all-important in science, of distinguishing essential (καθ' αὑτό) and accidental propositions, or, as we should now say with Mill, of eliminating chance from causal conjunc-

tions, and can only be solved by the methods of agreement and difference.

8] Ἀποφάνσεις. So read for ἀποφάσεις, the perpetual error of the scribes.

9] Perhaps for ποτέρως ἔχει τἀληθές, we should read ποτέρως ἔχει τὸ σύνηθες, i. e. ποτέρως εἴωθε λέγεσθαι. But τἀληθές, though an ill-selected word, may be the right reading, for it may refer to τὰς ἀληθεῖς δόξας, which occurs above. It would denote the real or symbolized meaning as opposed to the figure or imagery. The theorem that the side and diagonal of a square are incommensurate is demonstrated by Euclid, 10. 97, and is alluded to by Aristotle: Περὶ δὲ τῶν ἀιδίων οὐδεὶς βουλεύεται, οἷον περὶ τοῦ κόσμου, ἢ τῆς διαμέτρου καὶ τῆς πλευρᾶς ὅτι ἀσύμμετροι. Eth. Nic. 3. 3. We might suppose there was an allusion to the ambiguity of the terms, ἡ διάμετρος ἀσύμμετρος, which may express either that the diagonal and side of a square, or that the diameter and circumference of a circle, are incommensurate. The latter proposition was probably stumbled on by those who were seeking a method of squaring the circle; for they discovered that the area of the circle equals half the rectangle of the radius and circumference. But the interpretation given in the text seems better.

There is a similarly constructed period in Topica, 8. 3 : Τῶν δὲ ὅρων δυσεπιχειρητότατοι πάντων εἰσὶν ὅσοι κέχρηνται τοιούτοις ὀνόμασιν ἃ πρῶτον μὲν ἄδηλά ἐστιν εἴτε ἁπλῶς εἴτε πολλαχῶς λέγεται, πρὸς δὲ τούτοις μηδὲ γνώριμα πότερον κυρίως ἢ κατὰ μεταφορὰν ὑπὸ τοῦ ὁρισαμένου λέγεται· διὰ μὲν γὰρ τὸ ἀσαφῆ εἶναι οὐκ ἔχει ἐπιχειρήματα, διὰ δὲ τὸ ἀγνοεῖσθαι εἰ παρὰ τὸ κατὰ μεταφορὰν λέγεσθαι τοιαῦτ' ἐστίν, οὐκ ἔχει ἐπιτίμησιν. 'Of all definitions the most difficult to attack are those whose terms raise a doubt, firstly, whether they are ambiguous or unambiguous, and secondly, whether they bear their proper sense or are metaphors. The doubt whether they are ambiguous saves the definition from confutation as false, and the doubt whether they bear their proper sense saves it from condemnation as metaphorical.'

CHAPTER XVIII.

1] Ψευδὴς δὲ λόγος καλεῖται τετραχῶς· ἵνα μὲν τρόπον ὅταν φαίνηται συμπεραίνεσθαι μὴ συμπεραινόμενος, ὃς καλεῖται συλλογισμὸς ἐριστικός. Ἄλλον δὲ ὅταν συμπεραίνηται μέν, μὴ μέντοι πρὸς τὸ προκείμενον, ὅπερ συμβαίνει μάλιστα τοῖς εἰς τὸ ἀδύνατον ἄγουσιν. Ἢ πρὸς τὸ προκείμενον μὲν συμπεραίνηται, μὴ μέντοι κατὰ τὴν οἰκείαν μέθοδον· τοῦτο δέ ἐστιν ἐὰν ὁ μὴ ὢν ἰατρικὸς δοκῇ ἰατρικὸς εἶναι, ἢ γεωμετρικὸς μὴ ὢν γεωμετρικός, ἢ διαλεκτικὸς μὴ ὢν διαλεκτικός, ἄν τε ψεῦδος ἄν τε ἀληθὲς ᾖ τὸ συμβαῖνον. Ἄλλον δὲ τρόπον ἐὰν διὰ ψευδῶν συμπεραίνηται· τούτου δὲ ἔσται ποτὲ μὲν τὸ συμπέρασμα ψεῦδος ποτὲ δὲ ἀληθές. Topica, 8. 10. 'False proof is of four kinds: firstly, inconclusive or eristic proof: secondly, conclusive but irrelevant proof, which chiefly occurs in reductio ad absurdum: thirdly, relevant proof by an inappropriate method, i. e. proof that has a false pretence of being physiological or geometrical or dialectical, though it has a true conclusion: fourthly, proof from false premisses, whether the conclusion is true or false.' The first class is inconclusive syllogism. The second class is inconclusive confutation, including non causa pro causa and ignoratio elenchi (see ch. x, note 4). The third class is simulated pirastic proof or simulated scientific proof, and may be identified with one of the significations of accidental or incommensurate proof (ch. vi, note 5). The exposure of this class of fallacy is beyond the competence of pirastic, and demands science or at least education (see Appendix E). The fourth class is dialectic, sophistic, or pseudographic, according as the false premiss is a special opinion, a general maxim, or a special theorem. Perhaps Aristotle would also call it dialectic, if the general maxim was a really probable hypothesis. The first two classes exhaust the thirteen paralogisms. All the classes are sophistic, though the fourth class includes some members which are not. The sophistic members of the fourth class are discussed in chap. viii, where, however, they are not distinguished from the fallacies of the third class. Are there any confutations which fall under the third class and not also under the fourth, that is, which are sophistic and yet conclusive and constructed of true premisses? It is difficult to conceive any

thing that fulfils these conditions except the confutation of a geometer, who is seduced into advancing an ungeometrical thesis. He would scarcely do this deliberately, but he might in the heat of a discursive debate, and would then expose himself to a by-confutation (παρεξέλεγχος). We might, however, regard this as a case of non causa pro causa, that is, of the second class. See the mention of by-confutation in ch. xii, note 1.

2] Here the disproof of a conclusion is called counterproof, and spoken of as a solution of the argument in support of that conclusion. This is not only manifestly inadmissible, but is flatly contradicted by Aristotle himself in ch. xxiv. 'Something more than the exposure of a fault is required in solution, for the falsity of the conclusion may be demonstrated without explaining why the reasoning is fallacious. To solve Zeno's proof of the impossibility of motion, we ought not to try to prove the opposite, for though we gave ten thousand valid proofs, this would be no solution, for it would not expose where the falsity of his argument lies.' Elsewhere Aristotle clearly implies that antisyllogism or counterproof (he uses the synonymous term ἀντεπιχειρεῖν) is directed not against the conclusion but against a premiss. 'Επεὶ δὲ πᾶσα πρότασις συλλογιστικὴ ἢ τούτων τίς ἐστιν ἐξ ὧν ὁ συλλογισμός, ἢ τινος τούτων ἕνεκα (δῆλον δ' ὅταν ἑτέρου χάριν λαμβάνηται τῷ πλείω τὰ ὅμοια ἐρωτᾷν ἢ γὰρ δι' ἐπαγωγῆς ἢ δι' ὁμοιότητος ὡς ἐπὶ τὸ πολὺ τὸ καθόλου λαμβάνουσι)· τὰ μὲν καθέκαστα πάντα θετέον, ἂν ᾖ ἀληθῆ καὶ ἔνδοξα, πρὸς δὲ τὸ καθόλου πειρατέον ἔνστασιν φέρειν. Τὸ γὰρ ἄνευ ἐνστάσεως ἢ οὔσης ἢ δοκούσης κωλύειν τὸν λόγον δυσκολαίνειν ἐστίν. Εἰ οὖν ἐπὶ πολλῶν φαινομένων οὐ δίδωσι τὸ καθόλου μὴ ἔχων ἔνστασιν, φανερὸν ὅτι δυσκολαίνει. Ἔτι δὲ εἰ μηδ' ἀντεπιχειρεῖν ἔχοι ὅτι οὐκ ἀληθές, μᾶλλον ἂν δόξειε δυσκολαίνειν. Καίτοι οὐδὲ τοῦθ' ἱκανόν· πολλοὺς γὰρ λόγους ἐναντίους ἔχομεν ταῖς δόξαις οὓς χαλεπὸν λύειν· καθάπερ τοῦ Ζήνωνος ὅτι οὐκ ἐνδέχεται κινεῖσθαι οὐδὲ τὸ στάδιον διελθεῖν· ἀλλ' οὐ διὰ τοῦτο τὰ ἀντικείμενα τούτοις οὐ θετέον. Εἰ οὖν μήτε ἀντεπιχειρεῖν ἔχων μήτε ἐνίστασθαι οὐ τίθησι, δῆλον ὅτι δυσκολαίνει. Ἔστι γὰρ ἡ ἐν λόγοις δυσκολία ἀπόκρισις παρὰ τοὺς εἰρημένους τρόπους συλλογισμοῦ φθαρτική. Topics, 8. 7. 'All propositions are premisses of the final proof, or premisses of these premisses, as the particulars adduced in induction and similitude. These particulars must

be admitted if they are true, and the universal inference opposed by enstasis. To resist an inference without adducing an enstasis, real or apparent, is perversity, or irrational obstructiveness. To resist without even adducing a counterproof, is still greater perversity. Yet even this would be insufficient, for many proofs of paradoxes are hard to solve, like Zeno's about motion, and yet the respondent (in arguing on a different question) is bound to admit the opposite. If, then, the respondent refuses to admit a premiss without adducing either enstasis or counterproof, he is undeniably perverse. For logical perversity is withstanding proof without one of these modes of justification.' The same is implied in the Rhetoric : Τὰ δὲ πρὸς τὸν ἀντίδικον οὐχ ἕτερόν τι εἶδος, ἀλλὰ τῶν πίστεων ἐστι τὰ μὲν λῦσαι ἐνστάσει τὰ δὲ συλλογισμῷ..... ὕστερον δὲ λέγοντα πρῶτον τὰ πρὸς τὸν ἐναντίον λόγον λεκτέον, λύοντα καὶ ἀντισυλλογιζόμενον, καὶ μάλιστα ἂν εὐδοκιμηκότα ᾖ. ὥσπερ γὰρ ἄνθρωπον προδιαβεβλημένον οὐ δέχεται ἡ ψυχή, τὸν αὐτὸν τρόπον οὐδὲ λόγον, ἐὰν ὁ ἐναντίος εὖ δοκῇ εἰρηκέναι. δεῖ οὖν χώραν ποιεῖν ἐν τῷ ἀκροατῇ τῷ μέλλοντι λόγῳ· ἔσται δέ, ἂν ἀνέλῃς. Rhetoric, 2. 17. ' The portion of a speech which answers an opponent is not a separate kind of proof, but is a solution of his argument by enstasis and antisyllogism........The orator who speaks second should first encounter his opponent's argument by enstasis and antisyllogism, at least if it was effective. For as a person against whom we are prepossessed finds our mind closed against him, so does an argument after an effective speech of the adversary. Room therefore must be made in the hearer's mind for the coming proof, and this can only be by upsetting the adversary's argument.' Here ἀντισυλλογισμός is contrasted with ὁ μέλλων λόγος. It therefore can only signify opposition to the opponent's premisses : for if it was opposition to his conclusion it would be identical with ὁ μέλλων λόγος. This question is continued in the following note.

3] ' As was said before' must refer, not to Topica, 8. 8, quoted in last note, but to what immediately precedes. Ἡ ὧδε ἢ ὧδε, therefore, means that the ἀναίρεσις applies either to the premiss or to the conclusion. Here, then, we are in a difficulty : for no logician could suppose that an argument is solved by another argument in support of an opposite conclusion. The following seems to be the explanation. The disproof of the conclusion of

a prosyllogism, though no solution of that prosyllogism, is a solution of any subsequent syllogism in which the conclusion of that prosyllogism figures as a premiss. In fact, every premiss that the questioner wishes to obtain must be supported by induction, therefore every refusal of the answerer to admit a premiss is the rejection of an inductive conclusion. Ὅταν δ' ἐπάγοντος ἐπὶ πολλῶν μὴ διδῷ τὸ καθόλου, τότε δίκαιον ἀπαιτεῖν ἔνστασιν. Μὴ εἰπόντα δ' αὐτὸν ἐπὶ τίνων οὕτως, οὐ δίκαιον ἀπαιτεῖν ἐπὶ τίνων οὐχ οὕτως· δεῖ γὰρ ἐπάγοντα πρότερον οὕτω τὴν ἔνστασιν ἀπαιτεῖν. ...'Ἐὰν δ' ἐπὶ πολλῶν προτείνοντος μὴ φέρῃ ἔνστασιν, ἀξιωτέον τιθέναι· διαλεκτικὴ γάρ ἐστι πρότασις πρὸς ἣν οὕτως ἐπὶ πολλῶν ἔχουσαν μὴ ἔστιν ἔνστασις. Topica, 8. 2. 'When the questioner has made an induction by many particular instances, if the universal is not admitted, he has a right to ask for an enstasis or contradictory instance. Before he himself has adduced supporting instances he has no right to ask for contradictory instances. The induction must be made before the enstasis can be demanded. When many particulars can be alleged in support of a premiss and no contradictory ones against it, the universal proposition must be granted. For in dialectic that is a good proposition which is supported by many examples, and to which no exception can be alleged.' It appears, then, that enstasis and antisyllogism do not differ because one attacks a premiss and the other a conclusion, but because they attack the same premiss in a different manner. For more on the nature of enstasis see Appendix D.

CHAPTER XIX.

1] Thus: to speak of stones is possible, to speak of stones is speech of the speechless, therefore speech of the speechless is possible.

2] Συνεπίστασθαι is not explained by the lexicons, and we have no means of conjecturing the nature of the fallacy. But we may observe that it did not depend on any double meaning of ἐπίστασθαι, i.e. on homonymia, as we might imagine from what is said below, for we are here told it was a case of amphibolia.

3] Suppose Appius to be blind: then, to see Appius is possible, to see Appius is sight of the blind, therefore sight of the blind is possible.

When the conclusion is ambiguous, the sophist must take care to get it denied before he proves it, or it will be admitted and ridiculed as a truism. E. g. Πότερον δὲ ὁρῶσιν, ἔφη ὁ Εὐθύδημος, καὶ Σκύθαι καὶ οἱ ἄλλοι ἄνθρωποι τὰ δυνατὰ ὁρᾶν ἢ τὰ ἀδύνατα; Τὰ δυνατὰ δήπου. Οὐκοῦν καὶ σύ, ἔφη. Κἀγώ. Ὁρᾷς οὖν τὰ ἡμέτερα ἱμάτια; Ναί. Δυνατὰ οὖν ὁρᾶν ἐστι ταῦτα; Ὑπερφυῶς, ἔφη ὁ Κτήσιππος. Τί δέ; ἦ δ' ὅς. Μηδέν. Σὺ δ' ἴσως οὐκ οἴει αὐτὰ ὁρᾶν. Οὕτως ἡδὺς εἶ. Ἀλλά μοι δοκεῖς, Εὐθύδημε, οὐ καθεύδων ἐπικεκοιμῆσθαι. Euthydemus, § 67. 'Is what the Scythians and other people see able to be seen (able to see) or unable?—Able.—And what you see too?—What I see too.—Do you see our dress?—Yes.—Is our dress able to see (able to be seen)?—Certainly.—Why you don't mean to say—Yes I do. Did you think it was not able to be seen? What a noodle you are! Why, Euthydemus, you must be sleeping with your eyes open.'

4] A proposition or proof is said to be addressed to a term (πρὸς τοῦτο) when that term is the subject of the proposition or of the conclusion. Εἶναι μὲν συλλογισμὸν οὐδὲν κωλύει, πρὸς μέντοι τὸ Β οὐκ ἔσται διὰ τῶν εἰλημμένων.....Ὁ μὲν γὰρ συλλογισμὸς ἁπλῶς ἐκ προτάσεών ἐστιν, ὁ δὲ πρὸς τόδε συλλογισμὸς ἐκ τῶν πρὸς τόδε προτάσεων, ὁ δὲ τοῦδε πρὸς τόδε διὰ τῶν τοῦδε πρὸς τόδε προτάσεων. Ἀδύνατον δὲ πρὸς τὸ Β λαβεῖν πρότασιν μηδὲν μήτε κατηγοροῦντας αὐτοῦ μήτ' ἀπαρνουμένους. Analytica Priora, 1. 23. 'We may prove something, but not respecting this term, from these premisses. For all proof is from premisses, proof respecting a given term from premisses addressed to that term, proof connecting a given predicate with a given term from premisses addressed to that term, and relating to that predicate. When a premiss is addressed to a term, that term must be a subject on which the premiss imposes, or from which it removes, some predicate.' Ὅλως δὲ τὴν πρὸς τῷ μείζονι ἄκρῳ πρότασιν οὐκ ἔστιν ἀνασκευάσαι καθόλου διὰ τῆς ἀντιστροφῆς, ἀεὶ γὰρ ἀναιρεῖται διὰ τοῦ τρίτου σχήματος, ἀνάγκη γὰρ πρὸς τὸ ἔσχατον ἄκρον ἀμφοτέρας λαβεῖν τὰς προτάσεις. Anal. Priora, 2. 8. 'The contrary of the major premiss cannot be proved by the minor premiss and the contrary of the conclusion, for the proof is in the third figure, the minor term becoming the middle and being made the subject of both premisses.' Δῆλον δὲ καὶ ὅτι ἐν ἅπασι τοῖς σχήμασιν ὅταν μὴ γίνηται συλλογισμός, κατηγορικῶν μὲν ἢ στερητικῶν ἀμφο-

τέρων ὄντων τῶν ὅρων, οὐδὲν ὅλως γίνεται ἀναγκαῖον, κατηγορικοῦ δὲ καὶ στερητικοῦ, καθόλου ληφθέντος τοῦ στερητικοῦ, ἀεὶ γίνεται συλλογισμὸς τοῦ ἐλάττονος ἄκρου πρὸς τὸ μεῖζον, οἷον εἰ τὸ μὲν Α παντὶ τῷ Β ἢ τινί, τὸ δὲ Β μηδενὶ τῷ Γ. 'Ἀντιστρεφομένων γὰρ τῶν προτάσεων ἀνάγκη τὸ Γ τινὶ τῷ Α μὴ ὑπάρχειν. Anal. Priora, I. 7. 'In all the figures, when the premisses are inconclusive, if one is affirmative and the other universal negative, we get a conclusion by making the major term the subject and the minor the predicate. E. g.

    Some M is P,
    No S is M,
  ∴ Some P is not S,

for conversion of both premisses gives us the first figure.' [Aristotle employs conversion because he did not recognize the fourth figure. Conclusions in which the relation of the major and minor terms is inverted were called by the Schoolmen Indirect moods.]

Sometimes, however, the ὅρος πρὸς ὃν designates the predicate of the conclusion. 'Ἐν ἅπασι γὰρ τοῖς εἰς τὸ ἀδύνατον συλλογισμοῖς ἀνάγκη κοινόν τινα λαβεῖν ὅρον ἄλλον τῶν ὑποκειμένων, πρὸς ὃν ἔσται τοῦ ψεύδους ὁ συλλογισμός, ὥστ' ἀντιστραφείσης ταύτης τῆς προτάσεως, τῆς δ' ἑτέρας ὁμοίως ἐχούσης, δεικτικῶς ἔσται ὁ συλλογισμὸς διὰ τῶν αὐτῶν ὅρων. Anal. Priora, I. 29. 'In reductio ad absurdum we must take a third term distinct from those of the problem, and of this third term prove what is absurd. The contradictory of this conclusion and the other premiss of the reductio are the premisses of ostensive proof.' I. e. supposing no S is P to be proved ostensively thus,

    No M is P,
    All S is M,
  ∴ No S is P,

we may prove it indirectly by combining its contradictory. Some S is P, with either of the ostensive premisses, thus:

    No M is P,
    Some S is P,
  ∴ Some S is not M.
Or   Some S is P,
    All S is M,
  ∴ Some M is P.

In the former case, which is that which Aristotle examines, the

new term, *M*, is the predicate of the false conclusion: in the second case it is the subject. We may observe that in the first of the passages which we have quoted, Aristotle seems for the moment to have overlooked the third figure, for there the minor term (πρὸς ὅν) is the predicate, not the subject, of the minor premiss.

A proof is said to be addressed to a proposition (πρὸς τοῦτο) when that proposition is the conclusion or contradictory of the conclusion. 'Ἐν ἅπασι γὰρ τοῖς ἐξ ὑποθέσεως ὁ μὲν συλλογισμὸς γίνεται πρὸς τὸ μεταλαμβανόμενον, τὸ δ' ἐξ ἀρχῆς περαίνεται δι' ὁμολογίας ἤ τινος ἄλλης ὑποθέσεως. An. Pr. 1. 23. 'In hypotheticals the categorical reasoning is directed to prove the subsumption or condition (the antecedent or contradictory of the consequent) and the original problem is decided by an agreement or hypothesis making the problem depend on the subsumption.' "Ὅταν δ' ᾖ πρὸς τὸ ἀξίωμα καὶ τὴν πρότασιν μεῖζον ἔργον διαλεγῆται ἢ τὴν θέσιν, διαπορήσειεν ἄν τις, πότερον θετέον τὰ τοιαῦτα ἢ οὔ. Topica, 8. 3. 'When a premiss or proposition is harder to prove than the thesis to disprove, it may be doubted whether the respondent ought or ought not to concede the proposition.'

It appears, then, that πρὸς ὅ, when it denotes a term in a syllogism, excludes the middle; when it denotes a proposition, excludes the premisses. In the Analytica περὶ ὅ denotes the subject of demonstration, or minor term; ἅ the predicates, or major terms; ἐξ ὧν, not the middle terms, but sometimes the premisses, sometimes the axioms or syllogistic canons.

5] No English word expresses the ambiguity of δέοντα. For want of a better let us take the word necessary, then we have the syllogism: What is evil ought not to be done, what is evil is necessary, therefore what is necessary ought not to be done.

6] L. e. τὴν θέσιν διορθωτέον. 'Ἐρώτησις at other times denotes a premiss: here it denotes the thesis, or the question by which it is elicited. So in ch. xxii, 'Ὁ μὲν γὰρ ἔδωκεν ἐρωτηθείς, Ἐρωτήσας οὖν ὃ ἔχει, συνάγει ἐπὶ τοῦ ὅσα, Οἱ δ' εὐθὺς τὴν ἐρώτησιν ἀναιροῦντες, and in ch. xxiv, Λύουσι δέ τινες ἀναιροῦντες τὴν ἐρώτησιν. There is the same ambiguity about τὸ κείμενον. In Topica, 1. 4, Aristotle says that a premiss is properly introduced by the formula ἆρα, and a thesis by the formula πότερον, but he himself violates the rule shortly afterwards.

7] For ἔστιν read, or after ἔστω insert, ἀδύνατον.

CHAPTER XX.

1] Therefore he was beaten with eyes and you saw him with a stick. One syllogism will stand thus: What he was beaten with was what you saw him beaten with; what you saw him beaten with was your eyes; therefore he was beaten with your eyes. This we should call an ambiguous middle, if Aristotle in the text had not objected to the term. The other syllogism may stand thus: He was beaten with that with which you saw him; what he was beaten with was a stick; therefore that with which you saw him was a stick. Here the minor is ambiguous.

2] After σημαίνει ἕτερον we may supply or understand, τῷ μέντοι πνεύματι ἕτερον σημαίνει. Λεχθὲν σημαίνει ἕτερον is equivalent to φθόγγον σημαίνει ἕτερον. The passage shows that written signs of accentuation and breathing were an innovation when this treatise was composed.

3] The logician, who reduced all fallacies to equivocation, is probably the person criticized in ch. x, and very likely a Platonist.

4] This fallacy is alluded to in the Rhetoric, but is not explained. "Ἄλλος τόπος τὸ διῃρημένον συντιθέντα λέγειν ἢ τὸ συγκείμενον διαιροῦντα. Ἐπεὶ γὰρ ταὐτὸν δοκεῖ εἶναι οὐκ ὂν ταὐτὸν πολλάκις, ὁπότερον χρησιμώτερον, τοῦτο δεῖ ποιεῖν. Ἔστι δὲ τοῦτο Εὐθυδήμου λόγος, οἷον τὸ εἰδέναι ὅτι τριήρης ἐν Πειραιεῖ ἐστίν, ἕκαστον γὰρ οἶδεν. Rhet. 2. 24. 'Another source of fallacy is composition and division. As a proposition often seems the same when its parts are differently combined, we may combine them as suits our convenience. So Euthydemus argues: You know the fact that there is a trireme in the Piræus, for you know every separate element of the fact.'

5] This is no syllogism, as Aristotle seems to have thought; it is merely a pretence of stating in one sentence what had previously been stated in two. S is good, S is a shoemaker, therefore S is a good shoemaker. Here all the three terms reappear in the quasi conclusion. The same may be said of the next example. Evil is bad, evil is a thing to learn, therefore evil is a bad thing to learn.

6] For σπουδαῖον τὸ μάθημα read σπουδαία ἡ ἐπιστήμη. Μάθημα = τὸ μαθητόν or τὸ ἐπιστητόν.

CHAPTER XXII.

1] Energy or function (thought, sensation) is distinguished from production (κίνησις) because the former is complete in character at every moment of its existence, whereas the latter has not its complete character till it ceases. Pleasure, for instance, is pleasure at every moment, and the sum of a pleasant emotion only differs from the component parts in quantity. The parts are homogeneous to one another and to the whole. But the process called housebuilding is not completely housebuilding till it is finished. Before that time it is foundation-laying, wall-building, roof-constructing, and these stages differ in nature from one another and from the total operation. If the architect has built a house, he is not still building it; but the owner may have used it, and be still using it.

2] For ὃ ἔχει ἔλαβεν read ὃ ἔλαβεν ἔχει, or, ἔχει ὃ ἔλαβεν, and below for ὃ μὴ ἔλαβεν ἔχειν read μὴ ὃ ἔλαβεν ἔχειν.

3] 'Ἐπίτηρσις here signifies the thesis. It is rather an abuse of language to speak of solving a fallacy by contradicting the thesis. To contradict the thesis is not to solve the fallacy, but to admit that the confutation is valid. We were told in ch. xix. that we might, by way of solution, remodel the thesis, when the reasoning disclosed an ambiguity, but here the thesis is not remodelled, it is abandoned.

4] Solution points out the cause of a fallacy, and the cause ought to stand the criteria of causation. The solution ought to satisfy what Mill calls the method of difference. If the state of circumstances indicated by the solution deprives the elenchus of its cogency, the reversal of those circumstances ought to make it valid. No solution, therefore, is true, unless the elenchus becomes sound as soon as we correct the vices the solution indicates. But, in the above cases, we may concede the truth of what the solution alleges to be false, and yet the elenchus remains inconclusive.

5] 'Ἐγράφετο. So read for ἔγραφέ τις. A truth was written; what is written is what was written; therefore what is written is a truth. Here we may place the fallacy: What is bought in the market is eaten; raw meat is bought in the market; there-

CHAP. XXII.   NOTES.   153

fore raw meat is eaten. Or, better in Latin: Quod emisti, comedisti; crudum emisti; ergo crudum comedisti.

6] *Ἃ δὲ οὐχ ἅπαντα.* So read with one of the MSS. for τὸ δ' ἅπαντα. The construction is, ὃ μὲν οἶδεν, ἅπαν ἢ μαθὼν ἢ εὑρὼν οἶδεν· ἃ δὲ οἶδεν, οὐχ ἅπαντα ἢ μαθὼν ἢ εὑρὼν οἶδεν.

Similar to this is the reasoning: Food is necessary to life, corn is food, therefore corn is necessary to life. Food is taken collectively in the major premiss, distributively in the minor. The major does not mean, as Whately says, that some food is necessary to life, i. e. taking some in its logical sense, some particular food; for this would be false, as all food has its substitute.

7] Ὁ τρίτος ἄνθρωπος is the name of an argument directed against the doctrine of Ideas. If, wherever there are similar individuals, we require an idea to account for their common nature, we can set no limit to the multiplication of hypothetical existences. If the likeness of individual men to one another must be explained by an ideal man, then the likeness of the individual men to the ideal man must be explained by a second ideal, and so on, ad infinitum.

8] Ἔκθεσις is used in different senses. In the Analytics it means separating part of the denotation of a term, some of the members of a class, from the rest, and giving them a name. This is one way of reducing Baroko and Bokardo. For instance, let *P* represent the predicate or major, *M* the middle, and *S* the subject or minor; then in Baroko we have the following propositions:

All *P* is *M*,
Some *S* is not *M*,
∴. Some *S* is not *P*.

Separate the portion of *S* which is not *M* and call it *Z*: we then have the following:

All *P* is *M*,
No *Z* is *M*,
∴. No *Z* is *P*;

which is reduced as Camestres. This Aristotle describes as follows: Ἀνάγκη ἐκθεμένοις ᾧ τινὶ ἑκάτερον μὴ ὑπάρχει, κατὰ τούτου ποιεῖν τὸν συλλογισμόν. Ἔσται γὰρ ἀναγκαίως ἐπὶ τούτων. Εἰ δὲ κατὰ τοῦ ἐκτεθέντος ἐστὶν ἀναγκαῖος, καὶ κατ' ἐκείνου τινὸς, τὸ γὰρ

ἐκτεθὲν ὅπερ ἐκεῖνό τί ἐστιν. An. Pr. 1. 8. 'We must isolate that portion of the minor of which the middle and major are denied and make it a new minor. Then the premisses are necessary propositions; and whatever is universally true of the new minor is partially true of the old; for the old is the genus of the new.'

In the present passage ἔκθεσις signifies separating part of the connotation of a term from the rest, the specific from the individual or the generic from the specific; and we are reminded that this may be a purely mental or logical separation, not physical or real.

In the Metaphysica ἔκθεσις is used for real separation. Τοῦτο δ' ἐκίνησε μὲν Σωκράτης διὰ τοὺς ὁρισμούς, οὐ μὴν ἐχώρισέ γε τῶν καθ' ἔκαστον. Καὶ τοῦτο ὀρθῶς ἐνόησεν οὐ χωρίσας. Δηλοῖ δὲ ἐκ τῶν ἔργων· ἄνευ μὲν γὰρ τοῦ καθόλου οὐκ ἔστιν ἐπιστήμην λαβεῖν, τὸ δὲ χωρίζειν αἴτιον τῶν συμβαινόντων δυσχερῶν περὶ τὰς ἰδέας ἐστίν. Οἱ δ' ὡς ἀναγκαῖον εἴπερ ἔσονταί τινες οὐσίαι παρὰ τὰς αἰσθητὰς καὶ ῥεούσας, χωριστὰς εἶναι, ἄλλας μὲν οὐκ εἶχον, ταύτας δὲ τὰς καθόλου λεγομένας ἐξέθεσαν. Met. 12. 9. 'Attention to universals received an impulse from the Socratic definitions: but Socrates did not separate them from particulars, and he did well, as the result shewed. For universals are indispensable to science, but their separation from the objects of sense produces the difficulties of idealism. The idealists saw that substances, if there were any besides the objects of sense, must have a separate existence, and not knowing what else to assign, hypostatized universals.' Compare, 'Ἀλλ' ὁ μὲν Σωκράτης τὰ καθόλου οὐ χωριστὰ ἐποίει οὐδὲ τοὺς ὁρισμούς· οἱ δ' ἐχώρισαν, καὶ τὰ τοιαῦτα τῶν ὄντων ἰδέας προσηγόρευσαν. Met. 12. 4. 'Socrates assigned no independent existence to universals and the objects of definition. The Platonists separated them from the world of sense and called them ideas.'

9] The idealists supposed that the existence of ideas was an indispensable logical hypothesis. It was to them what the uniformity of nature is to modern logic. No ideas, no science, was their notion. Aristotle contradicts this in the Analytica: Εἴδη μὲν οὖν εἶναι, ἢ ἕν τι παρὰ τὰ πολλὰ, οὐκ ἀνάγκη, εἰ ἀπόδειξις ἔσται· εἶναι μέντοι ἓν κατὰ πολλῶν ἀληθὲς εἰπεῖν, ἀνάγκη. Οὐ γὰρ ἔσται τὸ καθόλου, ἂν μὴ τοῦτο ᾖ· ἐὰν δὲ τὸ καθόλου μὴ ᾖ, τὸ μέσον οὐκ

ἔσται, ὅστ' οὐδ' ἀπόδειξις. Δεῖ ἄρα τι ἓν καὶ τὸ αὐτὸ ἐπὶ πλειόνων εἶναι μὴ ὁμώνυμον. An. Post. I. 11. 'The existence of ideas or substantive unities independent of the world of sense, is not indispensable to demonstration: the existence of classes, or uniform relations (attributes) declarable of many individuals, is. Unless one and the same thing were predicable univocally of many, there could be no demonstration, for there could be no middle term to comprehend the minor.' In the text παρὰ is used in an unusual sense. In Aristotle τὸ ἓν παρὰ τὰ πολλά usually denotes the idea: here it denotes the universal. The doctrine that Aristotle here enunciates is Nominalism, i. e. that the similarity of universals to substances is merely grammatical (ἐν τῇ λέξει), the only point they have in common being their name, nomen substantivum. The words ἐπὶ πᾶσιν imply an exception, which, I suppose, refers to the active or objective reason (νοῦς ποιητικός).

10] Whately considers that the fallacy of figura dictionis consists in taking for granted that paronyms, i. e. nouns, verbs, adverbs, adjectives, derived from the same root, like design, designing, art, artful, project, projector, have a precisely correspondent meaning. In English this is not so, and the fallacy thence arising may be fairly classed under figura dictionis. But this was not Aristotle's view. In Greek, a more regularly constructed language, the meaning of paronyms, with very few exceptions, does exactly correspond; and paronyms (τὰ σύστοιχα) were a locus of dialectic, i. e. valid reasoning. Μάλιστα δ' ἐπίκαιροι καὶ κοινοὶ τῶν τόπων οἵ τ' ἐκ τῶν ἀντικειμένων καὶ τῶν συστοίχων καὶ τῶν πτώσεων· ὁμοίως γὰρ ἔνδοξον τὸ ἀξιῶσαι. Topica, 3. 6. 'The most effective and universally applicable topics are those from opposites and those from paronyms, for a proposition transferred to an opposite or a paronym is just as probable as in its original form.' This is another instance of the proximity (γειτνίασις) of dialectic and sophistry.

Paronymous words (παρώνυμα) are different modifications of the same root; like-figured words (ὁμοιοσχήμονα) are similar modifications of different roots. Homonymous words appear to denote things entirely identical; like-figured words appear to denote things belonging to the same class, order, or category; paronymous words appear to denote things variously correlated to the same standard of reference (πρὸς ἕν). In Greek the things

not the words are called ὁμώνυμα and παρώνυμα, so that these definitions would require modification.

CHAPTER XXIII.

1] For ἐμψυχον read ἀψυχον. Ἀποφήσαντα μὴ εἶναι (ἀψυχον) denotes the thesis, and is equivalent to φήσαντα εἶναι ἐμψυχον· Συμβαίνει denotes the conclusion of the confutation.

CHAPTER XXIV.

1] From this it might seem that every solution by διαίρεσις, as well as every solution by ἀναίρεσις, and every proposition of the questioner, was to be supported by induction: but Aristotle does not impose this obligation when speaking of any other fallacy.

2] Here the attribute (unknown) of the accident (about to be asked) is transferred to the subject (the summum bonum). It would be easy to state any of these fallacies so that the attribute of the subject should be transferred to the accident; e. g. if we inferred that because the summum bonum was known, therefore the question about to be asked was known. [The fallacy seems really to be amphibolia. The premiss, nescis quid sim te rogaturus, is employed as if it were, non novisti quod sum te rogaturus.]

3] The fallacy seems really equivocation, a confusion between the two senses of knowledge, old acquaintance, and recognition on a particular occasion.

4] In these two examples there is no syllogism, for all the three terms appear in the quasi conclusion. There is only a pretence of expressing in one sentence what had previously been expressed in two. The principle of the fallacy seems the same as that of the good shoemaker, which was put under the head of composition and division.

5] This excentric syllogism may be illustrated by the following: Oxygen combined with hydrogen is water; oxygen combined with hydrogen is oxygen, therefore oxygen is water. Or: Oxygen is gaseous; oxygen combined with hydrogen is oxygen; therefore oxygen combined with hydrogen is gaseous. The fallacy may be regarded as equivocation. In one premiss, four

multiplied by four means the product of the factors, in the
other, only the first-named factor.

6] For ἀναιροῦντες read διαιροῦντες. Ἐρώτησις here, as in eb.
xxii, is the thesis. But when we point out an ignoratio elenchi,
it is not necessary to remodel or abandon the thesis (ἀναιρεῖν).
It is sufficient to shew that it is not contradicted (διαιρεῖν).
One MS. reads οὐ διαιροῦντες. This seems to be the query of
an intelligent reader.

7] See ch. xx.

8] Here again (see ch. xxii, note 3) we have by implication
the strange expression of solving a fallacy by contradicting the
thesis. The syllogism seems to have been: A four is a small
number; a four multiplied by a four is a four; therefore a four
multiplied by a four is a small number.

9] Aristotle does not speak very accurately. He said in
eb. iv. that a term is ambiguous whether the plurality of signification is (1) proper, or (2) customary, or (3) merely arises in
combination.

10] From this expression it might seem that Aristotle considered the fallacy to belong equally to per accidens and to
composition.

11] The purport of the passage seems to require a mark of
interrogation after κακῶν.

12] Aristotle seems to mean that there would be a fallacy of
composition. But if Davus is good and belongs to bad masters,
the conclusion that something of the bad is good follows without
any fallacy of composition. Aristotle is in difficulties from refusing to admit that the genitive is ambiguous, at least has a
partitive and relative as well as a possessive force. Yet he repu-
diates as an impossibility the proposition, εἶναι τῶν κακῶν τι
ἀγαθόν. But what is there paradoxical in this unless its first
and most obvious, i. e. proper, meaning is, that some evil is
good, in other words, unless the genitive is partitive? This was
recognised by subsequent grammarians as its original meaning,
when they called it the genus-predicating case (γενικὴ πτῶσις).

13] If the expression is not ambiguous, how would Aristotle
solve the fallacy, What is of the animals is the property of the
animals, man is of the animals, therefore man is the property of
the animals? He could not refer it to any of the heads of fallacy,

but apparently would be obliged to deny the minor (see ch. xvii, Δῆλον οὖν ἐν οἷς ἀσαφὲς τὸ προτεινόμενον οὐ συγχωρητέον ἁπλῶς), which would be a very unsatisfactory mode of solution.

14] The fallacy per accidens has been generally misunderstood, which seems to shew that it is an ill-defined species. We might do well to drop it from the list and distribute its contents among the other classes. The principle which, in order to solve it, Aristotle brings to bear against the sophist, namely that the predicate of a predicate cannot be inferred of the subject, unless one of the premisses is an essential proposition or even a definition, is far too sweeping; and if admitted would upset nine-tenths of the syllogisms ever constructed. If we retain the class in order to comprehend the instances given in ch. v, i.e. all the cases of illicit process and undistributed middle that are not comprehended in consequens, it would be well to give the class a more appropriate name than accidens, and make one class represent both accidens and consequens.

CHAPTER XXV.

1] Whately, followed by Mill and De Morgan, makes per accidens the converse of secundum quid. He confines the second to the case where a term is first used with a limitation and afterwards without, and per accidens to the opposite case, where a term is first used without and afterwards with a limitation. But it is plain that with Aristotle secundum quid included both the case where a term has a limitation in the premisses and not in the conclusion, and vice versa; and both the case where the limitation is in the conclusion but not in the thesis, and that where it is in the thesis but not in the conclusion.

2] For ὑγιαίνειν read ἄρχειν.

3] So we must read with one of the MSS.: the others give τὸ γὰρ λαβεῖν ἀγαθὸν ἀγαθόν.

4] Νικᾶν. So read, in spite of MSS., for κρίνειν. Perhaps too, below, for δίκαιόν ἐστιν ἱκανῶς λέγειν, we should read δίκαιόν ἐστι νικᾶν λέγοντα, or δίκαιόν ἐστι νικᾶν ὃς λέγει.

CHAPTER XXVI.

1] See ch. v.

CHAPTER XXVII.

1] Ἐπεὶ τό γ' ἐρωτᾶν ἀμφίβολα καὶ τὰ παρὰ τὴν ὁμωνυμίαν, ὅσαι τ' ἄλλαι τοιαῦται παρακρούσεις, καὶ τὸν ἀληθινὸν ἔλεγχον ἀφανίζει, καὶ τὸν ἐλεγχόμενον καὶ μὴ ἐλεγχόμενον ἄδηλον ποιεῖ... Ἄδηλον γὰρ εἰ ἀληθῆ λέγει νῦν... Νῦν δὲ, διὰ τὸ μὴ καλῶς ἐρωτᾶν τοὺς πυνθανομένους, ἀνάγκη προσαποκρίνεσθαί τι τὸν ἐρωτώμενον, διορθοῦντα τὴν μοχθηρίαν τῆς προτάσεως. Ch. xvii.

CHAPTER XXVIII.

1] For ἀντιθέσεις read ἀντιφάσεις. The generic term ἀντικείμενον which follows, and which caused the false reading, is only used because ἀντίφημι has no perfect passive participle. If A and B are related as antecedent and consequent, that is, if all A is B, one form of fallacy is to assume that all B is A. This in hypothetical reasoning is to infer the truth of the antecedent from the truth of the consequent. Another form is to assume that all not-A is not-B. This is to infer the falsehood of the consequent from the falsehood of the antecedent. Δῆλον οὖν ὅτι πρὸς ἄμφω ἀντιστρέφει ἡ κατὰ τὴν ἀντίφασιν ἀκολούθησις ἀνάπαλιν γινομένη. Topics, 2. 8. 'Whether the original terms are affirmative or negative, in both cases the contradictories of the original terms have their sequence in an inverted order.' The false reading is probably the origin of the name of the famous conversion by contra-position. The logicians who used the name used it without a meaning, and were not troubled by the fact that in the rest of their system ἀντίθεσις had been translated opposition, not contra-position. In the above-quoted passage πρὸς ἄμφω ἀντιστρέφει γινομένη = ἐπ' ἄμφοιν ὁμοίως γίνεται.

CHAPTER XXX.

1] Ταὐτὰ, so read for ταῦτα. In the preceding line, after πάλιν, add, or understand, ἀνάγκη συμβαίνειν ὑπεναντίωμα.

2] For ἐπεὶ δ' read ἐπειδή.

3] Read, εἰ τὸ μὲν ἀγαθὸν γίνεται, τὸ δὲ κακόν, δύο γένοιτ' ἂν ἀγαθὼ ἢ δύο κακώ, or something similar.

4] Whately, forgetting that the names of the fallacies are taken from a treatise on Eristic, i. e. catechetical disputation, thinks that the questioning in plurium interrogationum is merely a rhetorical figure, and that this fallacy merely differs from homonymia because the orator, to give animation to his discourse, puts his assertions into the form of interrogations, making believe that he expects an answer. But the examples given shew that the peculiarity of plurium interrogationum is, that the premisses are in the form, A and B are X and Y, and that there is no ambiguity in the principal terms A, B, X, Y, but only in pronouns and syncategorematic words, such as they, themselves, both, all.

The error of treating two questions as one is independent of diction, and therefore Aristotle has placed this class among the fallacies extra dictionem: but as after this error has been committed no fallacy arises unless the questioner takes advantage of an ambiguity, it seems it ought to be classed with the fallacies in dictione. But throughout this treatise Aristotle seems inclined to differ from the logician, perhaps the theorist criticized in ch. x, who reduced all fallacies to equivocation.

CHAPTER XXXI.

1] Perhaps we should read, οἷον διπλάσιον ἄνευ τοῦ ἡμίσεος ἐν τῷ διπλάσιον ἡμίσεος.

2] Τὸ ἐν τῇ ἀποφάσει. So read for τὸ ἐν τῷ ἡμίσει.

3] Ταὐτό. So read for τοῦτο.

4] Σιμὸς and ῥαιβός lose part of their connotation when joined to substantives. Taken separately they mean something more than κοιλός; but σιμὴ ῥίς and ῥαιβὸν σκέλος mean no more than κοιλὴ ῥίς and κοιλὸν σκέλος. This must be the gist of the

passage, but it is not easy to get it from the text. If, with some MSS., we omit the words ἔνθα μὲν γὰρ τὸ σιμόν, ἔνθα δὲ τὸ ῥαιβὸν σημαίνει, we may read, προστιθέμενον δ' οὐδὲν κωλύει ἄλλο τὸ μὲν τῇ ῥινὶ τὸ δὲ τῷ σκέλει σημαίνειν. Bekker's reading, συμβαίνει instead of the first σημαίνει, is merely a conjecture of Pacius, and does not make the passage more intelligible.

5] The sophistic locus of tautology may be considered as a caricature of a dialectic locus. One fault which dialectic criticism finds with a definition is the introduction of superfluous words. Οὐκ ἔστι δὲ τὸ δὶς φθέγξασθαι ταὐτὸν ὄνομα τῶν ἀτόπων, ἀλλὰ τὸ πλεονάκις περί τινος τὸ αὐτὸ κατηγορῆσαι, οἷον ὡς Ξενοκράτης τὴν φρόνησιν ὁριστικὴν καὶ θεωρητικὴν τῶν ὄντων φησὶν εἶναι. Ἡ γὰρ ὁριστικὴ θεωρητική τίς ἐστιν, ὥστε δὶς τὸ αὐτὸ λέγει προσθεὶς πάλιν καὶ θεωρητικήν. Πάλιν εἴ τοῦ καθόλου εἰρημένου προσθείη καὶ ἐπὶ μέρους, οἷον εἰ τὴν ἐπιείκειαν ἐλάττωσιν τῶν συμφερόντων καὶ δικαίων· τὸ γὰρ δίκαιον συμφέρον τι, ὥστε περιέχεται ἐν τῷ συμφέροντι· περιττὸν οὖν τὸ δίκαιον. Καὶ εἰ τὴν ἰατρικὴν ἐπιστήμην τῶν ὑγιεινῶν ζώῳ καὶ ἀνθρώπῳ, ἢ τὸν νόμον εἰκόνα τῶν φύσει καλῶν καὶ δικαίων· τὸ γὰρ δίκαιον καλόν τι, ὥστε πλεονάκις τὸ αὐτὸ λέγει. Topica, 6. 3. 'It is not the recurrence of a word in a sentence that is to be condemned, but the reiteration of an identical predicate. Xenocrates is guilty of this when he says that wisdom defines and investigates truth, for to define is to investigate. The following definitions, which assert the particular after asserting the universal, are tautological. An equitable spirit is a willingness to have one's interests and rights reduced. Rights are included in interests and the word is superfluous. Medicine is the science of what is wholesome to animals and men. Law is the copy of the naturally beautiful and right. Right is included in beautiful.' Πολλάκις γὰρ λανθάνουσι τοῦτο ποιοῦντες (πλεονάκις λέγοντες τὸ αὐτό) καὶ ἐν τοῖς ἰδίοις καθάπερ καὶ ἐν τοῖς ὅροις. Οὐκ ἔσται δὲ καλῶς κείμενον τὸ τοῦτο πεπονθὸς ἴδιον. Ταράττει γὰρ τὸν ἀκούοντα τὸ πλεονάκις λεχθέν. Ἀσαφὲς οὖν ἀναγκαῖόν ἐστι γίνεσθαι, καὶ πρὸς τούτοις ἀδολεσχεῖν δοκοῦσιν. Topica, 5. 2. 'There is often a latent tautology in statements of property as well as in definitions. It is a fault, for it obscures the meaning, perplexes the hearer, and shows an incontinence of words.'

CHAPTER XXXII.

1] If for the neuter τοῦτο we substitute the masculine, which distinguishes the nominative and accusative, we find there is an ambiguous middle; and that the solecistic conclusion does not legitimately follow unless we substitute a false major or false minor premiss. Adopting the English collocation of the subject and predicate we have the following as the true syllogism:

Minor: Τὸ ὑποκείμενον ἐστιν οὗτος ὃν λέγεις αὐτὸ εἶναι.
Major: Οὗτος ὃν λέγεις αὐτὸ εἶναι ἐστι λίθος.
Conclusion: Τὸ ὑποκείμενον ἄρα ἐστι λίθος.

The solecistic conclusion requires either the false and solecistic minor,
  Τὸ ὑποκείμενον ἐστι τοῦτον ὃν λέγεις αὐτὸ εἶναι,
which with the true major,
  Τὸ τοῦτον ὃν λέγεις αὐτὸ εἶναι σημαίνει τὸ λίθον,
gives the conclusion,
  Τὸ ὑποκείμενον ἄρα ἐστι λίθον :
or the false major,
  Τὸ οὗτος ὃν λέγεις αὐτὸ εἶναι σημαίνει τὸ λίθον.

2] Εἰπεῖν. So read with one of the MSS. for εἶπεν. After οὗτος add ἢ τοῦτον. Then the complete sentence is, Ξύλον δ' εἰπεῖν οὗτος ἢ τοῦτον οὐδὲν διαφέρει, where οὗτος and τοῦτον merely represent cases, their gender being disregarded.

3] For τὸν λίθον σημαίνειν οὗτος, read λίθον σημαίνειν τὸ οὗτος. Here Aristotle assumes that the conclusion depends on a false major premiss; above he assumed that it depended on a false minor. As the reasoning relates not to things but to words, the realistic copula ἐστιν is replaced by the nominalistic copula σημαίνει.

4] We have MS. authority for omitting the article before λίθον. In the infancy of grammar Aristotle could not give a very lucid explanation from the want of technical terms: but he has sufficiently shewn that no solecism can enter a valid conclusion unless there was already a solecism in the premisses; and that the paralogism of solecism depends on the ambiguity of the neuter pronoun, which has the same form for the nominative and the accusative.

CHAPTER XXXIII.

1] Μεταφέρεσθαι is the characteristic of a dialectical as opposed to a scientific principle, or, within the limits of science, of an axiom (κοινὴ ἀρχή) as opposed to a thesis (ἰδία ἀρχή), that is, of a method as opposed to a doctrine. It is an ontological proposition, and has no relation to any one object of thought more than to any other. [Τῶν τετραγωνισμῶν] τὸν μὲν οὐκ ἔστι μετενεγκεῖν διὰ τὸ ἐκ τῶν ἰδίων εἶναι ἀρχῶν, τὸν δὲ πρὸς πολλούς, ἁρμόσει γάρ. Ch. xi. Kant would explain its universality by making it subjective, i. e. part of the framework of the logical faculty, only regarding as objective truths those which are specific and limited in range. The falsifications of dialectic maxims may be regarded as the κοιναὶ ἀρχαὶ of eristic. The character of transferability, therefore, is common to dialectic and eristic principles.

2] This was Dugald Stewart's opinion. He thinks the book of Sophisms the most useful part of the Organon, and that it supplies a very convenient phraseology for marking concisely some of the principal fallacies which are apt to impose on the understanding in the heat of viva voce disputes. However, he expressly excepts the fallacies in dictione as too contemptible to be deserving of any notice. *Philosophy of the Human Mind*, 2, 3. On the other hand, see the examples accumulated by Mill under the head of Ambiguity.

3] This idea, expanded by Wallis, is somewhat overpraised by Dugald Stewart, who was ignorant of its parentage. He transcribes the words of Wallis "for the benefit of those who may hereafter speculate upon the theory of wit." *Philosophy of the Human Mind*, Note M.

4] Read, τίς ὁ ὠνούμενος;

5] Read, ὁμοίως δὲ καὶ παρὰ τὸ συμβεβηκὸς καὶ παρὰ τῶν ἄλλων ἕκαστον.

6] Εἰπεῖν usually denotes rather the substance than the words of a speech: but in the Rhetoric, as here, it is used to designate diction. Οὐ γὰρ ἀπόχρη τὸ ἔχειν ἃ δεῖ λέγειν, ἀλλ᾽ ἀνάγκη καὶ ταῦτα ὡς δεῖ εἰπεῖν, καὶ συμβάλλεται πολλὰ πρὸς τὸ φανῆναι ποῖόν τινα τὸν λόγον. Rhetoric, 3. 1.

7] The meaning of μετατιθεμένης appears from the Analytics.

Τὸ δ' ἀντιστρέφειν ἐστὶ τὸ μετατιθέντα τὸ συμπέρασμα ποιεῖν τὸν συλλογισμὸν ὅτι ἢ τὸ ἄκρον τῷ μέσῳ οὐχ ὑπάρξει ἢ τοῦτο τῷ τελευταίῳ. 'Ανάγκη γὰρ τοῦ συμπεράσματος ἀντιστραφέντος καὶ τῆς ἑτέρας μενούσης προτάσεως ἀναιρεῖσθαι τὴν λοιπήν. An. Priora, 2. 8. 'Conversion here means the employment of the contradictory of the conclusion as a premiss to disprove the original major or minor premiss. For the contradictory of the conclusion combined with either of the premisses will upset the other.' Thus we shall have three syllogisms all equally probable and improbable.

All *M* is *P*,
All *S* is *M*,
∴ All *S* is *P*.

All *M* is *P*,
Some *S* is not *P*,
∴ Some *S* is not *M*.

Some *S* is not *P*,
All *S* is *M*,
∴ Some *M* is not *P*.

8] We have observed before that a syllogism with a false premiss may be either dialectic (εἰ γὰρ ἐκ ψευδῶν μὲν ἐνδόξων δέ, λογικός. Topica, 8. 12), or sophistic, or pseudographic. See ch. xviii, note 1. Grote has pointed out that under these circumstances it must be excessively difficult, not to say impossible, to draw a line between sophistic and dialectic proof. Certainly there is nothing here like extinction of species to establish a gulf between the genera, and the boundary, if there is one, can only be fixed somewhat roughly, as between right and wrong in morals, by the arbitration of common sense,—ὡς ἂν ὁ φρόνιμος ὁρίσειεν.

9] Τὸ δὲ γυμνάζεσθαι δυνάμεως χάριν, καὶ μάλιστα περὶ τὰς προτάσεις καὶ ἐνστάσεις. Ἔστι γὰρ ὡς ἁπλῶς εἰπεῖν διαλεκτικὸς ὁ προτατικὸς καὶ ἐνστατικός. Ἔστι δὲ τὸ μὲν προτείνεσθαι ἓν ποιεῖν τὰ πλείω, δεῖ γὰρ ἐν ὅλῳ ληφθῆναι πρὸς ὃ ὁ λόγος, τὸ δ' ἐνίστασθαι τὸ ἓν πολλά· ἢ γὰρ διαιρεῖ ἢ ἀναιρεῖ, τὸ μὲν διδοὺς τὸ δ' οὐ τῶν προτεινομένων. Topica, 8. 14. 'Facility comes by practice, and is chiefly shewn in proposition and enstasis. For dialectic power is the power of putting propositions and raising enstases. Pro-

position reduces plurality to unity; for the subject in dispute must be referred to a class. Enstasis resolves unity into plurality; for it distinguishes inconclusive from conclusive proof, or divides a universal proposition into particulars, of which some are granted and others denied.'

10] There is a similar statement in Topica, 8. 11. Εἴη δ' ἂν ποτε λόγος καὶ συμπεπερασμένος μὴ συμπεπερασμένου χείρων, ὅταν ὁ μὲν ἐξ εὐήθων συμπεραίνηται μὴ τοιούτου τοῦ προβλήματος ὄντος, ὁ δὲ προσδέηται τοιούτων ἃ ἐστιν ἔνδοξα καὶ ἀληθῆ, καὶ μὴ ἐν τοῖς προσλαμβανομένοις ᾖ ὁ λόγος. 'A complete proof is of inferior merit to an incomplete proof, if the premisses of the former are more improbable than the conclusion requires, and the premisses to be supplied for the latter are both probable and true and only remotely related to the conclusion.'

11] Ἔστι δὲ λόγον κωλῦσαι συμπεράνασθαι τετραχῶς. Ἢ γὰρ ἀνελόντα παρ' ὃ γίνεται τὸ ψεῦδος, ἢ πρὸς τὸν ἐρωτῶντα ἔνστασιν εἰπόντα· πολλάκις γὰρ οὐδὲ λέλυκεν, ὁ μέντοι πυνθανόμενος οὐ δύναται πορρωτέρω προάγαγεῖν· τρίτον δὲ πρὸς τὰ ἠρωτημένα· συμβαίη γὰρ ἂν ἐκ μὲν τῶν ἠρωτημένων μὴ γίνεσθαι ὃ βούλεται διὰ τὸ κακῶς ἠρωτῆσθαι, προστεθέντος δέ τινος γίνεσθαι τὸ συμπέρασμα. Εἰ μὲν οὖν μηκέτι δύναται προάγειν ὁ ἐρωτῶν, πρὸς τὸν ἐρωτῶντα εἴη ἂν ἡ ἔνστασις, εἰ δὲ δύναται, πρὸς τὰ ἠρωτημένα. Τετάρτη δὲ καὶ χειρίστη τῶν ἐνστάσεων ἡ πρὸς τὸν χρόνον· ἔνιοι γὰρ τοιαῦτα ἐνίστανται πρὸς ἃ διαλεχθῆναι πλείονός ἐστι χρόνου τῆς παρούσης διατριβῆς. Αἱ μὲν οὖν ἐνστάσεις καθάπερ εἴπαμεν τετραχῶς γίνονται· λύσις δ' ἐστὶ τῶν εἰρημένων ἡ πρώτη μόνον, αἱ δὲ λοιπαὶ κωλύσεις τινὲς καὶ ἐμποδισμοὶ τῶν συμπερασμάτων. Topica, 8. 10. 'There are four modes of preventing proof: first, the repudiation of a false premiss; secondly, an objection that silences the prover, for he is sometimes silenced by an objection not really fatal; thirdly, an objection that meets the premisses; for though the premisses are at first inadequate, some further addition might make them adequate. If the prover cannot complete the proof, he is silenced; if he can, only the original premisses are met. The fourth and worst enstasis is addressed to the time. For an objection may require a longer rejoinder than the time permits. Only the first of these enstases is solution, the rest are merely evasions and hindrances of proof.' The argumentum ad hominem of the schoolmen seems a translation of Aristotle's συλλογισμὸς πρὸς τὸν ἀπο-

κρινόμενον, but it does not mean the same thing, for the latter, it appears, is not addressed to the opinions but to the powers of the disputant. Argumentum ad hominem corresponds better with pirastic proof, the premisses of which are the opinions of the respondent. The argumentum ad verecundiam may refer to the locus of authority or to the locus for entrapping in paradox, the discrepancies of secret and avowed opinion (ch. xii).

CHAPTER XXXIV.

1] Σολοικισμός. So read for συλλογισμός, and σολοικισμοὺς for συλλογισμούς below. For this excellent emendation we are indebted to Pacius.

2] 'Ἡ μὲν πρόθεσις τῆς πραγματείας μέθοδον εὑρεῖν, ἀφ' ἧς δυνησόμεθα συλλογίζεσθαι περὶ παντὸς τοῦ προτεθέντος προβλήματος ἐξ ἐνδόξων, καὶ αὐτοὶ λόγον ὑπέχοντες μηθὲν ἐροῦμεν ὑπεναντίον. Topica, ι. ι. 'The aim of our inquiry is the invention of a method that shall enable us to reason with probable premisses on every problem that may be proposed, and to maintain any theses against attacks without self-contradiction.' Περὶ δ' ἀποκρίσεως πρῶτον μὲν διοριστέον τί ἐστιν ἔργον τοῦ καλῶς ἀποκρινομένου καθάπερ τοῦ καλῶς ἐρωτῶντος. Ἔστι δὲ τοῦ καλῶς ἐρωτῶντος οὕτως διαγαγεῖν τὸν λόγον ὥστε ποιῆσαι τὸν ἀποκρινόμενον τὰ ἀδοξότατα λέγειν τῶν διὰ τὴν θέσιν ἀναγκαίων, τοῦ δ' ἀποκρινομένου τὸ μὴ δι' αὑτὸν φαίνεσθαι συμβαίνειν τὸ ἀδύνατον ἢ τὸ παράδοξον ἀλλὰ διὰ τὴν θέσιν· ἑτέρα γὰρ ἴσως ἁμαρτία τὸ θέσθαι πρῶτον ὃ μὴ δεῖ καὶ τὸ θέμενον μὴ φυλάξαι κατὰ τρόπον. Topica, 8. 4. 'To determine rules for the answerer, we must first define the aims of the questioner and answerer. The aim of the questioner is so to conduct the reasoning as to force the answerer to the most improbable propositions necessitated by the thesis: the aim of the answerer to make the impossible or paradoxical propositions appear due not to himself but to the thesis. For it is a different fault to advance a wrong thesis, and after advancing it not to defend it as well as one might.' Κατὰ τρόπον here, and ὁμοτρόπως in the text, seem to mean, not consistently or without self-contradiction but, with a degree of probability that varies with the thesis. 'Ἐπεὶ δ' ὁ καλῶς συλλογιζόμενος ἐξ ἐνδοξοτέρων καὶ γνωριμωτέρων τὸ προβληθὲν ἀποδείκνυσι, φανερὸν ὡς ἀδόξου μὲν ὄντος

ἁπλῶς τοῦ κειμένου οὗ δοτέον τῷ ἀποκρινομένῳ οὔθ᾽ ὃ μὴ δοκεῖ ἁπλῶς, οὔθ᾽ ὃ δοκεῖ μὲν ἧττον δὲ τοῦ συμπεράσματος δοκεῖ. Topica, 8. 5. 'As premisses should be more probable and certain than conclusions, when the thesis is improbable, the answerer may refuse both all improbable premisses and all which though probable are less probable than the contradictory of the thesis.' Λόγον ὑπέχειν seems nearly the same as θέσιν φυλάττειν. Ὑπέχειν δὲ καὶ θέσιν καὶ ὁρισμὸν αὐτὸν αὑτῷ δεῖ προεγχειρήσαντα....Ἄδοξον δ᾽ ὑπόθεσιν εὐλαβητέον ὑπέχειν. Topica, 8. 9.

3] Throughout this treatise the questioner has represented the sophist; so that we were hardly prepared for the announcement that answering is the sophistic side of dialectic. The rest of the Topics, however, is written more from the point of view of the questioner; and the answerer appears as a sophist. Ἐπιτίμησις δὲ λόγου κατ᾽ αὐτόν τε τὸν λόγον καὶ ὅταν ἐρωτᾶται οὐχ ἡ αὐτή. Πολλάκις γὰρ τοῦ μὴ καλῶς διειλέχθαι τὸν λόγον ὁ ἐρωτώμενος αἴτιος διὰ τὸ μὴ συγχωρεῖν ἐξ ὧν ἦν διαλεχθῆναι καλῶς πρὸς τὴν θέσιν. Οὐ γὰρ ἔστιν ἐπὶ θατέρῳ μόνου τὸ καλῶς ἐπιτελεσθῆναι τὸ κοινὸν ἔργον. Ἀναγκαῖον οὖν ἐνίοτε πρὸς τὸν λέγοντα καὶ μὴ πρὸς τὴν θέσιν ἐπιχειρεῖν, ὅταν ὁ ἀποκρινόμενος τἀναντία τῷ ἐρωτῶντι παρατηρῇ προσενηρεδίζων. Δυσκολαίνοντες οὖν ἀγωνιστικῶς καὶ οὐ διαλεκτικῶς ποιοῦνται τὰς διατριβάς......Ἐπεὶ δὲ φαῦλος κοινωνὸν ὁ ἐμποδίζων τὸ κοινὸν ἔργον, δῆλον ὅτι καὶ ἐν λόγῳ. Κοινὸν γάρ τι καὶ ἐν τούτοις προκείμενόν ἐστι, πλὴν τῶν ἀγωνιζομένων. Τούτοις δ᾽ οὐκ ἔστιν ἀμφοτέροις τυχεῖν τοῦ αὐτοῦ τέλους. Διαφέρει δ᾽ οὐδὲν ἄν τε διὰ τοῦ ἀποκρίνεσθαι ἄν τε διὰ τοῦ ἐρωτᾶν ποιῇ τοῦτο. Ὅ τε γὰρ ἐριστικῶς ἐρωτῶν φαύλως διαλέγεται, ὅ τ᾽ ἐν τῷ ἀποκρίνεσθαι μὴ διδοὺς τὸ φαινόμενον μηδ᾽ ἐκδεχόμενος ὅ τί ποτε βούλεται ὁ ἐρωτῶν πυθέσθαι. Topica, 8. 11. "In criticising we must distinguish between the argument and the arguer. The badness of an argument is often imputable to the answerer who refuses to grant the premisses which would fairly confute the thesis. For it is not in the power of one of the disputants without the co-operation of the other to accomplish successfully their joint task. Accordingly, the questioner is sometimes forced to argue against the answerer instead of against the thesis, if the answerer takes every means of thwarting him with unscrupulous effrontery. This perversity makes the argumentation eristic......He is a bad associate who impedes the common work in reasoning as in any other occu-

pation. Both disputants attain their object in well-conducted argument, though not in eristic, for both cannot be victorious. It is equally reprehensible to spoil the common business by captious questions, and by refusing to admit what one really believes or pretending to misunderstand the questions.' Πρὸς γὰρ τὸν πάντως ἐνιστάμενον πάντως ἀντιτακτέον ἐστίν. Topica, 5. 4. 'The unscrupulousness of the respondent forces the questioner to be unscrupulous.'

It is not solely in the province of the answerer, however, that we may see the contiguity (γειτνίασις) of eristic and dialectic. A conclusive dialectic proof may be formed of false premisses. Ἔτι δ' ἐπεὶ γυμνασίας καὶ πείρας χάριν ἀλλ' οὐ διδασκαλίας οἱ τοιοῦτοι τῶν λόγων, δῆλον ὡς οὐ μόνον τἀληθῆ συλλογιστέον ἀλλὰ καὶ ψεῦδος, οὐδὲ δι' ἀληθῶν ἀεὶ ἀλλ' ἐνίοτε καὶ ψευδῶν. Πολλάκις γὰρ ἀληθοῦς τεθέντος ἀναιρεῖν ἀνάγκη τὸν διαλεγόμενον, ὥστε προτατέον τὰ ψευδή. Ἐνίοτε δὲ καὶ ψευδοῦς τεθέντος ἀναιρετέον διὰ ψευδῶν. Οὐδὲν γὰρ κωλύει τινὶ δοκεῖν τὰ μὴ ὄντα μᾶλλον τῶν ἀληθῶν, ὥστ', ἐκ τῶν ἐκείνῳ δοκούντων τοῦ λόγου γινομένου, μᾶλλον ἔσται πεπεισμένος ἢ ὠφελημένος. Δεῖ δὲ τὸν καλῶς μεταβιβάζοντα διαλεκτικῶς καὶ μὴ ἐριστικῶς μεταβιβάζειν, καθάπερ τὸν γεωμέτρην γεωμετρικῶς, ἄν τε ψεῦδος ἄν τ' ἀληθὲς ᾖ τὸ συμπεραινόμενον. Topica, 8. 11. 'As practice and mutual examination, not instruction, are the object of these argumentations, the dialectician must often prove a false conclusion, and employ false premisses: for if the thesis is true, the premisses of the confutation must be false. Even a false thesis must sometimes be confuted by false premisses: for the answerer may disbelieve the true premisses, and as the proof must be composed of his beliefs, he will be convinced but hardly enlightened. The proof, however, must be dialectic, not eristic, whether the conclusion is true or false: just as a proof by a geometer should be geometrical.' But dialectic proof may also be inconclusive or fallacious. We saw (ch. v, note 4) that the locus a dicto secundum quid is the common property of eristic and dialectic: we saw (ch. xii, note 1) that the dialectician does not abstain from the locus non causa pro causa: we saw (ch. xxii, note 10) that paronyms are in Greek a locus of dialectic, in English a locus of sophisms. It appears also that ambiguity is common ground to the dialectician and sophist. Χρήσιμον δὲ τὸ ποσαχῶς λέγεται ἐπεσκέφθαι.... καὶ πρὸς τὸ παραλογίσασθαι. Εἰδό-

τες γὰρ ποσαχῶς λέγεται, αὐτοὶ ἐρωτῶντες δυνησόμεθα παραλογίσασθαι, ἐὰν μὴ τυγχάνῃ εἰδὼς ὁ ἀποκρινόμενος ποσαχῶς λέγεται. Ἔστι δὲ οὐκ οἰκεῖος ὁ τρόπος οὗτος τῆς διαλεκτικῆς· διὸ παντελῶς εὐλαβητέον τοῖς διαλεκτικοῖς τὸ τοιοῦτον, τὸ πρὸς τοὔνομα διαλέγεσθαι, ἐὰν μή τις ἄλλως ἐξαδυνατῇ περὶ τοῦ προκειμένου διαλέγεσθαι. Topica, 1. 18. 'A knowledge of the various meanings of a term is useful, because it enables us when questioning to construct fallacies, if the answerer has not the same knowledge. This mode of reasoning is not characteristic of dialectic, and should be utterly avoided, unless there is no other possible means of attacking the thesis.' Elsewhere the locus is recommended without even this slight admonition. Ἔτι ἐὰν πολλαχῶς λέγηται, κείμενον δὲ ᾖ ᾗ ὣς ὑπάρχει ἢ ὡς οὐχ ὑπάρχει, θάτερον δεικτύναι τῶν πλεοναχῶς λεγομένων, ἐὰν μὴ ἄμφω ἐνδέχηται. Χρηστέον δ᾽ ἐπὶ τῶν λανθανόντων. Ἐὰν γὰρ μὴ λανθάνῃ πολλαχῶς λεγόμενον, ἐνστήσεται ὅτι οὐ διείλεκται ὅπερ αὐτὸς ἠπόρει ἀλλὰ θάτερον. Topica, 2. 3. 'If a predicate is ambiguous, prove it in the wrong sense if you cannot in the right. This is only practicable when the answerer fails to detect the ambiguity: otherwise he will object that the term is not used in the confutation in the same sense as in the thesis.' Finally, the advice to the geometer (ch. v, note 5), to decline answering before any but a geometrical tribunal, looks very like an admission that all pirastic is sophistic (see Appendix E).

4] This refers to ch. i. Ἐπεὶ δ᾽ ἐστί τισι μᾶλλον πρὸ ἔργου τὸ δοκεῖν εἶναι σοφοῖς ἢ τὸ εἶναι καὶ μὴ δοκεῖν, δῆλον ὅτι ἀναγκαῖον τούτοις καὶ τὸ τοῦ σοφοῦ ἔργον δοκεῖν ποιεῖν μᾶλλον ἢ ποιεῖν καὶ μὴ δοκεῖν. Ἔστι δ᾽, ὡς ἐν πρὸς ἓν εἰπεῖν, ἔργον περὶ ἕκαστον τοῦ εἰδότος ἀψευδεῖν μὲν αὐτὸν περὶ ὧν οἶδε, τὸν δὲ ψευδόμενον ἐμφανίζειν δύνασθαι. Ταῦτα δ᾽ ἐστὶ τὸ μὲν ἐν τῷ δύνασθαι δοῦναι λόγον, τὸ δ᾽ ἐν τῷ λαβεῖν.

5] The Topica begins with a classification of propositions and problems (theses). Πρῶτον οὖν θεωρητέον ἐκ τίνων ἡ μέθοδος. Εἰ δὴ λάβοιμεν πρὸς πόσα καὶ ποῖα καὶ ἐκ τίνων οἱ λόγοι καὶ πῶς τούτων εὐπορήσομεν, ἔχοιμεν ἂν ἱκανῶς τὸ προκείμενον. Ἔστι δ᾽ ἀριθμῷ ἴσα καὶ τὰ αὐτά, ἐξ ὧν τε οἱ λόγοι καὶ περὶ ὧν οἱ συλλογισμοί. Γίνονται μὲν γὰρ οἱ λόγοι ἐκ τῶν προτάσεων· περὶ ὧν δὲ οἱ συλλογισμοί, τὰ προβλήματά ἐστι. Πᾶσα δὲ πρότασις καὶ πᾶν πρόβλημα ἢ γένος ἢ ἴδιον ἢ συμβεβηκὸς δηλοῖ. Topica, 1. 4. 'We have first to examine the elements of the method, that is, the number and

170   NOTES.   Chap. XXXIV.

nature of the points to which arguments are addressed, and of the elements of which they are composed, and how they are obtained. The two questions are identical: for arguments are composed of propositions, and addressed to problems; and every proposition and problem is a genus, definition, property, or accident.'

6] The sources of proof are pointed out partly by describing the ὄργανα and partly by enumerating the loci. Τὰ μὲν οὖν γένη περὶ ὧν τε οἱ λόγοι καὶ ἐξ ὧν, διωρίσθω· τὰ δ' ὄργανα, δι' ὧν εὐπορήσομεν τῶν συλλογισμῶν, ἐστὶ τέτταρα, ἓν μὲν τὸ προτάσεις λαβεῖν, δεύτερον δὲ ποσαχῶς ἕκαστον λέγεται δύνασθαι διελεῖν, τρίτον τὰς διαφορὰς εὑρεῖν, τέταρτον δὲ ἡ τοῦ ὁμοίου σκέψις. Ἔστι δὲ τρόπον τινὰ καὶ τὰ τρία τούτων προτάσεις. Topica, t. 13. ' So much for the classification of problems and premisses. Operations subsidiary or instrumental to proof are four: the collection of propositions, the definition of equivocal terms, the discovery of similarities, the discovery of dissimilarities: and all four may be regarded as the collection of propositions.' Τὰ μὲν οὖν ὄργανα δι' ὧν οἱ συλλογισμοὶ ταῦτ' ἐστίν· οἱ δὲ τόποι πρὸς οὓς χρήσιμα τὰ λεχθέντα οἵδε εἰσίν. Topica, 1. 18. ' Such are the materials of proof: the maxims which will enable us to apply them have now to be enumerated.'

7] Arrangement and answering are treated of in the 8th book. Some of the precepts relating to solution appear to be lost.

8] Aristotle's desire to give an appearance of amplitude or development (πλῆθος) to his system has been very injurious to it. This has led him, with astonishing naïveté, to pretend to multiply the loci by repeating them for each of the predicables in a different order. He professes to do this for the sake of clearness; but it is difficult to conceive anything less luminous than the mode of exposition he has adopted. Μὴ λανθανέτω δ' ἡμᾶς ὅτι τὰ πρὸς τὸ ἴδιον καὶ τὸ γένος καὶ τὸ συμβεβηκὸς πάντα καὶ πρὸς τοὺς ὁρισμοὺς ἁρμόσει λέγεσθαι... 'Ἀλλ' οὐ διὰ τοῦτο μίαν ἐπὶ πάντων καθόλου μέθοδον ζητητέον. Οὔτε γὰρ ῥᾴδιον εὑρεῖν τοῦτ' ἐστίν, εἴθ' εὑρεθείη, παντελῶς ἀσαφὴς καὶ δύσχρηστος ἂν εἴη πρὸς τὴν προκειμένην πραγματείαν. Ἰδίας δὲ καθ' ἕκαστον τῶν διορισθέντων γενῶν ἀποδοθείσης μεθόδου ῥᾷον ἐκ τῶν περὶ ἕκαστον οἰκείων ἡ διέξοδος τοῦ προκειμένου γίνοιτ' ἄν. Topica, 1. 6. ' It should be observed, that the rules for proving property and genus and accident are

all applicable to the proof of definition: yet we must not try to establish a single body of rules of universal application. Such rules would be difficult to invent, and, if invented, would be very obscure and hard of application. By giving separate rules and appropriate methods for each predicable, we facilitate the examination of the different problems.' According to Alexander Aphrodisiensis, Theophrastus attempted to unite the canons of proof in a single system, and verified Aristotle's prediction: but against the failure of Theophrastus we may set the exposition of the methods of induction by Mill.

9] It is difficult to reconcile Aristotle's assertion with what we know had been done by Plato and Socrates and the Eleatics and Megarians. What he really performed in his dialectical treatise was to indicate a number of methodic principles or elements of method (τὰ κοινά); and it is probable that none of his predecessors had separated and extricated these from the specific propositions (τὰ ἴδια), or what some would call the material, as opposed to the formal, elements in which they are imbedded in actual ratiocination.

10] What the rhetoricians gave their pupils to learn by heart were, doubtless, not complete speeches, but finished portions of speeches, i. e. what Quintilian would have called loci communes, and the later Greek rhetoricians τόποι. Aristotle might have used the word here, and we may even suspect that he originally used it, for as the sentence now stands there is an awkward repetition of λόγους. But he was forced to use the latter word to distinguish the method of his predecessors from his own. For his own system is merely a list of loci. He has erred nearly as much by the omission of examples as his forerunners by the omission of rules. He has not even given us the maxims that group themselves about the different loci, although he admits that the exact form of these propositions is of the utmost importance to the disputant. Πρότασίν τε κοινὴν μᾶλλον ἢ λόγον εἰς μνήμην θετέον, ἀρχῆς γὰρ καὶ ὑποθέσεως εὐπορῆσαι μετρίως, χαλεπόν. Topica, 8. 14. 'A universal proposition is better worth remembering than a chain of proof: for a moderate command of principles and premisses is difficult to obtain.' He recommends however, like his predecessors, that whole arguments should be committed to memory. Πρὸς τε τὰ πλειστάκις ἐμπίπτοντα τῶν

προβλημάτων έξεπίστασθαι δεῖ λόγους, καὶ μάλιστα περὶ τῶν πρώτων θέσεων ἐν τούτοις γὰρ ἀποδυσπετοῦσιν οἱ ἀποκρινόμενοι πολλάκις. 'We should get by heart arguments on the problems that oftenest arise, particularly on the elementary theses; for here chance often makes the answers take an unlucky turn.' Ἀποδυσπετοῦσιν is a metaphor from dice. First principles are so difficult to elicit by questioning that the questioner may be baffled without any skill on the part of the answerer. [Compare the use of εὐπετές. Καὶ γὰρ ἰδεῖν αὐτὸν καὶ λαβεῖν παρὰ τῶν ἐρωτωμένων τὰς τοιαύτας προτάσεις οὐκ εὐπετές. Topics, 7. 5.] Δεῖ δὲ καὶ πεποιημένους ἔχειν λόγους πρὸς τὰ τοιαῦτα τῶν προβλημάτων, ἐν οἷς ἐλαχίστων εὐπορήσαντες πρὸς πλεῖστα χρησίμους ἔξομεν, οὗτοι δ' εἰσὶν οἱ καθόλου, καὶ πρὸς οὓς πορίζεσθαι χαλεπώτερον ἐκ τῶν παρὰ πόδας. Topica, 8. 14. 'We should have ready-made arguments for the conclusions that depend on the fewest premisses and yet are oftenest wanted, namely, the most abstract, and for those problems whose proof is difficult to extemporize.'

11] Read ἀλλὰ τριβῇ.

ADDENDA.

CH. VII, note 2. Ἐπισπᾶσθαι was a common term in the schools. E. g. Ἡ μὲν ἀμυδρὰ καὶ ἔκλυτος φαντασία οὐκ ἂν εἴη κριτήριον· τῷ γὰρ μήτε αὑτὴν μήτε τὸ ποιῆσαν τρανῶς ἐνδείκνυσθαι οὐ πέφυκεν ἡμᾶς πείθειν οὐδ' εἰς συγκατάθεσιν ἐπισπᾶσθαι. Sextus Empiricus, Adversus Logicos, I. 'A faint and weak sensation, according to Carneades, cannot be a criterion or ultimate evidence of truth: for, not clearly revealing either itself or its cause, it is not apt to persuade us or induce our assent.'

CH. VIII, note 6. Φαινομένους δὲ οὐχ ὑτῳοῦν ἀλλὰ τοῖς τοιοῖσδε. For the meaning of τοῖς τοιοῖσδε, compare, Οὐδὲ ἡ ῥητορικὴ τὸ καθ' ἕκαστον ἔνδοξον θεωρήσει, οἷον Σωκράτει ἢ Ἱππίᾳ, ἀλλὰ τὸ τοῖς τοιοῖσδε, καθάπερ καὶ ἡ διαλεκτική. Καὶ γὰρ ἐκείνη συλλογίζεται οὐχ ἐξ ὧν ἔτυχε, φαίνεται γὰρ ἄττα καὶ τοῖς παραληροῦσιν, ἀλλ' ἐκείνη μὲν ἐκ τῶν λόγου δεομένων, ἡ δὲ ῥητορικὴ ἐκ τῶν ἤδη βουλεύεσθαι εἰωθότων. Rhetoric, I. 2. 'Rhetoric, like dialectic, examines what is probable, not to any individuals, but to certain classes. Dialectical proof appeals, not to any opinions, for madmen have opinions, but to the opinions of those who want not understanding but evidence; and rhetorical proof to the opinions of those who are accustomed to deliberate.' Ἐκ τῶν λόγου δεομένων = ἐκ τῶν ἐνδόξων τοῖς λόγου δεομένοις, and ἐκ τῶν ἤδη βουλεύεσθαι εἰωθότων = ἐκ τῶν πιθανῶν τοῖς ἤδη βουλεύεσθαι εἰωθόσιν. For the meaning of τῶν λόγου δεομένων, compare, Οὐ δεῖ δὲ πᾶν πρόβλημα οὐδὲ πᾶσαν θέσιν ἐπισκοπεῖν, ἀλλ' ἣν ἀπορήσειεν ἄν τις τῶν λόγου δεομένων καὶ μὴ κολάσεως ἢ αἰσθήσεως· οἱ μὲν γὰρ ἀποροῦντες πότερον δεῖ τοὺς θεοὺς τιμᾶν καὶ τοὺς γονεῖς ἀγαπᾶν ἢ οὒ κολάσεως δέονται, οἱ δὲ πότερον ἡ χιὼν λευκὴ ἢ οὒ αἰσθήσεως. Topica, I. 11. 'We should not examine every problem or thesis, but only such as may be doubtful to a person who wants not intelligence but proof, not those which are doubtful to a person who wants castigation or

to a person who is defective in a sense. He who questions whether we should reverence the gods or love our parents wants punishment, he who does not know that snow is white wants an organ of sense.'

Ch. xi, note 2. Aristotle seems to have thought that, if we were in full possession of the ultimate conceptions, that is, the definitions of the ultimate terms, we should be able to predict the special propositions which are the ultimate basis of deductive science: that the conjunction of the terms A, B, C, &c. in all the primary objective theorems, A is B, B is C, C is D, is, to use the words of Kant, not synthetical but analytical, just as in geometrical theorems. Brown, in his celebrated treatise on Causation, has attempted to shew that, in the natural sciences at least, that is, in those that deal with changes or events, i. e. successions of phenomena, the ultimate immediate conjunctions are unpredictable, i. e. though constant juxtapositions, are inexplicable and mysterious. It is not quite clear what Aristotle considered to be the logical relation of the cause and effect in his causal definitions of natural phenomena; but, if we may judge from his expression, Διὰ γὰρ τὸ θαυμάζειν οἱ ἄνθρωποι καὶ νῦν καὶ τὸ πρῶτον ἤρξαντο φιλοσοφεῖν,......δεῖ δὲ εἰς τὸ ἐναντίον καὶ τὸ ἄμεινον κατὰ τὴν παροιμίαν ἀποτελευτῆσαι, Met. 1. 2, 'Men began to philosophize because they wondered, but the end of philosophizing should be something better, the cessation of wonder,' he seems to have expected that, in any province of inquiry whatever, if we carried the analysis far enough, when we arrived at the ultimate immediate conjunctions, whether of coexistent or of successive terms, we should find them neither inexplicable nor mysterious, but the evidently necessary result of determinate relations.

Κατὰ expresses causation (ὅλως δὲ τὸ καθ' ὃ ἰσαχῶς καὶ τὸ αἴτιον ὑπάρξει, ὥστε καὶ τὸ καθ' αὐτὸ πολλαχῶς ἀνάγκη λέγεσθαι. Met. 4. 18). Accordingly the proposition, τὸ A ὑπάρχει τῷ B καθ' αὐτό, means that all the conditions of the conjunction of A and B are contained in A and B themselves: that we are not to look for its cause in the interposition of any third independent term. The conclusions of science, as well as the first principles, are καθ' αὐτὰ ὑπάρχοντα, that is, τὸ καθ' αὐτὸ ὑπάρχειν is not confined to immediate conjunctions except so far as it excludes the inter-

ference of any foreign cause. We may add that in the expression, τὸ A ὑπάρχει τῷ B καθ' αὑτό, αὐτὸ is either the subject or the predicate, i. e. καθ' αὑτὸ means, as appears from Aristotle's definition of the two classes of καθ' αὑτὸ ὑπάρχοντα, either κατ' αὐτὸ τὸ A, or κατ' αὐτὸ τὸ B: e. g. γραμμὴ ὑπάρχει τριγώνῳ κατ' αὐτὸ τὸ τρίγωνον, but τὸ εὐθὺ ὑπάρχει γραμμῇ κατ' αὑτὸ τὸ εὐθύ.

Ch. XX, note 3. Eudemus, the disciple of Aristotle, informs us more than once that the theory of ambiguity (τὸ δισσόν) was invented by Plato. Παρμενίδου μὲν οὖν ἀγασθείη ἄν τις ἀναξιοπίστοις ἀκολουθήσαντος λόγοις καὶ ὑπὸ τοιούτων ἀπατηθέντος ἃ οὔπω τότε διεσεσάφητο; Οὔτε γὰρ τὸ πολλαχῶς ἔλεγεν οὐδείς, ἀλλὰ Πλάτων πρῶτος τὸ δισσὸν εἰσήγαγεν, οὔτε τὸ καθ' αὑτὸ καὶ τὸ κατὰ συμβεβηκός· φαίνεται δὲ ὑπὸ τούτων διαψευσθῆναι. Eudemus, quoted by Simplicius on Phys. Ausc. i. 3. 'We ought not to be surprised that Parmenides was misled by inconclusive reasonings and fallacies which in his time had not been exposed. For in his days no one had heard of equivocation, a method of solution first introduced by Plato, or of the distinction of subject and attribute which he overlooks.' See also ch. x, note 1.

Ch. XXXIV, note 3. Ἐπεὶ δὲ προσκατασκευάζεται πρὸς αὐτὴν ὡς οὐ μόνον πεῖραν δύναται λαβεῖν διαλεκτικῶς ἀλλ' ὡς εἰδώς. This should have been translated, 'Since it claims the power of catechizing or cross-examining not only dialectically but also scientifically.'

APPENDIX A.

PETITIO PRINCIPII.

Τὸ δὲ ἐν ἀρχῇ αἰτεῖσθαι καὶ λαμβάνειν ἔστι μὲν, ὡς ἐν γένει λαβεῖν, ἐν τῷ μὴ ἀποδεικνύναι τὸ προκείμενον. Τοῦτο δὲ ἐπισυμβαίνει πολλαχῶς. Καὶ γὰρ εἰ ὅλως μὴ συλλογίζεται, καὶ εἰ δι' ἀγνωστοτέρων ἢ ὁμοίως ἀγνώστων, καὶ εἰ διὰ τῶν ὑστέρων τὸ πρότερον· ἡ γὰρ ἀπόδειξις ἐκ πιστοτέρων τε καὶ προτέρων ἐστί. Τούτων μὲν οὖν οὐδέν ἐστι τὸ αἰτεῖσθαι τὸ ἐξ ἀρχῆς. Ἀλλ' ἐπεὶ τὰ μὲν δι' αὑτῶν πέφυκε γνωρίζεσθαι τὰ δὲ δι' ἄλλων (εἰ μὲν γὰρ ἀρχαὶ δι' ἑαυτῶν, τὰ δὲ ὑπὸ τὰς ἀρχὰς δι' ἄλλων) ὅταν τὸ μὴ δι' αὑτοῦ γνωστὸν δι' ἑαυτοῦ τις ἐπιχειρῇ δεικνύναι, τότε αἰτεῖται τὸ ἐξ ἀρχῆς.

Τοῦτο δέ ἐστι μὲν οὕτω ποιεῖν ὥστ' εὐθὺς ἀξιῶσαι τὸ προκείμενον, ἐνδέχεται δὲ καὶ μεταβάντας ἐπ' ἄλλα ἄττα τῶν πεφυκότων δι' ἐκείνου δείκνυσθαι, διὰ τούτων ἀποδεικνύναι τὸ ἐξ ἀρχῆς. Οἷον, εἰ τὸ Α δεικνύοιτο διὰ τοῦ Β, τὸ δὲ Β διὰ τοῦ Γ, τὸ δὲ Γ πεφυκὸς εἴη δείκνυσθαι διὰ τοῦ Α· συμβαίνει γὰρ αὐτὸ δι' ἑαυτοῦ τὸ Α δεικνύναι τοὺς οὕτω συλλογιζομένους. Ὅπερ ποιοῦσιν οἱ τὰς παραλλήλους οἰόμενοι γράφειν. Λανθάνουσι γὰρ αὐταὶ ἑαυτοὺς τοιαῦτα λαμβάνοντες ἃ οὐχ οἷόν τε ἀποδεῖξαι μὴ οὐσῶν τῶν παραλλήλων. Ὥστε τοῖς οὕτω συλλογιζομένοις συμβαίνει ἕκαστον λέγειν εἶναι εἰ ἔστιν ἕκαστον· οὕτω δὲ ἅπαν ἔσται δι' αὑτοῦ γνωστόν· ὅπερ ἀδύνατον.

Εἰ οὖν τις, ἀδήλου ὄντος ὅτι τὸ Α ὑπάρχει τῷ Γ, ὁμοίως δὲ καὶ ὅτι τῷ Β, αἰτοῖτο τῷ Β ὑπάρχειν τὸ Α· οὔπω δῆλον εἰ τὸ ἐν ἀρχῇ αἰτεῖται· ἀλλ' ὅτι οὐκ ἀποδείκνυσι, δῆλον· οὐ γὰρ ἐστιν ἀρχὴ ἀποδείξεως τὸ ὁμοίως ἄδηλον. Εἰ μέν τοι τὸ Β

APPENDIX A.

PETITIO PRINCIPII.

BEGGING the question[1], or, assuming the point to be proved, is a specific case of failing to demonstrate a theorem. This occurs in various ways, either when the reasoning is inconclusive, or when the premisses are less evident than the conclusion, or equally devoid of evidence with the conclusion, or when they are its consequents rather than its antecedents. For demonstrative premisses must be antecedent to the conclusion and more evident. None of these cases is begging the question. But some propositions being self-evident, others having a derivative evidence (for principles have their evidence in themselves, conclusions derive their evidence from other propositions), to attempt to make a proposition that is not self-evident evidence of itself is to beg the question.

This may either be done by directly assuming the conclusion or by assuming what is properly a conclusion from a proposition as a premiss to prove that proposition, proving, for instance, A by B and B by C when C can only be proved by A. For this amounts to proving A by A. An example of this is the pretended method of constructing parallels. Here the prover unconsciously assumes an operation which cannot be performed unless parallels have been constructed[2]. The proof therefore asserts a thing to be true if it is true, and if it were valid, all propositions would be self-evident, which cannot be.

When the conclusion, C is A, and the major, B is A, are equally deficient in evidence, there is not of necessity a begging of the question, but there is clearly no demonstration; for that cannot be a premiss of demonstration which is no more evident than the conclusion. But if the middle and minor, C and B, are so related as to be identical, either because they are con-

APPENDIX A.

πρὸς τὸ Γ οὕτως ἔχει ὥστε ταὐτὸν εἶναι, ἢ δῆλον ὅτι ἀντιστρέφουσιν, ἢ ὑπάρχει θάτερον θατέρῳ· τὸ ἐν ἀρχῇ αἰτεῖται. Καὶ γὰρ ἂν ὅτι τῷ Β τὸ Α ὑπάρχει δι' ἐκείνων δεικνύοι, εἰ ἀντιστρέφει. Νῦν δὲ τοῦτο κωλύει ἀλλ' οὐχ ὁ τρόπος. Εἰ δὲ τοῦτο ποιεῖ, τὸ εἰρημένον ἂν ποιοῖ καὶ ἀντιστρέφοι ὡς διὰ τριῶν [1].

Ὡσαύτως δὲ κἂν εἰ τὸ Β τῷ Γ λαμβάνοι ὑπάρχειν, ὁμοίως ἄδηλον ὂν καὶ εἰ τὸ Α τῷ Γ· οὔπω τὸ ἐξ ἀρχῆς αἰτεῖται, ἀλλ' οὐκ ἀποδείκνυσιν. Ἐὰν δὲ ταὐτὸν ᾖ τὸ Α καὶ τὸ Β ἢ τῷ ἀντιστρέφειν ἢ τῷ ἕπεσθαι τὸ Α τῷ Β· τὸ ἐξ ἀρχῆς αἰτεῖται διὰ τὴν αὐτὴν αἰτίαν. Τὸ γὰρ ἐξ ἀρχῆς τί δύναται, πρότερον εἴρηται ἡμῖν, ὅτι τὸ δι' ἑαυτοῦ δεικνύναι τὸ μὴ δι' αὐτοῦ δῆλον.

Εἰ οὖν ἐστι τὸ ἐν ἀρχῇ αἰτεῖσθαι τὸ δι' αὐτοῦ δεικνύναι τὸ μὴ δι' αὐτοῦ δῆλον, τοῦτο δέ ἐστι τὸ μὴ δεικνύναι, ὅταν ὁμοίως ἀδήλων ὄντων τοῦ δεικνυμένου καὶ δι' οὗ δείκνυται [2], ἢ τῷ ταὐτὰ τῷ αὐτῷ ἢ τῷ ταὐτὸν τοῖς αὐτοῖς ὑπάρχειν [7]· ἐν μὲν τῷ μέσῳ σχήματι οὐδετέρως [8] ἂν ἐνδέχοιτο τὸ ἐν ἀρχῇ αἰτεῖσθαι, ἐν δὲ κατηγορικῷ συλλογισμῷ ἔν τε τῷ τρίτῳ καὶ τῷ πρώτῳ.

Ἀποφατικῶς δὲ, ὅταν τὰ αὐτὰ ἀπὸ τοῦ αὐτοῦ καὶ οὐχ ὁμοίως ἀμφότεραι αἱ προτάσεις.

Ὡσαύτως δὲ καὶ ἐν τῷ μέσῳ, διὰ τὸ μὴ ἀντιστρέφειν [11] τοὺς ὅρους κατὰ τοὺς ἀποφατικοὺς συλλογισμούς.

Ἔστι δὲ τὸ ἐν ἀρχῇ αἰτεῖσθαι ἐν μὲν ταῖς ἀποδείξεσι τὰ κατ' ἀλήθειαν οὕτως ἔχοντα, ἐν δὲ τοῖς διαλεκτικοῖς τὰ κατὰ δόξαν. Anal. Prior. 2. 16.

vertible or because the middle involves the minor, the argument is a begging of the question. For the major premiss, B is A, might be proved by the minor premiss and conclusion if the middle and minor are convertible. If it cannot be, it is only from the comparative extension of the terms, not from any other relation. If they are convertible, we might, as was stated, prove the major premiss from the minor and conclusion, and we should have a circular proof of three propositions in which each would be alternately premiss and conclusion.

Similarly if the minor premiss, C is B, is no more evident than the conclusion, C is A, we have not necessarily a begging of the question, but we have a failure of demonstration. If, however, the major and middle terms are identical, because they are convertible or because the major is involved in the middle, then we have a begging of the question as before[8]. For begging the question arises, as was explained, when a proposition not self-evident is made to prove itself.

If then begging the question is making a proposition not self-evident prove itself, and this is a failure of proof, from the premiss being no more evident than the conclusion, because the premiss and conclusion either affirm two identical predicates of an identical subject or an identical predicate of two identical subjects, the question cannot be begged in the second figure in either of these ways, but only in the figures that give an affirmative conclusion, namely, the first and third[9].

In negative syllogisms there is a begging of the question in the first and third figures when an identical predicate is denied of two identical subjects, and it is not either premiss indifferently that begs the question but only the major[10].

In the second figure there is a begging of the question when two identical predicates are denied of an identical subject, and it is not either premiss indifferently that begs the question but only the minor, because the position of terms in the other premiss of negative syllogisms is not homologous to the position of terms in the conclusion.

Begging the question in scientific discussion is what really satisfies these conditions, in dialectic what has the appearance of doing so.

We have some further remarks in the Topica:—

APPENDIX A.

Τὸ δ' ἐν ἀρχῇ πῶς αἰτεῖται ὁ ἐρωτῶν καθ' ἀλήθειαν μὲν ἐν τοῖς Ἀναλυτικοῖς εἴρηται, κατὰ δόξαν δὲ νῦν λεκτέον. Αἰτεῖσθαι δὲ φαίνονται τὸ ἐν ἀρχῇ πενταχῶς. Φανερώτατα μὲν καὶ πρῶτον εἴ τις αὐτὸ τὸ δείκνυσθαι δέον αἰτήσει· τοῦτο δ' ἐπ' αὐτοῦ μὲν οὐ ῥᾴδιον λανθάνειν, ἐν δὲ τοῖς συνωνύμοις καὶ ἐν ὅσοις τὸ ὄνομα καὶ ὁ λόγος τὸ αὐτὸ σημαίνει μᾶλλον. Δεύτερον δὲ ὅταν κατὰ μέρος δέον ἀποδεῖξαι καθόλου τις αἰτήσῃ· οἷον εἰ ἐπιχειρῶν ὅτι τῶν ἐναντίων μία ἐπιστήμη, ὅλως τῶν ἀντικειμένων ἀξιώσειε μίαν εἶναι· δοκεῖ γὰρ ὃ ἔδει καθ' αὑτὸ δεῖξαι μετ' ἄλλων αἰτεῖσθαι πλειόνων. Τρίτον εἴ τις, τὸ καθόλου δεῖξαι προκειμένου, κατὰ μέρος αἰτήσειεν· οἷον εἰ πάντων τῶν ἐναντίων προκειμένου, τῶνδε τινῶν ἀξιώσειε· δοκεῖ γὰρ καὶ οὗτος, ὃ μετὰ πλειόνων ἔδει δεῖξαι, καθ' αὑτὸ καὶ χωρὶς αἰτεῖσθαι. Πάλιν εἴ τις διελὼν αἰτεῖται τὸ προβληθέν· οἷον εἰ δέον δεῖξαι τὴν ἰατρικὴν ὑγιεινοῦ καὶ νοσώδους, χωρὶς ἑκάτερον ἀξιώσειεν. *Η εἴ τις τῶν ἑπομένων ἀλλήλοις ἐξ ἀνάγκης θάτερον αἰτήσειεν, οἷον τὴν πλευρὰν ἀσύμμετρον τῇ διαμέτρῳ, δέον ἀποδεῖξαι ὅτι ἡ διάμετρος τῇ πλευρᾷ. Topica, θ. 11.

What begging of the question is to the philosopher we have examined in the Analytics: what it is to the dialectician we will now explain. It appears to occur in five ways. The first and most manifest way is when the very thing that should be proved is assumed. This cannot easily pass undetected when the terms are the same, but when synonyms are used, or a name and a circumlocution, it may escape detection. A second way is when a particular ought to be proved and the universal is assumed: as, for instance, if we have to prove that contraries are objects of a single science, and assume that opposites, their genus, are objects of a single science. It appears that what should be proved alone is assumed in company with other propositions. A third way is when a universal ought to be proved and the particular is assumed; as when what ought to be proved of all contraries is assumed of some. Here too it appears that what ought to be proved in company with other propositions is assumed alone. A fourth way is when we divide the problem to be proved and assume it in detail; as if we have to prove that medicine is the science of health and disease and successively assume it to be the science of each. A fifth way is when two facts are reciprocally involved and we assume the one to prove the other; as if we assume that the side of a square is incommensurate to the diagonal when we have to prove that the diagonal is incommensurate to the side.

NOTES TO APPENDIX A.

1] Aristotle examines the relation of the terms in a syllogism containing a petitio principii, and determines which premiss in each of the figures may be the petitio. In the first figure, if the principium, or conclusion assumed, is affirmative, either the major or minor premiss may be a petitio, and the middle term will be identical with the minor or major. If the principium is negative, the major premiss is the petitio, and the middle is identical with the minor. In the second figure the principium must be negative, only the minor premiss can be a petitio, and the middle term will be identical with the major. In the third figure, whether the principium is affirmative or negative, the major premiss is the petitio, and the middle is identical with the minor. All this is obvious from an inspection of the symbols of the figures. It does not throw much light on the nature of petitio principii, but for the satisfaction of the reader we give it in Aristotle's own words. Αἴτημα, petition, is the assumption without proof of a proposition which ought to be proved. It may or may not be opposed to the belief of the respondent. Hypothesis is, properly, an indemonstrable proposition. A relative hypothesis is a proposition which ought to be proved, but which is believed by the respondent and is assumed without proof. "Ὅσα μὲν οὖν δεικτὰ ὄντα λαμβάνει αὐτὸς μὴ δείξας, ταῦτ᾽, ἐὰν μὲν δοκοῦντα λαμβάνῃ τῷ μανθάνοντι, ὑποτίθεται, καὶ ἔστιν οὐχ ἁπλῶς ὑπόθεσις ἀλλὰ πρὸς ἐκεῖνον μόνον ἂν δὲ ἢ μηδεμιᾶς ἐνούσης δόξης ἢ καὶ ἐναντίας ἐνούσης λαμβάνῃ τὸ αὐτό, αἰτεῖται. Καὶ τούτῳ διαφέρει ὑπόθεσις καὶ αἴτημα· ἔστι γὰρ αἴτημα τὸ ὑπεναντίον τοῦ μανθάνοντος τῇ δόξῃ, ἢ ὃ ἄν τις ἀποδεικτὸν ὂν λαμβάνῃ καὶ χρῆται μὴ δείξας. An. Post. i. 10. 'What is capable of proof, but assumed without proof, if believed by the learner, is, relatively to the learner, though not absolutely, an hypothesis; if the learner has no belief or a disbelief, it is a petition; and this is the difference. Petition is an assumption opposed to the belief of the learner: or, still wider, a demonstrable proposition assumed without demonstration.' Αἴτησις τοῦ ἐν ἀρχῇ is an αἴτημα

APPENDIX A.

where the proposition assumed is the conclusion which ought to be proved.

2] It is not easy to say what is the vicious construction that Aristotle contemplates. Euclid postulates the power of drawing any circle from a given centre with a given radius, that is, the use of the compasses as well as of the ruler. Some geometer may have attempted the impracticable feat of solving the problem without the help of this postulate.

3] Perhaps for ἢ δῆλον ὅτι we should read διότι ἤ. Compare below, ἢ τῷ ἀντιστρέφειν ἢ τῷ ἔπεσθαι. Or we might read, εἰ δηλονότι, except that δηλονότι in the sense of 'that is to say' belongs to a later period of Greek.

4] The meaning of τρόπος is not obvious.

5] Assuming the conclusion to be affirmative, let us examine a syllogism in Barbara:—

> All B is A,
> All C is B,
> ∴ All C is A.

And let us first suppose that the major premiss is a petitio principii, i.e. that the proposition All B is A is identical with the proposition All C is A. This can only be because the terms B and C are identical.

Next let us suppose that the minor premiss is a petitio principii, i.e. that the proposition All C is B is identical with the conclusion All C is A. This can only be because B and A are identical.

The identity of the terms is their convertibility or their sequence (ὑπάρχει, ἕπεται). This, however, requires some limitation, for as the major is always predicated (ὑπάρχει, ἕπεται) of the middle and the middle of the minor, if this were enough to constitute petitio principii, every syllogism with a problematical premiss would be a petitio principii.

6] Perhaps for δείκνυται we should read δείκνύηται, which must otherwise be understood.

7] When the major premiss is the petitio, i.e. when

> B is A, and
> C is A,

are identical, we may apply the formula ταὐτὸ τοῖς αὐτοῖς ὑπάρχει,

A being ταὐτά, and B and C τὰ αὐτά. When the minor premiss is the petitio, i. e. when

C is B, and
C is A,

are identical, we may apply the formula ταὐτὰ τῷ αὐτῷ ὑπάρχει, B and A being ταὐτὰ and C τὸ αὐτό.

8] Οὐδετέρως. So read, disregarding the MSS., for καὶ τρίτῳ ἀμφοτέρως. As the conclusion of the second figure is always negative, it can never be begged by an affirmative premiss, such as the above-cited formulas imply.

9] In the third figure in Disamis,

Some B is A,
All B is C,
∴ Some C is A,

the major premiss may be a petitio principii, and we may apply the formula τὸ αὐτὸ τοῖς αὐτοῖς ὑπάρχει. The minor premiss can never be an assumption of the conclusion, for their terms are dissimilar [οὐκ ἀντιστροφοί. See below].

10] If the conclusion is negative, in Celarent of the first figure,

No B is A,
All C is B,
∴ No C is A,

and Bokardo of the third,

Some B is not A,
All B is C,
∴ Some C is not A,

the major premiss may be a petitio principii. The minor premiss cannot, because in these figures it is always affirmative; besides which, in the third figure the minor premiss and conclusion are not composed of similar terms in similar positions (οὐκ ἀντίστροφοι). We may here notice an inaccuracy of Aristotle, if the text is correct. An inspection of the symbols given above shews that the first and third figures require the formula ὅταν τὸ αὐτὸ ἀπὸ τῶν αὐτῶν (διαιρῆται), whereas the formula ὅταν τὰ αὐτὰ ἀπὸ τοῦ αὐτοῦ only applies to the second figure.

11] Ἀντιστρέφειν, i. e. ἀντιστρόφως ἔχειν. In the second

APPENDIX A.

figure the only possible petitio principii is in the minor premiss of Camestres:

> All A is B,
> No C is B,
> ∴ No C is A.

In Cæsare,

> No A is B,
> All C is B,
> ∴ No C is A,

no petitio principii is possible. Why not? Because the major premiss and conclusion are not composed of analogous or corresponding terms (οὐκ ἀντίστροφοι αἱ ὅροι). For ἀποφατικούς we should probably read some word expressing the mood which the moderns call Cæsare.

APPENDIX II.

NON CAUSA PRO CAUSA.

Τὸ δὲ μὴ παρὰ τοῦτο συμβαίνειν τὸ ψεῦδος, ὃ πολλάκις ἐν τοῖς λόγοις εἰώθαμεν λέγειν, πρῶτον μέν ἐστιν ἐν τοῖς εἰς τὸ ἀδύνατον συλλογισμοῖς, ὅταν πρὸς ἀντίφασιν ᾖ τούτου, ὃ ἐδείκνυτο τῇ εἰς τὸ ἀδύνατον[1]. Οὔτε γὰρ μὴ ἀντιφήσαντος[2] ἐρεῖ τὸ οὐ παρὰ τοῦτο, ἀλλ' ὅτι ψεῦδός τι ἐτέθη τῶν πρότερον οὔτ' ἐν τῇ δεικνυούσῃ, οὐ γὰρ τίθησι τὴν ἀντίφασιν. Ἔτι δὲ, ὅταν ἀναιρεθῇ τι δεικτικῶς διὰ τῶν Α Β Γ, οὐκ ἔστιν εἰπεῖν ὡς οὐ παρὰ τὸ κείμενον γεγένηται ὁ συλλογισμός. Τὸ γὰρ μὴ παρὰ τοῦτο γίνεσθαι τότε λέγομεν, ὅταν ἀναιρεθέντος τούτου μηδὲν ἧττον περαίνηται ὁ συλλογισμός. Ὅπερ οὐκ ἔστιν ἐν τοῖς δεικτικοῖς· ἀναιρεθείσης γὰρ τῆς θέσεως οὐδ' ὁ πρὸς ταύτην ἔσται συλλογισμός.

Φανερὸν οὖν ὅτι ἐν τοῖς εἰς τὸ ἀδύνατον λέγεται τὸ μὴ παρὰ τοῦτο καὶ, ὅταν οὕτως ἔχῃ πρὸς τὸ ἀδύνατον ἡ ἐξ ἀρχῆς ὑπόθεσις, ὥστε καὶ οὔσης καὶ μὴ οὔσης ταύτης οὐδὲν ἧττον συμβαίνειν τὸ ἀδύνατον.

Ὁ μὲν οὖν φανερώτατος τρόπος ἐστὶ τοῦ μὴ παρὰ τὴν ὑπόθεσιν εἶναι τὸ ψεῦδος, ὅταν ἀπὸ τῆς ὑποθέσεως ἀσύναπτος ᾖ ἀπὸ τῶν μέσων πρὸς τὸ ἀδύνατον ὁ συλλογισμός, ὥσπερ εἴρηται καὶ ἐν τοῖς Τοπικοῖς. Τὸ γὰρ τὸ ἀναίτιον ὡς αἴτιον τιθέναι τοῦτό ἐστιν. Οἷον, εἰ βουλόμενος δεῖξαι ὅτι ἀσύμμετρος ἡ διάμετρος, ἐπιχειροίη τὸν Ζήνωνος λόγον δεικνύναι, ὡς οὐκ ἔστι κινεῖσθαι, καὶ εἰς τοῦτο ἀπάγοι τὸ ἀδύνατον· οὐδαμῶς γὰρ οὐδαμῇ συνεχές[6] ἐστι τὸ ψεῦδος τῇ φάσει τῇ ἐξ ἀρχῆς.

Ἄλλος δὲ τρόπος, εἰ συνεχὲς μὲν εἴη τὸ ἀδύνατον τῇ ὑποθέσει, μὴ μέντοι δι' ἐκείνην συμβαίνοι· τοῦτο γὰρ ἐγχωρεῖ

APPENDIX B.

NON CAUSA PRO CAUSA.

The objection that a proposition is not the cause of a false conclusion, a formula often heard in controversy, is made in reply to a reductio ad impossibile in defence of the proposition contradicted by the framer of the reductio. For unless the opponent has contradicted the proposition the respondent will not deny that it is responsible for the conclusion, but will object to some other proposition; nor will he use the formula against direct disproof, for here the thesis is not employed as a premiss. Moreover in direct disproof by three terms, it cannot be said that the confuted thesis is irrelevant to the syllogism. This can only be said when a proposition may be eliminated without annihilating the syllogism, which cannot be the case in direct disproof, for without a thesis to be confuted there can be no confutation[1].

It is clear then that the formula can only be employed against reductio ad impossibile, when the thesis impugned is so related to the conclusion that it may be suppressed without destroying the conclusion.

The most obvious case of the irrelevance of the thesis to the conclusion is when the thesis is not connected by any middle terms with the conclusion, as we said in the Topics[4] in discussing the fallacy of non causa pro causa. We should exemplify this if, to disprove the commensurateness of the side of the square to the diagonal, we appended an argument for Zeno's theorem that there is no such thing as locomotion, pretending thereby to establish a reductio ad absurdum, for there is absolutely no connexion between this theorem and the thesis.

Another case is when the conclusion is connected with the thesis but is not its consequence. The connexion may be traced

APPENDIX B.

γενέσθαι καὶ ἐπὶ τὸ ἄνω καὶ ἐπὶ τὸ κάτω λαμβάνοντι τὸ συνεχές. Οἷον, εἰ τὸ Α τῷ Β κεῖται ὑπάρχον, τὸ δὲ Β τῷ Γ, τὸ δὲ Γ τῷ Δ· τοῦτο δὲ εἴη ψεῦδος, τὸ Β τῷ Δ ὑπάρχειν. Εἰ γὰρ, ἀφαιρεθέντος τοῦ Α, μηδὲν ἧττον ὑπάρχει τὸ Β τῷ Γ καὶ τὸ Γ τῷ Δ, οὐκ ἂν εἴη τὸ ψεῦδος διὰ τὴν ἐξ ἀρχῆς ὑπόθεσιν. Ἢ πάλιν, εἴ τις ἐπὶ τὸ ἄνω λαμβάνοι τὸ συνεχές. Οἷον, εἰ τὸ μὲν Α τῷ Β, τῷ δὲ Α τὸ Ε, καὶ τῷ Ε τὸ Ζ· ψεῦδος δὲ εἴη τὸ ὑπάρχειν τῷ Α τὸ Ζ· καὶ γὰρ οὕτως οὐδὲν ἂν ἧττον εἴη τὸ ἀδύνατον ἀναιρεθείσης τῆς ἐξ ἀρχῆς ὑποθέσεως. Ἀλλὰ δεῖ πρὸς τοὺς ἐξ ἀρχῆς" ὅρους συνάπτειν τὸ ἀδύνατον· οὕτω γὰρ ἔσται διὰ τὴν ὑπόθεσιν. Οἷον, ἐπὶ μὲν τὸ κάτω λαμβάνοντι τὸ συνεχὲς, πρὸς τὸν κατηγορούμενον τῶν ὅρων. Εἰ γὰρ ἀδύνατον τὸ Α τῷ Δ ὑπάρχειν ἀφαιρεθέντος τοῦ Α, οὐκ ἔτι ἔσται τὸ ψεῦδος. Ἐπὶ δὲ τὸ ἄνω, καθ' οὗ κατηγορεῖται. Εἰ γὰρ τῷ Β μὴ ἐγχωρεῖ τὸ Ζ ὑπάρχειν, ἀφαιρεθέντος τοῦ Β, οὐκέτι ἔσται τὸ ἀδύνατον. Ὁμοίως δὲ καὶ στερητικῶν τῶν συλλογισμῶν ὄντων. Φανερὸν οὖν, ὅτι τοῦ ἀδυνάτου μὴ πρὸς τοὺς ἐξ ἀρχῆς ὅρους ὄντος, οὐ παρὰ τὴν θέσιν συμβαίνει τὸ ψεῦδος. Ἢ οὐδ' οὕτως ἀεὶ διὰ τὴν ὑπόθεσιν ἔσται τὸ ψεῦδος ; Καὶ γὰρ εἰ μὴ τῷ Β ἀλλὰ τῷ Κ ἐτέθη τὸ Α ὑπάρχειν, τὸ δὲ Κ τῷ Γ, καὶ τοῦτο τῷ Δ· καὶ οὕτω μένει τὸ ἀδύνατον. Ὁμοίως δὲ καὶ ἐπὶ τὸ ἄνω λαμβάνοντι τοὺς ὅρους. Ὥστ' ἐπεὶ καὶ ὄντος καὶ μὴ ὄντος τούτου συμβαίνει τὸ ἀδύνατον οὐκ ἂν εἴη παρὰ τὴν θέσιν. Ἢ τὸ μὴ ὄντος τούτου μηδὲν ἧττον γίνεσθαι τὸ ψεῦδος, οὐχ οὕτω ληπτέον, ὥστ' ἄλλου τιθεμένου συμβαίνειν τὸ ἀδύνατον ἀλλ' ὅταν, ἀφαιρεθέντος τούτου, διὰ τῶν λοιπῶν προτάσεων τὸ αὐτὸ περαίνηται ἀδύνατον· ἐπεὶ τὸ αὐτό γε ψεῦδος συμβαίνειν διὰ πλειόνων ὑποθέσεων οὐδὲν ἴσως ἄτοπον· οἷον τὸ τὰς παραλλήλους συμπίπτειν, καὶ εἰ μείζων ἐστὶν ἡ ἐντὸς τῆς ἐκτὸς, καὶ εἰ τὸ τρίγωνον ἔχει πλείους ὀρθὰς δυεῖν. Anal. Prior. 2. 19.

APPENDIX B.

either from the attribute or superior term of the thesis, or from its subject or inferior term. As an illustration of a connexion with the inferior term, suppose the thesis to be, All B is A, the premisses, All D is C, All C is B, and the false conclusion, All D is B^6. If, eliminating the superior term A, we can retain the premisses, All D is C, All C is B, the conclusion, All D is B, is independent of the thesis. Again, let us trace the connexion to the superior term, and suppose the thesis to be, All B is A, the premisses, All A is E, All E is F, and the conclusion, All A is F^7. Here, too, the conclusion is unaffected by the suppression of the thesis. But when the impossibility is connected with the more remote of the two terms of the thesis, it will be the consequence of the thesis. When, that is to say, an inferior series of terms composing the ratiocination is linked on to the superior term of the thesis, so that the first impossible conclusion is, All D is A, the elimination of A eliminates the impossibility; and when a superior series is linked on to the inferior term of the thesis, so that the first impossible conclusion is, All B is F, the elimination of B eliminates the conclusion. Similarly when the propositions are negative. It is clear, then, that when the impossibility is not enchained to the remotest term of the thesis it is independent of the thesis, and when it so enchained it is dependent. Or may it not even then be independent? For if, instead of the thesis, All B is A, we had a thesis, All X is A, and the premisses, All D is C, All C is X, the impossible conclusion, All D is A, would still result; and similarly if the ratiocination consisted of a superior series of terms. As, then, in spite of the suppression of the first thesis the impossibility remains, is not the first thesis irresponsible for the conclusion? No. The independence of the conclusion and thesis does not mean that a different thesis might lead to the same conclusion, but that, if the first thesis were suppressed, the remaining existing premisses would of themselves involve the conclusion[9]. For the same impossibility may easily result from various theses: for instance, parallels may be proved to meet both from the thesis that if a straight line fall upon two parallel straight lines it makes the exterior angle greater than the interior and opposite angle upon the same side[10], and from the thesis that a triangle contains angles equal to more than two right angles[11].

NOTES TO APPENDIX B.

1] This is oddly worded. Perhaps we should read ὅταν προσαποφήσῃ τοῦτο ὁ δεικνὺς τὸ ἀδύνατον, or, ὅταν πρὸς ἀντίφασιν τούτου δεικνύηται τὸ ἀδύνατον.

2] 'Ἀντιφήσαντος. So read for ἀντιφήσας. One MS. gives ἀντιφήσας τις.

3] In a direct disproof of a thesis if we cancel the thesis, or rather the terms of which it is composed, we cancel an essential part of the syllogism.

4] This refers apparently to ch. v. of Sophistici Elenchi. If so, this passage must be a later addition, as we have seen (note to ch. ii) that the Analytica was written before the Sophistici Elenchi.

5] Things are said to be συνεχῆ, continuous, when the limit which separates them is common to both. Τὸ δὲ συνεχὲς ὅπερ ἐχόμενόν τι ἢ ἁπτόμενον. Λέγω δὲ συνεχὲς ὅταν ταὐτὸ γένηται καὶ ἓν τὸ ἑκατέρου πέρας οἷς ἅπτονται καὶ συνέχονται, ὥστε δῆλον ὅτι τὸ συνεχὲς ἐν τούτοις ἐξ ὧν ἕν τι πέφυκε γίγνεσθαι κατὰ τὴν σύναψιν. Metaphysica, 10. 12. 'Continuity is a species of holding on or touching. Two things are continuous when the two extremities by which they touch and hold together are one and the same. Continuity, therefore, is between things united at the point of contact.' Συνεχὲς δὲ λέγεται οὗ ἡ κίνησις μία καθ' αὑτὸ καὶ μὴ οἷόν τε ἄλλως· μία δ' οὗ ἀδιαίρετος. Metaph. 4. 6. 'Two parts are continuous whose motion is essentially and necessarily one and indivisible.' If we gave κίνησις a logical sense, in which sense κινεῖσθαι is sometimes used, two propositions would be συνεχῆ which must stand or fall together. We shall see however that Aristotle calls a thesis and conclusion συνεχῆ when their destinies are not thus implicated.

6] For example: suppose the thesis to be, Every animal lives; the premises, All snow is white, All that is white is an animal; the conclusion, All snow is an animal. Here the subject of the thesis is a part of the conclusion.

7] Suppose the thesis to be, as before, Every animal lives; the premises, All that lives is a plant, Every plant is insensible;

the conclusion, All that lives is insensible. Here the predicate of the thesis is a part of the conclusion.

8] 'Ἀρχῆς is emphatic. When we take an inferior series, ὁ ἐξ ἀρχῆς ὅρος, the extreme or remotest term, is the superior term of the thesis. When we take a superior series, ὁ ἐξ ἀρχῆς ὅρος is the inferior term of the thesis. Let the thesis be represented by $M N$, where M is the subject and N the predicate. The inferior series will be represented by $K L M$, the superior by $N O P$. For the validity of a reductio ad absurdum of the thesis $M N$, a ratiocination composed of the inferior series of terms must produce no absurdity until it embraces the superior term of the thesis, N: and a ratiocination composed of the superior series must produce no absurdity until it embraces the inferior term of the thesis, M. In the previous examples by combining the thesis with the conclusions we might obtain the further absurd conclusions, All snow lives, and Every animal is insensible, and the ratiocinations embrace the extreme terms of the thesis. But the reductio is not valid, because these are not the first absurdities that arise, for before introducing the thesis we had previously arrived at the same, or rather, equal absurdities, All snow is an animal, and All that lives is insensible.

9] We should add, ' or an equally impossible conclusion ;' for, as we saw in the last note, it is not exactly the same conclusion.

A reductio ad absurdum, being an assignation of cause, should stand the test of the method of difference. The impossibility that is found in the presence of the thesis should disappear in its absence. A similar consideration should guide us in determining to what class a fallacy should be referred. See ch. xxii.

10] I have assumed that in speaking of exterior and interior angles Aristotle uses these terms in the sense in which they are used by Euclid, 1. 29. A scruple as to his meaning is suggested by his saying that the lines will meet if the exterior angle is greater than the interior, when it is clear that they will equally meet if it is less: but this scruple vanishes when we observe that in the next hypothesis he says, that they will meet if the angles of the triangle are greater than two right angles, when he might just as well have said, unless they are equal.

11] Euclid, 1. 32.

APPENDIX C.

ENSTASIS, OR OBJECTION.

Ἔνστασις δέ ἐστι πρότασις προτάσει ἐναντία. Διαφέρει δὲ τῆς προτάσεως, ὅτι τὴν μὲν ἔνστασιν ἐνδέχεται εἶναι καὶ ἐπὶ μέρους, τὴν δὲ πρότασιν ἢ ὅλως οὐκ ἐνδέχεται, ἢ οὐκ ἐν τοῖς καθόλου συλλογισμοῖς. Φέρεται δὲ ἡ ἔνστασις διχῶς τε καὶ διὰ δύο σχημάτων, διχῶς μὲν ὅτι ἢ καθόλου ἢ ἐν μέρει πᾶσα ἔνστασις, διὰ δύο δὲ σχημάτων ὅτι ἀντικείμεναι φέρονται τῇ προτάσει, τὰ δὲ ἀντικείμενα ἐν τῷ πρώτῳ καὶ ἐν τῷ τρίτῳ σχήματι περαίνονται μόνοις. Ὅταν γὰρ ἀξιώσῃ παντὶ ὑπάρχειν, ἐνιστάμεθα ἢ ὅτι οὐδενὶ ἢ ὅτι τινὶ οὐχ ὑπάρχει, τούτων δὲ τὸ μὲν μηδενὶ ἐκ τοῦ πρώτου σχήματος, τὸ δέ τινι μὴ ἐκ τοῦ ἐσχάτου. Οἷον ἔστω τὸ Α, μίαν εἶναι ἐπιστήμην· ἐφ' ᾧ τὸ Β, ἐναντία· προτείναντος δὴ μίαν εἶναι τῶν ἐναντίων ἐπιστήμην, ἢ ὅτι ὅλως οὐχ ἡ αὐτὴ τῶν ἀντικειμένων ἐνίσταται, τὰ δὲ ἐναντία ἀντικείμενα· ὥστε γίνεσθαι τὸ πρῶτον σχῆμα· ἢ ὅτι τοῦ γνωστοῦ καὶ ἀγνώστου οὐ μία· τοῦτο δὲ τὸ Γ. Κατὰ γὰρ τοῦ Γ, τοῦ γνωστοῦ καὶ ἀγνώστου, τὸ μὲν ἐναντία εἶναι ἀληθές, τὸ δὲ μίαν αὐτῶν ἐπιστήμην εἶναι ψεῦδος. Πάλιν ἐπὶ τῆς στερητικῆς προτάσεως ὡσαύτως. Ἀξιοῦντος γὰρ τὸ μὴ εἶναι μίαν ἐπιστήμην τῶν ἐναντίων, ἢ ὅτι πάντων τῶν ἀντικειμένων ἢ ὅτι τινῶν τῶν ἐναντίων ἡ αὐτὴ λέγομεν, οἷον ὑγιεινοῦ καὶ νοσώδους. Τὸ μὲν οὖν πάντων ἐκ τοῦ πρώτου, τὸ δέ τινων ἐκ τοῦ τρίτου σχήματος. Ἁπλῶς γὰρ ἐν πᾶσι, καθόλου μὲν ἐνιστάμενον, ἀνάγκη πρὸς τὸ καθόλου τῶν προτεινομένων τὴν ἀντίφασιν εἰπεῖν. Οἷον, εἰ μὴ τὴν αὐτὴν ἀξιοῖ τῶν ἐναντίων πάντων, εἰπόντα τῶν ἀντικειμένων μίαν. Οὕτω δ' ἀνάγκη τὸ πρῶτον εἶναι σχῆμα· μέσον

APPENDIX C.

ENSTASIS, OR OBJECTION.

An enstasis[1], or objection, is a proposition proving the contradictory or contrary of a premiss. It differs from a premiss because it may be particular, while a premiss must be universal, at least for universal conclusions. An objection has two degrees, and is urged in two figures: it has two degrees because it proves either the contrary or the contradictory of the premiss; and it has two figures, because it proves the opposite of the premiss, and the opposite (at least if the premiss is negative) can only be proved in the first and third figure. If the premiss is a universal affirmative, the objection proves a universal negative or particular negative; in the first case the proof is in the first figure, in the second case in the third. Let A represent objects of the same knowledge, or simultaneously known, B contraries, C the knowable and unknowable, D opposites, E health and disease. If the premiss objected to is, All contraries are objects of the same knowledge, the objection may be either that no opposites are objects of the same knowledge, and the proof will be in the first figure,

No D is A,
All B is D,
∴ No B is A[2]:

or it may be that the knowable and unknowable are not objects of the same knowledge, and the proof will be in the third figure:

No C is A,
All C is B,
∴ Some B is not A[3].

Similarly if the premiss objected to is negative. For if it asserts that no contraries are objects of the same knowledge, we may

γὰρ γίνεται τὸ καθόλου πρὸς τὸ ἐξ ἀρχῆς. Ἐν μέρει δέ, πρὸς ὃ ἐστι καθόλου καθ' οὗ λέγεται ἡ πρότασις, οἷον γνωστοῦ καὶ ἀγνώστου μὴ τὴν αὐτήν· τὰ γὰρ ἐναντία καθόλου πρὸς ταῦτα· καὶ γίνεται τὸ τρίτον σχῆμα· μέσον γὰρ τὸ ἐν μέρει λαμβανόμενον, οἷον τὸ γνωστὸν καὶ τὸ ἄγνωστον. Ἐξ ὧν γάρ ἐστι συλλογίσασθαι τοὐναντίον, ἐκ τούτων καὶ τὰς ἐνστάσεις ἐπιχειροῦμεν λέγειν. Διὸ καὶ ἐκ μόνων τῶν σχημάτων τούτων φέρομεν. Ἐν μόνοις γὰρ τούτοις οἱ ἀντικείμενοι συλλογισμοί· διὰ γὰρ τοῦ μέσου οὐκ ἦν καταφατικῶς. Ἔτι δὲ κἂν λόγου δέοιτο πλείονος ἡ διὰ τοῦ μέσου σχήματος· οἷον, εἰ μὴ δοίη τὸ Α τῷ Β ὑπάρχειν διὰ τὸ μὴ ἀκολουθεῖν αὐτῷ τὸ Γ. Τοῦτο γὰρ δι' ἄλλων προτάσεων δῆλον· οὐ δεῖ δὲ εἰς ἄλλα ἐκτρέπεσθαι τὴν ἔνστασιν, ἀλλ' εὐθὺς φανερὰν ἔχειν τὴν ἑτέραν πρότασιν. Διὸ καὶ τὸ σημεῖον ἐκ μόνου τούτου τοῦ σχήματος οὐκ ἔστιν. Ἐπισκεπτέον δὲ καὶ περὶ τῶν ἄλλων ἐνστάσεων· οἷον περὶ τῶν ἐκ τοῦ ἐναντίου, καὶ τοῦ ὁμοίου, καὶ τοῦ κατὰ δόξαν· καὶ εἰ τὴν ἐν μέρει ἐκ τοῦ πρώτου ἢ τὴν στερητικὴν ἐκ τοῦ μέσου δυνατὸν λαβεῖν. Anal. Prior. 2. 26.

Περὶ δὲ λύσεων ἐχόμενόν ἐστι τῶν εἰρημένων εἰπεῖν. Ἔστι δὲ λύειν ἢ ἀντισυλλογισάμενον ἢ ἔνστασιν ἐνεγκόντα. Τὸ μὲν

APPENDIX C.

either object that all opposites are objects of the same knowledge, and then the proof is in the first figure:

All *D* is *A*,
All *B* is *D*,
∴ All *B* is *A*:

or we may object that some contraries, say, health and disease, are objects of the same knowledge, and then the proof is in the third figure:

All *E* is *A*,
All *E* is *B*,
∴ Some *B* is *A*.

If the objection has to prove the contrary of the premiss, the genus comprehending the subject of the premiss must be made the subject of the objection and receive a contradictory predicate. If the premiss is that no contraries are known together, the objection says that all opposites are known together, and we have the first figure, for the genus of the original subject is the middle term and the original subject the minor. If the objection has to prove the contradictory of the premiss, a species comprehended under the subject of the premiss must be made the subject of the objection, as knowable and unknowable are comprehended under contraries. Then we have the third figure, for the middle term is an inferior species comprehended under the minor. A premiss that gives an opposite conclusion is an objection, and such can only be applied in the first and third figures, for the second cannot give an affirmative conclusion. Besides, in the second figure more premisses would be necessary. If we objected to the proposition, All *B* is *A*, that No *A* is *C*, a second premiss must be expressed to make the disproof evident. But objection should be complete in itself and require no further premiss to be expressed [*]. For the same reason the second figure is the only one unfitted for proof by signs. We must at some future time examine the remaining modes of objection, namely, the objection of contraries, of similars, and of authority; and inquire whether an objection proving a contradictory cannot be raised in the first figure [a], or an objection proving a negative in the second.

Next to enthymeme (oratorical proof) real and apparent, solution remains to be explained. Solution is enstasis or counter-

… APPENDIX C.

οὖν ἀντισυλλογίζεσθαι δῆλον ὅτι ἐκ τῶν αὐτῶν τόπων ἐνδέχεται ποιεῖν· οἱ μὲν γὰρ συλλογισμοὶ ἐκ τῶν ἐνδόξων, δοκοῦντα δὲ πολλὰ ἐναντία ἀλλήλοις ἐστίν. Αἱ δ' ἐνστάσεις φέρονται, καθάπερ καὶ ἐν τοῖς τοπικοῖς, τετραχῶς· ἢ γὰρ ἐξ ἑαυτοῦ, ἢ ἐκ τοῦ ὁμοίου, ἢ ἐκ τοῦ ἐναντίου, ἢ ἐκ τῶν κεκριμένων. Λέγω δὲ ἀφ' ἑαυτοῦ μὲν οἷον, εἰ περὶ ἔρωτος εἴη ἐνθύμημα ὡς σπουδαῖος, ἡ ἔνστασις διχῶς, ἢ γὰρ καθόλου εἰπόντα ὅτι πᾶσα ἔνδεια πονηρόν, ἢ κατὰ μέρος ὅτι οὐκ ἂν ἐλέγετο Καύνιος ἔρως εἰ μὴ ἦσαν καὶ πονηροὶ ἔρωτες. Ἐπὶ δὲ τοῦ ἐναντίου ἔνστασις φέρεται οἷον, εἰ τὸ ἐνθύμημα ἦν ὅτι ὁ ἀγαθὸς ἀνὴρ πάντας τοὺς φίλους εὖ ποιεῖ, ἀλλ' οὐδ' ὁ μοχθηρὸς κακῶς. Ἐπὶ δὲ τῶν ὁμοίων, εἰ ἦν τὸ ἐνθύμημα ὅτι οἱ κακῶς πεπονθότες ἀεὶ μισοῦσιν, ὅτι ἀλλ' οὐδὲ οἱ εὖ πεπονθότες ἀεὶ φιλοῦσιν. Αἱ δὲ κρίσεις αἱ ἀπὸ τῶν γνωρίμων ἀνδρῶν οἷον, εἴ τις ἐνθύμημα εἶπεν ὅτι τοῖς μεθύουσι δεῖ συγγνώμην ἔχειν, ἀγνοοῦντες γὰρ ἁμαρτάνουσιν, ἔνστασις ὅτι, οὔκουν ὁ Πιττακὸς αἰνετός· οὐ γὰρ ἂν μείζους ζημίας ἐνομοθέτησεν ἐάν τις μεθύων ἁμαρτάνῃ. Rhet. 2. 25.

APPENDIX C.

proof. Counterproof will obviously be derived from the same repertories as proof. For the repertory of proof is the sphere of probabilities, and probabilities support opposite conclusions. Enstasis, or objection, as we said in the Topics, is of four orders: it is the allegation of co-ordinates, or of contraries, or of similars, or of authority. The allegation of co-ordinates is of two kinds. Suppose the enthymematic premiss objected to to be, that no love is evil, we either allege the genus of the subject, and object that all want is evil, or we allege a species of the subject, and object that a Caunian love is evil [6]. For an example of the allegation of contraries, suppose the enthymematic premiss to be, that a virtuous man is a benefactor to all his friends, we may object that a vicious man does not hurt all his friends [7]. For an example of the allegation of similars, suppose the premiss to be, that those who are injured always hate, we object that those who are benefited do not always love [8]. In the allegation of authority we quote the judgment of the eminent. Suppose the enthymeme to be, that ignorance is an excuse for the violation of law, and therefore intoxication is, we object that if this were true, Pittacus would have been wrong when he increased the penalty for offences produced by intoxication [9].

NOTES TO APPENDIX C.

1] Enstasis is either the solution of a fallacy by pointing out why the reasoning is inconclusive (διαίρεσις), or the disproof of a false premiss (ἀναίρεσις). It is the latter only that is now examined. Enstasis is neither the mere negation of a proposition, nor the assertion of the contrary or of the contradictory of that proposition, but is the major premiss of a syllogism by which the contrary or contradictory may be proved.

2] Were it not for this kind of enstasis and the locus of authority, the final appeal in dialectic, on the part both of questioner and answerer, would be solely to induction. But it seems the answerer might not only appeal to induction, but to a principle more abstract and universal than the proposition in dispute. But for the αὐτὸς ἔφα of Aristotle, one would have thought that this mode of disproof should be rather called antisyllogism than enstasis. From the modern sense of the word instance (instantia = enstasis) this kind of enstasis, in physical questions at least, seems to have early fallen into desuetude.

3] In the Topica we have an ethical example of this kind of enstasis. Ἔτι ὅταν μὴ ᾖ ἐναντίον τῷ γένει, σκοπεῖν μὴ μόνον εἰ τὸ ἐναντίον ἐν τῷ αὐτῷ γένει ἀλλὰ καὶ τὸ ἀνὰ μέσον. Ἐν ᾧ γὰρ τὰ ἄκρα καὶ τὰ ἀνὰ μέσον, οἷον ἐπὶ λευκοῦ καὶ μέλανος. Ἔνστασις ὅτι ἡ μὲν ἔνδεια καὶ ὑπερβολὴ ἐν τῷ αὐτῷ γένει, ἐν τῷ κακῷ γὰρ ἄμφω, τὸ δὲ μέτριον, ἀνὰ μέσον ὂν τούτων, οὐκ ἐν τῷ κακῷ ἀλλ' ἐν τῷ ἀγαθῷ. Topica, 4. 3. 'When the supposed genus of a term has no contrary, we should observe whether it is the genus not only of the contrary of the term, but also of the intermediate gradations. For (Proposition) contraries and their intermediate gradations belong to the same genus, as we see in colours. Objection: the contraries, excess and defect, belong to the genus evil, while their intermediate gradation, the mean, belongs to the genus good.' [This enstasis is clearly not valid; for good and evil are accidents, not genera, of the mean and extremes: the common genus is relative quantity.]

4] It is clear that an affirmative proposition may be disproved in the second figure. But Aristotle apparently would call such a disproof not enstasis but antisyllogism. Energetic brevity is a requisite of enstasis: its probative or subversive force must be instantaneously felt without further explanation. The second figure, therefore, being, as is here without much reason assumed, more intricate and cumbrous and requiring more enucleation than the others, is not short, sharp, and decisive enough for enstasis.

5] Enstatic disproof in the third figure may just as easily be stated in the first: otherwise, regarding the above-given disproof in the first figure as rather antisyllogism than enstasis, we might agree with Whately in calling the third the enstatic figure.

6] This class has been analysed in the preceding passage. Tò ἐνθύμημα seems, perhaps, rather to point to a conclusion than a premiss: but in this chapter enthymeme is used as the genus of παράδειγμα or induction, and every dialectical premiss is the result of induction.

7] Analysing this example as in the preceding passage, we must, as far as I can see, for our minor premiss borrow from the locus of contraries the maxim that the action of the virtuous is opposite and analogous to that of the vicious, and for our major transform the enstasis, that the vicious does not hurt every friend, into the equipollent proposition, that to act oppositely and analogously to the vicious is not to benefit every friend.

8] For our minor premiss we must borrow from the locus a fortiori, vel minori, vel pari, the maxim that those who are injured act oppositely and analogously to those who are served, and, for our major, transform the enstasis, that those who are served do not always love the benefactor, into the equipollent proposition, that to act analogously and oppositely to those who are served is not always to hate the injurer. Both these examples seem to apply the same maxim. (See, however, Topica, 2. 7, quoted below.) They shew that it is unsafe to assume, as is usually done, that the maxims or metaphysical principles of proof always occupy the position of major premisses.

9] The example is so carelessly given that it is not certain what analysis Aristotle intended. I conjecture the following: The premiss objected to is, that ignorance is an excuse: the enstatic syllogism is, Drunkenness is not an excuse (teste Pittaco), drunken-

ness is ignorance, therefore some ignorance is not an excuse. This kind of enstasis only differs from the first in the modality of the enstatic premiss. It has no intrinsic probability, derives no evidence from experience, but rests solely on the authority of Pittacus.

It seems an arbitrary arrangement to call disproof by the loci of contrariety and similarity, not antisyllogism but enstasis; and the illustrations are unfortunately chosen, for, without being told, we should never have suspected that they were taken from different loci.

Contraries are a locus common to the attack and the solution. Σκοπεῖν δὲ μὴ μόνον ἐπ' αὐτοῦ τοῦ εἰρημένου, ἀλλὰ καὶ ἐπὶ τοῦ ἐναντίου τὸ ἐναντίον· οἷον ὅτι τὸ ἀγαθὸν οὐκ ἐξ ἀνάγκης ἡδύ· οὐδὲ γὰρ τὸ κακὸν λυπηρόν· ἢ εἰ τοῦτο κἀκεῖνο. Καὶ εἰ ἡ δικαιοσύνη ἐπιστήμη, καὶ ἡ ἀδικία ἄγνοια. Εἰ δὲ τοῦτο μή, οὐδ' ἐκεῖνο....Οὐδὲν γὰρ ἄλλο νῦν ἀξιοῦμεν ἢ τὸ ἐναντίον τῷ ἐναντίῳ ἀκολουθεῖν. Topica, 2. 9. 'The questioner may quit the subject in dispute and examine its contrary. He may confute the thesis that the good is always pleasant, by the fact that the bad is not always painful, or vice versa, or the thesis that justice is knowledge, by the fact that injustice is not ignorance: the axiom assumed being that contrary subjects must have contrary predicates.' Similars are also a common locus. "Ἔτι ἐκ τοῦ ὁμοίως ὑπάρχειν....εἰ δύο δυσὶν ὁμοίως ὑπάρχει· εἰ γὰρ τὸ ἕτερον τῷ ἑτέρῳ μὴ ὑπάρχει, οὐδὲ τὸ λοιπὸν τῷ λοιπῷ· εἰ δὲ ὑπάρχει τὸ ἕτερον τῷ ἑτέρῳ, καὶ τὸ λοιπὸν τῷ λοιπῷ. Topica, 2. 10. 'Similars are another locus. If there is an equal probability that two subjects have respectively two predicates, if one has its predicate we may infer that the other has, and vice versa.' Aristotle justifies the example he has given of enstasis from similars by what he says in the Topica: Αἱ μὲν οὖν πρῶται δύο ῥηθεῖσαι (ἐναντίων) συμπλοκαὶ οὐ ποιοῦσιν ἐναντίωσιν· τὸ γὰρ τοὺς φίλους εὖ ποιεῖν τῷ τοὺς ἐχθροὺς κακῶς οὐκ ἔστιν ἐναντίον· ἀμφότερα γὰρ αἱρετὰ καὶ τοῦ αὐτοῦ ἤθους. Οὐδὲ τὸ τοὺς φίλους κακῶς τῷ τοὺς ἐχθροὺς εὖ, καὶ γὰρ ταῦτα ἀμφότερα φευκτὰ καὶ τοῦ αὐτοῦ ἤθους....Τὰ δὲ λοιπὰ πάντα τέτταρα ποιεῖ ἐναντιώσιν. Τὸ γὰρ τοὺς φίλους εὖ ποιεῖν τῷ τοὺς φίλους κακῶς ἐναντίον. Topica, 2. 7. 'The two first syntheses of contraries are not themselves contraries. Benefiting a friend is not contrary to hurting an enemy, for both are desirable and proceed from the same disposition; nor

APPENDIX C. 201

is hurting a friend contrary to benefiting an enemy, for both are undesirable and proceed from the same disposition. But the other four combinations, benefiting a friend, hurting a friend: benefiting an enemy, hurting an enemy: benefiting a friend, benefiting an enemy: hurting a friend, hurting an enemy; are all respectively contraries.'

The fourfold division of enstasis may be illustrated by a fourfold character of propositions and organa. Ἔστι δὲ πρότασις διαλεκτικὴ ἐρώτησις ἔνδοξος ἢ πᾶσιν ἢ τοῖς πλείστοις ἢ τοῖς σοφοῖς, καὶ τούτοις ἢ πᾶσιν ἢ τοῖς πλείστοις ἢ τοῖς μάλιστα γνωρίμοις, μὴ παράδοξος. Θείη γὰρ ἄν τις τὸ δοκοῦν τοῖς σοφοῖς, ἐὰν μὴ ἐναντίον ταῖς τῶν πολλῶν δόξαις ᾖ. Εἰσὶ δὲ προτάσεις διαλεκτικαὶ καὶ τὰ τοῖς ἐνδόξοις ὅμοια, καὶ τἀναντία κατ' ἀντίφασιν τοῖς δοκοῦσιν ἐνδόξοις εἶναι προτεινόμενα, καὶ ὅσαι δόξαι κατὰ τέχνας εἰσὶ τὰς εὑρημένας. Topica, 1. 10. 'A dialectic proposition is a proposition probable to all or to the majority of mankind; or an opinion of all or the majority of philosophers or the most eminent of them, not opposed to the opinion of the many; or a similar proposition respecting similar subjects; or an opposite proposition respecting opposites; or any doctrine of the arts.' Τὰς μὲν οὖν προτάσεις ἐκλεκτέον ὁσαχῶς διωρίσθη....Δεῖ δὲ προτείνειν καὶ τὰς ἐναντίας ταῖς φαινομέναις ἐνδόξοις κατ' ἀντίφασιν· χρήσιμον δὲ καὶ τὸ ποιεῖν αὐτὰς ἐν τῷ ἐκλέγειν μὴ μόνον τὰς οὔσας ἐνδόξους ἀλλὰ καὶ τὰς ὁμοίας ταύταις. Topica, 1. 15. 'The propositions to be collected are, as was said before, the opinions of the many or of philosophers, or the doctrines of the arts; and we may use any propositions that bear a certain relation to these, i. e. where opposite antecedents have opposite consequents, or similar antecedents similar consequents.' In fact, propositions respecting a given subject, and, mutatis mutandis, respecting similar or opposite subjects, might be treated as identical.

Enstasis was the only check on the inartificial induction by simple enumeration practised in dialectic. Ἐὰν γὰρ ἐπὶ πάντων φαίνηται διαίρεσιν προενέγκασιν ἢ ἐπὶ πολλῶν, ἀξιωτέον καὶ καθόλου τιθέναι, ἢ ἔνστασιν φέρειν ἐπὶ τίνος οὐχ οὕτως. Ἐὰν γὰρ μηδέτερον τούτων ποιῇ, ἄτοπος φανεῖται μὴ τιθείς. Topica, 2. 2. 'If all or many of the particulars into which a class is divided present an attribute, we may demand either an admission that it is true of the whole class, or an assignment of instances in which it is not

true. If the respondent does neither one thing nor the other, he is unreasonable.' (Antisyllogism was considered hardly sufficient) 'Ἔτι δ' ἐν τοῖς γένεσιν ἐπιβλεπτέον, διαιροῦντα κατ' εἴδη μέχρι τῶν ἀτόμων. Ἄν τε γὰρ παντὶ φαίνηται ὑπάρχον ἄν τε μηδενί, πολλὰ προσενέγκαντι ἀξιωτέον καθόλου ὁμολογεῖν, ἢ φέρειν ἔνστασιν ἐπὶ τίνος οὐχ οὕτως. Topica, 3. 6. 'Subdivision, as far as we can go, is useful; for whether we want an affirmative or negative proposition, we must first adduce particular examples in which it is true, and then challenge the respondent either to admit the general principle or to allege contradictory instances.'

A disputant who is more accustomed to defence than attack may quicken his wits when he has to attack by imagining himself on the defensive. Ἔτι τὸ πρόβλημα πρότασιν ἑαυτῷ ποιούμενον ἐνίστασθαι· ἡ γὰρ ἔνστασις ἔσται ἐπιχείρημα πρὸς τὴν θέσιν. Topica, 2. 2. 'The questioner may imagine the thesis to be a premiss against which he has to object as respondent: and his objection to the proposition as a premiss will be a confutation of the proposition as a thesis.'

A common formula for urging an enstasis, especially when it is directed against a major premiss and is a proposition which the opponent is particularly interested not to contradict, is to say that his argument proves too much: that, if good for anything, it proves so and so (the contradictory of the enstasis). In this case, instead of being put directly or ostensively, the enstasis assumes the form of a reductio ad impossibile.

APPENDIX D.

Κοιναὶ ἀρχαί, or, Method-founding principles.

§ 1. To understand the nature of the common principles (κοιναὶ ἀρχαί) is to understand Aristotle's conception of science, and, indeed, his conception of logic; for his logic is resumed in the contrast of science and dialectic, and this is the antithesis of common and peculiar principles (Ἴδιαι ἀρχαί). We propose in the following essay to collect some of the scattered indications of their nature; and the necessity of explaining more or less completely each passage as it is quoted must be our excuse if our observations seem to follow one another without much arrangement.

The most important passage is in the beginning of the Rhetoric:— 1, 2. 20

Τῶν δὲ ἐνθυμημάτων μεγίστη διαφορὰ καὶ μάλιστα λεληθυῖα σχεδὸν ἅπαντας ἐστὶν ἥπερ καὶ περὶ τὴν διαλεκτικὴν μέθοδον τῶν συλλογισμῶν. Τὰ μὲν γὰρ αὐτῶν ἐστι κατὰ* τὴν ῥητορικὴν ὥσπερ καὶ κατὰ τὴν διαλεκτικὴν μέθοδον τῶν συλλογισμῶν, τὰ δὲ κατ' ἄλλας τέχνας καὶ δυνάμεις τὰς μὲν οὔσας τὰς δὲ οὔπω κατειλημμένας. Διὸ καὶ λανθάνουσι τοὺς ἀκροατάς, καὶ μᾶλλον ἁπτόμενοι ἢ κατὰ τρόπον μεταβαίνουσιν ἐξ αὐτῶν· μᾶλλον δὲ σαφὲς ἔσται τὸ λεγόμενον διὰ πλειόνων ῥηθέν. Λέγω γὰρ διαλεκτικούς τε καὶ ῥητορικοὺς συλλογισμοὺς εἶναι περὶ ὧν τοὺς τόπους λέγομεν· οὗτοι δ' εἰσὶν οἱ κοινῇ περὶ δικαίων καὶ φυσικῶν καὶ περὶ πολιτικῶν καὶ περὶ πολλῶν διαφερόντων τῷ εἴδει· οἷον ὁ τοῦ μᾶλλον καὶ ἧττον τόπος· οὐδὲν γὰρ μᾶλλον ἔσται ἐκ τούτου συλλογίσασθαι ἢ ἐνθύμημα εἰπεῖν περὶ δικαίων ἢ φυσικῶν ἢ

* Κατὰ is here emphatic. Κατὰ τὴν διαλεκτικήν is equivalent to οἰκεῖα τῆς διαλεκτικῆς. We must distinguish between appropriate to dialectic and appropriate to a given subject-matter. Those principles are properly dialectical and compose a dialectical proof which are not peculiar to any subject-matter (κοιναί). Those which are peculiar to any subject-matter (ἴδιαι τοῦ πράγματος) are extra-dialectical, and constitute a proof scientific or pseudographic.

περὶ ὁτουοῦν· καίτοι ταῦτα εἴδει διαφέρει. Ὅσα δὲ, ὅσα ἐκ τῶν περὶ
ἕκαστον εἶδος καὶ γένος προτάσεών ἐστιν· οἷον περὶ φυσικῶν εἰσὶ
προτάσεις ἐξ ὧν οὔτε ἐνθύμημα οὔτε συλλογισμὸς ἐστι περὶ τῶν ἠθι-
κῶν· καὶ περὶ τούτων ἄλλαι ἐξ ὧν οὐκ ἔσται περὶ τῶν φυσικῶν·
ὁμοίως δὲ τοῦτο ἔχει ἐπὶ πάντων. Κἀκεῖνα μὲν οὐ ποιήσει περὶ οὐδὲν
γένος ἔμφρονα· περὶ οὐδὲν γὰρ ὑποκείμενόν ἐστι· ταῦτα δὲ, ὅσῳ τις
ἂν βελτίους ἐκλέγηται τὰς προτάσεις, λήσει ποιήσας ἄλλην ἐπιστήμην
τῆς διαλεκτικῆς καὶ ῥητορικῆς· ἂν γὰρ ἐντύχῃ ἀρχαῖς, οὐκ ἔτι διαλεκτικὴ οὐδὲ ῥητορικὴ ἀλλ' ἐκείνη ἔσται ἧς ἔχει τὰς ἀρχάς. Ἔστι δὲ
τὰ πλεῖστα τῶν ἐνθυμημάτων ἐκ τούτων τῶν εἰδῶν λεγόμενα τῶν κατὰ
μέρος καὶ ἰδίων, ἐκ δὲ τῶν κοινῶν ἐλάττω. Καθάπερ οὖν καὶ ἐν τοῖς
τοπικοῖς, καὶ ἐνταῦθα διαιρετέον τῶν ἐνθυμημάτων τά τε εἴδη καὶ τοὺς
τόπους ἐξ ὧν ληπτέον. Λέγω δὲ εἴδη μὲν τὰς καθ' ἕκαστον γένος ἰδίας
προτάσεις, τόπους δὲ τοὺς κοινοὺς ὁμοίως πάντων. Πρότερον οὖν
εἴπωμεν περὶ τῶν εἰδῶν. Rhet. I. 2.

.' ' Between rhetorical proofs the most important distinction,
a distinction which has been most commonly, not to say universally, overlooked, is one which also exists between dialectical
proofs: some are characteristic of rhetoric or dialectic, others
properly belong to certain special sciences or arts, whether such
sciences and arts are generally recognized or still remain to
be invented. If the science has not yet been established, the
theorems and proofs are not familiar to the audience to which
they are addressed; and if the prover adheres too closely to
the scientific method, he abandons the proper rhetorical or
dialectical method. This requires further explanation. ¹ Proofs
that properly belong to rhetoric and dialectic are applications of
a locus communis. Loci communes are principles that apply
indiscriminately to ethical, physical, political problems and
other heterogeneous spheres, as, for instance, the argument
a fortiori or a minori. A dialectical or rhetorical proof of this
character applies equally to ethical and physical questions and
other subjects different in kind. Intransferable (that is, not
properly rhetorical or dialectical) proofs are composed of propositions which relate exclusively to particular departments of
nature. For there are propositions respecting physical objects
which furnish no rhetorical or dialectical proof on ethical questions, and there are ethical propositions which furnish no proof
on physical problems, and so of the other provinces of science.

APPENDIX D. 205

The common principles give no scientific knowledge of any class of things, for they do not constitute the essence of any class: whereas the peculiar principles if well selected, though people may not be aware of the fact, go towards constituting a particular science, distinct from rhetoric or dialectic. For if the prover happens to hit upon first principles his proof is not rhetorical or dialectical but scientific. Most rhetorical proofs are composed of specific, that is, particular and intransferable propositions; only a minority are composed of common principles. A rhetorical treatise, therefore, like a dialectical treatise, must distinguish the specific principles of proof from the loci of proof. Specific principles are principles that exclusively belong to a particular class of problems; loci are methods (premisses) of proof that are equally applicable to all classes.'

In the last sentence instead of τοὺς κοινούς we should have expected τὰς κοινὰς [προτάσεις]. But this passage is one instance of a certain indecision in Aristotle's mind whether to treat the loci as premisses or as methods, as indicative or imperative, as categorical or hypothetical, as constituent principles (in the language of Kant) or as regulative, as objective or subjective, as laws of nature or as rules of procedure. He avoids, therefore, the unmistakeable term, προτάσεις, and uses the obscurer term, loci. However, even from the present passage, we may certainly infer that the word loci designates premisses. Aristotle does not say, Every proof has two elements; one is formal or dialectical, the other is material or extra-dialectical: but he says, There are two divisions, two separate classes, of proofs; one proof is properly dialectical, the other is not properly dialectical. As the specific or sectional character of the premisses is the differentia of the one class, the generic or catholic character of the premisses must be the differentia of the contradistinguished class. We shall see further on [§ 6] that one branch of dialectic may consist entirely of such syllogisms: but considering the subjects handled by the orator, it is clear that in oratorical proofs the maxims [τὰ κοινά] and specific facts [τὰ ἴδια] will be usually combined in the same syllogism. Aristotle would therefore have done better in a rhetorical treatise to found on the distinction of ἴδια and κοινά a division not of proofs (ἐνθυμημάτων) but of premisses.

Another proof that locus may denote a premiss we have in the fact that later on in the Rhetoric, not only the catholic principles or loci proper but the εἴδη or specific principles, which are perpetually called premisses, are designated by the term of loci. After giving a collection of specific principles (εἴδη) he says:— Εἷς μὲν οὖν τρόπος τῆς ἐκλογῆς καὶ πρῶτος οὗτος ὁ τοπικός· τὰ δὲ στοιχεῖα τῶν ἐνθυμημάτων λέγωμεν. Στοιχεῖον δὲ λέγω καὶ τόπον ἐνθυμήματος τὸ αὐτό.... Σχεδὸν μὲν οὖν ἡμῖν περὶ ἑκάστων τῶν εἰδῶν τῶν χρησίμων καὶ ἀναγκαίων ἔχονται οἱ τόποι. Ἐξειλεγμέναι γὰρ αἱ προτάσεις περὶ ἕκαστόν εἰσιν, ὥστ' [ἔχομεν] ἐξ ὧν δεῖ φέρειν τὰ ἐνθυμήματα τόπων περὶ ἀγαθοῦ ἢ κακοῦ ἢ καλοῦ ἢ αἰσχροῦ ἢ δικαίου ἢ ἀδίκου, καὶ περὶ τῶν ἠθῶν καὶ παθημάτων καὶ ἕξεων ὡσαύτως εἰλημμένοι ἡμῖν ὑπάρχουσι πρότερον οἱ τόποι. Ἔτι δ' ἄλλον τρόπον καθόλου περὶ ἁπάντων λάβωμεν. Rhet. 2. 22. 'One class of materials, and the class that should first be collected, are propositions such as I have given which (as contrasted with τὰ ἐξ ὑπογυίον, or the singular facts of each particular case) are in the nature of loci. We now proceed to the elements of proof, and by elements I mean [another sort of] loci. We are already in possession of loci on the particular subject-matters that are indispensable or useful to the orator: for we have made a collection of propositions and enumerated the loci respecting the expedient and honorable and right, and respecting characters and passions and dispositions. There still remain another sort of loci of universal application (the loci proper), which we now proceed to enumerate.' When, however, we find that the loci enumerated include etymology, division, definition, induction, it must be confessed that we seem to have rather a list of methods of reasoning than of premisses of syllogism. But the employment of each of these methods has to be justified by certain postulates, expressed or unexpressed; and if the loci are regarded as propositions, it is these postulates that are the loci. (This subject is resumed § 13.)

§ 2. We find frequent mention of common principles (τὰ κοινά) in the analysis of science under the name of Axioms. Ἀμέσου δ' ἀρχῆς συλλογιστικῆς θέσιν μὲν λέγω ἣν μὴ ἔστι δεῖξαι μηδ' ἀνάγκη ἔχειν τὸν μαθησόμενόν τι· ἣν δ' ἀνάγκη ἔχειν τὸν ὁτιοῦν μαθησόμενον, ἀξίωμα. Analytica Posteriora, 1. 2. 'Immediate syllogistic principles are either theses, that is, are indemonstrable,

APPENDIX D. 207

but not the necessary conditions of all inference: or axioms, that is, the common conditions of all inference.' If science as well as dialectic has both Ἴδιαι and κοιναὶ ἀρχαί, how, it may be asked, do they differ, and how can the κοιναὶ ἀρχαι be the distinguishing badge of dialectic [κατὰ τὴν διαλεκτικήν, § 1]? The answer is, that the common and peculiar principles exist both in science and in dialectic, but exist in an inverse ratio. In dialectic the common and abstract principles predominate, and the specific concrete facts are reduced to a minimum. In science the specific data predominate, and the common principles are reduced to a minimum, only those being admitted which are requisite to constitute a faculty of inference. Of course when dialectic investigation proceeds without, or with very scanty, specific data, the result can only be a Barmecide feast of abstractions such as we have in the Parmenides. Aristotle himself in his physical inquiries ('Physicam Dialecticæ suæ mancipavit'), forgetting his own canons, engages in a task which reminds one of that set by Egyptian taskmasters of making bricks without straw. But dialectic may command specific data in various proportions, and ranges over a wide field, touching sophistry on the one side and on the other approaching indefinitely near to science. Καὶ, μᾶλλον ἁπτόμενοι (τῶν ἰδίων) κατὰ τρόπον, μεταβαίνουσιν ἐξ αὐτῶν [τῆς ῥητορικῆς καὶ τῆς διαλεκτικῆς]. See § 1.

The common principles of science are identified with the common principles of dialectic. Ἐπικοινωνοῦσι δὲ πᾶσαι αἱ ἐπιστῆμαι ἀλλήλαις κατὰ τὰ κοινά (κοινὰ δὲ λέγω οἷς χρῶνται ὡς ἐκ τούτων ἀποδεικνύντες, ἀλλ' οὐ περὶ ὧν δεικνύουσιν, οὐδ' ὃ δεικνύουσι) καὶ ἡ διαλεκτικὴ πάσαις, καὶ εἴ τις καθόλου πειρῷτο δεικνύναι τὰ κοινά, οἷον ὅτι ἅπαν φάναι ἢ ἀποφάναι, ἢ ὅτι ἴσα ἀπὸ ἴσων, ἢ τῶν τοιούτων ἄττα. Analytica Posteriora, 1.11. 'The common principles express neither the subject nor the attribute of a theorem, but are the canons of demonstration; and are the common property of the particular sciences, of dialectic and of (metaphysic or) whatever science it is which investigates these propositions; Of two contradictories one or the other must be true; Equals from which equals are subtracted have equal remainders; and the like.' We must interpret this to mean that the common principles of science are included among the common principles of dialectic, not that they are coextensive. This is clear from the following

APPENDIX D.

considerations. The axioms, we saw above, are indispensable to reasoning; but many of the maxims cannot be indispensable, for science contrives to dispense with them, e. g. the maxims that constitute the unscientific formulae of reasoning by analogy or a fortiori. Secondly, an axiom is a necessary truth, a maxim may be merely a probability. Οὐκ ἔστι δ' ὑπόθεσις οὐδ' αἴτημα ὃ ἀνάγκη εἶναι δι' αὐτὸ καὶ δοκεῖν ἀνάγκῃ. An. Post. 1. 10. 'An axiom differs from an hypothesis or petition in being necessarily true and necessarily believed.' We know that dialectic only professes to rest on probabilities (ἔνδοξα), and we find in the Topics that this applies to the common as well as to the specific principles. E. g. Ἡ εἰ ἔστι μέν τι ἀμφοῖν ἀνὰ μέσον, καὶ τῶν εἰδῶν καὶ τῶν γενῶν, μὴ ὁμοίως δέ, ... ἔνδοξον γὰρ τὸ ὁμοίως ἀμφοῖν. Topics, 4. 3. 'If a term and its contrary are connected by gradations, it is a probable postulate that their genera, when not identical, are connected by similar gradations.' Thirdly, the axioms, as we saw above, are necessarily believed or self-evident; whereas some, at least, of the maxims require the evidence of induction. E. g. Δεῖ γὰρ τὰ ἐναντία ἐν τῷ αὐτῷ γένει εἶναι, ἂν μηδὲν ἐναντίον τῷ γένει ᾖ. Οὗτος δ' ἐναντίον τῷ γένει, σκοπεῖν εἰ τὸ ἐναντίον ἐν τῷ ἐναντίῳ. Ἀνάγκη γὰρ τὸ ἐναντίον ἐν τῷ ἐναντίῳ εἶναι, ἄνπερ ᾖ ἐναντίον τι τῷ γένει. Φανερὸν δὲ τούτων ἕκαστον διὰ τῆς ἐπαγωγῆς. Topics, 4. 3. 'Contrary terms have the same genus, unless there is a contrary to the genus. If there is a contrary to the genus, it ought to contain the contrary term. These postulates are evidenced by induction.' Even the laws of conversion require this support. Ἐπεὶ δ' αἱ ἀντιθέσεις τέσσαρες, σκοπεῖν ἐκ μὲν τῶν ἀντιφάσεων ἀνάπαλιν ἐκ τῆς ἀκολουθήσεως καὶ ἀναιροῦντι καὶ κατασκευάζοντι, λαμβάνειν δ' ἐξ ἐπαγωγῆς· οἷον εἰ ὁ ἄνθρωπος ζῷον τὸ μὴ ζῷον οὐκ ἄνθρωπος. Topics, 2. 8. 'There being four kinds of opposites (contradictories, contraries, privatives, relatives) to prove or disprove a sequence of two terms, we should observe whether their contradictories present a converse sequence (i. e. whether the terms admit of conversion by contraposition), and we must establish the law of conversion by induction. For instance, if all man is animal, all not-animal is not-man.' It is not necessary, then, to a dialectic maxim to possess the evidence or necessity of a scientific axiom.

APPENDIX D.

§ 3. The peculiar principles of science are definitions and hypotheses, that is, propositions asserting the existence of the things defined. Θέσεως δ' ἡ μὲν ὁποτερονοῦν τῶν μορίων τῆς ἀποφάνσεως λαμβάνουσα, οἶον λέγω τὸ εἶναί τι ἢ τὸ μὴ εἶναί τι, ὑπόθεσις, ἡ δ' ἄνευ τούτου ὁρισμός. Analytica Posteriora, 1. 2. 'Theses, or peculiar principles, are either hypotheses, that is, affirmations or negations of existence, or definitions.' Mill denies that definitions are an indispensable basis of science, and maintains that postulates (hypotheses) suffice as germs of scientific evolution. But, after pointing out that other logicians had combined the definition with a surreptitious postulate, he himself, when he maintains the self-sufficiency of the postulate, combines the postulate with a surreptitious definition. For without a definition the postulate is merely the proposition, X exists; and from such a proposition, without any explanation of the nature (definition) of X, it is impossible that any consequences can be deduced. The specific basis of science is a definition—postulate, that is, is composed of two distinct elements and cannot accurately be called either a definition or a postulate. On this point Aristotle has expressed the truth more exactly than either Dugald Stewart or Mill. Πᾶσα γὰρ ἀποδεικτικὴ ἐπιστήμη περὶ τρία ἐστί, ὅσα τε εἶναι τίθεται, ταῦτα δ' ἐστὶ τὸ γένος, οὗ τῶν καθ' αὑτὰ παθημάτων ἐστὶ θεωρητική, καὶ τὰ κοινὰ λεγόμενα ἀξιώματα, ἐξ ὧν πρώτων ἀποδείκνυσι, καὶ τρίτον τὰ πάθη, ὧν τί σημαίνει ἕκαστον λαμβάνει. Ἔνιαι μέντοι ἐπιστῆμαι οὐδὲν κωλύει ἔνια τούτων παρορᾶν, οἶον τὸ γένος μὴ ὑποτίθεσθαι εἶναι, ἂν ᾖ φανερὸν ὅτι ἔστι ... Καὶ τὰ πάθη μὴ λαμβάνειν τί σημαίνει, ἂν ᾖ δῆλα· ὥσπερ οὐδὲ τὰ κοινὰ οὐ λαμβάνει τί σημαίνει, τὸ ἴσα ἀπὸ ἴσων ἀφελεῖν, ὅτι γνώριμον. Ἀλλ' οὐδὲν ἧττον τῇ γε φύσει τρία ταῦτά ἐστι, περὶ ὅ τε δείκνυσι καὶ ἃ δείκνυσι καὶ ἐξ ὧν. An. Post. 1. 10. 5 'In all demonstrative science there are three elements: the subject, whose existence is assumed and whose essential laws are developed; the axioms, which belong alike to every science; and the attributes, whose definition is assumed and whose existence in the subject is the law we demonstrate. When any one of these is obvious, it will be neglected: if the existence of the subject is obvious, an hypothesis is not needed: if the definition of a predicate is obvious, it may be omitted. The meaning in the axiom of subtracting equals from equals is too plain for definition. But really there

P

210   APPENDIX D.

are always three elements of demonstration, the subject, the attributes, and the catholic canons of proof.'

Any classification of the sciences that we choose to adopt will serve as a classification of the specific principles of dialectic (ὄργανα, εἴδη). Aristotle gives one that has had a great currency both in ancient and modern times, though different from that which he adopts in his more philosophic writings. He says they may be roughly classed as physical, ethical, and logical (metaphysical). 'Έστι δ' ὡς τύπῳ περιλαβεῖν τῶν προτάσεων καὶ τῶν προβλημάτων μέρη τρία. Αἱ μὲν γὰρ ἠθικαὶ προτάσεις εἰσίν, αἱ δὲ φυσικαί, αἱ δὲ λογικαί. 'Ηθικαὶ μὲν οὖν αἱ τοιαῦται, οἷον πότερον δεῖ τοῖς γονεῦσι μᾶλλον ἢ τοῖς νόμοις πειθαρχεῖν, ἐὰν διαφωνῶσι· λογικαὶ δέ, οἷον πότερον τῶν ἐναντίων ἡ αὐτὴ ἐπιστήμη ἢ οὔ· φυσικαὶ δέ, πότερον ὁ κόσμος ἀΐδιος ἢ οὔ· ὁμοίως δὲ καὶ τὰ προβλήματα. Ποῖαι δ' ἕκασται τῶν προειρημένων, ὁρισμῷ μὲν οὐκ εὐπετὲς ἀποδοῦναι περὶ αὐτῶν, τῇ δὲ διὰ τῆς ἐπαγωγῆς συνηθείᾳ πειρατέον γνωρίζειν ἑκάστην αὐτῶν, κατὰ τὰ προειρημένα παραδείγματα ἐπισκοποῦντα. Topica, I. 14. 'Propositions and problems may be roughly thrown into three divisions, ethical, physical, and logical. Of ethical propositions the following is an instance: Should we obey our parents or the laws when their commands are inconsistent? of logical the following: Are contraries simultaneously known or not? of physical the following: Is the world eternal or not? And so of problems. To define these classes would not be easy, but we must endeavour to identify them by practice with the help of these examples.'

§ 4. In the Topica the word ὄργανα denotes the particular premisses (εἴδη). Aristotle elsewhere, or whoever named his logical treatises ὄργανον, uses the word in a different signification. In the Topica it signifies the materials (ὕλη) which are furnished to the artist, and the loci or maxims, as contradistinguished from the materials, represent the tools with which he works. But when the name of organon is given to the whole of logic, it denotes the latter, i.e. the loci or purely logical principles, which constitute an organ or faculty of cognition, co-ordinate with the natural organs of perception (κριτήρια), the eye, the ear, the hand, or with artificial organs of appreciation, the thermometer, chronometer, barometer.

When the problem is ethical or physical, there is a difference

APPENDIX D.

in kind between the organs and loci, and they present the contrast of special and catholic principles. But when the problem belongs to the third division, that is, when it is logical, the distinction disappears, the organa and loci coincide, and logical conceptions are the materials as well as the tools of the dialectician. Accordingly in another classification of problems Aristotle describes the third division (τὰ λογικά) as instrumental and subordinate theorems, that is, in terms which are equally appropriate to the loci. Πρόβλημα δ' ἐστὶ διαλεκτικὸν θεώρημα τὸ συντεῖνον ἢ πρὸς αἵρεσιν καὶ φυγήν, ἢ πρὸς ἀλήθειαν καὶ γνῶσιν, ἢ αὐτὸ ἢ ὡς συνεργὸν πρός τι ἕτερον τῶν τοιούτων. . . . Ἔνια μὲν γὰρ τῶν προβλημάτων χρήσιμον εἰδέναι πρὸς τὸ ἑλέσθαι ἢ φυγεῖν, οἷον πότερον ἡ ἡδονὴ αἱρετὸν ἢ οὔ, ἔνια δὲ πρὸς τὸ εἰδέναι μόνον, οἷον πότερον ὁ κόσμος ἀΐδιος ἢ οὔ, ἔνια δὲ αὐτὰ μὲν καθ' αὑτὰ πρὸς οὐδέτερον τούτων, συνεργὰ δέ ἐστι πρός τινα τῶν τοιούτων. Πολλὰ γὰρ αὐτὰ μὲν καθ' αὑτὰ οὐ βουλόμεθα γνωρίζειν, ἑτέρων δ' ἕνεκα, ὅπως διὰ τούτων ἄλλο τι γνωρίσωμεν. Top. I. II. 'A dialectic problem is either a practical (ethical) or speculative (physical) theorem, or is subservient to the decision of a practical or speculative question (logical). That is to say, the solution of some problems is useful for our guidance in action, as whether pleasure is to be pursued; that of others has no end beyond knowledge, as whether the world is eternal: another class are in themselves neither useful nor interesting but are ancillary to ulterior inquiries.'

§ 5. From our present point of view we may see that Whately's distinction of logical and extra-logical fallacies will not bear examination. He considers that some forms of fallacy, for instance, the fallacy of equivocation, are essentially extra-logical. Adopting the theory that logic is conversant not with things or ideas but with words, he says that, whenever to detect a fallacy it is necessary to understand the meaning of a word, the fallacy is extra-logical. The logician may happen to know the meaning of the word, but, if he does, he does so not as a logician, but as a moralist or mathematician, or in some other capacity. This is untenable. It is clear that the logician must know the meaning of some terms. He must at least know the meaning of all the terms of his own science. Unless a parrot can be a logician, no one can be a logician to whom the terms

universal, particular, antecedent, consequent, necessary, contingent, are mere words without meaning. This list may be extended almost indefinitely. If we reflect on what is discussed in logical treatises, we see that the logician requires all the conceptions as well as the vocabulary of—what till we find a better name we will call—ontology (τὰ λογικά). When, therefore, the problem belongs to the sphere of ontology, the logician, by his logical knowledge, will be able to detect any fallacy that depends on the meaning of the terms, and such fallacies will be purely logical. The dialectician, however, has a still wider range than the pure logician. He has to deal with all ethical or physical conceptions that fall within common cognition (ἔνδοξα, δοκοῦντα τοῖς πολλοῖς). Ethical or physical premisses, though special or particular propositions in one sense, that is, in respect of the subjects to which they apply, are common or universal opinions in another sense, that is, in respect of the minds by which they are entertained. Fallacies from the application of principles that lie beyond the range of ordinary information are extra-dialectical (ψευδογραφήματα). Whether ethical problems can furnish a pseudographema may be doubted. Even the physic of Aristotle's day, composed, as Bacon says with some truth, of vulgar notions loosely abstracted, could hardly furnish arguments beyond the competence of the dialectician. Accordingly the only examples of pseudographema that Aristotle gives, are, agreeably to the etymology of the name, geometrical.

§ 6. Without stopping to discuss the relation of logic in its modern sense to the logic (τὰ λογικά) of the Topics, assuming, moreover, that the latter (of whose nature Aristotle has scarcely given us any means of judging beyond the passages already quoted) is the science to which the maxims properly belong, we may regard it as more or less completely identical with ontology or metaphysic. We have already seen (An. Post. I. II, quoted in § 2), that the common principles are found alike in the particular sciences, in dialectic and in a certain universal science. The name of this science is not given, but we are elsewhere told it is metaphysic or philosophia prima. 'Επεὶ δὲ ὁ μαθηματικὸς χρῆται τοῖς κοινοῖς ἰδίως, καὶ τὰς τούτων ἀρχὰς ἂν εἴη θεωρῆσαι τῆς πρώτης φιλοσοφίας. Metaphysics, II. 4. 'As the mathematician only makes a limited application of the common principles, their

APPENDIX D. 213

adequate investigation belongs to metaphysic.' A paradox here arises. The common principles are the means by which the philosopher makes himself intelligible to the unphilosophic, they are the intellectual capital, the common sense, of the ignorant. Πρὸς δὲ τὰς ἐντεύξεις χρήσιμος ἡ πραγματεία, διότι τὰς τῶν πολλῶν κατηριθμημένοι δόξας οὐκ ἐκ τῶν ἀλλοτρίων ἀλλ' ἐκ τῶν οἰκείων δογμάτων ὁμιλήσομεν πρὸς αὐτούς, μεταβιβάζοντες ὅτι ἂν μὴ καλῶς φαίνωνται λέγειν ἡμῖν. Topica, I. 2. 'Dialectic is useful to the philosopher in his intercourse with the world, because, giving him possession of the creed of the uneducated, it enables him to reason with them on their own principles and to influence their opinions when he thinks them mistaken.' To say that the ignorant talk metaphysic without knowing it, and that metaphysical reasoning is the reasoning of the uneducated, seems paradoxical, and sounds like the sarcasm of a positivist. But though it is asserted that the principles of the ordinary public are in substance metaphysical, it is not maintained that they apprehend or state them with any precision. Ταῦτα γὰρ (τὰ κοινὰ) οὐδὲν ἧττον ἴσασιν αὐτοί (οἱ ἰδιῶται) κἂν δοκῶσι λίαν ἔξω λέγειν. Sophistici Elenchi, 11. 'The uneducated possess the common principles as well as the educated, though their expression of them may be very inaccurate.' Besides, the truth is, that all reasoning, scientific and unscientific, involves metaphysical principles; and unscientific reasoning is only called pre-eminently metaphysical, because it is composed in a larger proportion of those abstract principles which, either because they are innate or because they are the easiest and earliest generalizations, are of general acceptation, than of the specific facts which can only be learnt by a specially directed observation. Ἔτι δὲ πρὸς ἐνίους οὐδ' εἰ τὴν ἀκριβεστάτην ἔχοιμεν ἐπιστήμην ῥᾴδιον ἀπ' ἐκείνης πεῖσαι λέγοντας· διδασκαλίας γὰρ ἐστιν ὁ κατὰ τὴν ἐπιστήμην λόγος, τοῦτο δὲ ἀδύνατον ἀλλ' ἀνάγκη διὰ τῶν κοινῶν ποιεῖσθαι τὰς πίστεις καὶ τοὺς λόγους, ὥσπερ καὶ ἐν τοῖς τοπικοῖς ἐλέγομεν περὶ τῆς πρὸς τοὺς πολλοὺς ἐντεύξεως. Rhet. I. I. 'To some minds the most exact science would not enable us to convey persuasion. A teacher and a learner are implied in the proper scientific proof, and this relation may be out of the question. Then the catholic methods are the only means of persuasion or conviction, as I said in the Topica about the intercourse of the philosopher with the world.'

214   APPENDIX D.

Plutarch, or the author of Placita Philosophorum, says that the Stoics (who very likely took the doctrine from Aristotle) held that the axioms, or principles that constitute the logical faculty, are fully developed by seven years of age. Τῶν δ' ἐννοιῶν αἱ μὲν φυσικαὶ γίνονται κατὰ τοὺς εἰρημένους τρόπους καὶ ἀνεπιτεχνήτως, αἱ δ' ἤδη δι' ἡμετέρας διδασκαλίας καὶ ἐπιμελείας· αὗται μὲν οὖν ἔννοιαι καλοῦνται μόνον, ἐκεῖναι δὲ καὶ προλήψεις. Ὁ δὲ λόγος καθ' ὃν προσαγορευόμεθα λογικοὶ ἐκ τῶν προλήψεων συμπληροῦσθαι λέγεται κατὰ τὴν πρώτην ἑβδομάδα. 4. 11. 'Ideas are either natural, that is, acquired in the way we have mentioned (sensation and experience had been mentioned), and inartificial, or are artificial and the result of culture. The latter are specially called ideas, the former are specifically called anticipations (axioms). The reason, in virtue of which all men are called rational, is formed by the development of the anticipations in the first seven years of life.' In illustration of the statement that logical principles are metaphysical theorems, we might refer to the ontological inquiries on which the rudiments of logic are based in the Sophistes of Plato, to the position of the axioms in the Metaphysic of Aristotle, or to the metaphysical discussions in Mill's System of Logic, on the uniformity of nature, on the law of causation, on chance, &c. &c., which lay the foundation for his exposition of inductive method.

§ 7. After reviewing these general statements on the nature of the loci, if we proceed to examine the list of them given in the Topica and Rhetoric, our first impression is one of surprise. The loci given are not easy to reduce to any common principle, and their common principle, so far as it is perceptible, is not what we might have expected. From Aristotle's apparent identification of the maxims and axioms, we might have expected to find the maxims to be applications or specifications or corollaries of the axioms. For some reason or other, perhaps to reserve something for his immediate disciples, Aristotle has carefully avoided giving the loci in the form of propositions, so that it would be rash to assert that the propositions which he conceived to be grouped under the loci bear no relation to the axioms: but we may safely say that no such relation is obvious.

Many of the loci, most of those given in the Rhetoric, may

APPENDIX D. 215

easily be grouped under the category of correlatives. When unable to demonstrate the attributes of any term taken by itself, that is, when we have not materials for scientific reasoning (καθ' αὑτό, κατ' οὐσίαν), we still may reason dialectically (κατ' ἄλλο, κατὰ συμβιβηκός), by leaving the term and examining another term to which it stands in some definite relation, and then, mutatis mutandis, transferring the attribute of the second term to the first. The mutation to be effected, or the conditions of the transfer, may be supposed to be expressed in an axiom or topical maxim. Such correlatives are: Contraries, Similars, (giving rise to the methods of induction, analogy, argumentum a pari); Terms similar in quality and dissimilar in quantity (giving rise to the argument a fortiori and a minori): Parts (giving rise to the methods of partition and division): Elements, (giving rise to definition): Antecedent, Consequent, Name (giving rise to the argument from etymology), &c. &c. But the vast majority of loci in the Topica are of a different nature, and are held together by a different bond of union.

The nature of the arguments to be employed in a discussion, and of the rules for their invention, must be determined by the nature of the problem discussed or the thesis controverted. Every proposition that is supported or subverted must assert or deny a relation of subject and predicate, and this relation must be one of four, that is, if A is the predicate and B the subject, the proposition must assert or deny that A is an accident, or a genus, or a property, or the definition of B. Of course the definitions of accident, genus, property, definition, must decide respectively what is the nature of the proof required in support of any such conclusion. Aristotle accordingly breaks these four definitions into as many fragments as possible, presents them under as many different aspects as he can imagine, and calls these fragments and aspects of the definitions by the name of loci. But the theories of accident, genus, property, are all resumed in the theory of definition : for definition must be a truth or matter of fact (ἀληθὲς εἰπεῖν) like accident, and a law like genus and property, besides presenting its own peculiar characteristics. All the loci, therefore, that arise from these four definitions may be grouped under one head, the definition of definition. Πρῶτον οὖν θεωρητέον ἐκ τίνων ἡ μέθοδος. Εἰ δὴ λάβοιμεν πρὸς πόσα καὶ

APPENDIX D.

ποῖα καὶ ἐκ τίνων οἱ λόγοι, καὶ πῶς τούτων εὐπορήσομεν, ἔχοιμεν ἂν ἱκανῶς τὸ προκείμενον. Ἔστι δ' ἀριθμῷ ἴσα καὶ τὰ αὐτὰ ἐξ ὧν τε οἱ λόγοι καὶ περὶ ὧν οἱ συλλογισμοί. Γίνονται μὲν γὰρ οἱ λόγοι ἐκ τῶν προτάσεων, περὶ ὧν δὲ οἱ συλλογισμοί, τὰ προβλήματά ἐστι. Πᾶσα δὲ πρότασις καὶ πᾶν πρόβλημα ἢ γένος ἢ ἴδιον ἢ συμβεβηκὸς δηλοῖ. Topics, 1. 4. 'Let us first enquire of what branches the method is composed, and when we have classified conclusions and premisses, and shewn how to obtain the latter, we shall have accomplished our task. The classes of premisses and conclusions, that is, of propositions and problems, are identical; for every proposition and problem expresses either a genus, a property, or an accident.' Property is then subdivided into property and definition. Μὴ λανθανέτω δ' ἡμᾶς ὅτι τὰ πρὸς τὸ ἴδιον καὶ τὸ γένος καὶ τὸ συμβεβηκὸς πάντα καὶ πρὸς τοὺς ὁρισμοὺς ἁρμόσει λέγεσθαι....... Ὥστε κατὰ τὸν ἔμπροσθεν ἀποδοθέντα λόγον ἅπαιτ' ἂν εἴη τρόπον τινὰ ὁρικὰ τὰ κατηριθμημένα. Topics, 1. 6. 'The rules for property, genus, and accident all apply to definition: so that all the rules may be regarded as rules of definition.' Πρὸς μὲν οὖν τὸ συμβεβηκὸς διὰ τῶν τοιούτων καὶ οὕτως ἐπιχειρητέον. Μετὰ δὲ ταῦτα περὶ τῶν πρὸς τὸ γένος καὶ τὸ ἴδιον ἐπισκεπτέον. Ἔστι δὲ ταῦτα στοιχεῖα τῶν πρὸς τοὺς ὅρους· περὶ αὐτῶν δὲ τούτων ὀλιγάκις αἱ σκέψεις γίνονται τοῖς διαλεγομένοις. Topics, 4. 1. 'After these rules for disproving accident, the rules for examining pretended genus and property must be expounded. These will be elements of the method of testing definition. Genus and property are seldom themselves the final object of dialectic discussion.' Τῆς δὲ περὶ τοὺς ὅρους πραγματείας μέρη πέντε ἐστίν. Ἢ γὰρ ὅτι ὅλως οὐκ ἀληθὲς εἰπεῖν, καθ' οὗ τοὔνομα, καὶ τὸν λόγον (δεῖ γὰρ τὸν τοῦ ἀνθρώπου ὁρισμὸν κατὰ παντὸς ἀνθρώπου ἀληθεύεσθαι) ἢ ὅτι ὄντος γένους οὐκ ἔθηκεν εἰς τὸ γένος ἢ οὐκ εἰς τὸ οἰκεῖον γένος ἔθηκε (δεῖ γὰρ τὸν ὁριζόμενον εἰς τὸ γένος θέντα τὰς διαφορὰς προσάπτειν· μάλιστα γὰρ τῶν ἐν τῷ ὁρισμῷ τὸ γένος δοκεῖ τὴν τοῦ ὁριζομένου οὐσίαν σημαίνειν), ἢ ὅτι οὐκ ἴδιος ὁ λόγος (δεῖ γὰρ τὸν ὁρισμὸν ἴδιον εἶναι), ἢ εἰ πάντα τὰ εἰρημένα πεποιηκὼς μὴ ὥρισται μηδ' εἴρηκε τὸ τί ἦν εἶναι τῷ ὁριζομένῳ. Λοιπὸν δὲ παρὰ τὰ εἰρημένα, εἰ ὥρισται μὲν μὴ καλῶς δ' ὥρισται. Topics, 6. 1. 'The method of examining definition has five branches. We either shew, as in the case of accident, that the predicate is not true; or that the genus, at least the proximate genus, the dominant part of the essence, is

not given; or, as in the case of property, that the subject is not sufficiently distinguished; or, that the essence is not expressed; or, that the expression is inelegant.'

§ 8. We have seen that all the loci of solution by distinction (διαίρεσις), that is, all the means of exposing the inconclusiveness of a disproof, may be reduced to the definition of confutation. ['Η δὴ οὕτως διαιρετέον τοὺς φαινομένους συλλογισμοὺς καὶ ἐλέγχους, ἢ πάντας ἀνακτέον εἰς τὴν τοῦ ἐλέγχου ἄγνοιαν. Ἔστι γὰρ ἅπαντας ἀναλῦσαι τοὺς λεχθέντας τρόπους εἰς τὸν τοῦ ἐλέγχου διορισμόν. Sophistici Elenchi, 6.] We now see that the loci of confutation, and, therefore, also the loci of solution by antisyllogism and objection (ἀναίρεσις), are all reducible to another definition, the definition of definition. The former definition is the basis of what Cicero calls the logic of judgment, the latter of what he calls the logic of invention. See his Topics, ch. 2.

Though the definition of proof or disproof properly furnishes the loci of solution, yet the questioner as well as the respondent may sometimes appeal to this definition. This, however, is only when the respondent has raised the question, whether the proof is conclusive. 'Ἔτι ὥσπερ οὐδ' ἐν συλλογισμῷ λαμβάνεται τί ἐστι τὸ συλλελογίσθαι, ἀεὶ γὰρ ὅλη ἡ μέρος ἡ πρότασις ἐξ ὧν ὁ συλλογισμός, οὕτως οὐδὲ τὸ τί ἦν εἶναι δεῖ ἐνεῖναι ἐν τῷ συλλογισμῷ ἀλλὰ χωρὶς τοῦτο τῶν κειμένων εἶναι· καὶ πρὸς τὸν ἀμφισβητοῦντα εἰ συλλελόγισται ἢ μὴ τοῦτο, ἀπαντᾶν, ὅτι, τοῦτο γὰρ ἦν συλλογισμός· καὶ πρὸς τὸν ὅτι οὐ τὸ τί ἦν εἶναι συλλελόγισται, ὅτι ναί, τοῦτο γὰρ ἔκειτο ἡμῖν τὸ τί ἦν εἶναι. Ὥστε ἀνάγκη καὶ ἄνευ τοῦ τί συλλογισμὸς ἢ τοῦ τί ἦν εἶναι συλλελογίσθαι τι. An. Post. 2. 6. ' As in proving we do not define proof, for the terms of the syllogism are always related as whole and part, so in demonstrating a definition (defining) we ought not to assume among our terms a definition of definition; but as, if our proof is disallowed, we maintain it by defining proof; so if our proof of definition is disallowed, we may reply by defining definition. As we draw a conclusion independently of the definition of proof, so we ought to prove a definition (define) independently of the definition of definition.'

[To digress from our present subject, we may observe that the objection here raised by Aristotle to a mode of proving definition hardly seems to express his final view. Indeed it admits of an obvious answer. All dialectical proof is based, as we have just

218   APPENDIX D.

seen, on the definition of definition; a particular proof therefore, i. e. the proof of definition, may well rest on the same basis. For a further answer to this objection see § 13.]

That the questioner sometimes appeals to the definition of proof appears from another passage. Τὸ δὲ μὴ ἐνδέχεσθαι ἅμα φάναι καὶ ἀποφάναι οὐδεμία λαμβάνει ἀπόδειξις, ἀλλ' ἢ ἐὰν δέῃ δεῖξαι καὶ τὸ συμπέρασμα οὕτως. Δείκνυται δὲ λαβοῦσι τὸ πρῶτον κατὰ τοῦ μέσου ὅτι ἀληθές, ἀποφάναι δ' οὐκ ἀληθές. Τὸ δὲ μέσον [κατὰ τοῦ πρώτου ἀληθὲς] οὐδὲν διαφέρει εἶναι καὶ μὴ εἶναι λαβεῖν, ὡσαύτως καὶ τὸ τρίτον [κατὰ τοῦ μέσου]. Εἰ γὰρ ἐδόθη, καθ' οὗ ἄνθρωπον ἀληθὲς εἰπεῖν, εἰ καὶ [καθ' οὗ] μὴ-ἄνθρωπον ἀληθές, ἀλλ' εἰ μόνον [καθ' οὗ] ἄνθρωπον, ζῷον εἶναι μὴ-ζῷον δὲ μή· ἔσται ἀληθὲς εἰπεῖν, Καλλίαν, εἰ καὶ μὴ-Καλλίαν, ὅμως ζῷον μὴ-ζῷον δ' οὔ. An. Post. I.11. 'That of two contradictory predicates one must be false, is never expressed in demonstration, except when we wish to maintain the cogency of a proof. We maintain it successfully if we can shew that we have a major truly affirmed of a middle and not truly denied [and this middle similarly related to a minor]. If we have this, it is indifferent whether the middle can be truly denied of the major or the minor of the middle. For if all man is animal, and not not-animal [and Callias is man and not not-man], it follows that Callias is animal and not not-animal, even though not-Callias be also man, and not-man be also animal.' The passage is not very lucid, and a disputant would have very little chance of victory unless he could shew with rather more force and clearness than Aristotle in the text, that his reasoning was an application of the axiom, and therefore satisfied the conditions of proof. The passage, however, is interesting, as, compared with the one last quoted, it raises a strong presumption that in Aristotle's mind the axiom is identical with the definition of proof. If so, the antithesis between axiom and definition (two of the three classes into which he divides scientific principles) has a point where it vanishes, the axiom being transformable into the definition of syllogism.

§ 9. It seems that at one time Aristotle thought that the loci of invention (confutation) as well as the loci of solution might be obtained from the definition of proof. This seems to have been his theory when he wrote the Prior Analytic. After explaining the nature of syllogism and subdividing it into its

moods and figures, he tells us, in effect, that these may serve as so many sign-posts to guide us in our search for arguments. Πῶς μὲν οὖν γίνεται πᾶς συλλογισμὸς καὶ διὰ πόσων ὅρων καὶ προτάσεων καὶ πῶς ἐχουσῶν πρὸς ἀλλήλας, ἔτι δὲ ποῖον πρόβλημα ἐν ἑκάστῳ σχήματι καὶ ποῖον ἐν πλείοσι καὶ ποῖον ἐν ἐλάττοσι δείκνυται, δῆλον ἐκ τῶν εἰρημένων. Πῶς δ' εὐπορήσομεν αὐτοὶ πρὸς τὸ τιθέμενον ἀεὶ συλλογισμῶν, καὶ διὰ ποίας ὁδοῦ ληψόμεθα τὰς περὶ ἕκαστον ἀρχάς, νῦν ἤδη λεκτέον. Οὐ γὰρ μόνον ἴσως δεῖ τὴν γένεσιν θεωρεῖν τῶν συλλογισμῶν, ἀλλὰ καὶ τὴν δύναμιν ἔχειν τοῦ ποιεῖν. Anal. Priora, 1. 27. 'The nature of syllogism and the number and relations of its terms and premisses, and the figures in which any conclusion may be proved, have been explained. It remains to point out the sources from which we may obtain them and the method of discovering premisses for each conclusion: for we want not only to know the way in which proofs are produced, but to acquire a power of producing them.' He afterwards recapitulates in similar terms. Ἐν πόσοις μὲν οὖν σχήμασι καὶ διὰ ποίων καὶ πόσων προτάσεων καὶ πότε καὶ πῶς γίνεται συλλογισμός, ἔτι δ' εἰς ποῖα βλεπτέον ἀνασκευάζοντι καὶ κατασκευάζοντι, καὶ πῶς δεῖ ζητεῖν περὶ τοῦ προκειμένου καθ' ὁποιανοῦν μέθοδον, ἔτι δὲ διὰ ποίας ὁδοῦ ληψόμεθα τὰς περὶ ἕκαστον ἀρχάς, ἤδη διεληλύθαμεν. An. Priora, 2. 1. 'The number of the figures, the number and nature of the premisses, and the conditions of proof, the cardinal points in affirmative and negative proof, the universal methods of investigation, and the paths which we must follow in our search for evidence, have now been sufficiently explained.' The preliminary accumulation or registration of facts and materials is spoken of in the same terms as in the Topics. [Ἐκλαμβάνειν, ἐκληπτέον, ἐκλέγειν, ἐκλεκτέον, ἐκλογή, διαγεγραμμένα, διαγραφή.] The precepts indicating the ground to be reconnoitred, or the points to which our attention must be directed, are not called στοιχεῖα or τόποι, as in the Topics, but ἐπιβλέψεις, ἐπισκέψεις, or σκέψεις. E. g. φανερὸν δὲ καὶ ὅτι αἱ ἄλλαι σκέψεις τῶν κατὰ τὰς ἐκλογὰς ἄχρειοι πρὸς τὸ ποιεῖν συλλογισμόν. An. Prior. 1. 28. 'To ascertain other relations among the facts we have registered will be of no service in our reasonings.' Δῆλον δὲ καὶ ὅτι ὁποῖα ταὐτὰ ληπτέον τὰ [b] κατὰ τὴν ἐπίσκεψιν, καὶ οὐχ ὁποῖα ἕτερα ἢ ἐναντία. Πρῶτον μὲν ὅτι τοῦ μέσου χάριν ἡ ἐπίβλεψις, τὸ δὲ μέσον

[b] τὰ would be better omitted.

APPENDIX D.

οὐχ ἕτερον ἀλλὰ ταὐτὸν δεῖ λαβεῖν. Ibid. 'In scanning our materials we must try to find propositions with a common factor, because we want middle terms, which those only can give.' Συμβαίνει δὴ τοῖς οὕτως ἐπισκοποῦσι προσεπιβλέπειν ἄλλην ὁδὸν τῆς ἀναγκαίας. Ibid. 'To look for other relations would be to make an unnecessary search in paths where we cannot find what we seek.' The rules, introduced with such pretensions, only amount to this: After accumulating our materials we must look through them to find the terms of our proposed conclusion so related, respectively, to any third term as they are in any of the moods of any of the figures in which such a conclusion could be proved. When we have found this, we have found our proof. In this system it is evident that the moods of syllogism correspond in function to the loci of the Topica. A brief trial of the system would probably suffice to demonstrate its impotence, and the loci, probably, were a second and more successful attempt to found a method of invention. This order of succession of the systems is confirmed by the fact that τόπος, the technical term of the supposed second system, does not occur in the first; while ἐπίβλεψις, the technical term of the first, perpetually recurs in the second. If our supposition is correct, the following passage of the Analytic, which pretends to refer to the Topica as already composed, must be regarded as a subsequent interpolation. Καθόλου μὲν οὖν ὃν δεῖ τρόπον τὰς προτάσεις ἐκλέγειν, εἴρηται σχεδὸν δι' ἀκριβείας δὲ διεληλύθαμεν ἐν τῇ πραγματείᾳ τῇ περὶ τὴν διαλεκτικήν. An. Prior. 1. 30. 'We have given a summary account of the method of collecting materials. A more detailed account is to be found in my treatise on Dialectic.' It is to be observed that this passage only identifies the method of collection (ἐκλογή) in the two systems: it does not identify the ἐπιβλέψεις with the τόποι. They cannot be identified; for the one are deduced from the nature of the predicables, the others from the nature of syllogism. If the term ἐκλέγειν is here misapplied and refers not to the organa but to the loci, it is pretty certain that the sentence was not written by Aristotle.

We have supposed that Aristotle himself recognized the inefficacy of his first system. If successful, it would have been a triumph of simplification, for it would have founded the whole of dialectic on a single definition, the definition of proof.

§ 10. From many expressions of Aristotle it might appear that he would make the differentia between dialectic and science to consist in the fact that science is based on definitions and dialectic is not. Ἀντιστρέφει δὲ μᾶλλον τὰ ἐν τοῖς μαθήμασιν ὅτι οὐδὲν συμβεβηκὸς λαμβάνουσιν, ἀλλὰ καὶ τούτῳ διαφέρουσι τῶν ἐν τοῖς διαλόγοις, ἀλλ' ὁρισμούς. An. Post. 1. 12. 'The converse of a scientific proposition is often true because no accidental conjunctions are admitted as premisses in science, which herein differs from dialectic, but only definitions.' Ἢ εἰ μὲν οὕτως ὑπολήψεται τὰ μὴ ἐνδεχόμενα ἄλλως ἔχειν ὥσπερ ἔχειν [ὡς ἔχων?] τοὺς ὁρισμοὺς δι' ὧν αἱ ἀποδείξεις, οὐ δοξάσει ἀλλ' ἐπιστήσεται· εἰ δ' ἀληθὴ μὲν εἶναι, οὐ μέντοι ταῦτά γε αὐτοῖς ὑπάρχειν κατ' οὐσίαν καὶ κατὰ τὸ εἶδος, δοξάσει καὶ οὐκ ἐπιστήσεται ἀληθῶς. An. Post. 1. 33. 'When the belief of a necessary law is founded on definitions which serve as the basis of demonstration, the belief is not opinionative (dialectic) but scientific: whereas a belief in the same proposition, without the knowledge that it is deducible from the definition or essence of the terms, is not science but opinion.' Ἐκεῖνος δ' εὐλόγως ἐζήτει τὸ τί ἐστι, συλληγίζεσθαι γὰρ ἐζήτει, ἀρχὴ δὲ τῶν συλλογισμῶν τὸ τί ἐστιν. Διαλεκτικὴ γὰρ ἰσχὺς οὔπω τότ' ἦν, ὥστε δύνασθαι καὶ χωρὶς τοῦ τί ἐστι τἀναντία ἐπισκοπεῖν καὶ τῶν ἐναντίων εἰ ἡ αὐτὴ ἐπιστήμη. Δύο γάρ ἐστιν ἅ τις ἂν ἀποδοίη Σωκράτει δικαίως, τούς τ' ἐπακτικοὺς λόγους καὶ τὸ ὁρίζεσθαι καθόλου· ταῦτα γάρ ἐστιν ἄμφω περὶ ἀρχὴν ἐπιστήμης. Met. 12. 4. 'It was natural that Socrates should seek for definitions, for he wanted proof, and definitions are the foundation of proof. Men were not then aware of the resources of dialectic, which enable us to dispense with definitions in discussing the Socratic problems; and two procedures may be fairly assigned to Socrates, induction and definition; both of which aim at laying the foundation of deductive science.' From what has preceded, it appears that these statements must be accepted with some reserve. Dialectic as well as science is based on definitions, though on definitions of objects of a different order. The definitions on which science rests are definitions of a peculiar subject-matter and its attributes (ἴδια), those on which dialectic rests are definitions of fact, law, cause, experience, definition, proof, that is of certain catholic relations permeating every sphere (κοινά). Equipped with definitions of these shadowy abstractions, dialectic

APPENDIX D.

in entering the controversial lists with the sole purpose of constructing opinion can dispense with the more solid and concrete special information which scientific method requires for the evolution of genuine knowledge.

Unsubstantial, however, as are these abstractions, they occupy in this art the position of final causes, so that, from this point of view, the maxims may be regarded rather as imperative and hypothetical than as indicative or categorical. This character is suggested by the formula Δεῖ, which so often occurs in the Topics. (See end of § 7.) Another term, τὰ παρηγγελμένα, precepts of art, suggests the same conclusion. Τῶν δὲ πρὸς ταὐτὸν κατασκευαστικῶν τόπων οὐδεὶς χρήσιμος πρὸς ὅρον. Οὐ γὰρ ἀπόχρη δεῖξαι ταὐτὸν τὸ ὑπὸ τὸν λόγον καὶ τοὔνομα πρὸς τὸ κατασκευάσαι ὅτι ὁρισμός, ἀλλὰ καὶ τὰ ἄλλα πάντα δεῖ ἔχειν τὰ παρηγγελμένα τὸν ὁρισμόν. Topics, 7. 2. 'The topics for proving the identity of the subject and predicate do not suffice to prove definition; for if the predicate is a definition of the subject it must satisfy all the other prescribed conditions.' As in the arts or productive sciences, so in dialectic, we define the end we wish to accomplish (which here is the establishment of theorems of a certain character), and the maxims are corollaries or conclusions from those definitions, dictating the means to be employed *if* such objects are to be realized. Dialectic then, like science, is based on definitions, and, like practical science, on definitions of its final cause.

Kant treats the logical maxims as rather hypothetical and imperative than indicative and categorical, when, to explain, or explain away, the autonomy or legislative power of the speculative reason, he bids us regard her dicta not as a priori revelations of the laws of the external universe, but as precepts issued by reason for her own behoof, that is, in order to provide herself exercise for her own functions. Being a syllogistic faculty she bids us look at the world in such a way as will enable her to syllogize. For instance, she issues the precept of generalization and specification, i. e. she commands us wherever we have species or plurality to find their genus or reduce them to unity, and wherever we have generic unity to subdivide it into specific multiplicity, not because she knows a priori that nature is uniform or that things are arranged in classes and a hierarchy of

APPENDIX D. 223

law above law, but because, unless we contrive by some arrangement of the logical lenses to discern such a hierarchy of classes and laws, reason can have no scope for her inductive and deductive functions. The laws of the speculative reason (reflexionsgesetze), them, he makes, in effect, hypothetical rather than categorical. As far as I recollect, he avoids applying the term hypothetical to the laws of the understanding (verstandesgesetze): but as he perpetually refers them to the possibility of experience as their end and final cause, they may be, as a matter of fact, categorical, but, so far as his system explains them, they are only hypothetical, for such must be the character of conclusions deduced from the conception of an end.

§ 11. One application of dialectic is said to be the investigation of the first principles of science. Ἔτι δὲ χρήσιμος ἡ πραγματεία πρὸς τὰ πρῶτα τῶν περὶ ἑκάστην ἐπιστήμην ἀρχῶν. Ἐκ μὲν γὰρ τῶν οἰκείων τῶν κατὰ τὴν προτεθεῖσαν ἐπιστήμην ἀρχῶν ⁰ ἀδύνατον εἰπεῖν τι περὶ αὐτῶν, ἐπειδὴ πρῶται αἱ ἀρχαὶ ἁπάντων εἰσί, διὰ δὲ τῶν περὶ ἕκαστα ἐνδόξων ᵈ ἀνάγκη περὶ αὐτῶν διελθεῖν. Τοῦτο δ' ἴδιον ἢ μάλιστα οἰκεῖον τῆς διαλεκτικῆς ἐστίν· ἐξεταστικὴ γὰρ οὖσα πρὸς τὰς ἁπασῶν τῶν μεθόδων ἀρχὰς ὁδὸν ἔχει. Topica, 1. 2. 'Further, dialectic is useful for fixing the primary principles of the particular sciences. There are no theorems commensurate or coextensive with the principles of a (deductive) science that can furnish us premisses for the investigation, for the principles themselves are the primordial theorems; and therefore there are only the common principles to which we can appeal; and their application is the proper function of dialectic, or belongs to it more properly than to any other method. For its power of criticism makes it a method for determining the principles of all other methods.' We will not stop to ask how dialectic, the method of opinion, can be competent to investigate the principles of science (a question which Aristotle never suffi-

---

⁰ To avoid ambiguity Aristotle should have written, ἐκ τῶν οἰκείων ταῖς . . . . ἀρχαῖς.

ᵈ Τῶν ἐνδόξων is a term of vague meaning. If we are to accept the statement, we must interpret it to mean, ἐκ τῶν κοινῶν ἀρχῶν καὶ τῶν φαινομένων (τῆς ἐμπειρίας). Before dialectic method can become scientific both elements must be purified: the common principles must not be mere probabilities, and the specific data must not be mere rumours of the great public but exact observations, and, above all, quantitatively determinate.

ciently laid to heart), but assuming that dialectic includes all that is opposed to deductive science (ὁδὸς ἀπὸ τῶν ἀρχῶν), and that some severer branch of it, with a positive (κατασκευαστική), not merely a negative (ἀνασκευαστική) function, may be identified with inductive method (ὁδὸς ἐπὶ τὰς ἀρχάς), we will proceed to consider what is the character of the principles which it has to establish.

If the principles of science are definitions, it is evident that we cannot accept Mill's account of definition. After maintaining that propositions refer not to words or ideas, but to facts, he, somewhat inconsistently, makes an exception against the most carefully considered propositions, definitions. This cannot be admitted if we regard definitions as the result of inductive and basis of deductive science. If induction and science deal not with words but with facts, definition, the crown of induction and foundation of deduction, must also relate not to words but to facts.

Aristotle makes two orders of definition—verbal, which are all that Mill recognizes, relating to words, and real, relating to facts. The latter order is subdivided according as the term defined is that somewhat ideal object, something absolutely irresolvable and elementary, or something derivative and resolvable into antecedent terms. The latter class is again subdivided: it is either merely the precise statement or circumscription of a phenomenon, and corresponds to the conclusion of a syllogism in which the phenomenon is demonstrated; or it is a causal proposition giving the invariable and adequate antecedent of a phenomenon, and represents the premisses or the whole of the syllogism in which the existence of the phenomenon is demonstrated. Ὁρισμὸς δ' ἐπειδὴ λέγεται εἶναι λόγος τοῦ τί ἐστι, φανερὸν ὅτι ὁ μέν τις ἔσται λόγος τοῦ τί σημαίνει τὸ ὄνομα ἢ λόγος ἕτερος ὀνοματώδης, οἷον τὸ τί σημαίνει, τί ἐστιν ἢ τρίγωνον. Ὅπερ ἔχοντες ὅτι ἐστι, ζητοῦμεν διὰ τί ἐστιν.... Εἷς μὲν δὴ ὅρος ἐστὶν ὅρου ὁ εἰρημένος, ἄλλος δ' ἐστὶν ὅρος λόγος ὁ δηλῶν διὰ τί ἐστιν. Ὥστε ὁ μὲν πρότερος σημαίνει μέν, δείκνυσι δ' οὔ, ὁ δ' ὕστερος φανερὸν ὅτι ἔσται οἷον ἀπόδειξις τοῦ τί ἐστι, τῇ θέσει διαφέρων τῆς ἀποδείξεως. Διαφέρει γὰρ εἰπεῖν διὰ τί βροντᾷ καὶ τί ἐστι βροντή. Ἐρεῖ γὰρ οὕτω μὲν διότι ἀποσβέννυνται τὸ πῦρ ἐν τοῖς νέφεσι· τί δ' ἐστὶ βροντή; ψόφος ἀποσβεννυμένου πυρὸς ἐν νέφεσι. Ὥστε ὁ αὐτὸς λόγος ἄλλον

APPENDIX D.   225

τρόπον λέγεται, καὶ ὡδὶ μὲν ἀπόδειξις συνεχής, ὡδὶ δ' ὁρισμός. Ἔτι ἐστὶν ὅρος βροντῆς ψόφος ἐν νέφεσι· τοῦτο δ' ἐστὶ τῆς τοῦ τί ἐστιν ἀποδείξεως συμπέρασμα. Ὁ δὲ τῶν ἀμέσων ὁρισμὸς θέσις ἐστὶ τοῦ τί ἐστιν ἀναπόδεικτος. Ἔστω ἄρα ὁρισμὸς εἶς μὲν λόγος τοῦ τί ἐστιν ἀναπόδεικτος, εἶς δὲ συλλογισμὸς τοῦ τί ἐστι, πτώσει διαφέρων τῆς ἀποδείξεως, τρίτος δὲ τῆς τοῦ τί ἐστιν ἀποδείξεως συμπέρασμα. An. Post. 2. 10. Ἔστιν ὁ ὁρισμὸς ἢ ἀρχὴ ἀποδείξεως, ἢ ἀπόδειξις θέσει διαφέρουσα, ἢ συμπέρασμά τι ἀποδείξεως. Ibid. 1. 8. 'Definition is an exposition of essence, and one kind exhibits the signification of a name, or of a circumlocution, such as, triangular character, equivalent to a name. When we know that an object exists corresponding to the name, we may investigate its cause. .... Besides nominal definition there is real definition; a statement exhibiting the cause producing a phenomenon. The former kind indicated without proof: the latter is a demonstration of essence without a demonstrative form. When it is asked, Why does it thunder? the answer may be, Because fire is extinguished in a cloud. When it is asked, What is thunder? the answer may be, The extinction of fire in a cloud. Thus one and the same statement, disguised in form, becomes either a definition or a proximate demonstration. Another definition is the conclusion of an essential demonstration: as when we define thunder, a certain noise in the clouds. Another kind is the indemonstrable thesis or position of the immediate. Real definition, then, has three species: it is an indemonstrable statement of the essence, or a deduction of the essence without the deductive form, or a conclusion of a deduction of the essence.'
'Definition is either the premiss of demonstration, or the conclusion, or the whole demonstration dislocated.'

It is evident that the two last kinds present the contrast which obtains between colligation and induction. Colligation of facts is a term invented by Whewell to designate the explication of a conception or the precise circumscription of a phenomenon, which he regards as the final result of induction. Mill retains the term colligation but makes it merely a preliminary of induction, to which he attaches a new signification, making it connote the whole process of discovery of first principles (ὁδὸς ἐπὶ τὰς ἀρχάς). According to him the end of induction is the discovery of causal propositions, i. e. propositions which define

Q

the unconditional and inseparable antecedent of that consequent which was provisionally defined in colligation. If we use the term 'induction' to connote not the whole process but its result, it is clear that colligation is equivalent to Aristotle's definition which expresses the conclusion, and induction to his definition which expresses the premisses, of demonstration.

In the syllogism to which Aristotle refers, the major term represents the phenomenon or consequent, the minor term the cause or antecedent, and the middle term the causal definition of the major, indicating its relation of dependence on the antecedent or minor. The major premiss then is the definition of the attribute. Ἔστι δὲ τὸ μέσον λόγος τοῦ πρώτου ἄκρου, διὸ πᾶσαι αἱ ἐπιστῆμαι δι' ὁρισμοῦ γίγνονται. An. Post. 2. 17. 'The middle (in the ultimate syllogism) must be the definition of the major, which shews that the basis of science must be definition.' We may suppose that the definition of the primary subject or ultimate irreducible cause will appear as the minor premiss of a prior syllogism, but here Aristotle's logic is incomplete, leaving many questions unanswered, and it may be doubted whether the framework of the elementary syllogism is not too narrow to exhibit the mechanism of causation.

It is clear that the definition of an attribute may be a causal proposition, but it is not equally clear respecting primary subjects or elementary substances. Aristotle for the sake of symmetry calls these also causal, saying they are self-caused. Ἔστιν, ὥς ἔφαμεν, ταὐτὸν τὸ εἰδέναι τί ἐστι καὶ τὸ εἰδέναι τὸ αἴτιον τοῦ τί ἐστι. Λόγος δὲ τούτου ὅτι ἐστί τι τὸ αἴτιον, καὶ τοῦτο ἢ τὸ αὐτὸ ἢ ἄλλο. An. Post. 2. 8. 'To know the essence, as we said, is the same as to know the cause of the existence, for every thing has a cause, whether distinct from itself or identical.'

He elsewhere says that only substances are properly definable, and that attributes are definable only in a secondary and inferior degree. Φανερὸν οὖν ὅτι ὁ πρώτως καὶ ἁπλῶς ὁρισμὸς καὶ τὸ τί ἦν εἶναι τῶν οὐσιῶν ἐστίν· οὐ μὴν ἀλλὰ καὶ τῶν ἄλλων ὁμοίως ἐστὶ πλὴν οὐ πρώτως. Met. 7. 4. 'The primary and proper objects of definition are substances: attributes are only definable in a secondary degree.' But it is clearly a straining of language to call definitions of the uncaused or self-caused, causal propositions; and if the essential function of definition is the expression

of causation, we must reverse Aristotle's dictum and say that attributes or effects alone are properly definable, substances, at least elementary substances, only in a secondary degree.

We have now before us the character of the propositions which dialectic must establish if she is to lay the foundation of deductive science; and her loci of invention must be governed by this character, just as the loci for investigating accident, property, and genus were governed by the character of accident, property, and genus. It follows that the loci of definition in the Topica, none of which refer to the nature of causation, are useless for evolving scientific principles. For loci of invention, founded on the nature of causation, we must turn our eyes elsewhere.

§ 12. We must look for them in the modern method of induction: and as a comparison of its ultimate principles with the ultimate principles of dialectic will illustrate the conception of dialectic method, let us examine the former as stated in Mill's System of Logic, in his luminous exposition of the methods of agreement and difference.

Method of agreement. "The mode of discovering and proving laws of nature which we first examine proceeds upon the following axiom: whatever circumstance can be excluded without prejudice to the phenomenon, or can be absent notwithstanding its presence, is not connected with it in the way of causation." [This axiom is evidently a definition, or corollary from the definition, of cause or effect.] "The casual circumstances being thus eliminated, if only one remains, that one is the cause which we are in search of; if more than one, they either are, or contain among them, the cause: and so, mutatis mutandis, of the effect. As this method proceeds by comparing different instances to ascertain in what they agree, I have termed it the method of agreement; and we may adopt as its regulating principle the following canon:—If two or more instances of the phenomenon under investigation have only one circumstance in common, the circumstance in which alone all the instances agree is the cause (or effect) of the given phenomenon." For instance, let the problem be, to find the effect of a given cause: and let causes be represented by the capitals, A, B, C, &c., and effects by the italics, a, b, c, &c. "Suppose that A is tried

APPENDIX D.

along with B and C, and that the effect is abc; and suppose that A is next tried with D and E, and that the effect is ade. Then we may reason thus: b and c are not effects of A, for they were not produced by it in the second experiment; nor are d and e, for they were not produced in the first. Whatever is really the effect of A must have been produced in both instances" [definition, or corollary from the definition, of cause or effect]. "Now this condition is fulfilled by no circumstance except a. The phenomenon a cannot have been the effect of B or C, since it was produced where they were not; nor of D or E, since it was produced where they were not. Therefore it is the effect of A." [Why? In obedience to the celebrated principle of the sufficient reason, that every event must have a cause. This principle gives a categorical character to the otherwise hypothetical conclusion of the method of agreement. Mill derives it, under the name of the law of universal causation, from induction by simple enumeration, and speaks of it in terms similar to those in which Aristotle speaks of the axiom, as the most certain of our beliefs, and one capable of serving as a criterion by which all other beliefs may be tested. Ὅτι μὲν οὖν ἡ τοιαύτη πασῶν βεβαιοτάτη ἀρχή, δῆλον. . . . Διὸ πάντες οἱ ἀποδεικνύντες εἰς ταύτην ἀνάγουσιν ἐσχάτην δόξαν. Φύσει γὰρ ἀρχὴ καὶ τῶν ἄλλων ἀξιωμάτων αὕτη πάντων. Met. 3. 3. 'This is of all principles the most certain, and the one to which all demonstration appeals in the last resort; for it is the natural basis of all other axioms[a].' From the preceding analysis it appears that a single step of the method of agreement is an application of a definition and postulate by an agglutination of at least six elementary syllogisms.]

Next let the problem be, to find the cause of a given effect. "We may observe a in two different combinations, abc and ade; and if we know or can discover that the antecedent circumstances in these cases respectively were ABC and ADE, we may conclude by a reasoning similar to that in the preceding

---

[a] "A general proposition inductively obtained is only then proved to be true, when the instances on which it rests are such that if they have been correctly observed, the falsity of the generalization would be inconsistent with the constancy of causation; with the universality of the fact that the phenomena of nature take place according to invariable laws of succession." Mill on Positivism.

example that A is the antecedent connected with the consequent a by a law of causation. B and C, we may say, cannot be causes of a, since in its second occurrence they were not present; nor are D and E, for they were not present on its first occurrence."

Method of difference. "In the method of agreement we endeavoured to obtain instances which agreed in the given circumstance but differed in every other: in the present method we require, on the contrary, two instances resembling one another in every other respect, but differing in the presence or absence of the phenomenon we wish to study.... If the effect of $A B C$ is abc, and the effect of $B C$, bc, it is evident that the effect of A is a. So again, if we begin at the other end, and desire to investigate the cause of an effect a, we must select an instance, as abc, in which the effect occurs, and in which the antecedents were $A B C$, and we must look out" [ἐπιβλεπτέον] "for another instance in which the remaining circumstances bc occur without a. If the antecedents in that instance are $B C$, we know that the cause of a must be A. ... The axioms which are taken for granted in this method are evidently the following: Whatever antecedent cannot be excluded without preventing the phenomenon, is a cause or a condition of that phenomenon; whatever consequent can be excluded with no other difference in the antecedents than the absence of a particular one, is the effect of that one." [Definition, or corollaries from the definition, of cause or effect.] "Instead of comparing different instances of a phenomenon to discover in what they agree, this method compares an instance of its occurrence with an instance of its non-occurrence to discover in what they differ. The canon which is the regulating principle of the method of difference may be expressed as follows:—If an instance in which the phenomenon under investigation occurs, and an instance in which it does not occur, have every circumstance save one in common, that one occurring only in the former; the circumstance in which alone the two instances differ is the effect or cause, or a necessary part of the effect or cause, of the phenomenon. ... The method of agreement stands on the ground that whatever can be eliminated" (can be absent consistently with the existence of the phenomenon) "is not connected with the phenomenon by any law. The method of difference has for its foundation, that whatever cannot be

APPENDIX D.

eliminated, is connected with the phenomenon by a law." [Definitions, or corollaries from the definition, of causation.]

The preceding exposition suggests several observations. The foundation and keystone of inductive method, it appears, is the definition of causation. The foundation of dialectic method is the definition of definition. If a definition is a causal proposition, as Aristotle asserts in the Analytics, these two foundations ought to coincide. But when Aristotle enumerated the loci of definition in the Topica, he does not seem to have attained to the view which he explains in the Analytics, that the scientific definition of a phenomenon is the declaration of its cause. The principal branch of his Logic is founded on the definition of science, which is declared to be the knowledge of causes. 'Ἐπίστασθαι οἰόμεθα ἕκαστον ὅταν τήν τ' αἰτίαν οἰώμεθα γινώσκειν δι' ἥν τὸ πρᾶγμά ἐστιν, ὅτι ἐκείνου αἰτία ἐστί, καὶ μὴ ἐνδέχεσθαι τοῦτ' ἄλλως ἔχειν. An. Post. 1. 2. 'Science is the knowledge of necessary facts and their causes.' But instead of deducing from this conception the method of inductive science, a problem that asked the aid of the philosopher, he merely developes from it theorems respecting the nature of deductive science, a province which might have been safely left to the fostering care of the mathematicians. Hegel was full of the notion that certain metaphysical ideas were capable of being developed into regulative principles and furnishing methods of reasoning; but he never advanced beyond the haziest generalities, in which none but the cloudiest intellect could find satisfaction. It is to Mill that the honour belongs of solving the problem that had so long hovered before the eyes of philosophers, and shewing how the idea of cause can be developed into various methods of rigorous scientific inference.

Definition, which perhaps at some periods in the history of logic was unduly exalted as a scientific process, undergoes in Mill's System of Logic, along with syllogism, a deal of vilinihili-parvi-pauli-pili-nauci-flocci-fication, and is degraded from all her dignities. But for the ultimate foundation and evidence, and the sole foundation and evidence, of inductive method as expounded in this system, we are forced, as we have seen, to have recourse, reversing the bill of attainder passed against them, to definition and syllogism. Induction in its

APPENDIX D.

strictest sense seems to be merely the idealization or universalization of a singular fact, the transformation of the proposition, this ABC is followed by abc, into the proposition, all ABC is followed by abc. The faculty of making this transformation can, doubtless, not be identified with, or made dependent on, the syllogistic faculty. But if, as in Mill's writings, the word induction is used to signify the whole process of discovering first principles (ὁδὸς ἐπὶ τὰς ἀρχάς), then it appears, as we noticed when quoting his exposition, that every single step of induction is a crowd, at least an ample cluster, of syllogisms. Instead, then, of declaring with Mill, that all deduction is induction, it appears more accurate to assert that all induction is deduction.

The two elements, one general the other special, which Aristotle found in dialectic and demonstration, are also to be distinguished in inductive science. Inductive method, as we saw (§ 10) was the case with dialectic, assumes one definition and proves another. The definition assumed, that of causation, throws equal light on all inquiries, i. e. is a catholic principle (κοινὴ ἀρχή): the definition proved is a causal proposition, or law of causation in a special department of nature, and is a truth confined to a particular science (ἰδία ἀρχή).

Here we may resume a former topic. Aristotle objected (see § 8, quoting Anal. Post. 2. 6) to a proposed proof of definition, in which one premiss should express the conditions of definition, and the other assert their fulfilment, that every proof ought to have some apparent cogency prior to any express exhibition of logical rules and apparatus. If we consider the mode of reasoning in the methods of agreement and difference, we shall perceive that Aristotle's objection is by no means fatal, and that his requisition can be easily satisfied. The man who, assuming the validity of the methods of agreement and difference, shews the invariable and unconditional antecedent, let us say, for example, of dew, has demonstrated its definition without expressly invoking any logical or metaphysical canons. If an unconvinced critic demands further satisfaction, he may justify the process by appealing in the way Mill indicates to the axioms and canons of induction.

Another point that has been discussed will receive light from the same consideration. We observed (§ 1) that the dialectic

maxims may either be regarded as constitutive or as regulative, i. e. either as premisses or as methods. The same is true of the inductive canons. Possibly no inductive operator ever reasoned as Mill reasons to shew the cogency of his methods. The investigator of nature employs the methods without troubling himself about the metaphysical or ontological principles on which they are based. But if he would demonstrate the validity of the methods, these metaphysical or ontological principles must be expressed and furnish the premisses of proof.

§ 13. This seems the proper place for a few words concerning the celebrated question, whether definition is susceptible of proof? In the Topics Aristotle had asserted it is.

Ἀναιρεῖν μὲν οὖν ὅρον οὕτως καὶ διὰ τούτων δεῖ πειρατέον. Ἐὰν δὲ κατασκευάζειν βουλώμεθα, πρῶτον μὲν εἰδέναι δεῖ ὅτι οὐδεὶς ἢ ὀλίγοι τῶν διαλεγομένων ὅρον συλλογίζονται, ἀλλὰ πάντες ὡς ἀρχὴν τὸ τοιοῦτον λαμβάνουσιν· οἷον αἵ τε περὶ γεωμετρίαν καὶ ἀριθμοὺς καὶ τὰς ἄλλας τὰς τοιαύτας μαθήσεις. Εἶθ᾽ ὅτι δι᾽ ἀκριβείας μὲν ἄλλης ἐστὶ πραγματείας ἀποδοῦναι καὶ τί ἐστιν ὅρος καὶ πῶς ὁρίζεσθαι δεῖ. Νῦν δ᾽, ὅσον ἱκανὸν πρὸς τὴν παροῦσαν χρείαν, τοσοῦτον μόνον λεκτέον, ὅτι δυνατὸν γενέσθαι ὁρισμοῦ καὶ τοῦ τί ἦν εἶναι συλλογισμόν. Εἰ γάρ ἐστιν ὅρος λόγος ὁ τὸ τί ἦν εἶναι τῷ πράγματι δηλῶν, καὶ δεῖ τὰ ἐν τῷ ὅρῳ κατηγορούμενα ἐν τῷ τί ἐστι τοῦ πράγματος μόνα κατηγορεῖσθαι (κατηγορεῖται δὲ ἐν τῷ τί ἐστι τὰ γένη καὶ αἱ διαφοραί) φανερόν, ὡς εἴ τις λάβοι ταῦτα μόνον ἐν τῷ τί ἐστι τοῦ πράγματος κατηγορεῖσθαι, ὅτι ὁ ταῦτα ἔχων λόγος ὅρος ἐξ ἀνάγκης ἂν εἴη· οὐ γὰρ ἐνδέχεται ἕτερον εἶναι ὅρον τοῦ πράγματος, ἐπειδὴ οὐδὲν ἕτερον ἐν τῷ τί ἐστι τοῦ πράγματος κατηγορεῖται. Ὅτι μὲν οὖν ἐγχωρεῖ συλλογισμὸν ὅρου γενέσθαι, φανερόν. Topics, 7. 2.

'The disproof of a definition employs the foregoing topics. As to the proof, we must observe, in the first place, that definitions are rarely or never proved by the questioner in dialectic discussion, but are assumed as a basis of proof, as in geometry, arithmetic, and similar sciences. In the second place, the exact rules for the form and process of definition belong to another method, and we have now merely to say what may suffice for the present occasion. We say, then, that essence and definition are susceptible of proof. For if definition is a proposition declaring the essence of a thing, and is composed of all the predicates that say what it is, that is, of all its genera and differentiæ,

APPENDIX D.

it follows that if certain predicates fulfil these conditions in regard to a given term, the proposition in which they are resumed is the definition of that term, and there can be no other definition, for there are no other generic predicates. It is clear, then, that we may prove a definition.' This seems to be plausible enough, and may be made more so if a little differently worded. If we assume a priori that a certain relation of terms is the relation of effect and cause, or of phenomenon and definition, and find a posteriori by appropriate evidence that this relation exists between two given terms, we may conclude that these terms are related as effect and cause, or as phenomenon and definition. In the Analytic, however, Aristotle asserts that such a proof, which he calls hypothetical, is vitiated by a petitio principii. 'Ἀλλ' ἆρα ἔστι καὶ ἀποδεῖξαι τὸ τί ἐστι κατ' οὐσίαν, ἐξ ὑποθέσεως δέ, λαβόντα τὸ μὲν τί ἦν εἶναι ἐκ τῶν ἐν τῷ τί ἐστιν ἰδίων, ταδὶ δὲ ἐν τῷ τί ἐστι μόνα, καὶ ἴδιον τὸ πᾶν. Τοῦτο γάρ ἐστι τὸ εἶναι ἐκείνῳ. Ἡ πάλιν εἴληφε τὸ τί ἦν εἶναι καὶ ἐν τούτῳ; ἀνάγκη γὰρ διὰ τοῦ μέσου δεῖξαι. An. Post. 2. 6. 'Is definition susceptible of a hypothetical proof, if we assume as our major that the reciprocating or convertible combination of essential predicates is the definition; and as our minor, that certain predicates are essential, and, when combined, reciprocate with the subject; and then conclude that these predicates compose its definition? No: here, as in the former case, the minor premiss is a petitio principii.' Accordingly his definitive doctrine appears to be that definitions are indemonstrable. Ἡ τὰ πρῶτα ὁρισμοὶ ἔσονται ἀναπόδεικτοι. An. Post. 2. 3. ' The first principles are indemonstrable definitions.' Without controverting his assertion, that the proof of a definition is not demonstrative, we maintain that the reason he alleges is untenable. It is clear that if the prior definition assumed as a premiss in order to prove a definition is a definition of the same term, as in one of the modes of proving definition which Aristotle examines, there is a petitio principii, and, if the possession of the prior definition means anything beyond the power of rightly applying a name, or of recognizing an object when presented to sensation, such a proof hardly deserves the name which Aristotle concedes it, of dialectical (λογικός) proof. Οὗτος μὲν οὖν ὁ τρόπος ὅτι οὐκ ἂν εἴη ἀπόδειξις, εἴρηται πρότερον, ἀλλ' ἔστι λογικὸς συλλογισμὸς τοῦ τί ἐστιν. An. Post. 2. 8.

But in the hypothetical proof, or, what is a similar process, the establishment of causal propositions by the methods of induction, the definition assumed (that of essence or cause) is a general or metaphysical definition (αἴτιον), the definition to be established is a specific or scientific definition (ἴδιον). The things defined are quite disparate, the premisses are distinct from the conclusion, and therefore there is no petitio principii. How then did Aristotle come to imagine that there was this vice in the proof? The cause of the hallucination seems to have been his own tautological way of defining definition or essence. His account, in effect, amounts to this: Definition (τὸ τί ἦν εἶναι) is composed of—the elements of definition (τὰ ἐν τῷ τί ἐστι), or, essence is composed of—the elements of essence. From so tautological and unmeaning a premiss it would have been strange if any conclusion could be drawn without a petitio principii. That he was doubtful of the conclusiveness of his own reasoning we may infer from his adding another objection, which we have already discussed, § 8.

The true avenue to a possibility of error in the proof of essence or causation lies, as Mill has indicated, in the fallibility of observation. "But if we cannot artificially produce the phenomenon A, the conclusion that it is the cause of a remains subject to very considerable doubt......This arises from the difficulty of assuring ourselves that A is the *only* immediate antecedent common to both the instances. If we could be certain of having ascertained all the invariable antecedents, we might be sure that the unconditional invariable antecedent or cause must be found somewhere among them." This applies to the method of agreement, and the method of difference may be vitiated by similar non-observation.

Another method whereby it had been proposed to prove definition entirely a priori, namely, the method of division, is justly charged by Aristotle with involving a series of petitiones principii. Ὅτι δ' ἡ διὰ τῶν γενῶν διαίρεσις μικρόν τι μόριόν ἐστι τῆς εἰρημένης μεθόδου, ῥᾴδιον ἰδεῖν. Ἔστι γὰρ ἡ διαίρεσις οἷον ἀσθενὴς συλλογισμός· ὃ μὲν γὰρ δεῖ δεῖξαι αἰτεῖται, συλλογίζεται δ' ἀεί τι τῶν ἄνωθεν. Πρῶτον δ' αὐτὸ τοῦτο ἐλελήθει τοὺς χρωμένους αὐτῇ πάντας, καὶ πείθειν ἐπεχείρουν ὡς ὄντος δυνατοῦ περὶ οὐσίας ἀπόδειξιν γίνεσθαι καὶ τοῦ τί ἐστιν. An. Prior. 1. 31. 'Specification or subdivi-

APPENDIX D. 235

sion is a small item in the method of invention. Subdivision is a sort of feeble proof wherein the conclusion wanted is always assumed, and proof is only adduced of some antecedent proposition. This vice was not detected by those who first practised the method, and they would persuade us it was possible hereby to demonstrate definitions and primary laws.' To shew his meaning he supposes that the problem is to define man. We begin by an assumption that man is an animal, and after dividing animal into mortal and immortal, we prove conclusively that man is either mortal or immortal. This however is not the conclusion we want, and we make a second assumption that man is mortal. Ζῷον θνητὸν δὲ [εἶναι τὸν ἄνθρωπον] οὐκ ἀναγκαῖον ἀλλ' αἰτεῖται. Τοῦτο δ' ἦν ὃ ἔδει συλλογίσασθαι. Ibid. Then subdividing mortal animal into footed and not-footed, we can prove that man is either footed or not-footed: we want, however, something more positive than this, and are obliged as a third assumption to postulate that he is footed. Ὑπόπουν δ' οὐκ ἀνάγκη [εἶναι τὸν ἄνθρωπον] ἀλλὰ λαμβάνει. Τοῦτο δ' ἦν ὃ ἔδει πάλιν δεῖξαι. Ibid. And so on. It is evident that the defect of this method consists in its pretension to be entirely a priori or independent of experience, and the defect is removed as soon as we admit that experience or a posteriori truths are an essential element in the establishment of definition. This is given by Aristotle as the key of the enigma in the preceding chapter. Διὸ τὰς ἀρχὰς τὰς περὶ ἕκαστον ἐμπειρίας ἐστὶ παραδοῦναι. An. Prior. 1. 30. 'The specific principles of proof must be derived from experience.' A *petitio* is a premiss that is assumed without any evidence. Ὅταν τὸ μὴ δι' αὑτοῦ γνωστὸν δι' αὑτοῦ τις ἐπιχειρῇ δεικνύναι, τότ' αἰτεῖται τὸ ἐξ ἀρχῆς. An. Prior. 2. 16. But as soon as sensation or experience is recognized as an authentic criterion of truth, what was before an αἴτημα becomes an αἴσθημα, that is, a premiss evidenced by the most unexceptionable authority. Speaking of the method of division, Aristotle observes that its most important premisses are the arbitrary concessions of the disputant. Οὐδαμοῦ γὰρ ἀνάγκη γίνεται τὸ πρᾶγμα ἐκεῖνο εἶναι τωνδὶ ὄντων ......οὐ γὰρ δεῖ τὸ συμπέρασμα ἐρωτᾶν, οὐδὲ τῷ δοῦναι εἶναι, ἀλλ' ἀνάγκη (ἐξ ἀνάγκης?) εἶναι ἐκείνων ὄντων, κἂν μὴ φῇ ὁ ἀποκρινόμενος. An. Post. 2. 5. 'The conclusion of the process is defiaient in necessity: now a conclusion should not be a matter of ques-

tion or concession, but the inevitable consequence of the premisses, unaffected by concession or denial.' In the inductive method the decisive premisses are gained by interrogation, not of a disputant but, of nature: and a criterion, somewhat hastily rejected as unscientific, plays an essential part in the process. Τίς οὖν ἄλλος τρόπος [τοῦ τὴν οὐσίαν ἢ τὸ τί ἐστι δεικνύναι] λοιπός; οὐ γὰρ δὴ δείξει γε τῇ αἰσθήσει ἢ τῷ δακτύλῳ. An. Post. 2. 7. 'What other method remains? The definer, surely, does not point out the essence with his finger as an object of sensation?'

If, then, the colligative or phenomenal definition cannot be proved, we still maintain, looking at the modern methods of induction, that the more important, the inductive or causal definition, is capable of proof. The assumption, however, of so catholic a principle (κοινὴ ἀρχή) as the definition of causation, to say nothing of the admitted possibilities of error in observation, removes the proof from the sphere of deductive science or demonstration (ἀπόδειξις), which rests exclusively on axioms and ἴδιαι ἀρχαί, to that of dialectic, or, to speak more accurately, philosophic, method. So much for the limit of the power of the catholic or methodic principles working on the special data of experiment and observation.

§ 14. The reader may desire to have some specimens of the dialectic maxims, about which so much has been said. As we have stated, Aristotle avoids formulating them in the Topics; but the schoolmen coined them in abundance after his indications. The following are taken from Sanderson's Compendium. They are divested of all reference to the predicables, and to each maxim are appended certain limitations or exceptions, which he calls fallentiæ. In dialectic the falsity of the maxim, that is, its employment without due limitations and qualifications, though it led to a false conclusion, was not considered to make the argument sophistic; but we have stated our opinion (see notes to ch. viii), that in pirastic at least such false premisses constitute the proof a sophism.

Loci a causa et effectu:—

Posita causa, ponitur effectus, et sublata tollitur.

Fallit in causa impedita: ut gravia non semper descendunt, quia possunt ab aliquo impediente prohiberi.

Posito effectu, ponitur causa, et sublato tollitur.

Fallit in effectu permanente post causam; ut manet ædificium mortuo ædificatore: in effectu producibili a diversis causis; ut potest esse mors non epoto veneno: in effectu causæ quæ aliquando fuit; ut corruere potest ædificium superstite ædificatore.

Here we have the materials for the methods of agreement and difference, but the architect was wanting.

Loci a subjecto et accidente:—
Posito subjecto, ponitur accidens
Sublato accidente, tollitur subjectum.

Posito antecedente, concomitante, consequente, ponitur consequens, concomitans, antecedens: ut, si est eclipsis, est plenilunium.

Fallit si non est mutua necessitas; ut quamvis, si est eclipsis, est plenilunium, non tamen si est plenilunium, continuo erit eclipsis.

Loci ex oppositis et comparatis:—
Posito altero relatorum ponitur reliquum, et sublato tollitur.
Posito uno contrariorum, tollitur alterum.

Fallit in remissis qualitatibus; quia remissio qualitatis fit semper per admistionem contrarii.

Sublato uno contrariorum, ponitur alterum.

Fallit in contrariis mediatis; ut mel nec album nec nigrum est, sed flavum.

Contrariorum contraria est ratio; ut si frigus congregat heterogenea, calor secernit.

Fallit in ratione subjecti; ut quia sanitas convenit animatis, non propterea morbus inanimatis: et in causis quarum actio determinatur a dispositione materiæ; non enim emollit lutum frigus, quia indurat calor.

Posito altero contradictoriorum, tollitur reliquum, et sublato ponitur.

Similibus et proportionatis similia conveniunt et proportionalia; dissimilibus et improportionatis dissimilia et non proportionalia.

Fallit nisi intelligatur reduplicative, de similibus qua similia; omne enim simile est etiam dissimile: unde non sequitur corvum rationalem esse, quia Æthiops est rationalis.

Maximæ comparatæ rationis sunt istæ:—
Eorum quæ æque sunt aut non sunt talia, si unum est tale, et reliquum, si non est, nec reliquum.

APPENDIX D.

Si quod magis videtur esse tale, non est, etiam quod minus videtur esse, non erit; ut, non placuit omnibus Homerus, qui placebit Mævius?

Si quod minus videtur esse, est tale, etiam id quod magis; ut, fur si est suspendio dignus, certo dignior sacrilegus.

Loci a conjugatis (σύστοιχα):—

Quorum unum convenit alteri, eorum conjugatum unius convenit conjugato alterius et negative similiter; ut, si albedo est color, et album erit coloratum.

Fallit arguendo a concretis ad abstracta; ut, non propterea albedo est dulcedo, quia album est dulce: et arguendo ab abstractis ad concreta; ut, quia nulla albedo est dulcedo, non propterea nullum album erit dulce.

Loci a toto et parte:—

Posito toto, ponuntur partes.

Fallit in toto mutilato; ut potest esse homo, quantumvis amputato digito vel manu.

Sublato toto, partes tolluntur.

Positis partibus, ponitur totum.

Loci a divisione:—

Membrorum condividentium uno aut altero sublato, ponitur reliquum, et posito tollitur.

&c., &c., &c.

The criticism suggested by these numerous but inefficacious maxims is contained in a homely Greek proverb:—

Πολλ' οἶδ' ἀλώπηξ, ἀλλ' ἐχῖνος ἓν μέγα. 'Many tricks knows reynard; one good one suffices the hedgehog.'

APPENDIX E.

LIMITS TO THE COMPETENCE OF PIRASTIC.

It would not be surprising, if, after the performances of Socrates with the elenchus, some of the Socratici viri overestimated the power and value of pirastic. The professed function of pirastic is to examine a man's pretensions to a given science, although neither the examiner nor the auditory are themselves in possession of it; and in the infancy of all the sciences, and the absence of faculties or universities to pronounce on anybody's attainments, there was doubtless abundant scope for its exercise. In the Charmides, where pirastic as producing self-knowledge is discussed under the name of sobriety, [i. e. σωφροσύνη as opposed, not to ἀκολασία but, to χαυνότης or ἀλαζονεία, an ambiguity which we need not pause to discuss,] it is shewn that pirastic alone is not competent to the discharge of this function. To test a man's possession of a given science the examiner ought to possess not only the theory of science in general, i. e. logic, but also a knowledge of the theorems and methods peculiar to the particular science in question. Ὅτι μὲν δὴ ἐπιστήμην τινὰ ἔχει, γνώσεται ὁ σώφρων τὸν ἰατρόν· ἐπιχειρῶν δὲ δὴ πεῖραν λαβεῖν ἥτις ἐστίν, ἄλλο τι σκέψεται ὧν τινῶν; ... Οὐκοῦν ἐν τούτοις ἀναγκαῖον σκοπεῖν τὸν βουλόμενον ἰατρικὴν σκοπεῖν, ἐν οἷς ποτ' ἐστίν. Οὐ γὰρ δήπου ἔν γε τοῖς ἔξω ἐν οἷς οὐκ ἔστιν.—Οὐ δῆτα.—Ἐν τοῖς ὑγιεινοῖς ἄρα καὶ νοσώδεσιν ἐπισκέψεται τὸν ἰατρόν, ᾗ ἰατρικός ἐστιν, ὁ ὀρθῶς σκεπτόμενος.—Ἔοικεν.—Ἦ οὖν ἄνευ ἰατρικῆς δύναιτ' ἄν τις τούτων ποτέροις ἐπακολουθῆσαι;—Οὐ δῆτα.—Οὐδέ γε ἄλλος οὐδείς, ὡς ἔοικε, πλὴν ἰατρός, οὔτε δὴ ὁ σώφρων· ἰατρὸς γὰρ ἂν εἴη πρὸς τῇ σωφροσύνῃ.—Ἔστι ταῦτα.—Παντὸς ἄρα μᾶλλον, εἰ ἡ σωφροσύνη ἐπιστήμης ἐπιστήμη μόνον ἐστὶ καὶ ἀνεπιστημοσύνης, οὔτε ἰατρὸν

APPENDIX E.

διακρῖναι οἷά τε ἔσται ἐπιστάμενον τὰ τῆς τέχνης ἢ μὴ ἐπιστάμενος, προσποιούμενον δὲ ἢ οἰόμενον, οὔτε ἄλλον οὐδένα τῶν ἐπισταμένων καὶ ὁτιοῦν, πλήν γε τὸν αὐτοῦ ὁμότεχνον, ὥσπερ οἱ ἄλλοι δημιουργοί. —Φαίνεται, ἔφη.—Ἆρ' οὖν, ἦν δ' ἐγώ, τοῦτ' ἔχει τὸ ἀγαθὸν ἣν νῦν εὑρίσκομεν σωφροσύνην οὖσαν, τὸ ἐπιστήμην ἐπίστασθαι καὶ ἀνεπιστημοσύνης, ὅτι ὁ ταύτην ἔχων, ὅτι ἂν ἄλλο μανθάνῃ, ῥᾷόν τε μαθήσεται, καὶ ἐναργέστερα πάντα αὐτῷ φανεῖται, ἅτε πρὸς ἑκάστῳ ᾧ ἂν μανθάνῃ προσκαθορῶντι τὴν ἐπιστήμην; καὶ τοὺς ἄλλους δὴ κάλλιον ἐξετάσει περὶ ὧν ἂν καὶ αὐτὸς μάθῃ, οἱ δὲ ἄνευ τούτου ἐξετάζοντες ἀσθενέστερον καὶ φαυλότερον τοῦτο δράσουσι. Charmides, 40–43.

'That the pretended physician possesses some science, sobriety (pirastic) may discover; but before it can pronounce what science, that is, in what province, it must examine him, not in extraneous topics, but in his own province, that is, in questions of health and disease. But no one understands these except the physician, and if the sober-making man (dialectician) understands them, he must possess medical science as well as sobriety (dialectic). Sobriety (pirastic) then, or the science of science and nescience, cannot distinguish between the genuine physician and the pretended or self-fancied physician, nor between any genuine and false professor of science, except in her own sphere (logic), and must leave other artists to the judgment of their peers. The only use, then, of the science of science, is that it enables us to learn more easily and appreciate more completely any other science, as it enables us in each province to see science in addition to truth; and it will enable us to sift more thoroughly the pretensions of others to any other science that we ourselves may happen to have acquired.'

Aristotle asserts the same, though with some exceptions in practical matters. As a general rule, he says, to be competent to judge whether a man possesses a given science, we ourselves must have at least παιδεία, a sort of demi-science, an acquaintance with the leading principles and peculiar methods of the science in question. 'The physician can only receive his diploma and the geometer his certificate of proficiency from a board of physicians or geometers. But the title of physician may be given to those who have had an education (παιδεία) in medical science as well as to the professional physician. Ἔχει δ' ἡ τάξις αὕτη τῆς πολιτείας ἀπορίαν, πρώτην μὲν ὅτι δόξειεν ἂν τοῦ αὐτοῦ

APPENDIX E. 241

εἶναι τὸ κρῖναι τίς ὀρθῶς ἰάτρευκεν οὗπερ καὶ τὸ ἰατρεῦσαι καὶ ποιῆσαι ὑγιᾶ τὸν κάμνοντα τῆς νόσου τῆς παρούσης· οὗτος δ' ἐστὶν ἰατρός. Ὁμοίως δὲ τοῦτο καὶ περὶ τὰς ἄλλας ἐμπειρίας καὶ τέχνας. Ὥσπερ οὖν ἰατρὸν δεῖ διδόναι τὰς εὐθύνας ἐν ἰατροῖς οὕτω καὶ τοὺς ἄλλους ἐν τοῖς ὁμοίοις. Ἰατρὸς δ' ὅ τε δημιουργὸς καὶ ὁ ἀρχιτεκτονικὸς καὶ τρίτος ὁ πεπαιδευμένος περὶ τὴν τέχνην· εἰσὶ γάρ τινες τοιοῦτοι καὶ περὶ πάσας ὡς εἰπεῖν τὰς τέχνας· ἀποδίδομεν δὲ τὸ κρίνειν οὐδὲν ἧττον τοῖς πεπαιδευμένοις ἢ τοῖς εἰδόσιν. Ἔπειτα καὶ περὶ τὴν αἵρεσιν τὸν αὐτὸν ἂν δόξειεν ἔχειν τρόπον. Καὶ γὰρ τὸ ἑλέσθαι ὀρθῶς τῶν εἰδότων ἔργον ἐστίν, οἷον γεωμέτρην τε τῶν γεωμετρικῶν καὶ κυβερνήτην τῶν κυβερνητικῶν. Εἰ γὰρ καὶ περὶ ἐνίων ἔργων καὶ τεχνῶν μετέχουσι καὶ τῶν ἰδιωτῶν τινές, ἀλλ' οὔτι τῶν εἰδότων γε μᾶλλον. Ὥστε κατὰ μὲν τοῦτον τὸν λόγον οὐκ ἂν εἴη τὸ πλῆθος ποιητέον κύριον οὔτε τῶν ἀρχαιρεσιῶν οὔτε τῶν εὐθυνῶν. Ἀλλ' ἴσως οὐ πάντα ταῦτα λέγεται καλῶς διά τε τὸν πάλαι λόγον. ... καὶ ὅτι περὶ ἐνίων οὔτε μόνον ὁ ποιήσας οὔτ' ἄριστ' ἂν κρίσειεν, ὅσων τἆργα γιγνώσκουσι καὶ οἱ μὴ ἔχοντες τὴν τέχνην, οἷον οἰκίαν οὐ μόνος ἐστὶ γνῶναι τοῦ ποιήσαντος ἀλλὰ καὶ βέλτιον ὁ χρώμενος αὐτῇ κρινεῖ, χρῆται δ' ὁ οἰκονόμος, καὶ πηδάλιον κυβερνήτης τέκτονος. καὶ θοίνην ὁ δαιτυμὼν ἀλλ' οὐχ ὁ μάγειρος. Pol. 3. 11. 'The hypothesis that the people are qualified to elect and control the magistrates presents a difficulty, because to judge whether the medical functions have been rightly performed a man ought to be able to perform them himself, that is, ought to be a physician; and so in the other arts and sciences. As, then, a physician ought to be judged by physicians, so ought other functionaries to be judged by their peers. Now the title of physician may be given either to the person who practises, or to the person who combines practice with theory, or to the person who does not practise but has had an education in medical science. Some hold this position in every province, and are thought as competent to judge as the scientific. The same may be said in respect of the electoral power. Qualification to select requires knowledge, and a geometer can only be rightly selected by geometers, a pilot by those who know the pilot's art. If there are any functions and operations of which the uneducated are competent to judge, yet they cannot be more competent than the educated. According to this reasoning the people should not have the power of election or control; but perhaps it is open to objection,

both on other grounds and because there are certain operations of which the artist is not the sole nor the best judge, nor so good as a person who knows nothing about the art; as a house is better appreciated by the householder than by the architect, a rudder by the steersman than by the shipwright, a banquet by the banqueter than by the cook.' Περὶ πᾶσαν θεωρίαν καὶ μέθοδον ὁμοίως ταπεινοτέραν τε καὶ τιμιωτέραν δύο φαίνονται τρόποι τῆς ἕξεως εἶναι, ὧν τὴν μὲν ἐπιστήμην τοῦ πράγματος καλῶς ἔχει προσαγορεύειν τὴν δ' οἷον παιδείαν τινά. Πεπαιδευμένου γάρ ἐστι κατὰ τρόπον τὸ δύνασθαι κρίνειν εὐστόχως τί καλῶς ἢ μὴ καλῶς ἀποδίδωσιν ὁ λέγων. Τοιοῦτον γὰρ δή τινα καὶ τὸν ὅλως πεπαιδευμένον οἰόμεθ᾽ εἶναι, καὶ πεπαιδεῦσθαι τὸ δύνασθαι ποιεῖν τὸ εἰρημένον. Πλὴν τοῦτον μὲν περὶ πάντων ὡς εἰπεῖν τινὰ κριτικὸν νομίζομεν, ἕνα τὸν ἀριθμὸν ὄντα, τὸν δὲ περί τινος φύσεως ἀφωρισμένης· εἴη γὰρ ἄν τις ἕτερος τὸν αὐτὸν τρόπον διακείμενος τῷ εἰρημένῳ περὶ ἓν μόριον. Ὥστε δῆλον ὅτι καὶ τῆς περὶ φύσεως ἱστορίας δεῖ τινὰς ὑπάρχειν ὅρους τοιούτους, πρὸς οὓς ἀναφέρων ἀποδέξεται τὸν τρόπον τῶν δεικνυμένων χωρὶς τοῦ πῶς ἔχει τἀληθές, εἴτε οὕτως εἴτε ἄλλως. De Partibus Animalium, I. I. ' Every theory and method, however humble or exalted its function, has two degrees in which it may be mastered, one of which may be called science, the other education. Education makes a man a competent judge of the performances of the professional artist. Such a competence belongs to universal education, and indeed constitutes its criterion. But while some are thus competent to criticize in every province, others have a corresponding power in a limited province. Physiology then, like other sciences, must have certain canons by which, as by a standard of reference, a critic will judge a writer's method of demonstration, irrespectively of the truth of his doctrines.'

From this passage it is clear that, according to Aristotle, there are as many branches of education as of science; and that if he speaks of logic as education it is not as universal education but only as one of many branches, though perhaps one of the most important. Ὅσα δ' ἐγχειροῦσί τῶν λεγόντων τινὲς περὶ τῆς ἀληθείας ὃν τρόπον δεῖ ἀποδέχεσθαι, δι' ἀπαιδευσίαν τῶν ἀναλυτικῶν τοῦτο δρῶσιν. Δεῖ γὰρ περὶ τούτων ἥκειν προεπισταμένους ἀλλὰ μὴ ἀκούοντας ζητεῖν. Met. 3. 3. ' Discussions in the exposition of a physical system, respecting the method of demonstration to be

APPENDIX E.

required, betray a want of education in logic; for such questions should be previously determined, and not investigated in a physical treatise.'

The grand problem for the educated critic is the appropriate method of the particular science and the degree of accuracy (ἀκρίβεια) to be demanded in the demonstrations. Λέγοιτο δ' ἂν ἱκανῶς εἰ κατὰ τὴν ὑποκειμένην ὕλην διασαφηθείη. Τὸ γὰρ ἀκριβὲς οὐχ ὁμοίως ἐν ἅπασι τοῖς λόγοις ἐπιζητητέον, ὥσπερ οὐδὲ ἐν τοῖς δημιουργουμένοις.... Τὸν αὐτὸν δὲ τρόπον καὶ ἀποδέχεσθαι χρεὼν ἕκαστον τῶν λεγομένων· πεπαιδευμένου γάρ ἐστιν ἐπὶ τοσοῦτον τἀκριβὲς ἐπιζητεῖν καθ' ἕκαστον γένος ἐφ' ὅσον ἡ τοῦ πράγματος φύσις ἐπιδέχεται. Παραπλήσιον γὰρ φαίνεται μαθηματικοῦ τε πιθανολογοῦντος ἀποδέχεσθαι καὶ ῥητορικὸν ἀποδείξεις ἀπαιτεῖν. Ἕκαστος δὲ κρίνει καλῶς ἃ γινώσκει, καὶ τούτων ἐστὶν ἀγαθὸς κριτής. Καθ' ἕκαστον ἄρα ὁ πεπαιδευμένος, ἀπλῶς δὲ ὁ περὶ πᾶν πεπαιδευμένος. Ethica Nic. 1. 3. 'The exposition is adequate if it is as precise as the subject admits. For the same amount of exactitude is not to be required in all sciences any more than in all arts.... General statements, then, must be admitted in ethical science, for the educated critic varies in his demand of precision in the different provinces of science, and no more asks for demonstration from the orator than he accepts probabilities from the mathematician. Competence to judge requires knowledge of the subject-matter, and belongs in each province to the educated; universal competence, therefore, requires universal education.'

We have seen that sophistic proof as differing from paralogism depends on the employment of an inappropriate method or inadmissible evidence: the pretender to science proves a theorem by an unscientific method (ch. 6, note 5), or the questioner confutes the answerer accidentally, i. e. on topics not essentially connected with the department he professes to have mastered (ch. 18, note 1). The one case is simulated pirastic, the other simulated science (ch. xi). In neither can the sophism be detected by the ignorant judges (ἀκροαταί) of a pirastic controversy; for, as we have said before, we must not limit the simulation of pirastic to the employment of thirteen principles covering the defects of the thirteen paralogisms. It is clear that the admission of legitimate and exclusion of illegitimate

APPENDIX E.

evidence in proof of a scientific theorem or disproof of a man's pretensions to science is a function beyond the capacity of an ignorant jury and which requires an educated judge. 'Απαιδευσία γάρ ἐστι περὶ ἕκαστον πρᾶγμα τὸ μὴ δύνασθαι κρίνειν τούς τ' οἰκείους λόγους τοῦ πράγματος καὶ τοὺς ἀλλοτρίους. Ethica Eud. 1. 7. 'Those who are uneducated in a given department of science are unable to discriminate between the theorems and methods peculiar to it and those which are alien.' This explains the recommendation to the genuine geometer (ch. 6, note 5) to decline the piratic tribunal. A large branch, then, of sophisms, accidental or inappropriate confutations, and accidental or inappropriate demonstrations, are merely indicated, not examined, in the present treatise.

APPENDIX F.

THE QUADRATURE OF THE CIRCLE BY HIPPOCRATES, ANTIPHO, AND BRYSO.

As the quadrature of the circle by Hippocrates and the quadrature by lunules are the only examples which Aristotle gives of a pseudographema, it is desirable to examine them with some attention. The quadrature of the circle by means of lunules, i. e. spaces limited by the intersecting arcs of two circles, is as follows. We first invent a method of squaring a lunule:—

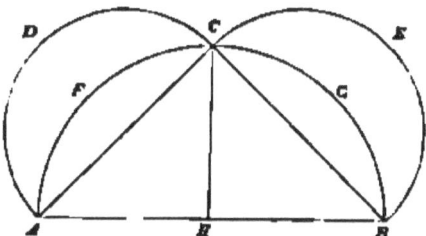

On the diameter AB describe the semicircle ACB; in this inscribe the isosceles triangle ACB; and on the sides AC, CB describe the semicircles ADC, CEB.

Because the angle ACB is inscribed in a semicircle, it is a right angle (Euclid, 3. 31), and the square of the hypotenuse AB is equal to the sum of the squares of the sides AC, CB (Euclid, 1. 47). But circles, or semicircles, are to one another as the squares of their diameters (Euclid, 12. 2), therefore the semicircle ACB is equal to the sum of the semicircles ADC, CEB. Take away from these equals the segments AFC, CGB which are common to each, and the remaining triangle ACB is

APPENDIX F.

equal to the sum of the lunules $ADCFA$, $CEBGC$, or the triangle ACH is equal to the lunule $ADCFA$. We therefore have found a rectilinear area equal to a given lunule.

According to Alexander Aphrodisiensis, Hippocrates applied this to the quadrature of the circle in the following manner:—

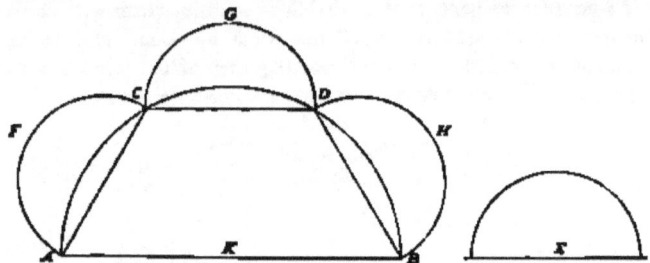

On the diameter AB describe the semicircle $ACDB$; in this inscribe three lines, AC, CD, DB, each equal to the radius AK (this is the same thing as inscribing a hexagon in the circle; Euclid, 4. 15). On these describe the semicircles AFC, CGD, DHB; and describe a fourth semicircle E equal to one of these.

Then because circles or semicircles are as the squares of their diameters (Euclid, 12. 2), the semicircle $ACDB$ is equal to the sum of the semicircles E, AFC, CGD, DHB. Take away the segments which are common to these equals, and the remaining rectilinear area $ACDB$ is equal to the sum of the semicircle E and the three lunules. But we discovered a method of determining a rectilinear area equal to a lunule; take away, then, from the rectilinear area $ACDB$ spaces equal to the three lunules, and the remaining rectilinear area will be equal to the semicircle E. Q. E. F.

What is the fallacy in this construction? This: it is true that we found a method of squaring a particular kind of lunule, that is, one whose upper arc was a semicircle and whose lower arc was the fourth of a circle; but we found no method of squaring such a lunule as we now have, i. e. one whose upper arc is a semicircle and whose lower arc is the sixth of a circle. This is clearly the quadrature by lunules, and therefore (see ch. xi) was not the method of Hippocrates. His method is described by Simplicius on Phys. Ausc. 1. 2, on the authority

APPENDIX F.

of Eudemus, disciple of Aristotle, a witness whose evidence on the question must be taken as decisive.

According to Eudemus, Hippocrates not only squared a lunule whose outer arc was a semicircle, but also lunules whose outer arc was greater or less than a semicircle. He then proceeded to square the circle in the following manner:—

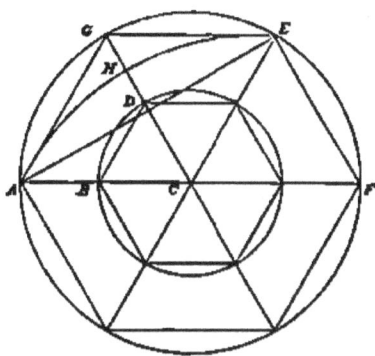

Let AC, BC be the radii of two concentric circles, and let AC^2 equal $6 BC^2$. In the inner circle inscribe a hexagon (Euclid, 4. 15). Producing the radii CD &c. to the outer circle, and joining AG, GE, &c., we inscribe a hexagon in the outer circle. Join AE, and on AE describe a segment AHE similar to the segment AG (Euclid, 3. 33). The inner circle plus the lunule $AGEH$ shall equal the triangle AGE plus the hexagon in the inner circle.

Because AEF, being an angle inscribed in a semicircle, is a right angle (Euclid, 3. 31), therefore AE^2 equals AF^2 minus FE^2 (Euclid, 1. 47). But AF^2 equals $4AC^2$; and FE, being the side of an inscribed hexagon, equals the radius AC (Euclid, 4. 15): therefore AE^2 equals $3AC^2$. But the radius AC equals the side of the hexagon AG or GE, and AC^2 by construction equals $6 BC^2$ or $6BD^2$. Therefore AE^2 equals AG^2 plus GE^2 plus $6BD^2$. But similar segments are as the squares of their chords [Hippocrates deduced this from the theorem that circles are as the squares of their diameters (Euclid, 12. 2)]: therefore the segment AHE equals the segment AG plus the segment

APPENDIX F.

GE plus the six segments of the inner circle. To these equals add the area inclosed by the arc AHE and the straight lines AG, GE; therefore the triangle AGE equals the lunule $AGEH$ plus the six segments. To these equals add the hexagon in the inner circle; therefore the triangle plus the hexagon equals the lunule plus the inner circle.

To complete the quadrature of the circle Hippocrates must have added: But we have shewn how to square any lunule: deduct, then, from the triangle and hexagon an area equal to the lunule, and the remaining rectilinear space is equal to the circle. Next construct a square equal to this rectilinear space (Euclid, 2. 14), and we have found a square equal to a circle. Q. E. F.

It is obvious that the fallacy of this is the same as that of the previous method. Hippocrates was the first who wrote a treatise of elementary geometry. Montucla (Histoire des Mathématiques) suggests what is very probable, that the construction was offered as a specimen of fallacious reasoning, and that Hippocrates as a geometer only intended to assert that we should solve the problem of squaring the circle as soon as we could square all the lunules as satisfactorily as he had squared certain definite lunules. This seems to have been Aristotle's view; at least he gives the proof by lunules, which has the same defect as the proof of Hippocrates, as an instance of abduction or reduction (ἀπαγωγή), i. e. a ratiocination which, though incomplete, advances one step towards the solution of a problem. 'Ἀπαγωγὴ δ' ἐστὶν ὅταν τῷ μὲν μέσῳ τὸ πρῶτον δῆλον ᾖ ὑπάρχον, τῷ δ' ἐσχάτῳ τὸ μέσον ἄδηλον μέν, ὁμοίως δὲ πιστὸν ἢ μᾶλλον τοῦ συμπεράσματος· ἔτι ἂν ὀλίγα ᾖ τὰ μέσα τοῦ ἐσχάτου καὶ τοῦ μέσου· πάντως γὰρ ἐγγύτερον εἶναι συμβαίνει τῆς ἐπιστήμης......Οἷον εἰ τὸ Δ εἴη τετραγωνίζεσθαι, τὸ δ' ἐφ' ᾧ E εὐθύγραμμον, τὸ δ' ἐφ' ᾧ Z κύκλος· εἰ τοῦ EZ μόνον εἴη μέσον τὸ μετὰ μηνίσκων ἴσον γίνεσθαι εὐθυγράμμῳ τὸν κύκλον, ἐγγὺς ἂν εἴη τοῦ εἰδέναι. An. Pr. 2. 25. 'Abduction is a proof whose major premiss is certain and whose minor premiss, though doubtful, is as certain or more certain than the conclusion, or whose minor premiss requires but few steps for its proof; for such a reasoning brings us one step nearer to knowledge. For instance, let P (major) be a square, M (middle) a rectilinear space, S (minor) a circle. If for the establishment

APPENDIX F. 249

of the minor premiss *SM* (the equation of the circle to a rectilinear area) only one step is necessary, the elimination of the lunules that enter into an equation we have discovered, this preliminary equation is an advance towards solving the problem *SP*, i. e. finding the equation of the circle to a square.'

An expression of Aristotle's that apparently refers to this subject (Τῷ γὰρ ἢ τὰ ἡμικύκλια περιγράφειν μὴ ὡς δεῖ, ἢ γραμμάς τινας ἄγειν μὴ ὡς ἂν ἀχθείησαν, τὸν παραλογισμὸν ποιεῖται [ὁ ψευδογράφων]. Topics, I. I. 'The pseudographema depends on semicircles being improperly described or lines improperly drawn') seems to indicate that Hippocrates or some one else introduced some further trick in the manipulation of the ruler or compasses.

Eudemus introduces his account of the quadrature of lunules (not the quadrature of the circle by lunules) in the following terms. Καὶ οἱ τῶν μηνίσκων δὲ τετραγωνισμοί, δόξαντες εἶναι τῶν οὐκ ἐπιπολαίων διαγραμμάτων διὰ τὴν οἰκειότητα τὴν πρὸς τὸν κύκλον, ὑφ' Ἱπποκράτους ἐγράφησάν τε πρώτως καὶ κατὰ τρόπον ἔδοξαν ἀποδοθῆναι, διόπερ ἐπιπλέον ἁψώμεθά τε καὶ διέλθωμεν. 'The quadrature of the lunules, which is regarded as no superficial demonstration because it is based on the essential properties of the circle, was invented by Hippocrates, and is generally admitted to be scientific, and deserves a fuller notice in a history of geometry.' Here ἐπιπολαίων seems a reminiscence of Aristotle's definition of sophistic principles: Οὐδὲν γὰρ τῶν λεγομένων ἐνδόξων ἐπιπόλαιον ἔχει παντελῶς τὴν φαντασίαν, καθάπερ περὶ τὰς τῶν ἐριστικῶν λόγων ἀρχὰς συμβέβηκεν ἔχειν (ch. viii, note 1): though Eudemus uses it to distinguish sophistic premisses, not, as Aristotle, from dialectic, but from scientific. Οἰκειότητα reminds of the οἰκεῖαι ἀρχαί which are characteristic of science.

Antipho inscribed a square in a circle, and in the four segments inscribed four isosceles triangles, in the eight smaller segments eight smaller isosceles triangles, and so on, ad infinitum. He then probably proposed some method of summing the series of triangles, and said that the sum of the series of triangles plus the inscribed square was the rectilinear area required.

Montucla observes that if he could have determined the law by which the triangles diminish in area, he might have summed

250   APPENDIX F.

the series and solved the problem. He therefore says that there is nothing sophistical or ungeometrical about the procedure of Antipho. It was by a similar method that Archimedes afterwards succeeded in squaring the parabola. He first inscribed a triangle in the parabola, then another in each of the segments, and so on, and proved that the area of the first triangle, the two second triangles, the four third triangles, &c., formed the progression $1, \frac{1}{4}, \frac{1}{16}$, &c., and that the sum of this series was $1\frac{1}{3}$. Thus the parabola which is the sum of these triangles is $\frac{4}{3}$ of the inscribed triangle or $\frac{2}{3}$ of the circumscribed parallelogram.

Probably if Aristotle had recognized the method of exhaustion, or limits, or infinitesimals, as a scientific procedure, he would have pronounced Antipho's reasoning not sophistic but pseudographic, or have conceded to it the name which he gave to that of Hippocrates, Reduction. As it is, he clearly considered it as sophistical and unworthy the attention of the geometer. His remarks are worth giving at length. Τὸ μὲν οὖν εἰ ἓν καὶ ἀκίνητον τὸ ὂν σκοπεῖν οὐ περὶ φύσεώς ἐστι σκοπεῖν. Ὥσπερ γὰρ καὶ τῷ γεωμέτρῃ οὐκ ἔτι λόγος ἐστὶ πρὸς τὸν ἀνελόντα τὰς ἀρχάς, ἀλλ' ἤτοι ἑτέρας ἐπιστήμης ἢ πασῶν κοινῆς, οὕτως οὐδὲ τῷ περὶ φύσεως...... Ὅμοιον δὴ τὸ σκοπεῖν εἰ οὕτως ἓν καὶ πρὸς ἄλλην θέσιν ὁποιανοῦν διαλέγεσθαι τῶν λόγου ἕνεκα λεγομένων, οἷον τὴν Ἡρακλείτειον......ἢ λύειν λόγον ἐριστικόν. Ὅπερ ἀμφότεροι μὲν ἔχουσιν οἱ λόγοι καὶ ὁ Μελίσσου καὶ ὁ Παρμενίδου, καὶ γὰρ ψευδῆ λαμβάνουσι καὶ ἀσυλλόγιστοί εἰσι, μᾶλλον δὲ ὁ Μελίσσου φορτικὸς καὶ οὐκ ἔχων ἀπορίαν, ἀλλ' ἑνὸς ἀτόπου δοθέντος τἆλλα συμβαίνει· τοῦτο δὲ οὐδὲν χαλεπόν. Ἡμῖν δὲ ὑποκείσθω τὰ φύσει ἢ πάντα ἢ ἔνια κινούμενα εἶναι. Δῆλον δὲ ἐκ τῆς ἐπαγωγῆς, ἅμα δὲ οὐδὲ λύειν ἅπαντα προσήκει ἀλλ' ἢ ὅσα ἐκ τῶν ἀρχῶν τις ἐπιδεικνὺς ψεύδεται, ὅσα δὲ μή, οὔ. Οἷον τὸν τετραγωνισμὸν τὸν μὲν διὰ τῶν τμημάτων γεωμετρικοῦ διαλῦσαι, τὸν δὲ Ἀντιφῶντος οὐ γεωμετρικοῦ. Οὐ μὴν ἀλλ' ἐπειδὴ περὶ φύσεως μὲν οὔ, φυσικὰς δὲ ἀπορίας συμβαίνει λέγειν αὐτοῖς, ἴσως ἔχει καλῶς ἐπὶ μικρὸν διαλεχθῆναι περὶ αὐτῶν, ἔχει γὰρ φιλοσοφίαν ἡ σκέψις. Phys. Ausc. I. 2. 'The question whether existence is one and unchangeable is not a physical problem; for as the geometer does not reason with one who denies his principles, but leaves him to be dealt with by some separate science or by some power that is a common element of all the sciences, no more does the physical inquirer. The examination

APPENDIX F. 251

of such a doctrine must resemble the confutation of a paradoxical thesis like the tenet of Heraclitus, or the solution of a sophistic proof. Such indeed are the reasonings both of Melissus and of Parmenides, for the premisses are false and the conclusions are illegitimate, though that of Melissus is the grosser and less suggestive of the two. For he starts from an inadmissible premiss and then obtains paradoxical conclusions; which is easy. We, then, postulate as a first principle, that the natural world, in whole or in part, is a scene of change. For this we may appeal to the evidence of observation; and we are not bound to encounter, even by way of solution, any doctrine except such as admits the principles of the science: just as the geometer is bound to examine the quadrature of the circle by segments, but is not bound to notice the reasoning of Antipho. However, as the thesis, though unphysical as regards its truth, is physical as regards the subject, let us examine it briefly. For the examination is philosophic and not merely dialectic.' Quadrature by segments is an apt description of the method explained by Eudemus, and doubtless refers to the method of Hippocrates. The contradiction of geometrical principles, which in Aristotle's judgment made Antipho's method ungeometrical, was either the assumption (now admitted) that the sides of a many-sided polygon coincide with the circumference of a circle, which contradicts the theorem that a straight line only touches a circle in a single point (Euclid, 3. 16), or (as this is rather the contradiction of a conclusion than of a principle) the assumption that, starting from the inscribed square, it is possible, by subdivision of the segments, to reach the circumference, an assumption which contradicts the principle of the infinite divisibility of space.

Bryso appears to have inscribed one square in a circle and circumscribed another, and to have said that as the circumscribed square was greater than the circle, and the inscribed square less, a third square that should be the mean between the two others would be equal to the circle; assuming that whenever two things are greater and less respectively than the same other things, they must be equal to one another.

It is plain that Bryso does not reason like a geometer; Antipho's reasoning approaches nearer to a pseudographema. Bryso's pemisses bear no relation to the principles of geometry;

Antipho's contradict them, but still lie without the geometrical sphere: for, whatever may be the case with natural philosophy, geometry, being in Aristotle's view a purely deductive science, takes no cognizance of any reasoning which calls her first principles in question.

With respect to the method of lunules and the method of Hippocrates, a difficulty suggests itself. The principle or method of these fallacies is evidently the omission of a limitation. Because we can square a particular kind of lunule, it is assumed that we can square every kind of lunule; that is, the arguments fall under the fallacy a dicto secundum quid ad dictum simpliciter. How then can it be said that the principle of these fallacies is not transferable to any other province?

It is true that lunules cannot be applied to the solution of ethical or physiological problems, but the suppression or substitution of limitations is practicable in every kind of discussion. If these fallacies are pseudographemas because the rest of their reasoning is geometrical, whereas Bryso's and Antipho's are entirely ungeometrical, it would seem that there is no intrinsic difference between a pseudographema and a sophism, only a difference in the accompaniments. But Aristotle speaks of them as different in kind. He apparently considers the fallacy of the pseudographemas to consist in the false geometrical proposition, that every lunule must belong to one of the classes whose quadrature has been given.

Works by the same Author.

THE PHILEBUS OF PLATO, with a revised Text and English Notes.

Oxford : at the University Press.

PHILEBUS, a Dialogue of Plato ; translated into English.

London : Longmans, Green, and Co.

THE LOGIC OF SCIENCE, a translation of the Later Analytics of Aristotle, with an Introduction and Notes.

London : W. Heath, New Oxford Street.

LECTURES ON THE HISTORY OF ANCIENT PHILOSOPHY.

By the Rev. W. ARCHER BUTLER, M.A., late Professor of Moral Philosophy in the University of Dublin. Edited by the Rev. WM. HEPWORTH THOMPSON, Master of Trinity College, Cambridge. 2 vols. 8vo. cloth, price 25s.

THE REPUBLIC OF PLATO.

Translated into English, with Analysis and Notes, by J. LL. DAVIES, M.A., and D. J. VAUGHAN, M.A., with Vignette Portraits of Plato and Socrates, engraved by JEENS from an Antique Gem. Printed on toned paper and bound in extra cloth, 18mo. price 4s. 6d. (The Golden Treasury Series.) Also 8vo. cloth, price 10s. 6d.

THE ILIAD OF HOMER.

Translated into English accentuated Hexameters, by SIR JOHN F. W. HERSCHEL, BART. K.H. M.A. F.R.S., etc. Extra demy 8vo. beautifully printed on toned paper, with Vignette, after the antique, by JEENS. Cloth extra, price 18s.

MACMILLAN AND CO. LONDON.

www.ingramcontent.com/pod-product-compliance
Lightning Source LLC
Chambersburg PA
CBHW021356230426
43666CB00006B/542